Don't Mention the 'Spor

CRYSTAL PALACE F.C. VERSUS THE WORLD

by Neil Witherow

First published in Great Britain in 2021 by Palace Echo
Publications through Kindle Direct Publishing.
© Neil Witherow 2021

ISBN: 9798519001571

Cover design: Mark Reynolds.
Editor: Chris Thorpe-Tracey
Palace Echo Logo: Ian Chapman

For Ray, for ever

With Grateful Thanks to the Main Contributors, Researchers and Interviewees

Kevin Barthrop
Anthony Bowden
Steve Browett
James Calder
Andy Carey
Steve Carleton
John Carter
Gary Chapman
Derek Collison
Carl Davies
Neil Everitt
Dominic Fifield
Nick Harling
Simon Higgins
Dave Hynes
Ian King
Dave Lewis
David London
Steve Martyniuk
Paul Smith
Andrew Wagon
Ian Weller
Martin Young

And also to everyone else involved in the production of this book, from advice, encouragement and inspiration to practical help and assistance. In particular, Chris Thorpe-Tracey and the rest of the loose/louche association of hugely-talented creative types known as The Monday Club: Jim Morrison, Les Carter, Marc Ollington and Tim Connery - of which I am proud to be a member, Mark Reynolds, Graham Nealon, Samantha Caplan, Cris Lehmann, Dan Weir, Terry Byfield, Kristy Smith. And especially to Sue Witherow, my wife, who has lived and breathed this book for as long as I have.

AUTHOR'S NOTE: CLUB AND PLACE NAME CONVENTIONS

Throughout the book, I have chosen to use the recognised English name for the places referred to and, wherever possible, I use the actual club name as it would be written in the native country. For example, I use Gothenburg to describe the Swedish city and IFK Göteburg when referring to the club, although there are occasional exceptions: where the club is better known by an anglicised or abbreviated form of their name - i.e. Internazionale is also written as Inter or Inter Milan. Also, if the club's name would natively be written in a non-western character set, such as Arabic or Chinese script, then I have defaulted to the most accepted English translation.

FOREWORD

Throughout my life, people have told me that I am ridiculously obsessed with Crystal Palace Football Club. First game 1969, season ticket holder all my adult life, 120 grounds visited… the list goes on. In 2010, I even bought the club with three other fans. But really, my dedication to CPFC is nothing compared to the incredible devotion to the club - and attending its matches - shown by Neil Witherow. He's absolutely Palace mad.

Over the years, I've bumped into Neil in such diverse places as Huddersfield and Hong Kong, Marpafut and Middlesbrough. He's the "man who's always there". His dedication to watching Palace seems to know no bounds and the list of obscure friendlies that he's managed to attend – involving long and complicated journeys – is quite remarkable. His wife Sue must be the most tolerant spouse in the world – but then she loves Palace too.

He's also been dressed as an Eagle as the club's mascot, edited a fanzine, been a moderator of a fans' message board… amongst a whole host of other stuff. And even when he's not doing something Palace-related he still seems to find time to watch football in Germany or at non-league clubs I've never heard of - where he photographs yellow hoses to post on Instagram. Extraordinary!

This quite unique account of travels over land and sea will make fascinating reading for all serious football fans – even if it makes most of us look like complete amateurs. Fans of bigger clubs – who have actually qualified for proper European tournaments on a regular basis – may be baffled.

One gets the feeling that Neil is still kicking himself for missing one particular game in North East Turkey that hardly anyone else attended. Hence the title of this book. Don't beat yourself up about it, mate, even the club's manager didn't bother to go to the home leg!

I can only hope that in our lifetimes Palace will finally manage to achieve qualification for a major tournament. An achievement so cruelly taken from us in 1991. If we do it and the first leg is away in an obscure country, against a team we've never heard of, in a town with no airport, terrible weather, and a two day journey to get there, there's one thing that I know for sure - Neil will be there and he will have another story to tell.

Stephen Browett, May 2021.

PROLOGUE

BLOWIN' IN THE WIND

Being stuck in a stationary cable car, swinging precariously in a strong wind, is an odd thing to blame on your football club. However, let the record show, I was in this predicament due entirely to Crystal Palace FC.

As we shuddered and swayed, I was desperately trying to think of something else, other than the increasing problems the cable car was having on its descent down the Italian side of the Matterhorn. I found my mind wandering back three months earlier to the fulfilment of my lifelong Palace dream.

The year was 1990 and, up until then, my greatest hope as a Palace fan was wanting to see us at Wembley in the FA Cup Final. Just to get there and be a part of that special day was my dream. Actually winning the FA Cup was altogether secondary for me. Call it the realism and ingrained pessimism forged by growing up in the seventies as a Palace fan. All I wanted was our day in the sun.

As a youngster I'd had the usual back-garden fantasies of actually playing for Palace and scoring the winning goal in the Cup Final. The League Cup wasn't even on my radar. I conveniently overlooked that the only position I had any sort of clue about was goalkeeper. And a very small clue at that.

When I was growing up, the day of the FA Cup Final became almost a religious ritual. Those were the days when it was the only domestic game to be shown live on television. It was always a major occasion in our household. My morning was spent writing a programme for the game and making a banner for our front door displaying my temporary allegiance for that day. No, I'm not going to tell you which teams they were.

From noon onwards, my older brother Ray, Dad and I watched the build-up with hushed reverence and rapt attention: *It's A Knockout, Mastermind, The Road to Wembley* for both sides – we sat entranced, drinking it all in. With half an hour to kick off, Mum would either go and visit my married sister, Christine or nip into Bromley, "As the shops will be nice and quiet." Only then would the living room curtains be drawn to enhance the atmosphere further. Brother and Father would get stuck into Dad's latest batch of homebrew, whereas my drink was 'Coola Cola' (delivered fortnightly by someone known only as 'the Corona man'). With nuts, crisps and sweets all readily to hand, we settled back to watch the game. I'd even stand for the National Anthem, much to my family's amusement.

The discussions were always the same, year after year. When 'Abide with Me' was played, Dad would recall the days when the crowd would be led in community singing for an hour and a half before kick-off; bemoaning the fact they didn't still do it. Ray would tell us what bets he'd had with his mates on the outcome of the game, but in deference to Dad, never how much he'd staked. And me, intensely jealous of what I saw being played out before me, would pipe up with the same old question: "Do you think it will be Palace's turn next year?" Dad's reply, his Nottingham accent burred soft by long years in the south, was always the same. "Every dog has its day, lad."

Eventually he was right, though not before Southampton broke my twelve-year-old heart with their FA Cup semi-final victory over us in 1976. Southampton are one of those teams Palace often seem to struggle against, especially when it matters most. Saints they ain't. Thirty years of hurt later, I still dislike them with a passion approaching that which I feel for the team most fans consider to be our club's biggest rivals, Brighton & Hove Albion.

The family Cup Final ritual faded with the passage of time, as these things tend to. My teenage years brought other distractions and Ray started a family, though most Cup Finals we did still try to make the effort. When league games began to be regularly televised, the magic was finally lost. While the desire to see Palace compete in the FA Cup Final remained fervent, it just seemed so unlikely. The high-flying team of the eighties that briefly topped the league quickly faded, giving way to a lower second tier club that seemed to struggle against relegation most years.

The rise back up to the top flight under young Manager Steve Coppell, also finally led to the realisation of the dream and an FA Cup Final appearance. It was just as well that I hadn't got too hung up on winning. After a glorious day out on the Saturday, which lived up to all my childhood hopes and dreams, we got beaten in a dour evening replay by Manchester United.

On the back of our cup exploits, the club had been invited to take part in the Cesare Pier Baretti Tournament in the Italian Alps during the following pre-season. The Eagles were in prestigious company as the other competing clubs were drawn from the cream of Serie A: Fiorentina, Sampdoria and Torino. Around seventy fans made the trip out to Italy.

The previous day, Palace had played Fiorentina in St. Vincent. In the day's break between matches, a few of us had gone exploring the region, hence our ill-advised cable car trip. Despite our current, hopefully temporary, predicament, we were having the absolute time of our lives following Palace in Europe. It didn't matter to us that it was just a minor pre-season competition. Could it get any better? Possibly not the best time to ask that question, as we dangled, several hundred feet above a very unforgiving rocky mountain slope.

The cable car started to move again and took a sickening lurch towards one of its support pylons. A huge wave of regret washed over me. Not because I was about to meet my maker, but because it finally sunk in just how close we'd come to doing this for real. We had been just seven minutes and the width of a post away from winning the Cup. And more importantly, as it now seemed, a bona-fide place in the UEFA European Cup Winners Cup.

Whether we would have had more fun in that competition than we did over those three days in Italy is debatable. Manchester United visited the exotic wilds of Hungary and had to brave a forty mile trip to Wrexham, en route to a Netherlands final and victory against Barcelona. Could Palace have matched that? Our form in the following season suggests we would have given it a damned good go.

The cable car finally creaked into its terminus and my new Palace dream was now crystallised: to watch Palace compete in a proper European competition abroad. Thirty years on and, just like Diana Ross, 'I'm Still Waiting'. During that period, we have been within realistic touching distance three more times.

By rights, I should have needed to come up with a new ambition later in that season as Palace stormed to a third-place finish in the league. It really should have been enough to secure a UEFA Cup place but, as so often with Palace, a swift kick in the unmentionables was the only reward. I'll cover the details of what happened a little later on, but there was to be no reward for our best ever season.

Even today, the perceived injustice still rankles with a great many Palace supporters. Indeed, it has come to be regarded as one of the pivotal moments in our history. Without the lure of European football, the club was unable to keep hold of talismanic goalscorer Ian Wright, who left early in the next season to pursue his own European and international ambitions. The deadly striking partnership of Ian Wright and Mark Bright – that had been a large part of the club's recent success – was disbanded. The decline became steadily more marked and eighteen months on, Palace were relegated from the top flight. All too quickly, my new ambition had begun to fade, just as my cup final hopes had in the dark days of the early eighties.

Although the relegation in 1993 was somewhat unlucky and was tempered by an immediate return as Champions, Palace could not keep a grip on their top flight status, yoyo-ing between the two divisions. In the winter of 1998, it became clear Palace was on another downward swing and the club was in the throes of a messy takeover. Out of the depths of this murky confusion came the unlikely second opportunity.

Our soon-to-be owner, Mark Goldberg, thought up a jolly wheeze to take Palace to a place they'd not been before. Confident that the protracted takeover would be completed, he started the formalities to enter Palace into the UEFA Intertoto Cup.

This was a competition that had been run since the sixties, but only achieved official UEFA status a couple of years before, when the prize changed from cash to places in the UEFA Cup (now Europa League). As such, UEFA made entry into the summer competition mandatory for each member country. English clubs that had shied away from the competition previously as it was held in the close season, were now obliged to enter.

Three unwilling English clubs – Wimbledon, Sheffield Wednesday and Tottenham Hotspur – found themselves under threat of European sanctions. The trio had to play six games in a group phase all over Europe, beginning in the middle of June. Each club fielded next to no regular first teamers, preferring a combination of youngsters and veteran loan signings. Alan Pardew even ended up captaining Spurs for their participation in the competition. Unsurprisingly, none of the English clubs progressed to the knockout stage.

Devoid of an actual trophy and widely regarded as a joke in English football, some of the crueller football commentators, including one who would end up managing us when the games were played, thought it highly amusing and appropriate that Palace were seeking to enter the 'Inter TwoBob' as it was dubbed by the British media.

The previous English entrants had gotten nowhere near the prizes of places in the UEFA Cup proper. There was little expectation that Palace – in dire trouble at the foot of the Premier League – would fare any better, even though the competition was now a straight knockout over two legs. For me, it was cruel for an entirely different reason: I would not be able to go.

I'd managed not to miss a competitive first team game for twelve years, due to a combination of luck, good health and, perhaps most importantly, understanding employers and family (notice how girlfriends aren't included on this list... that's a whole other book). Sometime in the afore-mentioned winter slump, I decided to forgo the considerable pleasures of the pre-season campaign and committed to take a long-planned for holiday of a lifetime to Disneyland, Florida with our good friends from Oldham.

The gang I'd often travelled with in the nineties: the Orpington Pissheads, met the Cooper and Megginson families on an away trip to Oldham in 1991. Whilst I wasn't with them that day, I was soon introduced and a firm friendship blossomed. One that continues to this day and even survived our relegation in 1993, when Oldham only moved above us on the very last day of the season.

The Coopers' eldest was 16 in 1998 and as such, he had exams to complete in the summer restricting when we could travel. I decided – just this once, mind – to give the pre-season games a miss and we booked up for the last two weeks in July. I mean what harm could it do?

Two days later at work, I went for a mid-morning 'comfort break', using the time productively to have a quick read of the sports section of the mailroom's tabloid newspaper. Then I read the fateful words: 'Crystal Palace are interested in entering the Intertoto Cup this summer', well, let's just say it was a good job I was already 'sitting comfortably' at the time. Though summer was still a long way off, my blood ran cold, while other bodily substances ran elsewhere. I just knew it would go ahead and it would clash with our trip.

Despite being relegated, The Eagles were seeded by virtue of being an English side and, as such, received a bye into the third round. The first leg of round three was to be played on Saturday 17th July – my nephew, Dean's wedding, at which I was to be best man. The second leg, as feared, fell right in the middle of the holiday.

The ties were pre-drawn right through to the final legs and the draw held a glimmer of hope that I might be able to dash back from America on a weekend return trip, should the Danish side, Lyngby, manage to qualify from the second round game. That fanciful and expensive notion died a death when the Danes were narrowly vanquished. The victors were the Turkish side, Samsunspor. Samsun is a port on the Black Sea – a twelve-hour drive from Istanbul on the Asian side of the Bosphorus. How bloody typical! Palace play in Europe for the first time and end up having to travel to a relatively inaccessible part of Asia.

As it transpired, the home leg was scheduled for the Sunday, so at least I was able to go to that, dragging the Oldham lot with me as their penance. That game ended in a scrappy 2-0 home defeat making the prospect of progressing further unlikely. It was, however, only a brief delay to the inevitable. My consecutive run of games came to a crashing halt the following Saturday and, yes, when kick off time came, I sulked like a baby who'd had his dummy stolen.

Even more so when it was pointed out to me that the game had already finished eight hours ago, due to the time difference. Samsunspor had won 2-0 again, although it took me two days to find out the result. In those early internet days and when mobile phones were too expensive to use abroad, I didn't find out until a trip to Epcot – Disney's 'future world' theme park – which had web-enabled computers available for use by the public.

Quite a few of my friends were amongst the 25 or so Palace fans who did make the trip. Of course, they have taken the mickey out of me quite mercilessly since, hence the title of this book. Twelve years unbroken service suddenly counted for nothing. If you didn't go to Samsunspor, well... could you even call yourself a

Palace fan? All these years later, a couple of them will still find ways of dropping Samsunspor into any conversation. The gits.

It could be argued that as the Intertoto was a UEFA recognised competition, then this should count as European Football. I'm sorry, but it's just not what I had in mind on that buttock-clenching trip down an Italian mountainside. It's my dream and I set the parameters.

Our final close-but-no-cigar moment came in 2016, when we reached the FA Cup Final again, facing Manchester United once more. Just one game away from a place in the Europa League group stages and a guarantee of not one, but three away European ties. Despite a mad 120 seconds of unbridled hope and joy when Jason Puncheon briefly put us ahead with ten minutes left on the clock, once again we failed to get our hands on the trophy. My dream lay in tatters.

There was one other really galling factor in this final missed opportunity: up until the year previous, losing the FA Cup to a side that had already qualified for Europe would have been enough to earn a place. It was just so Palace to miss out on this route by a single year.

So with all this personal heartbreak, why am I even thinking of writing a book about Palace's international exploits? It's a question I've thought long and hard about down the years. I've had a while to come up with an answer, given I originally started writing this book on and off – mostly off – in 2005.

Quite simply, the good times far outweigh the bad memories. Some of my very best times have been had following Palace abroad: from the Alps to America, Bastia to Berlin, Cape Town to Columbus… and that is just the ABC's. It is not just about me, though. There are some fantastic tales out there. Not just of the games, but of the extraordinary lengths that some of our fans have gone to just to get to these matches. Stories that are just begging to be brought together in a permanent record.

In what is Palace's most successful period, one when we are flooded with every turn with all sorts of media that micro-analyse almost every aspect of the club, I want to tell a different story. It may be niche, but I hope it is entertaining and will appear fresh and interesting to even the most devoted acolytes of our club history.

I look forward to hearing from you, as to whether I've achieved that aim, only please, just don't mention the 'Spor. Trust me, I have heard them all before.

1

THE ALTERNATIVE ITALIA '90

Say 'Italia 90' to most football fans of a certain age and the recollections will flow of that World Cup: of Gazza's tears; Toto Schillaci's eyes; Colombia's showboating keeper; David Platt's last minute wonder goal against the Belgians; a too-close-for comfort quarter-final against Roger Milla's Cameroon; and, ultimately, England losing a gut-wrenching penalty shootout to the West Germans.

Ask seventy or so Palace fans though, you might get an altogether different set of memories. During the later stages of the World Cup, the *Croydon Advertiser* (the local paper known, with affection, as the 'Adder') reported that as part of Palace's pre-season, we would be competing in the third Pier Cesare Baretti memorial tournament in Italy, together with Fiorentina, Sampdoria and Torino. Not a lot of detail surrounded the announcement, but it was more than enough to generate a great deal of fan interest.

The following week, the Palace fanzine of the time, *Eagle Eye* communicated, again via the Adder, that they would be running a coach to the tournament. They were swamped with interest and could have easily filled three coaches. I was one of the lucky fifty to get a place on board, as was my pal Johnny 'Bush' Wood. We agreed to share a tent to try and keep costs reasonable. For both of us, it was our first trip abroad to watch Palace.

Eagle Eye was at the forefront of the fanzine movement and was run by a collective of really lovely people. John Ellis and Tony Matthews headed up the editorial side, while Gary Chapman was the man in charge of the trip. There were several other *Eagle Eye* alumni on the coach, including Jason Axell, Phil Huffer, John and Annette Pateman. All of whom I had the pleasure of getting to know during the trip. I had just started up a small fanzine of my own called *Suffer Little Children*, which was written by and sold to people within Palace's Family Enclosure. There was no hint of any rivalry, though. They could not have been nicer or more helpful to me, indeed, I suspect it was one of the reasons that I made the cut for the trip.

Gary remembers that extracting information from the club about the tournament was no easy feat, having met with Palace Director Geoff Geraghty to discuss the planned trip:

> "Geoff himself was supportive and understanding, however, his message from the Chairman Ron Noades made clear that he wanted to stop us. I think he took it back to Mr Noades to say that we were all okay and no issues. Days after this meeting, however, Geraghty contacted us to say that the trip had been called off. I do recall contacting everybody to advise that Palace had said the trip was off, but I thought it may be a bluff. I was going to go ahead anyway and would they support us? Nobody pulled out but we agreed to keep quiet. We all took a big risk. A few days before, Palace contacted us again to confirm that the club were not going and we then knew it was definitely happening!"

In pre-internet days, getting information from Italy about a minor football tournament being held in the Alps was a real challenge. Luckily an *Eagle Eye* contributor, Stuart Dunbar, was working out in Milan and was able to provide assistance, but still there was some uncertainty about the venues for the games.

We set out from outside The Cherry Trees pub in South Norwood at 11.30am on Sunday 19th August, with pick-ups on route, catching the mid-afternoon sailing from Dover. Gary had advised the party against bringing any alcohol or wearing any Palace regalia, at least until we had crossed the Channel, to avoid unnecessary police interest. Even the coach firm and its drivers were initially unaware that it was a football trip.

The overnight journey through France was uneventful. Our coach drivers, Ivan and Percy, would occasionally point out sites of interest. It became clear, after a while, that these points of interest were almost exclusively battlefields and war memorials. After a while, their detailed knowledge of the exact numbers of casualties became rather unnerving.

In the dead of night, we stopped for a rest break in a mountainous area. Immediately an impromptu football match broke out on the petrol station's forecourt. The other customers at the rest stop, many of whom were asleep in their vehicles, got a rude awakening when one of the players was dispossessed by a stray traffic cone. The braying laughter and cries of "Are you Pardew in disguise?" echoed across the hills. This was swiftly followed by "Son of Aylott!" when the ball was accidentally lumped on to the carriageway. That might have been me.

Part of the reason for the stop was so that we could travel through the Mont-Blanc pass in daylight. The scenery in the Chamonix region is simply stunning, although our drivers doggedly continued with their War Memorial notifications. I'm feeling a bit guilty at having a little bit of fun at their expense here: both guys were absolutely superb throughout the trip and even took us on an unscheduled tour of Paris on the way home. The size of the whip-round at the end of the journey reflected their efforts.

We arrived in mid-morning at St. Vincent, a small, but extremely picturesque town in the Aosta Valley in the Piedmont region of Italy. The tent proved to be a good call as most of the accommodation in the town was already taken. The campsite on the slopes of Mount Zerbion, just outside the town, ended up taking in most of our coach party.

As it was the day of our first match against Fiorentina, who were the current trophy holders, tents were erected in double-quick time. After a long trip, we urgently needed to seek out some suitable liquid refreshment. It was, after all, a mid-afternoon kick off. On the way back to town, we encountered some young Fiore fans, heading for the campsite. They seemed quite wary of us, at first. Was this going to be a legacy of the troubles at the World Cup? One guy went as far as to unveil his West Ham Hooligans T-shirt. When they realised that we were far more interested in sharing a chat and a beer than having a fight, they became very friendly. We agreed to meet up later.

Once in town, we came across a bar with a Sussex Eagles flag draped outside. It was owned by a car-load that had made their own way down through France, arriving the day before. They regaled us with a tale of gate-crashing the evening training session, followed by a lively night in the local Casino. While we were there, several Palace players wandered by, but seemed almost embarrassed by our presence.

Shortly after that, Palace Manager Steve Coppell walked past the bar with Mr Noades and his son. Despite giving Copps a hero's welcome, we got barely a flicker of a smile in return. Our Chairman maintained a stony face throughout, ignoring our presence. This was too much for a couple of the Sussex Eagles who called him out. Still no response.

At this point, John and Gary entered the bar. They had just had their own encounter with Uncle Ron and received an official presentation of a Cold Shoulder. It seems that he was not just upset that the coach party had travelled at all, but accused us of causing bother in the town the night before. Something that had led to the involvement of the local Carabinieri. John and Gary made him aware that the coach had only arrived that morning, however, he wasn't having any of it. It must be said, the Sussex chaps were looking rather sheepish at this point.

Johnny Bush and I wandered off to score match tickets and bumped into Steve again, this time without the Chairman in tow, and he was a lot more amenable. With the Fiorentina support now arriving in droves, we decided to stay at the ground and drink there. The Tournament programmes were a lavish, glossy affair, but were surprisingly free, although the staff wouldn't let you have more than one copy. A lot of collectors back home were going to be disappointed at this rate.

The ground was small and open, equivalent to lower non-league at home, but beautifully maintained. Both sets of fans, including the young chaps from the campsite, happily mingled and sang each other's songs. It's fair to say that Juventus and Brighton both got a vocal shoe-ing that afternoon. Their chant "Se non Salti, Juventini, Oh-ay! Oh-ay!" ("If you don't jump, you must be Juventus") became the earworm of the whole trip.

Fiorentina's line-up boasted some World Cup stars in the Beatle-haired Romanian Marius Lăcătuş and the Brazilian playmaker Dunga, who was accorded his own special song to the tune of the *Can Can* about the apparently outlandish size of his member.

The tournament was a knockout format, with Sampdoria and Torino playing in Aosta, a larger town in the region, where the final was to be held. The losers would play off for third and fourth place in St Vincent. This game was also being televised live back in England on the Croydon Cable channel.

Palace took the lead through the head of Gary O'Reilly on 18 minutes after a truly woeful punch out from the keeper. Four minutes later, O'Reilly gave away a disputed penalty which the allegedly over-endowed Dunga converted. Just before the half-hour, O'Reilly gave Nigel Martyn a hospital ball and Borgonovo nipped in for the second. The second half was quieter, as pre-season games often are. Some truly awful refereeing decisions went against Palace and multiple substitutions on both sides disrupted the flow of the game. No more goals were forthcoming and thus, The Eagles would be staying in St Vincent for their second game.

Towards the end of the game the chant went up "If they played in Kuwait City, we'd be there" aimed squarely at the Chairman. The Iraqi invasion and occupation of Kuwait had taken place earlier that month. The song was a culmination of the events earlier in the day.

We retired to a bar to watch Torino demolish Sampdoria 4-1 with our new 'La Viola' friends. Their English was embarrassingly good, and the conversation flowed easily over pasta and beer. They had a theory about the poor officiating:

"The referee was only following orders" they told us with a knowing laugh. "Baretti was a former Fiore president. It would not be right if we were not in the final of his Memorial."

The barman agreed, although he spoke no English. He was able to make it quite clear he thought it was a ridiculous penalty and signalling with his fingers that it should have been 1-1. Our friends suddenly turned dismissive: "He would always say that. He is Juve."

I assumed they were joking about this minor episode of apparent corruption. However, having since read *The Miracle of Castel di Sangro* by Joe McGinniss, I began to have my doubts. I later found that La Viola had made the final in every year they had entered the Tournament.

Tuesday dawned bright, although with a stiff breeze. We hung around the campsite knocking a ball around, while getting to know a few Palace lads calling themselves the Orpington Pissheads, whom I ended up travelling away with a fair bit in the early nineties: Paul and John James, Kelvin Blackman, his girlfriend Claire Baker and Martin Young. The ball was soon booted into a field of scary looking cattle (not by me, this time) which brought a swift end to the game.

It was there that I first met Laurie Dahl, who had missed out on a seat on the coach so had made his own way. Laurie and I would go on to become a part of the *Eagle Eye* editorial team. When that fanzine ended in 1994, we co-founded the *Palace Echo* fanzine together, which ran for a further twelve years.

As the sun rose higher, the rarefied mountain air made just sitting outside the tent feel like an effort. Surprising, then, that we should elect to go on a trip even higher into the Alps on our day off. Gary arranged for the coach to take a party to the ski resort Cervinia, on the Swiss-Italian border near the Matterhorn.

There were about twenty of us on this mountain excursion, others electing to stay and play football against the Italians, or go swimming in the local pool. A couple of hardy souls even made it all the way down to Turin some fifty miles away. Cervinia was the site of the cable car incident. We really should have known better; warning signs were there right from the off.

Spying the cable car station, next door to the coach park, we piled off and decided on a bit of peak-bagging. The Matterhorn, glinting majestically in the midday sunshine, was calling to us. The attendant seemed incredibly reluctant to sell us any form of ticket. She spoke no English at all, just kept pointing to a chalkboard with writing that none of us could understand. Finally, she relented and sold us a ticket to Plan Maison, the first base station. No summiting for us, but the view from there would surely be worth it.

Another clue we missed was that whilst we were dressed in gear more appropriate for the beach, the skiers in full salopettes, who had just come off the mountain were looking at us with sheer incredulity. We set off and initially we naively thought the gondola was stopping obligingly so we could admire the view. In fact, it was struggling with the increasingly gusty wind as we ascended. It took twenty-five minutes to get to first base, a journey that would usually take just ten.

Undaunted, we left the landing station and went out onto the mountainside. Not only was it a lot windier than it was in Cervinia, it was colder. Much colder. Just four degrees Centigrade according to the gauge as opposed to the mid-twenties below.

We still decided to walk out a fair way from Plan Maison and get some photos. The wind was so strong, not only were we having trouble keeping upright, but it was picking up sizeable sharp stones and whipping them onto our bare legs. However the sun was shining and we were having fun. If only that piercing siren emanating from the landing stage would stop.

The cold made us abandon our attempt to get up to the snowline a few hundred feet higher. We staggered back to the landing stage. As we entered the building, we were hustled, at indecent speed, straight onto a cable car. The service was being shut down, due to the ever-increasing wind and this was the last car out of Dodge. Had we missed it, we would have had to walk several kilometres back down to the town. That annoying ear-splitting shriek was obviously an evacuation warning.

The ride down, as already recounted, was utterly terrifying. Much worse than the ascent. The café staff from the landing station, who must have done the trip daily, were openly praying. It's no wonder we tried to focus on something other than the descent.

We made it down eventually and the coach took us back to St Vincent. Back at the campsite, our hastily erected tent, like many others, had blown over. The wind had freshened considerably there too. A smiley German camper named Roger, helped us put it back up. The rest of the afternoon was spent attending Palace's training session back at the stadium. There we also discovered the store cupboard that held the programmes was unlocked. The place was looted in moments.

The evening is a blur, it started off with a pizza and a couple of bottles each of the young local wine, that proved to be deceptively strong. We made a tactical withdrawal to the campsite, whilst we still had a few motor skills left and retired for the night. I was unable to sleep though as "The trees were going round" and got up to try and clear the dizziness. Several witnesses tell me that I started climbing trees and then clambered up onto the rusty roof of the toilet block, yelling my head off about "going to get the ball back!" I have no memory of any of this.

The next morning was hell. We were due to check out at ten, but neither Johnny nor I could lift our heads. Once again, Roger to the rescue, he helped us pack up, while his wife made us a chamomile tea hangover cure. It was then that we realised that, ill or not, there was no physical way we could carry all our stuff and those newly 'acquired' load of programmes back up the hill to the town square.

Just as I was making a decision about ditching the tent or programmes, our Guardian Angel Roger reappeared and drove us, programmes and all, up to the coach load-in. I showed my immense gratitude for his kindness, by throwing up his wife's chamomile concoction in the back of his car. The smile never left his face.

The lads who had taken on the Italians at football yesterday were having a rematch after the game had ended 9-9. The second game finished 6-4 to us and both were enjoyed by none other than Ron Noades and Assistant Manager Alan Smith, who stood on the touchline taking photos and chatting to other spectators. His attitude towards our travelling party had totally thawed, as Gary remembers:

"The day after that first game, we were in Main Street and I saw Mr Noades out walking. I went up to him in my best Cook Report style and door-stepped him: 'Hi Mr Noades, I am Gary Chapman and you tried to ban me from organising this trip. When you look at everybody now and at the game, what do you think now?' I can't recall his exact response, although it wasn't angry or nasty. We told him that we were playing the Italian supporters and he came along with Alan Smith. He saw that we were all representing the club superbly."

Despite our best intentions, neither Johnny Bush nor I made it to the supporters rematch. Tony and Percy, seeing our abject state, had taken pity on us. They allowed us to stay in the coach where we spent what seemed like an age, just lying on the floor of the coach feeling ridiculously ill in baking midday heat. Eventually, thirst drove us out of the coach and we discovered it was time to head to the game anyway.

There seemed to be more Sampdoria fans present for this game, hardly a surprise in geographical terms, with Genoa being much closer than Florence. They, too, were more than happy to mingle with us and exchange souvenirs. Our friends from Florence had found a vantage point to watch the first part of the game, without having to pay to get in. They were heading off to the final before our game would be over, although disappointment was in store, as they lost 2-1 to Torino. Someone even managed to get 'Glad All Over' played as the teams came out.

Sampdoria also boasted their fair share of Italia '90 talent. They had just signed the blond Russian Oleksiy Mykhaylychenko, who quickly moved onto Glasgow Rangers the following year. Also in their starting line-up were three Italian internationals, Pietro Vierchowod, Marco Branca, who had a brief spell at Middlesbrough in the late nineties and Roberto Mancini, who needs no introduction. There was one other name on the team sheet who went on to be very familiar in England and at Palace: a certain Attilio Lombardo, who was a non-playing substitute that day.

It was Branca who struck first in the game after only eight minutes and Sampdoria had most of the first half. Palace struck back ten minutes into the second period, when Glyn Hodges rifled a screamer from twenty yards. Palace had strong claims for a late penalty waived away after a foul on Eddie McGoldrick. The game went to straight to penalties after the regulation ninety minutes, which went to sudden death. Perry Suckling saved first, then Rudi Hedman was the unlikely hero of the hour, securing the win for The Eagles.

The mood on the terraces throughout the game had been festive, with conga lines and Mexican waves breaking out at will. The 'Right Side-Left Side' song became 'Pizza v Spaghetti'. Mr Noades was again mentioned in despatches with the chant: "Are you proud of us Ron Noades?" which returned a cheery thumbs-up. The Genovese contingent even gave us a rendition of "We hate Brighton" in English, which sparked off yet another conga.

At the end of the game, the players were cheered off like Roman gladiators, none more so than Rudi. We conga'd our way back to the coach, waiting to start the journey home. As Tony Matthews put it in a brilliant article about the trip in *90 Minutes* magazine: "When you support Crystal Palace and you finish third, you dance!" Prophetic words indeed.

The season commenced with a low-key draw away at Luton Town, somewhere else we weren't supposed to go – although around 2,000 Eagles managed it. The Hatters had a controversial 'Home Fans Only' membership scheme in place at the time, but it was in tatters by the start of that season. From there, Palace leapt up the table, going unbeaten until November. Mark Bright and Ian Wright spearheaded our greatest league season to date, finishing third behind Arsenal and Liverpool. Also winning the Zenith Data Systems Trophy at Wembley for good measure.

A third-place finish should have been enough to see us into Europe. However, UEFA and the English FA had other ideas.

Between 1985 and 1990, all English clubs had been banned from European competition as a result of the Heysel stadium disaster. At the European Final in 1985 between Liverpool and Juventus, serious crowd disorder led to the collapse of a wall on the terrace, which caused the deaths of 39 Italians and Belgians. The finger was pointed firmly in the direction of a small section of the Liverpool support and, as a result, the English clubs served a five-year ban from all European competition.

This may also go some way to explaining why the club and authorities had been so nervous about the St Vincent coach trip. It was the first travel of English club support into Europe since the ban had been lifted. As already noted, it was uncomfortably close to Turin – home of Juventus.

Although the ban on English clubs had expired, Liverpool's own ban was for an undefined period. This was amended to another five years. As a result of their absence, England clubs had slipped right down the UEFA rankings and thus only had one space allocated in each competition.

As the season entered its final phase, Palace won away at Leeds United, our nearest challengers for third place, and were now firmly on course for the available UEFA Cup slot, by virtue of the fact that the ineligible Liverpool were in second. Just as we began to believe, UEFA dashed our hopes.

Early in 1991, the English media started to call for Liverpool's ban from European competition to be lifted at the end of that season. This idea gained momentum via a number of high profile television pundits. UEFA admitted that informal discussions with the club and the English FA had taken place. By April, the decision, supported by the English FA, was made to lift Liverpool's ban with immediate effect. The season was over 80% complete at this stage and suddenly the goalposts had been moved.

Discounting the period during which all English clubs were exiled, Liverpool's individual ban amounted to one season. To put it into perspective, that season Dynamo Dresden had been banned from European competition for two seasons for their fans getting a game abandoned in a European quarter-final. Five years later, Spurs served a one season punishment for fielding an under-strength side in the Intertoto.

It is not possible to directly correlate the softening of the authority's stance on the club directly with the utterly tragic events at Hillsborough in 1989, when 96 Liverpool fans needlessly lost their lives in a terrace crush. However, many Palace fans still believe it was an influential factor.

No-one outside South London spared a thought for Palace, whose European hopes had been shattered so late in the season. It still beggars belief that there was no formal representation to either the FA or UEFA from the Club about the ramifications of this late decision to re-admit Liverpool. Outwardly, the strength of response was for our Manager, Steve Coppell to call the English FA 'Chocolate Soldiers' and the Chairman also laid blame at the FA's door saying that he thought Palace's case had been underplayed in UEFA meetings – if indeed it had been recognised at all. In a radio interview with *Capital Gold*, he seemed more concerned by the loss of an estimated million pounds income, but there was no talk of appealing the decision. Why Ron Noades did not kick up an almighty fuss is a secret he carried to his grave.

As *Eagle Eye* pointed out in their book *We All Follow The Palace*:

> "The FA could and should have asked for special dispensation for Palace. Germany was a reunified country, yet two East German teams were still permitted to enter the UEFA Cup. It should not have been beyond the wit of the FA to call for a preliminary game between Palace and the fourth team in the old German League: Chemie Halle. A team not considered good enough for entry into the Bundesliga."

For the record, Chemie Halle (now known as Hallescher FC) did not progress from the first round going down 4-2 on aggregate to Torpedo Moscow.

There was a strong rumour that the lack of any challenge was due to ongoing negotiations with the FA to include a redeveloped Selhurst Park as the second London venue for the 1996 European Championships hosted by England. In the event, there was no second London venue chosen for Euro 1996. To this day, despite several changes of ownership of club and ground, the redevelopment of Selhurst remains a painfully slow and drawn out process.

Palace take on Fiorentina in the Italian Alps - August 1990

The *Eagle Eye* coach crew - August 1990
[Photo: Gary Chapman]

2

THE ANGLO-ITALIAN JOB

It's strange to think that since my first amazing Italian experience over thirty years ago, a senior Palace side has yet to return there. That said, there have been Italian Youth tournaments since, in which Palace have been represented and our youngsters have acquitted themselves very well against the world's biggest clubs.

Back in 1971, one of Palace's most notable historic moments came against Internazionale (Inter Milan) during the post season Anglo-Italian Inter-League Clubs Competition. Palace faced off against the Italian giants twice, in home and away legs. After a 1-1 draw at home, we went to the San Siro and won 2-1, becoming only the second English side to ever win there, following Birmingham City's 1961 triumph in the Inter-Cities Fairs Cup. It would be another 32 years until another English club won there, when Arsenal thumped Inter 5-1 in the Champions League.

First staged in 1970, the Anglo-Italian Tournament was a curious beast that ran for four seasons. The competition was conceived after both countries found themselves with enlarged wage bills, due to the extension of the close season to accommodate the 1970 World Cup. The first post-season tournament was a financial success, with all competing teams turning a profit. This created an appetite for more, so the tournament became an annual event.

A format was developed with many innovations, but these were not always successful. Squad numbering was introduced; a choice of two substitutes from five and a penalty shoot-out to settle drawn games, these were all welcomed, however the radical idea of a league point for each goal scored proved controversial. The grouping and league system takes some following. The competing clubs were divided into three groups, each containing two from each country. Each English team met its respective Italian opponent on a two-legged home-and-away basis but did not play the side from their own country.

Palace were not involved in the first tournament, which was won by Swindon, although the final against Napoli was abandoned after 79 minutes due to 'politically motivated' crowd trouble. The scoreline, a remarkable 3-0 to the Wiltshire side, was allowed to stand.

As a result of the violence, which saw 40 police officers and 60 fans injured, Napoli were banned from all European competition for two years.

In 1971, Palace were joined by Swindon, as defending Champions and five other First Division sides, although Blackpool had just been relegated. Stoke City, Huddersfield Town and West Bromwich Albion completed the English complement. They were up against Roma, Inter Milan, Cagliari, Bologna, Hellas Verona and Sampdoria.

Palace got the worst possible draw and had to face current champions Inter, and Cagliari, the 1970 champions. West Bromwich Albion were the other unlucky English team. Palace started well and led the group by beating Cagliari 1-0 at Selhurst. The Sardinian side included the legendary Luigi Riva, star of the Italian National side that finished runners-up to Brazil at the Mexico World Cup the previous year. In front of 19,326 at Selhurst, Bobby Tambling scored the only goal. Three days later, Palace faced Inter at home, in front of the *Match of the Day* cameras.

The team changes childishly scrawled on the paper team sheet would suggest I was there. I'd like to be able to say I remember something of it, but sadly not. This would have been one of my earliest visits to Selhurst Park. My first had come in September 1970 when my Dad's team Nottingham Forest were the visitors. Dad, his mate Bill Gant and I had seats in what was known as the New Stand back then (subsequently the Arthur Wait Stand). Ray was on the Holmesdale terrace with his mates. I was wearing a little red and white rosette. Yes, red and white… I was still following in my father's footsteps at that point.

It only took a 2-0 Palace win that day to get me to change my allegiance, as only a fickle six-year-old can. The same had happened to my father in 1965 with Ray. Second Division Palace were responsible for a fifth round FA Cup giant killing, beating First Division Forest 3-1 at Selhurst. Poor old Dad. Still, I think he had the last laugh as he got to see his beloved Forest win the Football League in 1978 and then the European Cup twice in his lifetime.

Not long after my first game, Ray began to take me on the Holmesdale, when he wasn't working as a wedding photographer. I had a little home-made platform to stand on and we went to so many games together whilst I was growing up. Ray played a couple of trial games in goal for Palace's youth team, but despite keeping clean sheets, he was not taken on. Despite this rejection, his passion for Palace and football in general was infectious. I was quickly and deeply hooked.

I often think of how Ray might have enjoyed going abroad with me to watch Palace. His young family meant he was happy and secure at home when I started to travel. He was one of the founders of Palace's Family Enclosure in 1988 and we worked there, as a family, throughout the seasons in the top flight in the early nineties. Devastatingly, in 1999, Ray was taken from us way too early after a long, but spirited struggle with cancer. He was only fifty.

Back to the Inter game, with or without me in the crowd. Alan Birchenall fired Palace into an early lead and the Italians took a while to get going, with Palace missing a hatful of chances. Get going they did, however, when Roberto Boninsegna, another Italian World Cup star, scored a superb solo effort. Palace Manager, Bert Head, crowed: "We should have won it in the first half. This game today would have made a great final."

At the beginning of June, Palace travelled to Italy for the two second legs. Palace were no match for Cagliari on Sardinian home soil, falling 2-0 to goals from 'Gigi Riva, who still retains God-like status on the island. Due to the goal-scoring points system, the result effectively ended Palace's chances of progressing to the final stages of the competition.

Palace moved on to the mainland and the San Siro, where Inter had not lost since November. Despite the odds, Palace amazed everyone. "Bobby Tambling kept a promise here tonight when he gunned in two great goals and lifted Crystal Palace to a stunning two-goal victory over Italian Champions, Inter Milan," wrote Norman Giller in the *Daily Express*.

Tambling had something of a point to prove, having been written off not only by Chelsea, who he had recently left, but also by sections of the press, who had upset him by misquoting his age. The striker protested that, at 29, he was not yet at the veteran stage. Giller agreed saying that he looked like a 'coltish thoroughbred' as he scored with either foot. With his summation though, one wonders about the sobriety of the Express correspondent as he claimed: "By the time the final shots were fired Palace had built themselves a reputation for greatness that will live long in the memory of this soccer-mad city."

The victory was made all the sweeter as Palace's captain Steve Kember was affected by a stomach bug and Birchenall, scorer in the home leg, wasn't fully fit. Palace went into half-time leading but were quickly pegged back by Tarcisio Burgnich after the break. John Jackson was called on for one of his 'stonewall' performances, before Tambling silenced the San Siro.

Our heroics were not given due reward. The other English sides had much easier games and scored with ease. Palace finished fifth out of the six, with only WBA below us. Harry Miller in the *Daily Mirror* called our placing "a tragedy". Bert Head echoed that, saying: "I felt sorry for my players that they are not in the final. They deserve to be there." Blackpool lifted the trophy after putting their miserable league form behind them to defeat Bologna 2-1 in extra time.

Sports Journalist Nick Harling was one of a small number of Palace fans who travelled to Italy along with Chris Wright (later to find 'fame' as the leader of the

Palace Action Campaign that became something of a thorn in Ron Noades' side in the early eighties). Nick has some fascinating memories of the trip:

> "About six of us went on the trip to Italy on the cheap in a van. Roger, a mate of Chris's, came along to help him with the driving. We were also joined by Marilyn, a Liverpool fan we had befriended at the 1970 World Cup in Mexico. Sadly, I can't remember who the others in the van were, but they were more interested in the beach. I do recall we had to leave right after the final whistle of the Inter home game. Time was tight and we travelled through the night.
>
> Only Chris and I actually went to Sardinia. It was a 13-hour overnight ferry from Civitavecchia on the mainland, which none of the others fancied. I remember being extremely impressed by Riva but have no recollection of his goals.
>
> Chris was well in with the players, so we chatted to them after the game, especially Alan 'Birch' Birchenall, with whom Chris was very friendly. Bert Head also made us very welcome... we didn't have time to interact with the locals because of our tight schedule. We went to the island, saw the game and hurried back early the next morning to head to Milan.
>
> It was my first visit to the San Siro but, if anything, I seem to recall that I found it more awe inspiring on subsequent visits as there was a smaller crowd there for Palace's game. Frankly, Inter had much bigger things on their plate. Tambling's winning goal was a long range worldie. The crowd did not take it well. There were boos, catcalls and hisses from the cognoscenti."

After that game, Nick stayed in Italy with his girlfriend at the time, whilst the others headed home. He even went to the final in Bologna, much to the disgust of the girlfriend who was out there on a family holiday.

Again, the 1971 tournament did well financially, with crowds up a third on its inaugural year, ensuring its continuation the following year. The Palace home game against Inter established a tournament record for a game staged in England.

Palace skipped a year, but the format of the tournament they came back to in 1973 was very different. The points per goals rule had gone, in the wake of Blackpool's early 10-0 thrashing of Lanerossi Vicenza in 1972, which practically guaranteed another final placing. This time however, they lost 3-1 to Roma, meaning the cup left English shores for the first time.

Other changes to the format saw the competition expanded to eight teams from each country and the group structures were also enlarged. Now, teams would not play each other home and away, instead a draw was made, so each club had two home games and two away against different opposition.

The biggest change of all – and one that, arguably, hastened the tournament's demise – was that the games were no longer post-season. Palace, in particular, were singled out for severe admonishment by the British press, as it was felt these games would prove a distraction to our relegation dogfight. The same could be said of similarly struggling Manchester United, who had signed on, ostensibly to quell the feeling on the Italian side that the bigger English clubs were not taking the competition seriously.

Attendances were down across the board and at Selhurst only 13,500 people attended the two home ties, against 44,800 in 1971. Also, clubs from both countries started to field weaker sides, choosing to blood youngsters rather than risk key players. Unlike Manchester United, however, Palace did well in the group stage, winning both home games.

First up was Hellas Verona, who were dispatched 4-1 with goals from Martin Hinshelwood, Bobby Bell and a brace from Alan Whittle. The second Selhurst game saw John Craven hit a hat-trick – the first ever in the competition – which was enough to see off Lazio 3-1. The two away games in the group saw Derek Possee head home the only goal at Bari. He then netted twice in a 2-2 draw at Fiorentina. It was good enough to qualify for the semi-final. It was just a shame that our league form was not equivalent. Palace were relegated at the end of the season, with the semi-final still to play.

The semi was a two-legged affair, but there was no Italian opposition for Palace to face, instead a two-legged affair against Newcastle, before we could savour a final against either Bologna or a rematch with Fiorentina. Palace earned a goal-less draw in the home leg but were thrashed 5-1 by the Magpies in the return, with Jim Cannon scoring the consolation. Newcastle went on to win the final 2-1 against Fiore, thus adding this trophy to their previous European honour; the Inter-Cities Fairs Cup, which they won in 1969.

Nick Harling did not travel to the games in Italy this time. Although even after the depressing relegation, he believes he did attend both legs of the semi-final, although neither have stuck in his memory.

No longer in profit, the Anglo-Italian Tournament folded, to re-emerge three years later as a semi-professional tournament. Local side Sutton United were the only English side to win it in 1979. After 1982, the competition was rebranded by the Italians and they dropped the involvement of the English sides altogether. The tournament ceased again in 1986.

The tournament was revived yet again for the 1992/3 season, ostensibly as a replacement for the Full Members Cup in England. A trophy that Palace had actually lifted in 1991 during their 'annus mirabilis'.

This time the premise was that the 24 English second tier sides would play off amongst themselves within groups of three across three games. The groups were arranged geographically to create interest in local derbies and mitigate travel costs, insofar as possible. The winners of each group would go to meet the eight Italian Serie B sides that came through their own qualification process.

The first year, one of the English groups had to be decided on the toss of a coin, as West Ham United and Bristol Rovers had identical records. The Hammers progressed but went out in the following group, Derby County topped the English sides in that group, and played an all-English two-legged semi-final against Brentford, winning through on away goals. The Rams succumbed to 3-1 Cremonese at Wembley, the new home of the final. Ex-Palace striker Marco Gabbiadini was their goalscorer.

Palace were relegated from the Premier League on the last day of the 1992/3 season, so once again we renewed our acquaintance with this tournament. Manager Alan Smith had already condemned it as "ill-conceived" before a ball had been kicked, mindful of the fixture pile-up it would create. Palace were placed into a group with Charlton and Millwall, who had already played out a 2-2 draw. When Palace faced the Addicks at the Valley it had become almost a sudden death scenario. A defeat would mean Palace could not qualify, leaving the Millwall fixture as a dead rubber for us.

The game was played in the September international break, meaning Palace were without most of the first-choice defence. The dream of Italy effectively died within sixty seconds of the start as Charlton took the lead. Paul Williams, getting some stick from the home fans for being a 'Charlton reject', clawed one back for Palace, but only straight after Charlton had scored their second. Any hope of comeback was dashed when Chris Armstrong was sent off for a violent challenge, just before the break.

Amongst the away support, there was a strong feeling that the in-form Palace striker had been targeted from the off. Charlton knew that they had to face Palace three times more in the coming weeks; once in the league and also in a two-legged League Cup draw. There were several niggling challenges and off-the-ball digs on him that went largely unpunished, before the sending-off. Charlton scored twice more in the second half, leaving Millwall with a mountain to climb at Selhurst.

The men from the New Den needed to win by four clear goals to qualify outright. Although we had nothing to play for, Palace rescued themselves from the ignominy of finishing bottom of the group, with a 3-0 win. Goals came from Williams, a penalty from the not-yet-banned Armstrong and a last- minute David Whyte effort. In truth, the goal tally should have been much higher. Millwall's debutant goalkeeper, Carl Emberson, had been sent off in the penalty incident and 'Wall had not named a substitute 'keeper. Left winger Lee Luscombe had to deputise between the sticks, but Palace gave him an easy ride with some wildly off-target shots.

Armstrong was subsequently banned for two of the following three games against Charlton, but if they had, indeed, engineered his absence it totally backfired. Palace raced to a 3-1 lead in the first leg of the Cup, following up with a gritty goalless away draw in the league five days later. The final straw was Armstrong himself grabbing the only goal of the second leg, on his first game back! Whilst I am indulging in schadenfreude, it should also be noted that Charlton finished bottom of their group in the next stage of the Anglo-Italian Tournament. Brescia were the eventual winners of the trophy that season, defeating Notts County 1-0.

The competition staggered on for two more years. Palace were promoted at the end of 1993/94, thus did not take part the following year. Though it is doubtful they would have entered anyway, as the English group qualifying stage had been scrapped and participation was by invitation. Notts County went back to Wembley as English finalists in 1995 and this time triumphed 2-1 over Ascoli. When Palace found themselves back in the second tier for the 1995/96 season, there was no appetite to enter a competition now infamous for its truly shocking disciplinary record. Genoa lifted the trophy for the final time beating Port Vale 5-2.

Palace have had four more encounters with Italian clubs to date: all friendlies at Selhurst. In 2003, a friendly in the September international break was arranged against Brescia. Palace raced to a three goal lead, but were pegged back in the second half, eventually losing 4-3. Not before Palace Manager Steve Kember was involved in a side-line altercation with his rather corpulent opposite number. With the Palace support only occupying the Main Stand, the Italian coach was subjected to rather heartless chants of "Who ate all the pasta?" from right behind the bench, which further increased his ire. The handshakes between benches at the end of the game seemed begrudging at best.

The following season we welcomed Sampdoria to Selhurst. Our former favourite, Lombardo was coaching their reserve side at the time, but did not make the journey over with the senior side, for a much-hoped-for curtain call. The Genovese side dismissed newly-promoted Palace with an ease that belied the 1-0 score line.

In 2005, Inter Milan were invited to Selhurst to participate in a marquee match marking Palace's Centenary Season. Early rumours suggested that this would be a two-legged affair with a return game in the San Siro. These were quickly dismissed when the Chairman, Simon Jordan, explained the cost was almost too high to get the Italians to play us here, let alone back in Milan.

With a week to go before the game and with the game already sold out, the Italians publicly threatened to pull out. The reason given was that they did not feel safe after the July 7th terrorist attack on London. Frantic back-room negotiations took place, including, no doubt, further costs for Palace to increase security for our honoured guests. All this drama took place whilst Palace were out on tour in Germany.

Although the game did go ahead, it was a rather muted affair for a supposed Centenary celebration. Palace didn't really look like they would ever trouble Inter, who ran out comfortable 2-0 winners with goals from young Nigerian striker Obifemi Martens and Greece's midfield star of Euro 2004, Giorgis Karagounis.

Our last home encounter with an Italian side was Lazio in 2013. Veteran German international Miroslav Klose scored the only goal of the game for the visitors.

So ends Palace's Italian adventures to date. I very much hope it is not a final end: I yearn soon to return there with a senior Palace side in some capacity. The trip in 1990 remains among my fondest football memories and began a personal fascination with watching Palace play abroad whenever and wherever I could.

The Gijon Minibus party begins to assemble at Sutton - August 1991
L-R: Richard Moore, Dave Stovell, Me, Nicki Carey, Rick Ballantine, Robbie Tobin, Andy Carey, Pete Jones, Nigel Campey.

3

BUSMAN'S HOLIDAY

Early in the 1991 close season, Palace announced their pre-season plans, which included three overseas trips. Palace News, the free Club newspaper, simpered about these games being good preparation for when we did get to play in proper European competition, ignoring the controversy surrounding the circumstances of our non-qualification that season.

After Italy, I was desperate for another adventure. Palace had played a Gibraltar XI to inaugurate their stadium towards the end of the previous season, without giving any prior notice to supporters. This caused some upset amongst the regular travellers, who were denied the chance to go for a few days in the sun. Their main bone of contention seemed to be that the Club had publicised two post-season friendlies in May within the home programme immediately prior to the trip, yet not made any mention whatsoever of the match on The Rock. The game finished in a 2-2 draw.

The first of the three trips announced was the traditional Scandinavian training camp in Sweden, which had taken place every season since 1987 under Steve Coppell's management. It was a very popular pre-season destination for English clubs at the time.

These trips would be interspersed with games every couple of days against local teams midway through their summer season. In theory, you'd think that this might provide some form of competition, but the standard of football there was such that scorelines often more closely resembled cricket scores in Palace's favour. Good practice for the strikers, at least.

Before the days of budget airlines, Sweden was an incredibly expensive country to visit. Also, with no internet, just getting news of the games was difficult without someone on the inside. Very few fans travelled across to these tours, although Palace were not completely without representation on the terraces. Local members of Scandinavian Eagles supporters' group would be in attendance, whenever they had managed to get notice of the games.

Of more interest to the travelling faithful was a one-off friendly out in Greece against AEK Athens and our participation in the Costa Verde (Green Coast) Tournament hosted by Spanish side Sporting Gijon. Palace Travel offered trips to both. This was a firm of travel agents based at Selhurst Park, which had some connection with the Club that was never quite explained.

Finances for most travellers dictated that we choose one trip or the other. Anything involving flights was certainly out of my wallet's reach back then, so I plumped for a less official mini-bus trip to Spain, organised by Rick Ballantine – one of Palace's regular away travel crew.

Club photographer Neil "Mr Cad" Everitt and Kevin Barthrop - an away regular and keen groundhopper - chose the official Athens trip which left on the Saturday evening of a 3-2 defeat in a friendly at Fulham. Kevin recalls how the official trip didn't go quite to plan:

"We were told to check in at 9.40pm only to find that the plane was due to take off at 12.40am, an hour later than stated in the trip itinerary. Neil and I decided to go airside and get a pre-flight pint. Upon getting my beer, I looked up to see that our flight had been delayed until 2.20am!

By the time we finally arrived at our Athens Hotel it was 9.30am Greek time. It was too late to sleep, so we hit the sights in the morning. Great views but hard work at 90 degrees in the shade. The next sight was a Taverna for lunch and more beers, before continuing with the sightseeing in the afternoon.

Monday was matchday and at 5pm we headed for the Metro. We arrived at the ground to find it deserted. It turned out that kick off was at 9pm to avoid the worst of the heat. Something else that was unclear from the official itinerary. We retired to the nearest bar, returning to the ground at 8.15pm.

We entered the ground just as Palace players were walking onto the pitch to be greeted by a chant, in English, of "Crystal Palace! Fuck off!" from the AEK fans. Charming! Although the players seemed quite amused by it."

AEK scored first, but were quickly pegged back by a thunderbolt volley from Andy Gray. In the second half Palace began to dominate with a short passing game aimed at retaining possession, unlike the long ball game that was associated with the team at the time. Kevin was in shock:

"I could scarcely believe I was watching Palace. Ian Wright had a lively second half, but was subject to some particularly crude tackling – including one absolute shocker – which got him riled up. The next time he received the ball, just inside his own half, he burst forward beating five Greek players on the way to the box. Just when it seemed he had lost control, he managed to flick the ball into the path of Mark Bright, who finished with a sublime chip. Even the AEK fans warmly applauded the goal before throwing their polystyrene seat cushions in the air to signal their disgust that their own team."

It should have been enough for the win, except for some interminable and unwarranted injury time in which Athens took full advantage by equalising with the last kick. Then was back to the bar for Kevin to meet up with Neil, who was doubling as the official Clubcall reporter (CPFC's premium rate 0898 telephone information line), as well as photographer that evening.

> "The barman was so happy to see us again that he gave us free beers and said he hoped
> Palace would be back again soon in the European Cup... if only."

Two trips down and one to go for the first team. The three team Costa Verde Tournament in Northern Spain was the final one on the overseas agenda. The other sides competing were the hosts: Sporting Gijon, fifth in the Spanish top flight the previous season, and Bulgarian side, Levski Sofia, who had finished sixth in their domestic league.

Again, concrete information about the tournament was scarce. The venue for both games was known, but the travelling party had been told that Palace would be playing on the Monday and Wednesday. This meant leaving directly after the Club XI friendly at Sutton on the Saturday evening to ensure we would get there in time.

Rick did a brilliant job pulling this trip together, from organising the 15-seater Minibus and who would drive it; the ferry crossing; right down to getting a route from the AA that avoided expensive motorway tolls. No satnav or GPS back then. The cost was dependent on how many people he could get interested, but it needed a minimum of twelve to keep it affordable. Understandably Rick only wanted people who he could trust on the trip, so the invite was made to regular Palace travellers he knew well.

This raised eight: Robbie Tobin, Andy Carey and Rick from the away travel club, their mates Dave Stovell, Richard Moore and Nigel Campey (who had been in St. Vincent) plus away regulars Shaun Ellis and myself.

To make up the numbers, Rick asked us to invite any Palace friends that we could personally vouch for. I chipped in with Alan Jones, who I knew from my Sunday football club, and his brother Pete who happened to be over from Thailand where he lived. Andy Carey also persuaded his wife Nicki to come. The final space was filled by someone I will refer to only as The Sniffer, I'm not even sure I ever knew who invited him. Whoever it was, they quickly disowned him once the trip got going.

Andy Carey had fallen into conversation with Ron Noades in the bar at Sutton. The Chairman seemed impressed that a dozen of us were travelling:

"What flight are you on?"

"Flight?" replied Andy. "We are driving down in a minibus that leaves in about ten minutes."

For once, Mr Noades was lost for words.

35

Problems started almost as soon as we left Sutton. It was a different era back then; smoking was permitted in hire vehicles and Rick was fine about it as we only had three smokers onboard. Two of these were reasonably discreet, lit up infrequently and made sure their smoke did not bother others. The Sniffer made no such consideration.

He chain-smoked constantly, not caring who got a lungful of the smoke from his particularly noxious brand of cigarettes. He pretended not to hear any comments aimed in his direction. Then the van began to fill with a petrol-like smell. Rick was worried it was a fuel leak.

"Can anyone else smell that?"

"Yeah, it seems to be coming from the back" came the reply.

Several pairs of eyes turned and alighted on The Sniffer, who was hunched over, repeatedly cranking his huge petrol lighter open like a flick-knife, but without igniting it. He was dreamily inhaling the fumes.

"Well, you can pack that right up." said Pete, himself a smoker, sitting across from him.

"What the hell is he doing?" I demanded to know from the driver's seat, eyes still on the road.

"Hey, I just love the smell of the fuel" came The Sniffer's response.

Quite how he wasn't left at the side of the A3, I'm not certain. I'm not sure I would have had Rick's patience with him. The Sniffer continued to chain-smoke though, and every time he lit up, another short blast of lighter fuel would fill the van. When he wasn't smoking he would sniff, cough and spit out of the window. I couldn't tell if he was doing it maliciously or just too self-absorbed to care about anyone else.

The ferry departed Portsmouth at midnight and arrived in Cherbourg at around 7am. We drove south, not always on the prescribed route, but in the right general direction. Through Rennes and Nantes, before stopping for a late lunch in the pretty port town of La Rochelle. The expensive harbourside restaurants were way above my budget, so I made do with sandwiches and snacks. The Sniffer was aghast to find that there was no McDonalds and moaned continuously for the next leg of the journey down to Bordeaux.

We stopped again at a service station, someone produced a ball and we had a kickabout to stretch our cramped legs. So keen was I for the trip to happen, that I had volunteered to be one of the drivers right from the outset. What I had not told anyone was that I had never driven on the right side of the road before. How difficult could it be, most of my stint would be on a wide straight dual carriageway with no navigation required until we hit the Spanish border, three hours away.

It wasn't my lack of experience driving abroad that became an issue, but my inability to keep my eyes open. It had been 36 hours since I'd had some proper shut-eye. The combination of the unchanging pine forest and traffic-free, white concrete road quickly lulled me into a stupor. The rest of the van appeared to be dozing too, so no chatter to focus on either.

I was aware of hitting the back of the headrest and waking with a start to find the van was now in the outside lane about to meet the central barrier. My last recollection was of being in the inside lane.

"Did you just fall asleep?" asked Nicki accusatorially.

"No – just stretching my back." I lied, badly.

Andy realised that I needed some stimulation and abandoned his own nap to chat to me for the rest of my stint. In truth, my heart was racing from the adrenaline spike caused by the realisation of what I had nearly done. There was no way I would be able to drift off again.

Crossing the Spanish border was something we were dreading, expecting to get hauled off the bus and questioned. Rick marshalled the paperwork and passports, telling us under no circumstances was anyone to mention football if asked about the nature of our journey. We worried for nothing. They didn't even ask for our passports and we crossed into Spain without stopping

The plan had been to stop just over the border in San Sebastian for the night. Booking budget accommodation from the UK had again proved impossible so we were winging it. San Sebastian seemed extremely busy for a Sunday evening as we headed for the seafront, thinking it the most likely place to find hotels. Instead we found something else entirely.

In the mid-nineties, there was a far-fetched advert for a small car – I forget which brand – with two young girls, who turn out of a side-street and accidentally find themselves as part of a carnival parade. That is exactly what happened to us. It was like something out of a dream, but I definitely wasn't asleep now: we were in the middle of a full-on fiesta. All I could see was puzzled looks from the celebrants on the float in front and a man on stilts in the side-mirror. The police had now realised something was amiss and began running over to us. It was time to get the heck out of Dodge.

I threw the van down the first side road I saw, scattering some pedestrians, who were doubtless surprised to see a minibus barrelling down the one way street in the wrong direction. Fearful of being pursued by the local constabulary and the inevitable scolding that would follow, I rapidly headed out of town west along the coast road.

A little further along, we tried again for accommodation, but everywhere was booked out – or maybe they just didn't like the look of us. Rick took over the driving and I made a bed up across the unused seats at the back, packing the gap with our luggage bags. The Sniffer cast envious eyes at the makeshift bed and said he would be having the next lie-down.

"That is for drivers only" came the swift reply from Rick.

The Sniffer sulkily lit up again, ensuring the gas went unlit for a longer time and then blew his smoke towards my prone form. I was too tired to care and quickly fell into a deep sleep.

It was now gone midnight and another stop proved fruitless, if noisy, as a very drunken Spaniard serenaded the van, believing he had the operatic prowess of Placido Domingo. He didn't. It was agreed that we would push on through the night to Gijon with Richard at the wheel.

Fitfully dozing, I awoke suddenly at a strange angle, pressed into the back of the seat. It was pitch-black and I could just about make out Richard's voice from the front over the roaring engine.

"It just keeps getting steeper and steeper" he said incredulously. Indeed the van seemed to be almost vertical as I struggled against gravity to pull my head forward. The bus eventually levelled out and, in the chatter that followed, I gathered that the AA route had recommended the shortest route across the Cantabrian mountains. Unfortunately it was on roads that were more suitable for goat-herding. This wasn't the only scary ascent or descent that night. Richard did a truly heroic job to get us safely to Gijon.

The milky light of dawn was just breaking as we reached the outskirts of the city at 6.30am, a mere 37 hours since we left Sutton. The stadium was pretty much the first thing we encountered as we neared the city centre. We popped into the car park for a closer look, the first thing we saw was a poster informing us that the Palace games were actually on Tuesday and Wednesday. We had departed earlier than we needed to and could have broken the journey up more sensibly. It didn't go down well with any of us, but now we had something else to deal with.

We had attracted the attention of the local police who, after a chat that neither side really understood, escorted us to the hotel where the players were staying. Not much use at that time of the morning. We parked up and went in search of an English breakfast. Eggs, hot dog sausages and bread were as good as it got, the concept of bacon apparently alien to that café's cook. Though coastal, this part of Spain evidently saw few English tourists.

The players' hotel was way beyond our budget, but they helpfully directed us to a more modest hotel along the main shopping street. Here, they said they were happy to accommodate us, but had nowhere for us to park the bus. Further enquiries suggested the only place to park it would be back at the Stadium car park, which doubled as a long-term lorry park. We also had to wait until the rooms were ready at noon, despite all of us being desperate for a shower and a bed. Time crawled by until we were allowed to check in.

At that point the elephant in the room needed to be addressed. Who would be rooming with The Sniffer? His 'trip sponsor' was suddenly nowhere to be seen, so Alan and Pete took one for the team. Everyone else heaved a sigh of relief. In fact, the Jones Brothers did a great job on The Sniffer for the rest of the trip, tactically steering him away from others when he was being even more annoying than usual.

After ablutions and a quick nap, I decided to go exploring with Alan to find some local food before heading to the ground for the game between our opponents. Some of our party hadn't gone to bed at all, but straight out on the beers instead and thus, not everyone made the game.

On the walk up to the ground we passed a stand selling club memorabilia, also on the display was some rather grim Nazi paraphernalia. Being much younger and dafter back then, some of us adopted the 'Basil Fawlty' approach to mockery instead of expressing our disgust in a more serious manner.

The El Molinon stadium was impressive, literally translated it means 'the big windmill'. The stadium capacity was 45,000 and had played host to three World Cup games in 1982. The most famous of these was the West Germany v Austria stitch-up, which allowed both teams to progress. The stadium was built with no attempt at uniformity which, whilst fostering individuality, led to some odd sightlines. This hadn't yet become a problem, however, as the ground had never seen a capacity crowd. A minor tournament involving Crystal Palace was unlikely to change that fact.

The game was one-way traffic, the home side were far better in all departments than the Bulgars, except one. The level of thuggery and cynicism shown by the Sofia side. It did not bode well for our game the next day, with Palace being so close to the start of their season. Sporting ran out 5-0 winners and we enjoyed spending time on the terrace with their "Ultra-Boys". They were happy enough to chat to us once they realised we were supporting their team for the night and the usual souvenir exchanges took place.

A curious feature of the tournament was the need for a penalty shootout after such a resounding win and Sporting actually lost the spot-kick contest. We didn't have a clue what this meant for Palace, but assumed it must be a good thing. After the game we headed for Fotogramas bar, tucked away in a backstreet. The route to and from our hotel was defined by signposts that had been bent out of shape by a few of our crew who'd passed by earlier. They were not convinced that we would find our way without a visible trail to follow.

The following day was spent at the beach enjoying the sunshine, before heading back to the ground for Palace's game against the bolshy Bulgars, who lived right down to expectations. The game had not captured the Spanish imagination with only 1,100 in the stadium. The bus crew, plus four other travellers did their best to inject some colour into proceedings with a pre-match balloon launch that delighted the local children.

The game itself was a battle, often crude and brutal, with Palace giving as good as they got. Geoff Thomas opened the scoring on ten minutes with a bizarre overhead kick that floated over the goalkeeper like a chip rather than taking the net pegs out. Levski hit back almost immediately through Petrov. Before the game reached the twenty-minute mark, Thomas had struck a long range rocket for Palace to retake the lead. Palace set about Sporting's goal tally as Eddie McGoldrick and then Mark Bright found the woodwork.

The second half saw the usual raft of substitutions which can disrupt the flow of any friendly, but not before Palace had increased the lead thanks to one of the early subs: Stan Collymore. His tricky low cross set up John Salako, who dispatched with a diving header at the back post. Cue the second round of substitutions. There were no more goals, but plenty more fouls. An awful challenge on John Humphrey, which required him to go off, set off a huge melee.

As the final whistle sounded, there was no shirt-swapping or handshakes, just another mass brawl. The referee brandished a card like a semaphore in the midst of a storm. It was impossible to tell what had happened from the sidelines, but we got the lowdown later.

Such was the ill-will that Palace appeared not to want to take part in the penalty shootout, but eventually relented, winning 4-3 with Andy Woodman saving well and Ian Wright putting the final penalty to bed.

I had been asked by the Club's Publications Department to file the official Clubcall report and headed back to the players' hotel to do so and also to try and figure out what had gone on at the end. Alan Smith, the Assistant Manager at the time, was quick to collar me.

"Look we don't want any news of Geoff's sending off to get back home," he warned.

"Well, consider that done because I've already written the report and didn't know we'd had anyone sent off." I replied.

With that Alan's face broke into a grin and handed me a beer. He proceeded to tell me that one of the Bulgars had spat in Richard Shaw's face at the final whistle and Geoff, as Captain, had remonstrated in time-honoured fashion by chinning him. Despite the mass brawl going on, the Referee had spotted both the spit and the punch, so both players got their marching orders.

"It'll affect his England place if it gets out." Alan underlined.

"No worries there." I confirmed. "Geoff is one of my most favourite players."

(And he still is.)

The card-less report was eventually phoned through on the hotel's public phone, once Andy Woodman had finished telling his mum about his shootout heroics. I also took the opportunity to clarify what the significance of the penalty shootout was. As far as anyone knew, it was worth an extra point in the table. If true, it put Palace top of the group going into the final game, but no-one appeared certain.

I rejoined our happy crew, now swelled by a couple of the Palace fans who had made their own way to Gijon: Dave Hynes and Steve Carleton. Steve had been through the mill on the trip having gotten beaten up on the journey and looked rather pale. We all celebrated the win until the small hours, not caring that we had to be up early for checkout the next morning. A boozy evening was enlivened by a group of bullfighters in full regalia, who came into the bar late on. They were clearly used to being revered wherever they went and didn't appreciate the hoots of derision from our group.

The now obligatory last day hangover was another doozy, but not as bad as the previous year in Italy or those of the chaps who'd been on the brandy and chocolate milk cocktails. I could, at least, function. The weather had turned and it was grey and wet, so no more beach for us. We whiled away the time guarding the bus, which was now full of our bags ready for the long trip home after the game. We had discussed staying an extra night to do the mountain drive in the daylight this time, but decided to pay the motorway tolls instead. The friendly car park attendant bore an uncanny resemblance to Benny Hill and provided good value entertainment directing the traffic with some wild gestures.

We had also decided that, although Sporting's Ultra-Boys had been friendly enough at Monday's game, there was a distinct feeling that, should Palace be leading, they might be less accommodating. We bought tickets in the seated section instead of the terrace. Another balloon launch was accompanied by the sound of the 'Euro horns' (what we now know as vuvuzelas) that we had purchased. These plastic droning horns had long been part of the soundscape of European football, but fell out of favour during the nineties. The 2010 World Cup in South Africa brought them to the attention of the football stage again, where they were absolutely reviled by everyone except the African nations. There would be no revival for them in Europe.

Palace started the game brightly but fell behind midway through the first half when Paul Bodin was caught out of position and Luhovy converted the cross. Palace had two strong penalty shouts denied, before Sporting had a second chalked off for handball. Luhovy managed to grab a second despite being wildly offside leaving Palace two goals down at the break.

Palace reverted to their more traditional 4-4-2 formation and within five minutes had pulled one back, when Eddie McGoldrick's cross was turned into his own net by Muniz. This time, the rash of substitutions didn't disrupt the game, in fact as far as Palace were concerned, they improved it. With fifteen minutes left, Stan Collymore headed home from a corner and Palace were level.

The game finished and we waited for the tournament-deciding penalty shootout, instead the trophy was brought out and promptly awarded to Sporting! Ian Wright led the protests then stormed off, followed by several of his team-mates. Mark Bright was left to sheepishly lift the runners-up trophy. Ultimately, the Ultra-Boys lived up to their Sporting name and chanted "Crystal Palace" approvingly as what was left of our team applauded them.

We headed back to the van with a sour taste in our mouths, but our spirits were lifted by the sight of scores of children taking our balloons home with them. As we sat in traffic, we also spotted a ghostly-white Steve, full of beer and bonhomie, dancing his way along the pavement without a care in the world.

No-one was looking forward to the all-nighter ahead of us in the bus, but the move to the motorways paid dividends. A journey that had taken us nearly five hours on the way was reduced to three. A driver change break allowed me time to phone through the Clubcall report, while Andy Carey entertained the locals with his newly-acquired Euro horn. It was 1am, but he saw it as justified revenge for Placido Domingo. This argument might have carried more weight if we had stopped in the same village.

By using the toll roads, the whole journey was much quicker and we arrived back in Cherbourg a good few hours before the sailing we were booked on. A very pleasant evening of food, beer and table football was enjoyed by the bus crew. In the bar on the boat, The Sniffer piped up:

"This trip has been brilliant. Where are we all going next year?"

It was a race to see who got there first; Andy Carey won.

"We might be going somewhere, but you *ain't* coming with us!"

I'm not sure if he took this advice literally, but I never saw the bloke again at another Palace match. Come to think of it, I don't remember seeing him at a match before the trip either.

Levski and Palace take the field for a bruising encounter - August 1991

Mark Bright lifts the Runners-up trophy in Gijon - August 1991

4

ACROSS THE GREAT DIVIDES

The following season was one of change, though sadly not for the better. With the Club unable to offer him European football, Ian Wright decided his future lay elsewhere and joined Arsenal in a £2.5million deal in September. Alan Smith, interviewed by Edmund Brack in 2021 for the *VAVEL.com* website, explained:

"It derailed us massively [not qualifying for Europe] and what followed was that we ended up selling Ian Wright. The players were realising at that stage that they were pretty good.

I think missing out on any further progression, when we did finish third in the league, had a knock-on effect in the changing room. I think it also unsettled Steve [Coppell] a little bit; he was probably thinking, 'How much further can I take the club?'

Steve was so loyal to Palace and he loved the club, but there was a time when Tottenham were interested in him. There was also talk at the time of Steve becoming England Manager, so there was a lot of anxiety around the club that you could see brewing."

After an audacious failed attempt to prise Alan Shearer away from Southampton, Wright's eventual replacement, Marco Gabbiadini, never settled at Palace after his £1.8 million transfer from Sunderland. He was off to Derby County before the season ended. Palace finished tenth and ended the season with the unlikely strike partnership of Mark Bright and defender Chris Coleman. For the second year in a row, the summer signings were less than stellar and failed to address the deficiency up front.

The 1992 close season brought forth two foreign tours, the routine trip to Sweden, however before that Palace were invited to become the first foreign team to play in South Africa after the end of the apartheid regime. You have to wonder whether Palace would have been invited had a recently-surfaced rumour been more widely-known at the time. The story goes that Palace hosted an impromptu game at the Mitcham Training ground against Sundowns (now known as Mamelodi Sundowns) in 1986, during apartheid.

At the time, the South African club was owned by flamboyant playboy Zola Mahobe, who decided to fly his entire team and partners to England for the FA Cup Final. It was while they were here that the game is alleged to have taken place, in contravention of the United Nations ban on sporting links in force at the time. The game was said to be completely unofficial, with dustbins being used as goalposts and refereed by their coach. There was no press coverage, we don't know which players took part and the score remains unknown. Two years later, after bankrolling the Sundowns to promotion and a cup win, Mahobe had to relinquish the club, following his conviction for bank fraud.

The 1992 tour was a highly prestigious two-game affair against South African National League Champions, Kaizer Chiefs and their fiercest rivals, Orlando Pirates. The games were played over two consecutive days of a weekend and the whole tour was a huge event for the country. The Palace team were warmly welcomed at the airport by scores of Chiefs fans, including their Zulu Witchdoctor mascot. It was a raucous greeting at 6.30am, which the Palace staff seemed utterly unprepared for, having just come off a twelve hour flight. The waiting TV crews captured their bewilderment in all its glory!

The Chiefs game took place in Johannesburg at the First National Bank Stadium on the Saturday in front of a crowd of over 50,000. This ground was later to host the 2010 World Cup Final, although it was much improved by then. The next day, Palace had to fly to Durban for the match against the Pirates, even though they were also a Johannesburg side based in Soweto. Palace did, however, hold a training session at the Orlando Stadium.

Palace won the first game, a 3-2 thriller, with a brace from Mark Bright – continuing his 22 goal form from the previous season – and a diving header from John Salako. The following day Palace lost 2-1 to the Pirates, with 45,000 packed into Kings Park in Durban. The result was put down to a combination of fatigue and some outrageous refereeing decisions. Mark Bright scored the consolation goal.

I'd had a promotion at work and could have afforded to go on the official trip, however, there were certain events in the year where my attendance was mandatory. One of those was the Marks and Spencer Annual General Meeting, which happened to fall on the same date that the trip left the UK. I was scuppered. Three people who did go, making their own way out there, were Claire Baker, Kelvin Blackman and Martin Young, who had all been on the *Eagle Eye* coach to Italy in 1990. This was a very different trip though, as Martin relates:

"The mad idea of going on this trip came in the pub after our weekly game of five-a-side. The trip was announced pretty late so we had to move fast. A friend of Kelvin's was a travel agent and pulled together a trip for around £1,000 each for 10 days.

We flew out to Johannesburg on 14th July, also my birthday and we stayed four days there. It was, umm, interesting. Our hotel was in the red light district and someone was shot in the hotel on our first night. We had gone out for a meal and when we came back there were people outside milling around everywhere. We'd spoken to some guys in the bar before we went out. Nelson Mandela was free, but there it was still very much 'white rule' at that time. The ANC and Inkatha were jockeying for position. It was a very volatile city at the time.

We had dropped our bags when we arrived and then went to explore. We had the feeling it wasn't the best part of town when we went into a petrol station and the goods were covered over with tarpaulins. We had to ask for what we wanted from the guy behind the counter and he would get it for us. We were only after a couple of cans of Coke.

We went back to the hotel bar and got friendly with a couple of barmen. There were also some British ex-pats there and some old-boy Afrikaaners as well. They asked what we'd been up to that afternoon. They were horrified, we been wandering around in one of the very worst parts of the city centre. We still went out again though, in the same district, to a really nice Chinese restaurant above a shop, although this time taking taxis as advised.

On another occasion, we were in the bar and Kelvin wanted to go to a shop opposite. He was advised to go alone and quickly. Also to leave his watch behind, only take very little money and one of us had to watch him all the way from a window. One of the Afrikaaners was definitely a product of Apartheid and did not like us talking to the black bar staff. For us, this was really weird. Obviously, we knew something of the situation beforehand, but to experience it first hand was quite disturbing.

There was one other guy called Paul out there with us, who had been in touch with Kelvin. I ended up sharing a room with him. He wasn't used to our drinking style, so we didn't see too much of him.

We managed to get tickets for the first game through our hotel, so that wasn't a problem. I remember getting in and then wandering around inside the ground. Somehow we managed to find ourselves downstairs next to the dressing rooms. The door opened and Ron Noades walked out. We had the very briefest of conversations, but he wasn't particularly pleased to see us! We ended up being shepherded out to the pitch side and then walked back up through the stands.

The Jo'burg crowd seemed to be more keen on the skills on display than the actual game. Any showboating would send them crazy! They took a huge, friendly interest in our black players, especially Mark Bright and John Salako. They were certainly aware of Salako's African background and he was the poster boy.

We flew down to Durban the next day and it was a different world. So much more laid-back and everyone seemed to get on. It was a far more youthful city where the new generation seemed to have much more of a say. We stayed in a reasonable hotel there and I particularly recall the huge number of street sellers that would set up each day along the seafront. It was a big tourist hotspot, not just for South Africans.

For the second game, we didn't have tickets so went in early. Suddenly it felt like there was several thousand people staring at us. It was quite obvious we weren't local, but it was all very friendly. Then some stewards thought they would shift us around to the main stand where *there were a few Palace fans dotted around, together with some British ex-pats supporting us for the day.*

I remember talking to some African guys and their first realisation about this team called Crystal Palace was due to the Cup Final against Manchester United, a couple of years before. All the Africans seemed to be either Man Utd or Liverpool followers.

Whilst we were in Durban, a shark-sized hole in the shark net that guarded the beach was discovered which upset quite a few people who'd been swimming there earlier! We flew home from Durban and shortly after we got back, I recall reading about someone who been attacked by a shark just up the coast from there."

Ron Noades hailed the ground-breaking South African trip as "absolutely marvellous from start to finish. Easily the best tour I have been on." No sooner than Palace were back in the Northern Hemisphere, than they were whisked off again to Sweden for an altogether more low-key tour.

The bone-hard African pitches had taken their toll on the squad, who were carrying several injuries. Sweden was a five-game tour in the space of seven days and saw a further reduction in the number of fit players. It got to the point in the final game at Målilla, where Palace had to make three substitutions in the first ten minutes. Andy Woodman ended up playing up front (and scored!) and the side played the whole of the second half with just nine men. Still won 5-0 though.

On his way home from the airport, Alan Smith called into a Sunday morning Club XI friendly at Chipstead. It's fair to say, he had seen little sleep the night before. Thus I'm not sure how serious he was when he told Andy Carey and myself, that had we been out there, we'd have got a game! As you can imagine those words have haunted me ever since.

With key players missing, the start to the league season went from indifferent to poor and before long the rumblings started that the pre-season schedule was to blame. The striker issue was finally addressed with the £1million purchase of Chris Armstrong, a highly rated prospect from Millwall. However, this was swiftly followed by the exit of Mark Bright, with Paul Williams coming the other way. Chris Armstrong did well on his step up to the division, but Paul Williams failed to score a single goal. Palace ended up being relegated on the final day of the season, after seemingly being safe the previous Saturday.

Relegation saw Steve Coppell leave as Manager after nine years at the helm. Alan Smith took over. Out went the mammoth Scandinavian tours to be replaced by a more fitness-focused training camp in Portugal, with just a couple of practice matches at the camp against Portuguese and Spanish opposition. Palace did, however, play two overseas friendlies in that mid-season. Well I say two, but I'm not quite sure if the game on the Channel Islands qualifies.

Palace's home game against Middlesbrough fell over the November international weekend. Back then games in the second tier were only postponed if one or other of the sides had three or more players unavailable, which Palace did. Anxious to keep the momentum of our good start going, Smith took the squad out to Guernsey for a prestige friendly to mark the centenary of the island's Football Association.

The exhibition game against a representative island side, which included a couple of Matt Le Tissier's brothers, was an unequal contest with Palace running in eight goals without reply. Chris Armstrong rattled in four, Paul Mortimer grabbed two, David Whyte and Simon Osborn scored from the penalty spot – something Palace had unduly struggled with over the past couple of seasons.

Again, Palace did not publicise the game beforehand, despite the section in the previous home programme entitled 'Important Fixture Announcement'. This only dealt with the 'Boro game being postponed and other changes due to TV coverage.

One fan did get to see the game. Paul Smith had taken advantage of the free weekend to visit his relatives on the island, without prior knowledge of the game. Paul wrote an account of his serendipity in *Eagle Eye*.

"We made our way to the ground for a 2.30pm kick off as the ground had no floodlights. The venue was the 'Wembley' of Guernsey, known as 'The Track'. Despite its official name of The Cycling Grounds, the pitch was actually ringed by a go-cart track! The weather was wet, windy and miserable. We decided to pay £2 to sit in the stand. Alternatively we could have just parked on the track and watched the game from our car, just like they did with those blue Invacars at Stamford Bridge in the seventies.

The crowd numbered about 800, not bad for an island with a population of 50,000. There were even a couple of Palace shirts sprinkled about. Thankfully Palace were too strong and quick for the local side, otherwise my relatives would have taken the mickey all weekend.

The highlight of the weekend for me was still to come. Going into 'Town' – the capital St Peter Port – for a Saturday night out with my girlfriend, we came across the team in the White Hart pub and The Monkey nightclub downstairs. What followed was rather surreal. After years of being on the other side of the fence, the team were now at every turn. There was no escaping them.

One minute I was ordering drinks next to Nigel Martyn at the bar, then Paul Williams was apologising for bumping into me. Also apologising was Alan Smith, who felt we could have won the Everton League Cup game a few days before. We'd lost 4-1!"

Paul's article shed some light on one of the mysteries of the time. Shortly after the trip, right back John Humphrey was unexpectedly shipped out on a loan to Reading with the Club being tight-lipped about the reason. Paul had noticed him behaving in a rather unsober fashion in the nightclub. This apparently culminated in an 'incident' the following day, which was considered to be a serious breach of Club discipline. After three months in Berkshire exile, Humphrey finished the season back in the Palace first team.

The second trip was out to Northern Ireland at the end of January 1994. Palace had been knocked out of the FA Cup third round, away at Wolverhampton Wanderers, who then unkindly repeated the feat a week later in the league. This meant no game for a fortnight, although we had league games in hand, the clubs we were due to play were involved in the fourth round of the cup. A friendly was hastily arranged with Derry City on the Wednesday of the first week, not least to give Paul Stewart, our new loan signing from Liverpool, some game time with his new team-mates.

Palace had played out in Derry five years before, just after the start of our first season back in the top flight. Back then, I had begged the Away Travel Club to run a coach, but the Troubles were seen from here to still be very much a part of life in Northern Ireland, with Derry being known as a particular hot spot. Consequently, despite several other enquiries, there was no appetite to arrange official travel and I didn't fancy travelling there on my own.

Although the city is in Northern Ireland, the club has played in the Irish Republic's League of Ireland since 1985. The move required special dispensation from the Irish Football Association and FIFA. As its stadium was situated in a staunchly republican area once known as "Free Derry", with a history of deep scepticism towards the Royal Ulster Constabulary in the local community, Derry received special permission from UEFA to steward its own games. The presence of the RUC was regarded as more likely to provoke trouble than help prevent it.

Palace had come from behind to win that first Derry game 4-2 with Geoff Thomas scoring twice, once from the spot, with Alan Pardew and Mark Bright also on target. Palace received a warm reception from the home fans at the end of the game. The *Derry Journal* hailed the game as "the best friendly at Brandywell since City came back into senior football, four years ago" noting that "too often friendlies are so boring that watching paint dry is more appealing. But this was a game to remember."

This time round, with some experience of travelling abroad to see Palace games, together with a greater understanding of the region having attended a wedding there, I would have definitely gone. Trouble was, I didn't know about it. It was my own fault: this time the fixture had been mentioned in the *Croydon Advertiser* on the previous Friday. Also, in my mind, Andy "Wags" Wagon played a bit part here, although he strenuously denies it to this day.

Wags is now one of my very best mates, we've travelled to watch Palace in so many far-flung outposts: Vancouver, Cape Town, Hong Kong, Grimsby… this was, however, quite early days in our friendship. Wags worked at Gatwick Airport, near to his Crawley home. So, on finding out about the game, he acquired himself cheap flights. He assumed I knew about the game and that he'd probably see me out there. Sadly for me, he didn't check. To this day, I claim this as a major oversight on his part. Wags maintains, in those pre-mobile days, that he didn't know how to contact me, outside of seeing me in the pub on a matchday.

Blissfully unaware of the game and, ironically, with plenty of holiday time accumulated which my firm had been nagging me to take, I was sat at my desk working when I could have been on another trip. Meanwhile, Wags was having the craic:

"I travelled over with Tom "Tommy Two-Pints" South. We flew into Belfast City Airport on the Tuesday, before the game the following day. Upon clearing the airport we headed for the train station immediately noticing the Protestant murals on the houses nearby. I was only 19 at the time and quite naïve about 'the Troubles', so it was quite a disconcerting sight.

We checked into our guest house near Botanic and went out for a few beers. It hadn't occurred to us that Belfast was pretty much shut down at night; there was very little open. We found a nightclub that was open and happy to serve us. There was only about six people in there. These two girls started to chat to us and when they heard we were there for football, they had one question for us:

'Rangers or Celtic?'

'Umm, Rangers.'

And that was the last we saw of them.

Then we went for a Chinese. The restaurant had a Karaoke machine. It was the first time I'd done Karaoke. Good job there was only about six people in there too. Coming out of there we walked straight into an Army Patrol which really freaked us out. Soldiers on the street on patrol was not something I was used to seeing on the mean streets of Crawley. They looked us up and down, decided we were not the drunks they were looking for and walked away.

We took the train across to Derry the next day and found a hotel. We headed to the ground about six o'clock, unaware of the significance of its Bogside location. We found a bar and the first thing they wanted to know was:

'Are you Squaddies?'

'No, we're Palace fans here for the game and flying back tomorrow.'

Suddenly everything was fine. We had a few beers and after a while, chatted to the locals about the game. I was young and had no real clue about the tensions there."

The game was played in appalling weather. Just as in 1989, Palace fell behind, but quickly equalised through Dean Gordon. Palace were on top thereafter and Paul Stewart grabbed the winner. The now-traditional warm Derry reception greeted the players after the game. Wags remembers that the Palace travelling fans ended up drinking with the team:

"After the match, we were invited back to the club where the players were drinking. Alan Smith bought us a round, as did Gareth Southgate. I ended up chatting to Gareth about our *mutual hometown. After that things get a bit hazy! I do remember the next morning I awoke next to a massive Pizza that I have absolutely no recollection of buying.*

On the Taxi ride back to the station, the cabbie pointed out where the soldiers fired the first shots of Bloody Sunday, which I knew only as a U2 song. On the plane home I was sat next to Nigel Martyn, who it turned out hated flying. Head in a sick bag for most of the journey:

'It's not nerves' he explained to me.

'Just air-sickness with the turbulence.' "

One wonders how Nigel coped after his Leeds side were involved in a minor plane crash, taking off from Stansted a few years later.

The trip did Palace's league form no harm at all, going unbeaten in the next eight games and only losing two games for the rest of the season. One of those was on the last day having already been crowned Champions. As part of their reward, the team went on a post season tour to southern Spain, playing three games whilst there. Another encounter with a Gibraltar XI, which resulted in a 1-0 win, followed by a 1-0 defeat by Marbella and a 2-0 win over a Malaga XI.

Then 1994/95 saw Palace back in the Premiership, by way of preparation the maxim: 'If it ain't broke…'' came into play and the team returned to Portugal for a training camp, plus a practice game against an unknown local side.

At the turn of 1995, in what was proving to be a difficult league season, Palace were invited to play in an all-expenses paid prestige game out in Hong Kong over an international weekend in late April. Palace allegedly beat off several other teams who were interested.

The problem was that although Palace's league form was poor, they had reached the semi-finals in both Cups, leading to something of a fixture pile-up at the end of the season. Alan Smith asked whether Palace could pull out, but the organisers weren't having any of it. Even when Aston Villa, themselves not totally safe at this point, offered to go instead.

The day after the 2-1 league defeat away at Champions-elect, Blackburn Rovers, Palace would find themselves travelling on a twelve hour flight to the colony. Or rather the reserves and fringe players would. Already decimated by international call-ups and injuries, Smith took the decision not to take any of the players who had featured in that game. He did, however, go on record as saying:

"I'm knackered and I could have done with a weekend in the garden. The players are dead tired. They've had two cup semi-finals, two Easter games and the Blackburn match. The players badly want a rest. We have an absolutely vital match against Forest next weekend and that has to come first."

The game took place on the Sunday at the Happy Valley Stadium in front of an 8,000 crowd. Palace would return there 22 years later, in front of considerably more people. Happy Valley included some guest players in their line-up, including Jan Molby and Nigel Clough, but it was the makeshift Palace side that took the lead through Bruce Dyer.

Happy Valley equalised after a fine individual goal, although the scorer of this wonder strike remained uncredited in the UK reports. The game finished 1-1 in normal time. Palace then had to go through a further 30 goal-less minutes of extra-time, before eventually losing 6-5 in a penalty shootout. The Club took away £30,000 prize money from the 72-hour Asian excursion.

No amount of money could save Palace though, as they finished fourth from bottom, the one season that four teams were relegated. This gave them the unwanted and oft-repeated record of finishing in the last four of each of the competitions they entered. (It's also a stat that isn't strictly true as pedantic fans like me will be quick to tell you. Palace got knocked out in the quarter-final of the London Five-a-Sides.)

The relationship between Manager and Chairman had broken down long before the end of the season, so it was no surprise when Smith was sacked. Once again, Palace were heading into a pre-season at a lower level and without a Manager in place.

Palace take on IFK Göteburg at the Ullevi Stadium - November 1997

The Lonely Goths take to the pitch - November 1997
[Photo: Dave Lewis]

5

THE LONELY GOTHS

Palace's managerial position was eventually filled in a novel way. Ray Lewington and Peter Nicholas were promoted as 'joint coaches' and Steve Coppell nominated as Director of Football. Some cynical observers felt that this was just a mechanism for Mr Noades to have greater influence on the team, especially when it came to selection, but there was no real evidence of this. What there had been was a 'fire sale' of players post-relegation and, worryingly, there was also no immediate sign that the income generated would be used to rebuild the team.

The 1995 pre-season training camp was out in Turkey, with two games played. One of those games was against a team with a higher pedigree than the Portuguese opposition we'd faced in the previous two years. Altayspor. The game finished 1-1, with Palace winning 4-0 against lower league Muğlaspor, two days before.

These training camp games were not really suited to building a trip around, for a couple of reasons. There was no certainty of any matches being played and, perhaps worse, no guarantee of getting access to any that were. For this reason, a double-header in the exotic lands of South Wales suddenly seemed to fit the bill as a 'foreign' tour.

A Palace first XI took on Swansea on a Friday evening, followed by a Club XI at Inter Cardiff on the Saturday afternoon. Martin Young, Paul James, Dave "Safety" Lewis and Wags all crammed into my Astra, on one of the hottest days of the year. We arrived thirsty in late afternoon and grabbed the first Bed & Breakfast that was advertising vacancies. Then we set out for a pre-match drink, ending up at the harbourside complex. The offices had just turned out and the bar was full of attractive young ladies in skimpy summer wear. There was beauty to behold at every turn and I'm still not sure how we dragged ourselves away to the game. It's fair to say we had sunk a skinful in a short space of time.

To say the away terrace at the dilapidated Vetch Field was sparsely populated would be a gross understatement. Our slightly late arrival doubled the numbers. There were about thirty Palace fans at the game, but most had opted for the seats along the side. The walk to the ground hadn't cleared our heads in the slightest. We sat on the terracing and unloaded our frustrations on the Chairman with regard to his lack of spending on the team.

There were several silly songs referencing the Golf Course he had recently bought and the Outhere Brothers' summer hit was re-appropriated as

"Boom! Boom! Boom! Let me hear you say: Noades Out – NOADES OUT!"

On that crumbling terrace, a jokey and extremely juvenile drunken alliance of the 'Kick Noades Out Brigade' or "K.N.O.B." was formed. Mr Noades responded, later in the season, by calling us 'morons' and 'a minority'.

A year later, during a friendly at Notts County, 'Uncle Ron' joined us and painstakingly answered any questions put to him throughout the second half. It was a good job he had not thought to try that approach at the Swansea game, we were way too drunk to have had a serious chat with him.

The game ended 1-1 and we changed before heading into town for more beer and some Welsh nightlife. The doormen at 'The Quids Inn" disco pub eyed us suspiciously, but after a bit of banter let us in. It turned out many of the team were already there and they'd heard our drunken chants from the pitch. Richard Shaw was the first to buy us all a beer.

It seemed that our anti-Noades protest had found resonance within the squad. Iain Dowie told us he wouldn't be staying at the Club, due to broken promises. Local boy Chris Coleman was getting absolutely mobbed, but found a moment to also buy us a beer, smiling enigmatically when we asked whether he would be staying. It was clear to us that the fire sale wasn't over yet.

On the walk back to our lodgings, Wags actually fell asleep whilst walking forward. As he pitched forward, he managed to kick a huge kerb stone knocking it clean out of the ground. He's a tall lad with plenty of weight behind him, even back then, but I still don't know how he managed that. His foot was sore in the morning, although not as sore as Safety's head.

We were all suffering in the hangover department. I'd woken up early and, realising I was in trouble, took a double dose of soluble aspirin and went outside for some fresh air. This sorted me out, which was just as well as I was driving, but the others had to be raised from their respective rooms well past the 10am checking out time by a grumpy landlord, everyone having missed breakfast.

As Martin, Wags and I sat on the wall outside, waiting for everyone else to get their act together, Martin told a ridiculously poor joke, which Wags attempted to laugh at, but it turned into a projectile vomit. The timing could not have been more perfect as a wedding party were just walking past in all their finery. Their looks of absolute horror at Wags' freshly rendered pavement art only set him off once again.

Safety finally emerged looking like hell and fell asleep as soon he got in the car, head lolling out of the window. He woke on the outskirts of Cardiff and proceeded to anoint my car with several 'go faster' stripes. When we arrived, he refused to budge from the car and ended up laying across the back seats, slowly stewing as the temperature rose higher and higher.

Inter Cardiff's ground was the old athletics track, which is almost exactly where the Cardiff City Stadium was built a decade later. We were just checking out the car parking situation, before heading off in search of a pub, when we got invited into their Directors' Bar instead. As we were driving straight home after the game, I couldn't have a drink. Although the other three didn't much feel like one either, they struggled on manfully.

We met up with Andy Carey and Rick Ballantine, who seemed in better shape than our lot. Safety finally dragged himself into the football ground, to ironic cheers, with about fifteen minutes to kick off. He still looked like death warmed up.

The game was a dull affair in the scorching sun. It was heading for a goalless draw, but Palace grabbed a late winner. Cardiff were playing Burnley in a pre-season friendly just across the road at Ninian Park, which had kicked off slightly later. I suggested that we head over and catch the final few minutes. Despite it being a new ground for most people in the car, no-one could muster the enthusiasm.

On the drive home, we tried frantically to remember the excellent song we had made up the night before about Mr Noades spending all our money on a golf course, but to this day, no-one can recall it.

The joint coach experiment didn't last long. After a half season of indifferent results, in came Dave "Harry" Bassett. The new manager bounce became a fully blown upswing and Palace almost won promotion. We narrowly missed out on automatic, losing a crunch game with Derby on our last visit to the Baseball Ground. Then Steve Claridge's shin did for us in the last minute of the Play Off final at Wembley.

Dave Bassett was clearly a fan of the Scandinavian treadmill approach to pre-season and Palace played five games in Norway, winning them all, mostly by some margin. Towards the end of the season, Bassett left for a chance to manage struggling Nottingham Forest in the Premier. Steve Coppell, who'd had a brief and unhappy sojourn in charge of Manchester City, took over and managed to get Palace back into the Premier via the play-offs. Harry, meanwhile, was heading the other way with Forest.

The 1997 pre-season took place just a little further afield than Scandinavia, with Finland being the destination. A four-game tour, which ended in a 5-0 win against the intriguingly named Santa Claus FC. The club is based just inside the Arctic

Circle in Rovaniemi, the capital of Lapland, which goes some way to explaining its name.

Palace started the season reasonably well, with Attilio Lombardo – our marquee signing from Juventus – the standout player. Our home form was cause for concern, having failed to win a league game at Selhurst thus far. The day before the 1-1 draw with Aston Villa at home, prior to the November international break, the *Advertiser* announced that Palace would be travelling for a friendly the following Thursday, against IFK Göteburg.

"Anyone for Sweden?" I asked, as I walked in the Cherry Trees that Saturday. Most people laughed, but Safety piped up: "Yeah, I've got a week off, I'll have some of that." I had no idea whether I could get time off, but what started as a joke had turned swiftly into temptation.

Flight prices to Gothenburg were over £500 one-way, so we swiftly parked the idea. But the next day: Enter the Wagon. Partially redeeming himself for his Derry misdemeanour, Wags rang to say he had just heard a radio advert describing £99 fares London to Stockholm with some company called Ryanair. He was not able to come himself, but still thought he would pass it along. Good lad.

Neither Safety nor I had ever heard of Ryanair – this being the relatively early days of the budget airline. We felt it was worth further investigation. Turns out that price was for a return trip providing we stayed two nights, which we would need to do if we flew via Stockholm. Even better! Once establishing we could get easily get a train between Stockholm and Gothenburg, we decided to risk it. The train would end up costing five pounds more than the flight! My next hurdle was to negotiate some short notice time-off.

Come Wednesday afternoon we found ourselves at Stansted Airport in good time for the 4.20pm flight to Stockholm South. The location of said airport turned out to be over 70 miles south of Stockholm involving a bus transfer into the City. Ah well, still couldn't argue with the price.

With the time difference, we arrived fairly late into Sweden's Capital city. Our digs for the night turned out to be a homestay with 'Mr and Mrs Sodastream'… at least I think that's what they said. We managed to have a decent night out, but woke not just our hosts but pretty much the whole block trying to work their lock at 3am. Alcohol may possibly have been impairing our motor skills.

We had a reasonably early start the next day, so had little sleep. Breakfast was served in our room, wheeled in on a little trolley. It was simple fare: muesli, cold sausage, and a lump of cheese that would have comfortably fed the street. The sausage reeked of garlic and tasted way worse. Even the family's dog would go nowhere near it.

The 10am train was of a standard that puts current British trains to shame. Fine drizzle and mist prevented us from seeing much of the Swedish countryside, so I took the opportunity to catch up on my sleep.

We arrived at the advertised time of 13:30 and after a visit to the station's tourist information had secured a cheap hotel for the night. Dropping our bags, we headed out to the stadium to grab some photos while it was still light. The Ullevi stadium complex was only a few minutes away. An oval-shaped stadium with a sweeping curved roof dominated the skyline. First though, we passed a smaller ground, that looked rather like Wimbledon's old Plough Lane home. This was the Gamla Ullevi where other Swedish sides, and occasionally IFK, played home games. At this point, we didn't know exactly where Palace would play that evening, but were obviously hoping for the main stadium.

The smaller ground was shuttered up, so we headed for the main ground following helpful signs in English to the ticket windows. There was not much sign of life here either and we began to get apprehensive. One of the windows appeared to be lit and staffed by an older lady engrossed in her knitting. She eyed us with suspicion.

"Two tickets for the Palace game tonight, please." She scowled and muttered: "Not this week"

We begged her to check, she crossly looked at her newspaper. "No game today." And went back to her knitting.

The blood froze in our veins. Had we come on the wrong day? Palace had asked me to phone in a Clubcall report when they heard I was thinking of going but I couldn't remember actually confirming the date of the game. We headed for the main reception where our fears were immediately allayed:

"Yes, there is a game tonight."

"Yes, it's against Crystal Palace."

"Yes, it's here at the main stadium."

A more welcome hat-trick, I can scarcely remember.

The club official was rather amazed that anyone had travelled from England and kindly let us go pitch-side to take photographs inside the stadium.

It became obvious that the grumpy grandma had thought we'd said Paris – as in Paris St Germain – the club IFK were due to face in the Champions League in a fortnight's time. Safety isn't one to easily forgive and forget though. To this day he refers to her as 'that silly old bag' whenever the incident is retold.

With the Swedish League being played during the spring and summer, IFK needed match practice. We later found out why Palace had been keen on a mid-season game abroad. The Club was in negotiation to bring in Tomas Brolin to bolster the squad. He was supposed to have played for Palace that night, but injury prevented his appearance. Once he was injury-free he did, indeed, join Palace a couple of months later. Fit he wasn't, fat he was and roundly mocked for it by the English media. The club official obligingly told us where the supporters club bar was and assured us that we'd be warmly welcomed. Indeed we were and whiled away the rest of the afternoon chatting to the locals, keen to impress us with their knowledge of English football.

The floodlit stadium seemed even bigger and more impressive as we walked up for the game. The capacity was 38,000 though I doubt more than a thousand came to the game. There were a few other Palace scarves dotted around belonging to Scandinavian Supporters Club members, but it appeared that Safety and I were the only travellers from England.

Palace fielded the strongest side they had, allowing for international call-ups, but went down 2-1. IFK took the lead in the first half, with Neil Shipperley, continuing a good run of goalscoring at the time, equalising just after the break. A poor mistake from Kevin Miller allowed IFK to score an all-too-easy winner. Despite that, Palace had given a good account of themselves, worthy of our efforts to be there.

After the game, we returned to the stadium reception to phone through the Clubcall report, as previously arranged. Our friendly official was waiting for us with a bundle of team sheets and club souvenirs. The rest of the evening was spent getting some long-overdue food onboard and listening to a band in the Auld Dubliners bar.

The next day we had some time to kill before our train, so we went out sightseeing. We ran into Assistant Manager, Ray Lewington and it took us a while to convince him that we had actually travelled over for the game. He felt the game was a useful run-out, no injuries from the greasy surface, just a few post-match hangovers to contend with. I picked up an orange IFK away top as a souvenir of the trip. It had to be the away shirt, their blue and white striped home strip was just too similar to that of Brighton.

In the sports shop, we ran into assistant manager Ray Lewington. In his second stint at Palace as assistant to Roy Hodgson, Ray's wearing of shorts however cold the weather became something of a trademark. Although on this occasion, he was dressed in a tracksuit, he was carrying a pair of Palace shorts. We thought it rather odd at the time to have brought a pair of shorts into a sports shop, but now the reason seems clear. He was simply worried about the weather getting too warm while he was out.

While we were away, Palace signed Michele Padovano from Juventus. The first in a long list of expensive signings, supposedly funded by new investor Mark Goldberg, who made no secret of his desire to eventually buy the Club from Mr Noades. Amidst the uncertainty of the ownership overtures and Lombardo getting injured whilst on international duty, Palace's form fell off a cliff. Eight straight league defeats from the start of 1998 to mid-March saw Palace plummet to the bottom of the table. Steve Coppell stepped down to be replaced, bizarrely, by Attilio Lombardo.

The cause was already as good as lost and there was little improvement under the Italian's player-management, but at least he did manage to win a home game. Derby County were our prey and the home crowd celebrated afterwards like we'd actually won a trophy.

The slew of signings could not arrest the slide: Tomas Brolin, Valerian Ismael, Matt Jansen, Marcus Bent, Patrizio Billio and Sasa Curcic were all added to the roster. They weren't all bad: Jansen, Bent and Curcic quickly became fan favourites, but still we plummeted out of the top flight anyway.

The Club officially changed hands in the close season, but not before Mr Noades finally did get an official credit for managing the team for the last three games, alongside Ray Lewington and Brian Sparrow. Mr Noades bought Brentford FC with some of the £23million he'd received for the Club.

Mark Goldberg threw even more money at securing someone he regarded as a top-of-the-line Manager to try and ensure an immediate return to the Premier League. Terry Venables was his target and, after long negotiations, finally got his man to sign on for his second managerial stint at the Club. Albeit after he had finished being a TV pundit in France at the World Cup.

At face value, it was a major statement of intent, but supporters with long memories recalled the acrimony of Venables' departure from Palace in 1980 and his continual transfer raids on our players in his new job at Queens Park Rangers. Despite his solid track record as a Manager, not least of the Euro '96 England team, there was disquiet amongst the fanbase. As one burly fellow put it, at the Fans Open Day:

"Welcome back, Terry. Don't shit on us again."

The touring party in the Samsun Directors Box (Dave London centre back row) - July 1998. [Photo: Dave London]

Palace try to recover from an early setback - July 1998 [Photo: Dave London]

"Nice to see you made it then, Tel": Training at the 19 Mayis Stadium - July 1998 [Photo: Dave London]

6

DON'T MENTION THE 'SPOR

It is time to address the elephant in the room or, in this case, the book: Samsunspor. I've already detailed in the prologue just how Palace came to be entered in the 1998 UEFA Intertoto Cup and why I didn't go on the trip.

Palace were already 2-0 down from the home leg, so the chances of progressing were not high. It seemed the game was being treated as a pre-season friendly rather than a competitive game, as far as the home side were concerned. Palace were lucky not to be even further behind when the Turks missed a penalty. Much had been made in the press of our new Manager deciding to miss the home leg. He wanted to squeeze in a family holiday instead of taking up his role at Palace immediately after his television commitments ended.

It was difficult to know what was in the Manager's mind. On one hand Venables was on record as saying that he was not keen on Palace's entry into the competition and actively tried to get us pulled out once he had accepted the job. On the other, his programme notes for the match go to some lengths to make it sound like he would be there. Tucked away in the first league programme within the 'Summer Diary' was a rather waspish confirmation that he had, indeed, missed the game: "Terry Venables is on a short holiday after his World Cup exertions, although 11,000 spectators do attend causing the kick-off to be delayed by fifteen minutes."

Any suggestions Venables had made about non-participation ran into a wall of defiance from both UEFA and the English FA, even though we were no longer a part of their Premier League. Pressure was brought to bear because in the three years that the Intertoto Cup came under UEFA's auspices, English teams had only competed once – in 1995 – and then not taken it seriously. Palace had applied and England's return to the competition heralded by UEFA. No other Premier club had applied, so it would be a major embarrassment to all concerned if Palace pulled out, despite no longer being a top flight club.

In spite of the compunction expressed by the new management, the size of the crowd proved there was a real appetite for European football at Selhurst. The Club had taken the decision not to open the Arthur Wait Stand, which ultimately caused the delay to kick-off. The lack of preparedness was not just noticeable in the team: the upper tier of the Holmesdale had no refreshments and the programmes sold out well before kick-off.

There was also a lot of interest shown in the away leg, though much of that waned when the game ended up being in a relatively inaccessible part of the world. In the week before the game, when it was confirmed who our opponents would be, the Club had organised an official tour at an eye-watering price of £800, excluding VAT. Even allowing for the accessibility issue, that was too steep.

Samsun was not considered to be a tourist destination. The guidebooks of the day had nothing good to say about this industrial port on the Black Sea. They used adjectives like 'smelly', 'grimy' and 'filthy'. 'A place to travel through, rather than linger.' Even today, Samsun is notorious for poor air quality and its biggest claim to fame is a historical event, when Mustafa Kemal Atatürk, the founding father of the Republic of Turkey, began the War of Independence there in 1919.

In spite of the apparently unattractive nature of the destination, there were those who were still desperate to be part of Palace's first official European adventure. They chose to look for alternative routes more suitable to their budget. Wags was part of four-man 'Team Kebab'. Not the cultural misappropriation it might appear to be, but rather a challenge to see how many they could eat between them on the trip (31). They flew to Istanbul, hired a car and drove twelve hair-raising hours mainly through darkness to Samsun. Also in that car was Cris Lehmann, editor of *One More Point*, who wrote an excellent chronicle of their adventure in issue #26 of the Palace fanzine.

Another group elected to fly into Ankara and faced a mere six-hour road trip in a hired minibus up to Samsun. Anglo Italian veteran Nick Harling was in that party, covering the game in his capacity as a sports journalist. With no other English papers sending reporters, Nick had his work cut out.

Another car set out from England with the intention of driving across Europe, as the driver Carl Davies remembers:

"Originally there were four of us going. One good mate who is a Wycombe fan and two other Palace lads. One dropped out because he couldn't get the required time off and another after the home leg result. So we were down to two. I said to him 'Shall we go for it?' and he said 'I've got the time off – let's drive over'. It was my car and I'd be doing all the driving.

We left fairly late on the Monday and took the car on the Chunnel. We hadn't booked anything and we thought we'd have loads of time. We'd worked out it was 2500 miles and would take around 40 hours to drive it and we'd do around 8-10 hours a day, so we weren't killing ourselves. We decided to stop the first night in Lille.

Then we did what you just shouldn't do and had a monster night out. We got absolutely, completely smashed. At some point in the evening my mate mustered up the courage to ask

'Are we really doing this? You know you aren't going through and it's going to be bloody horrendous driving back.' By the time we went to bed we were already talking ourselves out of it.

The following morning, we were completely hungover, feeling rotten. My mate broached the subject again and came out with the immortal line:

'I know you love Palace, but there'll be other times when you can watch them in European competition. This is madness!'

And he was absolutely right – well, apart from the other opportunities bit so far – so we just drove home. Even if we did perform a miracle and get through, we wouldn't get back in time for the next round in either Belgium or Bremen.

My wife's face was a picture when I pulled back into the drive. I looked like I'd been away for two weeks, I was still so hungover. Had I known then that we wouldn't get back into Europe anytime soon, I'd have gone on the official club trip. I certainly played around with that in my head. It was around £800 from memory which was a lot of money to find. As the week wore on, I must confess that it did bother me that I wouldn't be there."

Fourteen people did go on that official tour, most booking before the result of the home leg was known. Amongst their number was 23-year-old Dave London, who recalls how he came to be on the official trip and his experience on his first overseas trip to watch Palace:

"I previously discovered that National Express coaches could cheaply take me to further afield grounds and games – initially in Scotland, and then across mainland Europe – Milan, Bruges, Amsterdam and Paris, seeing games at stadiums I had only seen in magazines or on TV, with some sightseeing thrown in. A friend had also got me hooked on travelling to watch England games abroad, again usually on coaches. It didn't bother me if the coach took 24 hours each way to Katowice in Poland or Rome in Italy. It was cheap, reliable and I enjoyed the adventure.

To me, Palace entering the Intertoto sounded fantastic. I had never even seen Palace play abroad, but I had read about pre-season trips in Europe of previous years in the Eagle Eye fanzine and it sounded like these trips were great fun. I thought surely someone would run a coach again. I hadn't missed a home or away game in six years at that point, so I just had to be one of the fans going to this! If not, then a scheduled 'Eurolines' National Express coach would get me there. When we learned of the opposition, I realised a coach trip to see Palace's first ever game in Europe wasn't going to happen.

The next day I borrowed my Dad's atlas to see where Samsunspor actually was. It really was in the middle of nowhere! I phoned the American Express Travel Centre in Croydon. Unfortunately the news was not good: the only places in Turkey to which they sold flights were Istanbul and Ankara. They were 450 and 250 miles away from Samsun respectively with little in between along the way. Apparently, Samsun does have its own airport, but it was only used for internal domestic flights.

Oh well, at least I could go to the home game, but I was gutted. Then on the Friday before the home leg, the Croydon Advertiser mentioned that the club would be running a supporters trip to the away leg, travelling with the team.

I had to call the club for more details, which they duly faxed across to my work. I was already imagining something akin to the expensive 'day trip' flights that were run to England away matches: the sort that cost in the region of £300 for a straight there and back in a day experience. Way more than my usual budget of £100 for an abroad coach trip.

The fax arrived and I immediately poured over the details, but no price was shown so I phoned again:

"Seven hundred and fifty pounds per person" came the reply. I had a split second to make a decision. Stay or go? Miss it and hope we get through to the next round which would be within my usual budget. I made my mind up before my brain could register the cost. I was going to see Palace in Europe. In Turkey. I did wonder just how many other fans would be going at that price.

My friends thought I had a death-wish going to Turkey, mentioning Manchester United's trip there a few years before, where the players and fans were roughly treated. The atmosphere was like an intimidating cauldron and with the infamous 'Welcome to Hell' banner much discussed. Most of the advice was: 'Just be careful!'

The itinerary arrived a couple of days before the trip and I was impressed at how organised it was. The game itself was scheduled for Sunday at 9pm as it would be too hot for an afternoon kick off. The flight would leave Stansted at 8.30am on Saturday morning. It was a small private plane and would have to stop at Vienna airport for an hour to refuel. This meant we would not arrive at Samsun until 5pm.

On Saturday morning, I got up at silly o'clock and headed to Stansted airport, although not the main terminal, instead a small building accessed off an airport perimeter road. My passport was checked, and I waited in the lounge, I was the first there! Gradually over the next hour, a mixture of supporters, various CPFC staff, players, and team management arrived. I took the chance to get a few photos with a few players and management, who I knew were friendly and approachable.

Palace Communications Manager, Pete King, was also on the trip. Armed with his camera, as official photographer for the trip, he was outdoing my own click-happy efforts, enthusiastically welcoming and arranging photos of everyone. One was a group photo of the fans on the trip, so we quickly got put together and got to know each other. I think there were twelve 'fans' on the trip, mostly lifelong, 'not-missed-a-game-in-years' types. When it was time to go, we simply walked across the tarmac to board the plane waiting nearby.

The players knew the game and piled on first, heading to the back of the plane. The management got on next and, like good kids on a school trip, the fans sat together at the front of the plane. I was sat next to an older chap called Peter. He really loved to talk and he was absolutely nuts about Palace! He had even made sure his house on Whitehorse Lane had the perfect view overlooking Selhurst Park. He'd been supporting Palace for decades and even played for the amateur third team as a youngster.

He also loved talking with enormous pride about his son, Simon, who ran a successful mobile phone business. That summer, his son would be getting his first advertising board for his phone company on the front of the Arthur Wait Stand roof. I became friends with Peter over the next couple of years, seeing him regularly on the coaches to away games. A couple of years after this trip, the penny dropped that Peter was the father of Simon Jordan!

On the plane after the refuelling stop, I took my chance to get the CPFC pennant —to which I'd added match details using Letraset — signed by the players. It was the perfect opportunity to work my way up the rows of seating and not to miss anyone.

Finally we landed at Samsun, got our passports stamped and boarded a luxury coach, which I presume our hosts had arranged. It was a half-hour drive from the airfield to our hotel and it was a bit of an eye opener. It was a pretty basic area, I'm not saying it was a ramshackle shanty town, but there were some poor, underdeveloped areas, particularly on the outskirts of the town.

The hotel was on the seafront right by the centre of town and was four star – definitely the best accommodation in town. I was told that in European competition, the host team provide the hotel and they had done a good job for us.

Within fifteen minutes of checking in at the hotel, it was back onto the coach for a twenty minute ride to the teams' evening training session. Under UEFA regulations, every team is entitled to do this before the game on the stadium pitch. Being pre-internet, I had no idea what to expect. I would best describe it as being 'Soviet style' – a running track around the pitch, a covered seated stand on one side, and uncovered concrete steps on the other three sides which curved at each end of the ground.

Although it was evening, it was still very hot and muggy, but the players did their training on the pitch. It wasn't much more than what you'd see in a warm-up to a game. They couldn't do much in the way of set piece routine practice, because there were people from the host club in the stands watching what was taking place. During training, as dusk began to fall, across the hillside in the distance you could hear the 'call to prayer' from the Minarets, which was very atmospheric.

Back at the hotel, the squad and fans dined together, in a large conference room with the players together on one side and everyone else on the other. The difference being that everyone else got wine with our dinner and the players didn't. Unsurprisingly, the players ate quickly then went back to their rooms, whilst the rest of us enjoyed our meal for a bit longer. Not everyone was at the dinner though: Terry Venables, Steve Coppell and Pete King were taken by taxi to a special 'friendship dinner' that Samsunspor had laid on for their English guests; a nice sign of respect.

After dinner, most of us went to the hotel bar for evening drinks. It was a lovely bar on the top floor of the hotel and had a great panoramic view of the town and the seafront all lit up at night. Amongst the fans there was lots of talk about not having ice in your drinks in case it gave you an upset stomach. And the bar was also handing out complimentary small bowls of fruit salad, which looked tempting, but most of us were too cautious and politely declined, while trying not to offend the hospitality being shown. I got the impression that foreign visitors were a rarity to the town, and the hotel was going out of its way to make us feel special.

After an hour or so, Steve Coppell and Pete King arrived in the hotel bar, back from the friendship dinner they had attended and we got talking about their evening. Terry Venables hadn't been in reception when they were due to leave, so they had to go without him. Half an hour later, Venables appeared in the bar. He apologised to the others and explained that after getting back from training he'd fallen asleep in his room!

The evening in the hotel bar wore on, then suddenly Clinton Morrison tried to sneak in. He said he couldn't sleep so decided to go for a walk around the hotel, but unluckily for him all the team management were in the bar. He was caught in the act and sent back to his room straight away. Venables seemed to see the funny side, after all, Clinton had a huge grin on his face and you couldn't be angry with such a likeable young guy. At about midnight I went to bed.

Matchday arrived and at 10am the coach set off again from the hotel for training at the stadium. However, Palace were not allocated the stadium pitch this time, just a scrappy piece of grassed land next to it. It was already scorchingly hot sunny weather again. The players did the lightest training you could imagine in the only bit of shade they could find. You worked up a sweat just walking in the heat. The locals were watching the light training through the fence from the street adjacent, so again no chance of practicing any tactics.

As the players were doing very little, I took a walk around the ground and I found a merchandise stall set up selling Samsunspor souvenirs, even though there was still ten hours before kick-off. I bought a pennant, scarf and pin badge.

The coach returned us to the hotel at midday, and we were told we had the rest of the day to ourselves until 6.30pm when we would head off for the game. I had a bit of experience of exploring towns abroad from having watched England away games, so I made sure I was wearing no football colours before heading into town. My overall impression was that it was a bit shabby and run down, but not massively dissimilar to a French Riviera town. The locals were very friendly and although there wasn't much to see, it was good to get a feel of the place. I found a sports shop selling Samsunspor shirts, so I had to buy one of those.

As we were wandering, we came across half a dozen Palace fans including Cris Lehmann and his gang, so we all went for a beer at an outside café. Everyone was really enjoying the experience and was looking forward to the game. We agreed that Palace needed to score the first goal or the tie would be dead!

After an hour or so, my group of fans walked back to our hotel. We had to get our luggage together as, after the game, we would be heading straight on to the airport.

At half past six, we got aboard our transport to the ground: the playing squad and coaches went together on the luxury team coach. The fans, plus Steve Coppell and the club staff went on a large minibus where I sat next to Steve Coppell. On the way, Steve was asked about the places he travelled to when he played for England. He didn't go to Turkey with England, but he did reel off quite a list of countries. Steve also made a funny observation that outside every little bar on the way, there would be a little man sitting on a stool outside the door, and a lady sweeping the pavement with a broom. Sure enough, the very next one we passed had that exact scenario.

When we got to the stadium, the team coach went to one end and our minibus drove up to the main Directors entrance. We didn't have any match tickets and there was quite a throng surrounding the minibus. We had to leg it into the entrance as quickly as possible to make sure we all stayed together as a group.

We went up some marble steps and came out in what was like the 'Royal Box' part of the main stand, marble floors, padded seats and right on the halfway line. I was very pleased to be seated here, as the rest of the ground was very basic. It was a safe place to be and a great view. We took our seats across a couple of rows and then I noticed Cris and his friend had managed to sneak in on the back of our group and were also in the VIP section. We took some photos of each other, including one with my massive Palace 'St George' flag. After doing that, someone important said I should put it away now, out of respect to our Turkish hosts. Steve Coppell was asked by the hosts to sit in the very front row of the Directors Box, which were actual armchairs, alongside the Chairman and President of the club as their VIP guest.

I managed to get hold of some team sheets (there were no programmes) so I was more than happy with the arrangements for the game. The team sheets were copies of a typed sheet on headed paper, and listed such greats as Endwotthy (Edworthy), Mollins (Mullins), Herisdanson (Hreidarsson), Shipperky (Shipperley), M'Kardie (McKenzie) and "Ordishan" (Ormshaw, our reserve keeper).

As kick-off approached, the noise in the ground got louder and louder, even though the crowd was under 8,000. The PA system played music best described as 'tribal beats' and it was really pumping up the home fans.

The teams came out, from an underground stairway inside the athletics track behind the goal. All we could hope for was for Palace to keep it tight and score the first goal to make a real cup tie of it.

Unfortunately, Samsunspor scored the opener after less than 3 minutes – a deep cross-shot caught Kevin Miller off his line. He scooped the ball away only to an oncoming forward who squared the ball to Serkan who scored. With Samsunspor now 3-0 up on aggregate, they were content to let Palace have most of the ball, and Palace largely spent the rest of the first half passing it sideways with little attacking intent.

At half time we were invited into the boardroom by our hosts to drink traditional Turkish tea – small, strong shots in tulip-shaped glasses.

The second half was slightly more promising, Palace did show some attacking intent, only to leave massive gaps at the back. Kevin Miller was to thank for keeping the score down. Clinton Morrison came on as a sub and smashed a shot against the underside of the crossbar, only for it to bounce back out rather than down and in. It was our best chance of the game. In the last minute, with Palace pretty much resigned to their fate, the defence was exposed, and Serkan scored again, this time with a delicate chip over Miller.

At the final whistle, all manner of press and TV crews ran onto the pitch to photograph and interview the victorious Samsunspor players and the home crowd were very jubilant. To beat an English team and progress further in the competition was a big feat for this club.

The Palace players gave a quick clap in our direction and hastily departed down the tunnel. This fast exit made the press over the coming days, until skipper Marc Edworthy drew the matter to a close by apologising in the pages of the Croydon Advertiser the following weekend.

We thanked our hosts in the Directors' Box, and I scampered around collecting up discarded team sheets for fans back home.

On the minibus journey back to the airport, Steve Coppell did complain that the Chairman and President he was sat next to in the ground smoked enormous cigars all game, which he really didn't like.

We got to Samsun airport at about midnight local time, but it was still hot and balmy. About fifteen minutes after we arrived, the players and management joined us in the departure lounge. As we were the only airplane leaving Samsun airport that night, there was almost no hanging around and we boarded for the long flight home through the night. The air hostesses, who had been with us throughout the whole of the trip since the outward leg, had bought plenty of cans of local beer. Despite it being a night flight home, several were consumed by the Palace supporters on the plane. Sensibly, I left all the players and staff alone, having had loads of interaction with them during the trip, as they were clearly tired and needed to be left amongst themselves.

The plane did stop off for an hour to refuel in the middle of the night, but everyone was too tired to get off and we landed back at Stansted at 4.30am, exhausted but having had the experience of a lifetime."

That wasn't quite the end of the Intertoto as far as two Palace fans were concerned. Unable to go to Samsun, Rob Ellis and Andy 'Essex' Curtis had booked a trip to Germany. They had taken a rather large gamble on Palace and a much smaller gamble on Werder Bremen both making it through to the semi-final. In doing so Rob had to overcome the additional problem of messing up existing holiday plans with his girlfriend, Caroline. It's unclear whether Essex ever admitted to his other half that Palace weren't actually going to be playing out there. Whilst Bremen easily disposed of Belgian club Lommel 5-2 on aggregate, it became clear that Palace progress was not happening, so they switched destination to Dortmund, a more familiar city, thanks to Rob's long time love for BVB.

In case you're thinking this was an extremely odd trip to make, I should explain a little more about Rob, Essex and my gang of mates, who've made travelling to Germany for football a regular habit. Especially when Palace have a free weekend. This was in the early days of such trips and, indeed, Belgium rather than Germany used to be our preferred destination. The existence of £25 return flights to Brussels with Virgin Express had a lot to do with this preference. Soon enough, the other budget airlines got in on the act of ridiculously cheap fares and our options opened up further.

On matchday, Rob and Essex ended up in a Dortmund bar watching Bremen trounce Samsun 3-0 on TV. The game was held at Bremen's training ground, which would have been an extremely disappointing venue had Palace got through. Bremen made similarly short work of the away leg with another 3-0 victory. They faced FK Vojvodina from Serbia in the final game, the reward being qualification to the first round proper of the UEFA Cup. The Germans narrowly won the first leg 1-0, but were trailing 1-0 in the away leg until their German international Torsten Frings fired the winner.

Werder were joined in the first round by fellow Intertoto qualifiers Bologna and Valencia. Bremen went out in the second round to losing finalists Marseille, who had beaten Bologna on away goals in the semi-final. Valencia fell to Liverpool on away goals.

The bright new start promised by Mark Goldberg and Terry Venables never got going, not helped by a stream of odd signings. Almost invincible at home, but unable to win away, Palace failed to mount any serious sort of promotion challenge. Around Christmas time, while he was away in Australia, dark rumours began to surface about the creditworthiness of the new Chairman. The share price of MSB International, the recruitment consultancy in which Mark Goldberg's fortune was tied up, had tumbled drastically. It had also become clear that Ron Noades had only sold control of the club, but had retained ownership of the ground.

Once Goldberg returned, a fire sale of playing assets began and Venables lost his job, not so much due to the indifferent results but because the club could simply no longer afford him. Steve Coppell took over as Manager for a third time, as the Club spiralled into administration in early March. No points deductions back then, but the club was in a sorry mess financially and Coppell did well to keep Palace clear of any serious threat of relegation.

CPFC's Number 1 supporter in China - July 1999
[Photo: Dom Fifield]

Fan Zhiyi attracting a media scrum wherever he goes - July 1999
[Photo: Dom Fifield]

7

CHINA IN OUR HANDS

With Palace in administration, an overseas tour looked unlikely in the 1999 close season. Nothing could be further from the truth, as Palace ended up playing a series of games in China. Early in his short managerial tenure, Venables had signed two Chinese internationals, Fan Zhiyi and Sun Jihai. It was the first transfer deal involving Chinese nationals moving to England and caused no little media attention in both countries. It transpired that as part of the transfer deal, Palace had been asked to tour China.

It also seemed to the Club Administrator, Simon Paterson, like a good opportunity to put the Club in the shop window to prospective Chinese investors. The problem would be financing the trip, but former shirt sponsor Virgin Atlantic Airlines came to the rescue. Keen to publicise their new route to Shanghai, they agreed to fly the club out. For the period of the tour, Virgin were once more our shirt sponsor.

The tour was announced in mid-June and it was immediately an appealing, if daunting, trip. My brother-in-law, Andy "Gibbo" Gibson, had recently had some experience of touring in China and was keen to go back, so we began to look at options. Phil Alexander had recently been appointed Managing Director, following the departure of Goldberg and his entourage. Phil was kind enough to provide some background details. He confirmed that the Club would not be able to put on a supporters' trip but was happy to send us the proposed itinerary, advising that it still was a work-in-progress. We started to look at the costs involved of running our own trip. We could get there easily enough, but the vast distances that the team was travelling cross-country meant that we would need a number of costly internal flights.

We had just about worked out a way to do it, albeit for over £1,500 per person, when the schedule changed again. This meant that we'd have to miss one of the games, as there seemed to be no scheduled flights between the cities on the days in question and not enough time to travel by train. We asked Phil how the club would be travelling and he told us that the Chinese travel agency handling the tour were looking to charter a plane. We asked whether they would allow us to buy any spare seats, but understandably no-one wanted the additional hassle this would cause. In the end, a charter wasn't needed, but another amendment to the schedule sent the cost of flights alone over the £2,000 mark and we reluctantly gave up on the trip.

The internet was just about establishing itself back then and a number of Palace websites and email newsletters had sprung up. I had started the *Palace Echo* website myself, earlier that year. The most popular service was the email newsletter CP-FRIS (*Crystal Palace – Fast Results Information Service*) run by Ray Bateup. He had the idea to email out the results to overseas supporters as soon as he could physically do so after the game. This service was joyously welcomed by many of our more far-flung expats. It quickly expanded into a news service and not just for ex-pat fans. It became a vital tool for disseminating information about the administration. Soon, Ray was sending emails every day. No more waiting for Friday's *Croydon Advertiser*.

It was through this medium that most Palace fans followed the tour. Dominic Fifield, a young football journalist and Palace fan, who had been an intern in the club's Publications Department, was asked to undertake the role of Press Officer on the tour. By rights, Terry Byfield, who was Head of the Department, should have gone to China, but he was not at all keen on flying, so Dom was asked to step in. Dom, who these days is a senior football writer with *The Athletic*, after twenty years at *The Guardian*, remembers his amazement at being asked to accompany the squad:

"I had started my year-long traineeship at The Guardian in June. My association with Palace resulted from a work experience placement in 1997 when I was working out what I wanted to do for a living. I'd written to Palace, Capital Gold and the Croydon Advertiser. My letter happened to land just as James Coome, the Palace programme editor, was off to Australia for a month in the middle of the Premiership season. They took me in the following Monday, I had a week with James, then I did the programme for the following month while he was away. James showed me the ropes, taught me to use an Apple Mac and how to deal with the printers. At the end of the month, James returned and I was free again.

A month later, they came back to me and asked whether I would come back for the rest of the season and help James out on a short-term contract. It was quite a stressful time, with the takeover going on and Lombardo coming in as Manager. They released me at the end of the season and I went off to University to do a year-long post-grad degree in journalism.

I still did some work for the club on a matchday, doing Clubcall interviews and then writing them up for the following programme. That was the extent of my relationship with the club, I had no reason to imagine that I would get to go to China. Terry Byfield rang me to let me know I'd be getting a call from Phil Alexander, asking me whether I could go to China for two weeks. It was ridiculously short notice. I've no idea how they rushed through my visa. I was slightly perturbed as to how The Guardian might react, but they were happy for me to be in with a football club. My Mum drove me down to the training ground at Streete Court with an old suitcase."

With no official club website – one of the casualties of the Administrators' cost cutting – Dom's daily reports to CP-FRIS from the camp were followed avidly back home.

The tour of China began with a gruelling ten-hour flight to Shanghai. The visit was the first tour of any real length by a British football club to the country and attracted great interest in the Chinese State media, who were on hand to greet the team, along with Fan Zhiyi. Dom recalls that his first experience of China was that it was a very different world:

"The squad was packed into three minibuses bound for the team's hotel about five miles away. The twenty-minute journey proved too much for one bus, which was carrying thirteen people including the Palace management. Having stalled the van at a traffic light, our unfortunate driver failed to restart the engine and drifted uncomfortably across three lanes of traffic, some of which was oncoming, before coming to a halt underneath a motorway flyover. The temperature outside was near 30 degrees, prompting a handful of the occupants to jump out of the vehicle, carefully avoiding the oncoming traffic which tended to veer across the road haphazardly.

Meanwhile the driver opened a flap in the floor of the minibus, revealing the engine in all its dubious glory. There were exposed wires, an empty water tank and a dipstick that quite patently hadn't seen any oil since the van was made. Unfortunately, such novelties soon became hidden behind plumes of thick black smoke, prompting a mass evacuation from the bus.

A policeman appeared from nowhere and urged the driver, rather forcibly, to keep trying to move on. The officer then wandered over to the players and staff asking: 'Fan Zhiyi? Fan Zhiyi?' Had the Chinese national captain been on our bus, the official might have pushed us all the way to the hotel.

To his credit, the driver did eventually restart the bus, but was all too aware that if he stopped again the engine would fail. The next few moments were interesting – the embarrassed chauffeur beeping his horn at every junction to ward off any traffic that might be in our way, legitimately or not. He was eventually thwarted by a toll booth and the Eagles staff were back out on the road, waiting for back-up to arrive. When it did, thirteen people crammed into a six-seater, although it was luxury compared to what had gone before."

Welcome to China, indeed. Palace trained at Shanghai Stadium that evening and it became clear just how revered Fan is in his native Shanghai.

"He is followed wherever he goes by a cluster of soccer enthusiasts and adolescent girls. Apart from the policeman, the first question the hotel staff asked was 'Fan Zhiyi good, no?' He is worshipped and, if he does not relish it, it appears he is well used to the attention. A crowd gathered by the gates of the training ground, come to watch their hero play with the

Brits. They were rewarded when Fan scored the winning goal in a training game. A cheer went up which had not greeted the other four goals scored. As he left, he was mobbed by yet more adoring fans."

Palace moved onto Beijing for a game against Beijing Gouan, who had finished third in the league last season and were currently fourth in mid-season. The clubs were competing for the China Telecom International Cup at the Workers Stadium. The day before the game, the travelling party were treated to a barbeque at the British Embassy, then on to an authentic 'Peking Duck' dinner in the evening:

"After the extravagances of the night before, it came as no surprise that the Peking Duck didn't feel quite so spectacular in the morning. Wayne Carlisle, who had been one of those brave enough to try a slice of duck brain, was one of a number who'd spent the night with their heads down the toilet, others suffered the duck's revenge later in the day. Kevin Miller was so poorly he didn't make the game."

It wasn't only Fan and Sun who were attracting local attention. Even our young Press Officer, who had acquired the nickname 'Laptop', wasn't immune:

"My autograph is looking more professional by the day. I have developed a rather nonchalant, almost disdainful look, as I scribble my name on whatever is handed to me. Who says fame can go to the head?

My name would often appear in the programmes... well, I say 'programme', they were more like A4 glossy pamphlets, all in Chinese script, except for the Palace squad names which would appear with quite phonetic spellings. My name would be amongst the playing staff, in the same way as Steve Kember, Gary Sadler and Vic Bettinelli were."

Palace may not have been favourites, given that this was their very first game of pre-season and Gouan were midway through theirs, but they took home the China Telecom International Cup after beating the hosts 2-1. The Eagles' goal-scorers were Clinton Morrison and Sun Jihai; which would prove to be his first and only goal for Palace. Such was the suspect quality of the huge, multi-faceted trophy, that it did not even survive the on-pitch celebrations in one piece.

Many of the Palace staff celebrated the fine win well into the night, ending up at a Karaoke bar. Some preferred to nurse their still-sensitive stomachs and others were simply too exhausted after playing in the wet and muggy conditions. The following day was a day off from training and a coach trip to the Great Wall and Ming Dynasty tombs had been organised. The day was rounded off with a lavish buffet in the company of Beijing Guoan, the Chinese FA and the British Embassy.

The next day was Steve Coppell's birthday. His first gift was a 5.45am alarm call for the flight back to Shanghai, where Palace were to play the city's second team, Shanghai 02, the next day. It was also a return to training for the team, but with full-sized football pitches being something of a rarity in China at that time, their training venue was in a suburb some way out of the city, as Dom recalls:

"It was clear we were leaving the traditional tourist track well behind. We passed through paddy fields and grim industrial areas, lined with shanty towns and rubbish tips. A group of children were swimming in a lake of dirty water, next to a tip, while yards way an elderly gentleman fished. This was, perhaps, our first glimpse of the other China – the one which had yet to bow to western influence. The road signs no longer bothered with English translations – no westerners wanted to see this.

After a journey of such contrasts, the training ground was surprisingly civilised. A modern arena, probably holding around 15,000 spectators but the ends behind each goal were blocks of flats. Indeed, people actually lived in basement accommodation below the main stand."

The team had recovered from the journey, though one player was distressed to find there was no toilet paper in the gents. Training went well and the locals turned up to watch, as word of the conquerors of the capital's finest had spread.

"Back at the hotel, it was time for the Manager to celebrate. He was presented with a cake by Mr Liu of GreatGate (the club's tour guides while in China) before the management team went out on the town – the players had to abide by an 11pm curfew, though there was no-one around to enforce it!"

The second matchday dawned and if the coaching staff had any ill effects from the night out, they were well concealed at the morning training session, again some distance from town. Dom, however, was, in his own words, "all over the place!"

Another player fell foul of the lack of toilet paper until Mr Liu saved the day in the nick of time. Lunch was taken back at the hotel before a 2.30pm departure, however another mini-crisis was about to strike, courtesy of the Press Officer:

"Who needs crowd congestion, motorway traffic jams or broken-down coaches when you can have a press man falling asleep in his hotel room and keeping everyone waiting? I single-handedly delayed kick-off by fifteen minutes.

In my defence, we were working twenty hour days. It was absolutely brutal. I came back that morning after training – God knows why they were training on the day of a game because it was so hot – I lay on my bed, closed my eyes and suddenly it was four hours later. Phil Alexander was ringing me on the room phone. I just picked up my laptop and ran downstairs. Everyone was sitting on the coach outside and I was still dressed in the shorts and t-shirt from training. I sat behind Steve Coppell, who was not impressed, I was extremely apologetic. It was simply sheer exhaustion from the long hours, the heat and humidity. We had no staff with us, everybody was doing everything."

The game was meant to be behind closed doors, but around a thousand spectators managed to gain entry, despite a military presence on the gate. Others were able to watch from their houses at either end of the ground.

The match, when it finally got underway, was a see-saw affair. Palace conceded early but got straight back into it through Andrew Martin. After the Chinese had a goal struck off for offside, Palace took the lead through Richard Harris. Early in the second half, Shanghai equalised from the penalty spot. With the spartan crowd baying for the introduction of Fan and Sun, James Hibburt claimed the winner for Palace. The audience had to settle for watching their local heroes warm up behind one goal.

There was to be no extended post-match celebrations as Richard Branson was flying in the next morning and the Palace party were to be there to greet him on the runway. The inaugural scheduled flight from London Heathrow to Shanghai landed an hour late at 10.15am. The squad, kitted out in their Virgin sponsored shirts, were there to meet Branson as he descended the aircraft steps. Fan and Sun, first in line to welcome the entrepreneur to Shanghai. He then greeted the other players as the press photographers jostled, none too gently, for the best positions.

Once Branson was on his way, it was time for the squad to fly to Kunming in the South West of China. Although there had been little issue with the internal flights between Beijing and Shanghai, this five-hour journey was less smooth:

"Steve Coppell was anxious that Jamie Smith not be told that we would have to refuel halfway. Smith is a bad flier and had considered taking the train. However, the prospect of an eighteen-hour rail journey made him think again. Whilst we were waiting in the lounge, two other flights had been delayed. The staff wrote the reasons for the delay on the board in the check-in area and when the phrase 'delayed due to mechanical problems' appeared there was an audible groan. Jamie Smith's head sunk into his hands. Our plane did not suffer such problems, but it was tiny for such a long flight. The meatballs at dinner left a lot to be desired as well.

We stopped off near Three Gorges to refuel. The wave of heat that struck as we stepped onto the runway had a few players looking apprehensive, but Nicky Rizzo in particular was annoyed. He wasn't the best flyer and was perturbed to find himself sat beside live chickens in baskets in the cabin. As the plane made its final approach – a bumpy set-down, having been buffered non-stop for the previous two hours – a mobile phone went off behind him. The gentlemen answered and proceeded to chat merrily away as the plane bounced to a halt on the tarmac. Having taken to heart the standard warnings about turning mobiles off, the thought that our plane's navigational systems might be scrambled by a cellphone pushed already chicken-wary Nicky over the edge. The next forty minutes were spent trying to calm him down. The second leg of the trip was appreciably shorter and less eventful."

Although the party arrived at their hotel close to midnight, a full dinner buffet was awaiting them. After a day acclimatising, it was onto matchday number three. The Zhidong Stadium was the venue for the game, as well as the morning training session. This was also where Dom's mistaken celebrity status came a cropper:

"We were greeted by a Chinese man dressed head to foot in Palace kit from last season, none of which had apparently been made by Adidas. He had bought it at the market and was besotted by the club. He insisted that every member of the side have their photograph taken

with him. Then he went and had the film developed and proudly reappeared with prints for all the players. Meeting his heroes had made his day and he turned up again after the game to thank the team once more.

He was a star. A star with some sense, mind you. He asked me for a signature and, when I scribbled Dom Fifield on his autograph book, he wanted me to point to my name on the matchday magazine. Unlike in Beijing, I am officially Terry Byfield in this programme, but he was having none of it. Even with no English he could tell that my name was nothing like that of the official club press officer. I beat a hasty retreat..."

There was another delay to kick-off – not the fault of Dom, this time – as the match organisers battled with last-minute red tape.

Although the stadium was impressive, the pitch was uneven and rough. Rough also summed up the style of play that the second tier club, Yunnan Hongta, employed that evening, urged on by over 17,000 fans. A friendly it was not and many injuries were sustained throughout the game, through a combination of poor pitch, physicality and bad luck. Hayden Mullins was even hospitalised with a gashed ankle after a particularly brutal tackle.

Palace took the lead twice through Lee Bradbury and Clinton Morrison, but were pegged back both times and the game finished level. The match was decided by a penalty shoot-out, which Palace lost 8-7. If the reception on the pitch had been poor, the adulation that greeted the team as they made their way back to the hotel was not.

"As the coach crawled through the crowd, there were smiling faces everywhere, the chants and hooting started up again. The fans waved, cheered and snapped as we slowly drove back the short distance to the hotel. It must feel like this when you've won the FA Cup, not lost a meaningless pre-season friendly. The scenes were amazing – it was a carnival to celebrate the visit of Fan, Sun and Crystal Palace. It was a joy to watch and, in a small way, be part of. It summed up the way the club had been welcomed in China."

The squad had enjoyed Kunming with its fresher climate and relatively smog-free air, compared to the major cities of Shanghai and Beijing. It was with some regret, at 5.30am the next day, that they embarked on the most gruelling leg of the journey within China.

Their final game was against Dalian WanDa, a remote city in the north near Harbin, with a large Russian population. 'Near' should perhaps be in inverted commas; the game was taking place three hours away in Da Qing. Some miscommunication had occurred and no-one was happy about this, having already endured another long two-legged flight in another tiny plane. The road between the two places was desperately poor and the coach drive, under police escort, was hair-raising at times.

There was further misapprehension upon arrival at the hotel, which had prepared a seven course meal for the team, instead of the requested afternoon snack. The feast was scheduled for 6.15pm, but the party was scheduled to attend a formal banquet with their opponents at 7pm. Given the players' dietary requirements it was difficult to avoid causing offence.

Communication of any sort in the remote region was also difficult: just one phone in the hotel from which international calls could be made, very little mobile phone service, and no internet. For a club in Administration this was a particular issue, as the Administrator, Chairman and Managing Director were all on the touring party, completely cut off from Selhurst Park.

The exhibition game against Dalian, Sun's former club located some 1,000 kms away, had become of major local political significance in Da Qing, but the pitch was in a shocking state, uneven and bone-dry. The baking hot conditions were hardly ideal either. The game was the centrepiece of the opening events of the Da Qing Games and, as such, the team who had arrived some three hours before kick-off had to warm-up around various athletics events and entertainments.

"I went out with the players for the pre-match inspection of the pitch. I had been issued the same Adidas training gear as the players. I was pottering around looking at the dreadful turf and suddenly I realised all the players had gone back in to escape the smouldering heat. Then, fans at the far end, starting chanting "Shui-Jing-Gong!" at me, which meant 'Crystal Palace' in Mandarin. To my shame, I responded by doing the 'Dean Austin' clap, applauding with hands over head but held horizontally. I turned back to find Steve Coppell and Steve Kember watching me from the mouth of the tunnel and Kember was just shaking his head."

Given the unusual pre-match build-up, it was little surprise that the game ended goal-less. The 28,000 capacity crowd vented their displeasure at Dalian's performance, throwing empty water bottles onto the pitch. It had become clear that the majority of the crowd were there for Fan and Sun, rather than any of the other sporting or cultural displays. The carnival atmosphere that existed was very much dampened down by the game, in which Palace were the better side throughout. Palace's dominance of the game was justified by a 4-2 win in the post-match penalty shootout.

The party did not linger after the game as they were heading back to Harbin, although the journey away from the immediate area of the stadium was hampered by autograph hunters repeatedly breaking into the bus as it sat in traffic.

From Harbin, the squad made their way back to Shanghai via another long flight. Steve Coppell carried on towards home, via Hong Kong, in what must have been an absolute marathon of air-travel. Coppell was not the only squad member missing when the team finally returned home after a final day in Shanghai. Sun Jihai, as had been widely speculated by the Chinese media throughout the tour, had re-signed for Dalian WanDa. His last ignominious activity as part of the Palace squad was to pull up exhausted early on in a training run. Despite all the rumours, however,

Fan did return to Palace, after playing in an exhibition game for Shanghai Shenhua against Manchester United. He played for Palace for a further two years before joining Dundee in the summer of 2002.

It was touch and go whether Palace would be allowed to commence the 1999/2000 season in administration, but the Football League was eventually persuaded that a deal to sell the club was on the horizon. It turned out to be a very remote horizon. It would be almost a year before Simon Jordan eventually bought Palace. The season had been something of a struggle but Steve Coppell managed to keep The Eagles in the second tier. One factor credited for his success was having been able to blood many of the youngsters who'd be called upon during this hard season, in that first tour to China.

Clinton Morrison on target in China - July 1999
[Photo: Dom Fifield]

A cup-winning start against Shan'xi GouLi - July 2000
[Photo: Dom Fifield]

Match action in Nanchang against Guangzhou Songri - July 2000
[Photo: Dom Fifield]

8

RE-ENTER THE DRAGON

With Palace spending the whole year in Administration, a trip to anywhere more exotic than the bankruptcy court seemed unlikely. However, Palace had managed to retain Fan Zhiyi and another trip to China had been tentatively arranged. With the future uncertain, the club seemed to have made few concrete plans, never mind the fans.

On 5th July 2000, it was announced that Simon Jordan, former owner of PocketPhone Shop, had bought the club in an audacious move. He bought the club from Jerry Lim who, as the Administrators' preferred purchaser, had completed the deal only to sell it immediately on, at half a million pounds premium, to Mr Jordan.

Despite a severe lack of senior first team members available, it was confirmed that the China trip would now go ahead and, following some frantic last-minute arrangements, nineteen footballers, two coaches, a physio, a fitness instructor, a kit man, an ex-chairman, a chief exec and Dom Fifield, once again fulfilling the role of press officer, assembled at Heathrow for a trio of games against Shan'xi Gouli, Guangzhou Songri and a prestigious game against the Chinese national team.

Dom had recently been taken on full-time by *The Guardian* but they were again more than happy for him to take ten days leave and this time he did file the odd story for them while there.

Dom recalls there was also some suggestion that money had changed hands to help the club through the later months of administration and therefore Palace were obligated to fulfil the tour. There was a distinct feeling that no-one really wanted to be there, though and it felt very much like an after-thought.

The full playing roster should have been 21 players, but Matt Gregg's girlfriend was on the point of giving birth and extremely nervous flyer Jamie Smith mysteriously managed to lose his passport when it came to arranging Chinese visas. The eventual travelling squad was comprised of only five players from the previous year and the rest were mostly youth teamers on the fringes of first team consideration, by dint of the long, crippling administration period. Simon Rodger and Fraser Digby were the senior players in the squad, while even Hayden Mullins and Clinton Morrison were considered to be old hands, despite their relatively tender age.

The new owner, Simon Jordan, decided that his time was better spent on turning around the club at home, rather than glad-handing in China. Not that he wouldn't be taking a very keen interest in the trip, as both Steve Coppell and Dom Fifield were soon to discover.

The flight from Heathrow was with Air China rather than Virgin and the travelling party were less than impressed with the dysfunctional state of the seat-back consoles and range of films on offer. Most eventually electing to sleep.

Arriving in Beijing, the party took a short internal flight to Xi'an. After the experiences of the year before, this was the flight that the most seasoned travellers were dreading, but apart from a bumpy landing all went comparatively well. It was the ride to hotel that held greater terrors, as Dom Fifield explained in his *CP-FRIS* reports:

"Having boarded the coach and with a police escort leading the way, all seemed clear for a relaxing twenty minute trip from the airport into the city centre to our hotel. One major junction later and with buttocks clenched all around, the memories of life on China's roads came flooding back.

It's hard to say what speeds we reached on that trip to the hotel. Certainly we never went below 35mph, which is just as well seeing as if we had slowed down much more than that we would have been overtaken on all sides by agricultural vehicles driven by farmers who had also left the iron on at home. At one point, we found ourselves tearing down the wrong side of a dual carriageway as traffic scattered ahead of us, the police escort honking his horn and castigating anyone who had the bare-faced cheek to be driving on the correct side of the road. Occasionally I glanced round, half expecting to see a trail of debris in our wake, only to find other tractor drivers making merry in our slipstream. Every death-defying swerve into oncoming traffic prompted screams of terror from the players and hoots of laughter from our Chinese hosts. At one point we sent two cyclists scurrying as we barged our way between them at 50mph.

'You wouldn't like to drive here in Xi'an, no?' grinned 'Dave', our host.

'Not on a bike' came the polite version of my reply.

On our arrival at the hotel, the team were mobbed by supporters and press alike. Fan, who'd just met up with the team having already been in China for the summer, commanded an impromptu standing ovation in the reception. Steve Coppell was immediately thrust into a press conference alongside the Chinese national team Manager and the Coach of Shan'xi Guoli – a Brazilian fellow who has steered them to top of the First Division and possible automatic promotion.

The Chinese national coach was Bora Milanovic, formerly with Mexico, the US, his native Yugoslavia and Costa Rica. His mission was to lead the Chinese to the forthcoming 2002

World Cup, being held in Asia for the first time. It was unthinkable that the Chinese should miss out on the world's biggest party when it was being held on their doorstep. Recent results had been patchy and his relationship with his Chinese masters was uneasy. One Chinese reporter asked him at the conference why he was always smiling and whether Chinese supporters might be given something to smile about some time soon. It seemed that the country was expecting, nay demanding, a hammering."

Team selection for the imminent Shan'xi Gouli game was giving Steve Coppell something of a headache, with no left-back in the squad and Fan Zhiyi insistent that he was unable to play, suffering from the common complaint of "sore ankle, too hot" with the emphasis placed firmly on the second complaint. Dom Fifield light-heartedly reported the discussions in the first of his now-traditional daily missives to CP-FRIS as follows:

"As the management team were sitting discussing selection at the bar this evening, the lone pianist started tinkling away at what turned into an epic version of her only tune. It was that bloody Celine Dion song, the theme tune from Titanic.

'Listen Steve,' piped up Gary Sadler. 'They're playing our song.'

'Do you think they can declare?' asked Vic, turning his attention to the game against the Chinese national team on Thursday.

At least there was some good news over dinner. A telephone call from Simon Jordan to Coppell confirmed that Arsenal's Tommy Black and Julian Gray should be joining the club for around £1m. They will be the first players to join the Eagles since 1998, although it would be better if they could be flown straight out to China to take part on Thursday.

'Someone send for the cavalry' sighed one of the management team.

'No, sod it. Let's be positive. We'll beat this lot tomorrow and then show the national team what we're made of on Thursday.' That's the attitude."

The tone of this bulletin prompted Mr Jordan to write a page-long email to Dom, critical of the 'negativity' he felt was prevalent throughout his report. This was, perhaps, the first sign that the times were most definitely a-changin' at Selhurst. Dom recalls the heart-sinking moment when Phil Alexander knocked on his hotel door asking to see the email:

"It seemed to me that the main problem that the Chairman had with my bulletin was that it dwelt too much on the Administration, how we didn't have any players, how the club is on its knees. He wanted that air-brushed out of history and that we have moved on from that. That was completely his prerogative. The fact was that nobody at the club was pre-checking what I was sending.

The previous year, I had complete free rein, then Simon Jordan came in and this wasn't his baby. It was someone else's adventure, he wanted it over, get it done and come back so we could focus on new signings and the like. Looking back now, I don't actually see my tone changing dramatically in the subsequent emails, maybe I didn't talk about administration as much, but the nature of it was still quite flippant. It certainly didn't become professional journalism, or even club in-house journalism, overnight, which I suspect is what the Chairman actually wanted.

I got on the bus that morning and Steve Coppell was sitting on the seat in front of me and turned to me and asked:

'So, have you had an email, this morning?'

'Erm, yeah I have.'

It seemed that my email was one of a longer list of things that the new Chairman had taken the Manager to task over. You could see then that the relationship wasn't going to last."

The news of the signing of the two young players from Arsenal also caused Dom some embarrassment:

"Over a drink with the management, I'd been told on the quiet that we had bought these two players. Later that evening, I had to do a Clubcall interview with Hayden Mullins in my room. After the conversation he asked whether it was true that we were signing someone? I confirmed the news to him but asked him not to broadcast it as the club were still keeping it quiet at this point.

'Yeah, no worries at all' said Hayden, before bellowing to his roommate further down the corridor:

'HEY CLINTON, WE'VE SIGNED JULES AND TOMMY!'

My reply to Hayden was unprintable."

The first full day in Xi'an began with training at the Shan'xi Stadium, a vast arena, capable of holding up to 60,000 people, with a running track and long jumps distancing the pitch from the stands. The two sides were covered and this was to be the inaugural game under their new floodlights. It was a fine stadium, although the players were not particularly happy with the long length of the grass, the heat and humidity.

As last year, Fan Zhiyi was attracting the most attention, given a hero's welcome everywhere he went, although his spending time with the national side inevitably led to much transfer speculation. At the press conference, a local journalist asked him if he wanted to play for another club, either in China or abroad. His reply was that he had signed a four-year contract at Palace and so he couldn't. The answer drew a wry smile from Steve Coppell.

It was tribute to the Palace management that their much-deliberated line-up notched up a reasonably comfortable 2-0 win in front of 24,000 spectators. Steven Hunt and Roscoe D'sane getting the goals in the first half. D'sane also collected the 'man of the match' award as the PA incongruously blared out 'The Marseillaise'.

The coach back to hotel left without Steve Coppell, Phil Alexander and Dom Fifield, at the inexplicable insistence of the police, so the three repaired to a nearby restaurant for a beer before being picked up by a police car. Steve was then forced to make the journey back to the hotel sitting in the boot. What amounted to a line in Dom's report was picked up by the Evening Standard who ran a page-lead story back in England.

The following morning was given over to relaxing and a trip to see what has been called the eighth wonder of the ancient world, the Terracotta Warriors. Some of the players preferred to stare at their hand-held gaming devices than the historical wonders right in front of them. The afternoon was spent with a brief training session back at the stadium, with children training on the track as the players went through their routines on the pitch. The stand above the players' entrance was packed with locals desperate to catch a glimpse of Fan, who had been mobbed as the bus had pulled up.

In the evening, tour organisers Great Gate took the staff out for a meal and plied their guests with the local spirit, leaving the Press Officer with a monumental hangover on the morning of the China game.

After a short morning training session in searing heat, for once the smog lifted and there was clear blue sky. Prior to the game, Phil Alexander and Peter Morley attended a meeting with the President of the Chinese Football Association and the Governor of Shan'xi Province. Both parties were very enthusiastic about strengthening the ties between Palace and China, with an exchange of players and coaches a possibility, given the latter's desire to perform well in both the Asian Games and the World Cup.

A young Palace side had played a Chinese National XI once before. In late August 1997, a touring squad visited Palace's Mitcham training ground. Both Sun and Fan took part in that match. This game put them both firmly on Palace's scouting radar, along with striker Hao Haidong. Manager Steve Coppell was quoted as saying: "They have several players who would survive in the Premiership. Two of the substitutes they brought on at half-time were outstanding." He was referring to Haidong and Fan, although the *Eagles Magazine* that covered the game continually referred to Fan as 'Fang'.

Despite scoring twice, through Steven Thomson and Clinton Morrison in the first half, China replied with five goals in the second period. These included a brace each for Sun Jihai and Hao Haidong. Steve Coppell had sent out a young side but had also included new coaching assistant Ray Wilkins in the side. Coppell said afterwards, "If I'd have known they'd be that good, I would have put out a much stronger team."

Fan and Sun signed in August 1998, but Hao Haidong was also supposed to have signed for us in the November. He left China for trials here, but the deal was not completed. It's unclear why he didn't sign in the end. One theory is that his club, Dalian WanDa, were demanding too high a fee. Others think that Palace's reluctance to release yet another potentially key player for the Asian Games played a part. Of course, it could have been one of the earliest signs that Mark Goldberg's finances were faltering.

Haidong did make it into English Football at the tail-end of his career, signing for Sheffield United in 2005 from Dalian for the nominal sum of £1. Injuries meant he only made a single substitute appearance for the Blades, in the 2006 FA Cup; a 2-1 defeat to Colchester United. He did some coaching with their Youth Academy before retiring and returning to China. He hit the headlines again in 2020 when he spoke out against the Chinese Government on human rights issues.

Back to the 2000 tour. In the stadium there were fewer people for the second game, but the welcome for Fan and the players was as noisy and passionate as ever. Milutinovic had apparently spent the last two days studying videos of our match on Tuesday. This game was vital for him; his job being on the line, despite only being appointed eight months before. He desperately needed a convincing win under his belt. With 100 million people tuning in to the live match coverage on Chinese television, for once, the pressure was firmly on him and his team to perform, rather than Palace.

He got the result he needed, albeit not the hammering that some quarters were demanding and the 3-1 scoreline doesn't tell the full story of a game that saw Palace given a standing ovation as they left the field. Indeed, Palace took the lead when an unmarked Clinton Morrison stretched to reach and then convert Stephen Hunt's perfect cross. This setback was met by a hail of plastic bottles from the stand mostly aimed at the China dugout. The lead lasted fourteen minutes. Though Palace had looked untroubled, they were caught out by an offside flag that never came and an equaliser ensued. Two more goals either side of the break sealed the game for the hosts.

In Dom's estimation it was a magnificent night for Crystal Palace's reputation in China. The players did themselves proud and the supporters in the stadium cheered their every move as they warmed down after the game. Friends were won here by the spirited, committed and thoroughly professional performance, belying the relative inexperience of the Palace side.

The following day the squad left Xi'an for Nanchang. Dom recounts an interesting day, mostly for unpleasant reasons, that encapsulated Palace's life on tour in China:

"A busy, strength sapping day of travelling which has taken us from one corner of China to another, via Shanghai. The journey would have been hard enough but the lads are dropping like flies with various stomach complaints. Being struck down with stomach cramps and diarrhoea at 30,000ft on a Chinese internal flight is, well, interesting to say the least.

If nothing else, the day has provided an opportunity to meet some of the younger players, who have otherwise lived in dread of me pulling a Clubcall interview on them. They went to Xi'an's biggest shopping centre in the morning, situated under the main square on two levels, but found prices almost identical to those back home. The arcade was geared very much to Westerners and almost all the squad came home empty handed although full of Kentucky Fried Chicken. Fan picked up two push scooters, the kind of which cost around £100 I am told in London. Over here they are nearer £30 and the vast majority of the lads have placed orders with him before we return to England – what with the kit skips and 30-odd scooters, the baggage attendants at Air China must be dreading next Tuesday.

Chris Sharpling was the first to succumb to the stomach ailments; he was up all night, apparently, and needed to be attended to by physio Gary Sadler. The next to go – to the amusement of the lads – was kitman Vic Bettinelli who found good use for my hotel carrier bag on the journey to Xi'an airport. To a chorus of 'Huuueyy' and 'heave ho, here we go' from the back of the bus, Vic retained his dignity and kept his breakfast down – until we arrived at the airport where he made a mad dash to the toilet. He's had a bad day.

The driving was as hair-raising as ever, although it has become vindictive as well. At one point, an army car actually joined our convey today, forcing itself between the police car and the bus and zooming along at our terrifying tempo. The bus driver was not having this and literally edged the car to one side, towards the hard shoulder of the motorway, before accelerating past. It was little short of stock-car shunting; verging on dodgems tactics. But the army guy didn't give up. Instead of seeing sense, realising he was up against a complete nutter of a chauffeur here and staying well back in the carnage which generally trails in our wake, he came back for more. At high speed, he motored down the inside, nipped across between coach and police car and out into the fast lane to our left. The coach driver tried in vain to veer into his slip stream, presumably to finish him off this time by catapulting him into the oncoming traffic on the other side of the central reservation, but the game was up. The army man turned off at the next round-about. Our driver spat out of the window in frustration.

Upon arrival at Xi'an airport, a few of the squad picked up replica Terracotta Warriors from the tacky gift shops in the foyer. All the prices were reduced from cheap to bargain because Fan was with us – although the Chinese star was not having the best of days. As we left the hotel, surrounded by autograph hunters, he was handed a piece of paper by the clerk, which he duly signed like all the rest. Unfortunately it was an unpaid telephone bill – even Fan cannot get away with that over here – and he was forced to apologise sheepishly before paying a visit to the cashier. Still, he managed to swing us all business class seats on the flight to Shanghai.

The journey to Nanchang took only 55 minutes, but try telling that to young goalkeeper Lee Kendall. He is the Nicky Rizzo or Jamie Smith of this year's tour, his fear of flying making him an obvious target for the other members of the squad. To this end, it was unfortunate he found himself sitting above the wheels of the small-scale aircraft, forced to listen to the *creaking and feel the lurching as the undercarriage coped with the landing gear. Some of the others had a field day at his expense.*

Arriving at Nanchang the squad found their hotel to be of a questionable standard, particularly in the hygiene department, with biting insects being a particular nuisance. The food was also an issue: chicken claws, chillied beef on skewers and white things that scared the living daylights out of some of the squad – prompting most to stick to toast, which is sweet and almost tastes like a tea cake. 'They must think it's a bit odd, don't you think,' said young midfielder Michael Fowler. 'We've been travelling all day on empty stomachs and we turn up at their hotel and order two rounds of toast.' He had a point."

It should be taken into account that these tours were in the very early days of Western football teams touring in China. Nutrition was just one of the problems facing the squad.

"The level of chaos was unbelievable, the local authorities didn't anticipate the level of interest that there would be and certainly there was not a lot of organisation from our end either. It was so improvised. Steve Coppell was trying to source cheap white bread and jam for the players' pre-match meal. It was a logistical nightmare back then, although now it is brilliant. I've covered Chelsea there in pre-season and the sports scientists are all over it. Back then, the hotels were expecting us to sit down and have seven courses whenever we had a meal. That summed up the level of chaos."

The game in Nanchang against Guangzhou Songri was scheduled for Monday afternoon, when the expected temperature would be in the mid-thirties. It's fair to say that the squad were dreading it, although at least they'd arrived on the Friday which allowed some time to acclimatise. To that end, the weekend training sessions were being taken in the afternoon.

"Nanchang does not have its own league side, the city is football crazy and the main Renmin Square sports two giant screens, one of which broadcasts live Chinese league games every Saturday afternoon. Large numbers of schoolchildren watched Palace train, occasionally uniting in a chorus of 'Fan Zhiyi' followed by the Mandarin for 'Give us a goal'. He duly obliged, to loud cheers."

Due to several ongoing issues, Palace also decided to change hotels over the weekend. It was Vic's birthday and it was celebrated by a lively night out, watching cabaret at the local theatre:

"When we arrived, it was clear the media were also attending in force. There were television cameras and snappers everywhere, with one journalist actually delivering his report in the middle of an act by a woman singing Whitney Houston. The autograph hunters were everywhere, while Fan was granted his customary reception, the lights focusing on him as he took his seat in the front row of the auditorium. Gradually a few other Palace players meandered into the hall having been brought by minibuses from the hotel.

The show kicked off with dancers, cabaret acts, a Korean speaking in Chinese and singing the Carpenters in pidgin English, and even a comic – although that probably lost a bit in non-translation. We all clapped at the right times and smiled for the flash bulbs.

Things really picked up when a portly old fruit took the microphone and started a rendition of a song by Ricky Martin which brought the house down, particularly when he started thumping his chest on the chorus and pouring water all over his head. That turned to jugs of beer – there was no logic to this part of his act as he was presumably lost in his music – and, for good measure, kit man Vic Bettinelli jogged on to the stage and emptied a champagne bucket over the singer.

Dressed in a golden waistcoat, the cabaret king took to Vic, did an encore and was covered from head to toe once again by the kit man, to the delight of the audience. From then on, anything could have happened. Clinton and Vic did some of their own dancing routines on stage, with the latter gleefully picking up one of the other dancers and doing a twirl, while Jimmy Hibburt's rendition of Bryan Adams' 'Everything I Do, I Do It For You' – complete with husky voice – had to be heard to be believed. He has since been nicknamed 'Elvis' and, after training in the heat today, was considering giving up football to become a nightclub singer. It didn't take long to persuade him that maybe that wasn't the best idea.

Back to the action. When Fan decided against participating on stage, our seven-foot tall kit man was then hauled up to perform some keep-me-ups, which he did to great effect despite wearing flip-flops... until, to howls of laughter from the floor, Fan appeared stage left to empty another champagne bucket all over our main attraction.

After the fire breathing and a less-than-convincing whistling act ('Colonel Bogey' has definitely sounded better) a cake appeared on scene and all the performers entered. Our guide David was called on stage and asked Vic to accompany him to blow out the candles. The cast and hall erupted into a chorus of 'Happy Birthday to You' and the kit man delivered a rather shocked, but appropriate speech thanking everyone on behalf of Crystal Palace. It went down a treat. With the whole crowd participating now, the stage was transformed into a dance floor and all the players, staff and performers danced away to some decidedly dodgy Euro bop tunes.

When the Palace lads eventually left, they were given a rousing farewell and clapped out of the theatre. 'I told the lads we'd have a quiet night,' said the boss with a smile on his face. In the end it was a top-quality night."

The final matchday arrived against Guangzhou Songri. They had been relegated from the Chinese Premier League the previous season and were struggling in the lower league this year. They were expected to be the weakest of the opposition faced on the tour. The awful pitch and the heat were expected to have a major influence on the outcome. Even walking around town this morning was difficult. Palace were also without Clinton Morrison and Simon Rodger.

The tour ended with a deserved win, although the winner from Steven Thomson only came four minutes from time. Sean Hankin had opened the scoring for Palace in the first half, only to be pegged back after an outrageous dive from the Chinese side's Brazilian striker, that almost sparked a diplomatic incident when the Referee saw fit to award a penalty, when an Oscar would have been more appropriate.

In the end, justice was seen to be done on a truly awful pitch in unbearable heat. The opposition had been as disappointing as predicted but was equalled by the unexpectedly poor turnout of spectators. A win is a win, though. Post-match celebrations were slightly tempered by an early start for home.

Dom remembers there was a final sting in the tale upon arrival at Heathrow.

"As the players waited patiently around the luggage pick-up, a panicked Heathrow official sprinted across the room muttering something to himself. It quickly transpired that the small collection of bags already claimed were all that had been in transit. Virtually every member of the touring party was missing some part of his inventory. All the skips were still sitting proudly in Beijing with Palace's dirty kit inside; there are games on Thursday and Friday and most of the players will not have their boots available. It was a highly inappropriate way to end what had been a successful tour."

As part of my research for this book, I had the pleasure of speaking to Dom again, who I first met during his first days at Palace, as I was also working on a matchday in the Publications Department. Dom is well-known today for his work at *The Athletic*. As well as generously giving me his permission to reproduce his reports verbatim, in spite of his self-consciousness of those very early journalistic efforts, our conversation gave Dom the opportunity to offer some new reflections of the two Chinese tours:

"I am amazed that the club assumed that I would have the hang of what to do as a Press Officer. I had to attend the pre- and post-match press conferences and assemble the ridiculous fold-up advertising backdrop with all its magnetic strips. I had no clue – utterly a fish out of water. Re-reading those reports, especially from 1999, God only knows how they let me get away with writing that stuff. To offer that level of detail from the inside and to take the piss quite often was unbelievable. The Administrator had no interest in it. There was no-one there to say 'you can't do this, this is not the image we want to portray'. I was so young and naïve, I had no concept about who might read it or how it was received. That first year, it wasn't even picked up by the Evening Standard. The Hayters Press agency did a few bits, but not very much.

These days you have fly-on-the-wall documentaries on Netflix and Amazon, yet they are so sanitised and controlled. This was a student, effectively, writing whatever he wanted from the most secretive country in the world about whatever he wanted. These days, football clubs are the most secretive businesses out there. It's just unthinkable that it would ever happen again or that it even did. We were a nondescript second tier club that no-one really cared about. I felt sorry for Steve Coppell, he was trying to get the team ready for pre-season and not dealing with the logistical nightmares – it was amateur hour in so many ways.

I was basically writing a blog and, to me, a blog at that time was a jokey little commentary, but it was for a professional football club. Ridiculous. An amazing experience for me personally, but, at times, quite ridiculous."

Copps and Dom "Laptop" Fifield
[Photo: Dom Fifield]

The sun sets on the Furiani Stadium as Palace warm-up - March 2001

Welcome to the posh seats! Paul Field makes the most of the Bastia Directors Box
- March 2001

9

CLUB MED

The new ownership at Palace brought forth sweeping changes. After the relative success of the China Tour, two disastrous friendlies spelled the end for Steve Coppell's third reign as Manager. A 4-0 defeat by Reading, at the training ground – supposedly behind closed doors – and a humiliating 6-0 reverse to Millwall at the New Den saw the new Chairman lose patience. Alan Smith was installed as his replacement. A slew of signings and loans followed: Neil Ruddock, Andy Morrison and Jamie Pollock being particularly eyebrow-raising.

The season got off to a slow start, but picked up in the autumn and, by the turn of the year, Palace were handily placed for a run towards the play-offs and in the semi-final of the League Cup. The season pivoted on a 5-0 semi-final defeat to Liverpool at Anfield. Palace had won the first leg 2-1 at Selhurst but were crushed in the return. League form suffered and after a run of six defeats, Palace fans were staring fearfully at the relegation places.

Dougie Freedman had returned to the club in the October and was joined on deadline day by another former favourite, David Hopkin. In an effort to get some playing time under the injury-plagued Hopkin's belt and to introduce him to his new team-mates before the final run-in, Alan Smith took the team away to SC Bastia for a friendly over the March international break.

I hadn't been able to make an overseas trip since Gothenburg in 1997, so I was hungry for some foreign adventure. The problem here was that the Friday evening game was only announced to supporters on the Thursday morning, a mere 32 hours before kick-off. I was game, due to be off work on Friday anyway and could drive over. However, I was not sure where in France Bastia was to be found. Time to hit the internet.

Oh. Bastia was not on the French mainland: it's the capital of the island of Corsica. Located south of Marseille and west of Pisa in the Mediterranean Sea. Driving would involve an eleven hour overnight non-stop journey through France and then a ferry which took another eleven hours. The times of the sailings meant it was not possible to make kick off, even if I could have afforded £500+ fare.

Whilst doing the travel research, my pal Paul "Paf" Field had got in touch professing his interest in doing the trip, if I could work out a way that wouldn't cost a month's mortgage payment. I was struggling at this point, there were no direct flights from London to Corsica. Given our time constraints, the best flight involved changing in Paris but came in at over £500.

I finally worked out that if we left at 7pm and drove to Paris, we could pick up the next morning's 9am scheduled Air France flight from Orly Airport. The cost of the flights and a return on the Eurotunnel was £275, well over what I had set as my maximum for travel. I consulted Paul. He was onboard, if a bit amazed that I was prepared to effectively drive through the night. We decided to go.

One small potential obstacle needed to be overcome first. I say overcome, but in reality it was simply ignored. My partner-now-wife Sue was away with work on a residential course that week, which culminated in taking some important exams that day, so effectively incommunicado. I knew she was looking forward to a long weekend of R&R for us both, without a Palace game to attend, and had planned a special Sunday dinner.

It was probably just as well I was somewhere beneath the English Channel as she arrived home to find my note which read:

"Palace have got a friendly in France tomorrow, well, Corsica (look it up, I had to). Paf and I are driving down there now and will be gone for most of the weekend. Sorry it's all a bit last minute, typical Palace. See you Sunday. X"

I knew she would get it eventually, after all, we met on an away coach to Grimsby in 1987 and Sue is as passionate about Palace as I am. I was just relieved that I was not available to receive her immediate reaction to my note! Back then, mobiles wouldn't work abroad without ringing to amend your contract and that was expensive. So I was effectively out-of-contact for the whole weekend.

We took the night drive to Paris quite easy. It was about 10pm when we got to Calais. It was the first time I'd driven across using the Tunnel and was perturbed to realise the exit road throws you straight out onto a motorway, where we were confronted by a sign with one word: Péage. Our rusty schoolboy French ground into action and, after a brief spat about whether this word meant 'beach' or 'toll', it quickly became obvious, that every exit on the road towards Paris had a toll booth. Trouble is neither of us had a French Centime between us, never mind a Franc.

We stopped at the first opportunity, but the joy and convenience of cash machines in service stations had not reached our continental cousins. We managed to change up a tenner into 100 Francs with another English driver, who was 'fairly sure' the toll booths took credit cards. We approached the first toll booth and our hearts sank as the display read 108 francs!

"Crédit Carde, Monsieur?" I offered hopefully.

I didn't understand a word of the response, but it must have been something along the lines of:

"That will do nicely, sir."

With considerable relief, we were back on our way.

The rest of the journey was fairly uneventful, other than the over-zealous petrol attendant who wanted to hold both my passport and my credit card as insurance against me doing a bunk after refuelling. We arrived at Orly airport at 4.30am, just in time for the long-term car park to open and get a couple of hours shut-eye in the car. I awoke to the sound of my mobile phone alarm and noted – with some surprise – how remarkably refreshed I felt. Paul was in less good humour, mumbling about the loudness of my snoring. It must have been the noise of the planes going over.

When we entered the airport, it became apparent that I had forgotten to put the clock on my phone forward by an hour. This wiped out our plan for a leisurely breakfast, exchanging it for a charge to the boarding gate instead. We just about managed to grab a coffee and croissant before boarding the thankfully slightly delayed flight to Bastia.

After a pleasant hour's flight, we stepped off the plane into twenty degree heat and a gentle Mediterranean breeze. Nothing like the dreary weather we had left behind in London and, indeed, the fact we had flown over snow-capped mountains on our descent had led us to believe it would be a lot chillier.

The transfer bus into town was in a poor state, which made the fiver each we paid for a ten minute ride seem extremely poor value on a trip that was already well over budget. On the outskirts of the city we got our first glimpse of the Stade de Furiani – home of Sporting Club Bastia. The ground had a strangely unfinished look, with a single terrace running around the pitch and a single two-tier roofless stand, topped by a row of imposing floodlights. We were shamefully unaware of the tragedy that had occurred there nine years before, when a terrace had collapsed, killing eighteen people. The ground seemed to be located in the middle of a light industrial area. Most worryingly of all, we failed to spot any local bars in the vicinity.

We secured some shabby but serviceable accommodation in the centre of town. The most welcome factor was the price: £25 for two nights. In the room, we quickly changed into clothes more suitable for the climate, whereupon Paul came across a packing fail:

"Damn! I've brought my Jamie Fullarton shirt out, instead of my Clinton Morrison one."

Paul's company had sponsored the Palace shirts a year previous when we were deep in Administration and he'd collared quite a few of the match-worn jerseys.

"Never mind" I said "We signed Jamie Fullarton from Bastia, so it might come in handy with the locals."

Little did we know.

Off to explore the delights of Bastia. Our attire immediately attracted attention, though not so much our Palace shirts, rather the fact we were wearing shorts. The locals were done up as though it was winter and they remained so for the whole weekend. Our reception among the bar-keeps of Bastia was decidedly mixed. One Maître d' insisted that every table outside was "reserveé" and that we should go inside, despite the place being completely empty.

When we did find somewhere to sit outside – a trendy establishment that promised lively nightlife later – the waiter refused to run a tab. It was apparent that he did for other tables, yet presented us with a bill for every drink. When he finally gathered that we were no flight risk, we had decided this was going to be our last one there, so he ended up having to do a bill for us. To say he was not best pleased would be an understatement.

Before we left, however, there was one thing we had to do. We'd both been putting it off, having had similar bad experiences in French bars, but we couldn't wait any longer. We finally had to visit a French toilet. I went first. But upon entering the single unisex cubicle, I had a very pleasant surprise: it was a beautifully tiled and surprisingly large space with art deco posters. It was spotless, apart from a small glass table next to the toilet bowl, which was covered with ash where people had been resting their ciggies.

Paul went in after me and came out giggling.

"That was not ash!"

He continued to smirk at my innocence all the way to the next bar.

We realised we'd come full circle and were now in the bar underneath our hotel. The barman wanted us to try the local brew, Pietra – a beer made from chestnuts. It was utterly foul, he saw our faces and wordlessly began pouring us two lagers bearing a look of wounded pride. We struck up a conversation with him in broken Franglais about our trip but he wasn't keen on Le Foot.

One of the locals in the bar, a dead ringer for then-Liverpool Manager Gerard Houllier, became interested in our conversation and firmly declared that the game was:

"Demain" (tomorrow) – wagging his finger at us as though we were naughty schoolchildren.

"Non, monsieur. Ce soir" (this evening) we responded.

The local paper was consulted and after much eyebrow raising and gallic shrugging, he finally agreed that the match was indeed "Ce Soir". He then downed his drink and grabbed his coat and let off a volley of rapid-fire French to his puzzled colleagues. Although we understood not a single word, his meaning was transparently obvious. "Sorry chaps, there's a game on tonight. I've got to go and break it to the missus!" I felt his pain. His colleagues watched him go, exchanging knowing smiles and rueful shakes of the head with us, which we took to mean: "He's as barmy as you two."

The barman had recommended the 'Bar of the Four Roads' as a good place to drink before the game and it was now gone 5pm, so time to head down there. We took some photos outside with Paul's Palace flag, before he spied the team coach in the distance. We risked life and limb crossing a main road, a field and a railway line, to beat them to the gates and give them a proper welcome… only to realise as we got there, this was the Bastia team arriving.

Trudging back to the bar to finish our abandoned beers and collect our bags, we agreed to wait by the gates for our boys, as there was no way we would survive another mad dash like that. The flag was pinned up at the gates and we waited for our team. Out of nowhere, we heard a female Geordie voice calling to us. Not exactly what you'd expect to hear in Corsica. It turned out that Christine, Bastia's English interpreter, had spotted Paul's Fullarton shirt. She told us that she used to be Jaime's French tutor. We spent a pleasant few minutes chatting with Christine, who was still in touch with Jaime via email. She pointed out a few of the Bastia hierachy milling about at the entrance and said they were amazed to see that Palace fans had made it over for the game.

While we were chatting, the Palace team coach drew up from the other direction which caught us unawares, but we still managed to let them know we were here. Vic Bettinelli recognised us and popped over to say hello, but most of the players seemed absolutely stunned by the fact that we were there at all.

Christine had a word with Bastia's Club President, who very graciously invited us to watch the game from the padded seat comfort of the Directors' Box and attend the post-match reception as their guests. An invitation we were delighted to accept.

Given our current league predicament, a very enjoyable, stress-free game ensued. The fact that both sides were without a win in at least six games – and were also experiencing a similar goal drought – made it all the more amazing that the game finished up 4-3. Palace took the lead early on, through Dougie Freedman. Bastia responded with two within a minute. Palace had a Clinton Morrison goal ruled out for offside, before he finally equalised early in the second half, converting after a thunderous Simon Rodger effort smacked the post and fell kindly for him. Clinton then scored again, yet once more fell foul of the offside flag. Bastia retook the lead when Faderne completed his hat-trick and added a fourth. Substitute Steve Kabba scored from the penalty spot, after being hauled down from behind having rounded the keeper as he was about to tap into an empty net.

At the post match reception we met Alan Smith and Ray Houghton and also had the chance to have little chats with most of the players. The main topic of conversation was not the game, but yesterday's flight over. It had been a catalogue of disasters. First the plane was late leaving London for Paris Charles de Gaulle, which meant a Thursday evening rush crawl around the infamous Paris ring-road – le Peripheriqué – to get to Orly airport and find that the flight down to Bastia was also delayed.

Just as they were coming into land at Bastia, being seriously buffeted by very high winds, the pilot decided to abort the landing just fifty feet from the runway.

"I don't mind telling you, man, I was screaming. I thought I was gonna die!" was Clinton's take on the moment. Even Alan Smith confirmed that in all his years of air travel, it was the worst incident he'd ever experienced.

The plane was then diverted to Ajaccio, some 160 kilometres away on the other side of the island. A road transfer across the island was out of the question at that time of night, so they stayed in hastily- arranged accommodation there, finally making it to bed at 4am. Even then the fun wasn't over as the next morning it took them three hours to cross the island in a coach, over a winding mountain pass, that took them up above the snow line. Hearts were in mouths, once more.

Alan Smith kindly invited us and some of the Bastia people, including Christine and her partner Serge, to join the team meal in Bastia. We ended up travelling back to Bastia centre on the team coach, chatting to Hayden Mullins' agent, who'd had a large hand in arranging the game. He was keeping the troops entertained with his purple wide-checked suit and Cockney banter.

The meal was arranged in one of the more expensive restaurants overlooking a pretty marina, which we hadn't ventured to earlier in the day. Even if we had, it was well above our price range. Paul and I sat opposite Alan Smith and Ray Houghton and very much enjoyed their company over a few glasses of red. Alan, who had been abroad for most of the week, appeared to be very relaxed. He was pleased with the way the game had gone and felt that it was good to come away with the team occasionally. We agreed with him, but asked for more notice next time, which made him chuckle saying he only knew they were definitely coming on Wednesday.

At 1am we decided to call it a night and went to pay, but Alan insisted that the meal was on the Club, which was a lovely touch. On leaving, we bumped into a few of the players who had left the restaurant a while back to check out the local nightlife. They were none too impressed, but upon talking to them it transpired that they hadn't got further than the end of the marina and certainly hadn't found the joint we'd lunched in, all of a hundred metres around the corner. When we walked past now, the place was absolutely heaving with Bastia's young and beautiful. Tempted – but too tired – we headed for the hotel and hit the hay.

Our flights home were early on Sunday, so we had the Saturday to ourselves. The weather had turned, so no trip to the beach, however we did get to see the start of the Corsican rally in the main square. We were hoping to find a bar that might be covering England's friendly with Finland that afternoon, but even the Irish Bar didn't have Sky Sports. We knew our luck was out. Returning to our hotel, there was an unexpected, but nevertheless very welcome, invite awaiting us from Christine and Serge to join them for dinner at their apartment. The meal and company were both lovely.

Christine and Serge dropped us back to the square around midnight and we set off to enjoy the nightlife that had eluded the players the previous night. We crawled back to the hotel at 3.30am, having been earlier reminded by Serge to put our watches forward. Just as well he did, or we would have had another mad scramble to the airport, having been blissfully ignorant of the fact that French Summertime starts on the same day as British.

We awoke surprisingly early, considering the late night. Since bus times back to the airport were not complimentary to our flight , we elected for a cab, which turned out to be a hideously expensive £30. It really was a rollercoaster of a trip where finances were concerned.

The noon flight to Paris was uneventful, even the Le Peripheriqué was well behaved. Certainly more so than my tummy as the weekend's excess began to catch up. An urgent need sent me scurrying into a petrol station, which I feel I should note, more than lived down to our original expectations of French toilets. An unwelcome hour and a half's delay at the Eurotunnel was shortened by a spot of entirely accidental queue-jumping. By 8pm, we were home. I walked up the path, half-expecting to be greeted by packed suitcases. Luckily for me, the weekend was a long enough time to process my disappearing act, although I did note Sue hadn't saved me any dinner.

This bonus game did not have a massive impact on Palace's form. With two games to go, after a 2-0 home defeat against Wolves, Palace were left needing snookers to survive and Alan Smith was dismissed. Steve Kember was put in temporary charge to make the best of what seemed to be an almost impossible job.

Hope was restored after a fabulous 4-2 away win at Portsmouth, which in turn put the Hampshire club in some jeopardy. The following Sunday lunchtime, Pompey cruised to an easy home win over Barnsley, wiping out Palace's slight goal difference advantage. Meanwhile Palace were deadlocked until the 87th minute when Dougie popped up to score the winner against Stockport County.

Palace fans then had to endure an agonising five minutes as the game that would decide our fate was running behind. Those five minutes felt more like fifty as time crawled by. Huddersfield Town, who had started the day seemingly pretty safe, were losing at home 2-1 to Birmingham. If the game ended that way, the Terriers would be going down.

Finally, a joyful explosion of noise and relief rang out around Edgeley Park, as news of the final score from Huddersfield came through. Palace had avoided relegation by the skin of their teeth.

The Chairman wasted little time in trying to put things right in the close season, though there was no reward for Steve Kember, after he'd pulled the club back from the brink of disaster. Steve Bruce was quickly installed as Manager. The choice of pre-season destination was fully in the hands of Mr Jordan for the first time and he chose to take the club back down to the Mediterranean. This time to Marbella, where he also had a home. Fine by me, Mr Chairman.

The club's press release announced that we would be competing for The Marbella Cup in a round-robin tournament with NK Čakovec from Croatia and HIT Gorica from Slovenia. The tournament was to take place at Marpafut International Elite Football Centre, which had just opened that January at a cost of £6.5m. So far, so good. But quickly problems started to appear.

The club was promoting its own exclusive supporters trip, staying in the team hotel, at a cost of £2,000 per person. It also became apparent that Marpafut was not open to the public. Clarification was sought from the Club as to whether fans travelling under their own steam would be able to get into the games. Initially they were quite coy, clearly hoping to direct interest towards their own hideously expensive package trip. The late, great Ian "Chocky" Chapman, a Palace regular who had gone to live in southern Spain, even went to scope the place out and reported back that you could still get a decent view of the main pitch from outside the complex.

Chocky was something of a legend on Palace's most popular online bulletin board : *cpfc.org* (a.k.a. 'The BBS') which was run by Dave Campbell and a team of moderators, which included both Chocky and myself. When he communicated his findings on that forum the club realised the game was up. They agreed to make special arrangements for all spectators to attend. What these would be was not specified but it was good enough for me.

At that time, my personal finances were at something of a low ebb. I'd also been on two long-haul holidays with Sue that summer. A fortnight in Barbados came about as a result of winning the club's Lifeline Lottery Holiday Voucher Prize, but it still cost a pretty penny. The reason for an earlier short notice week to Bali – the day after the Stockport game – had its roots in my 'disappearance' to Bastia. I even missed the Surrey Senior Cup Final for it!

Sue had used up most of her holiday on those two trips, whereas I was working part-time and had a more flexible employer. Sue decided to give it a miss, so Safety became my travelling companion for this trip. Accommodation in high season was proving too costly for our budget, so we agreed to camp, on the proviso that we found a proper campsite with showers. Chocky had assured me that there were plenty in the region.

A number of fans had booked Thursday to Sunday to take in both games. Then the fixtures began to change. The Slovenians had run into problems with visas and they were replaced by NK Osijek, another Croatian side. This also led to the game originally scheduled for the Saturday being moved to the Sunday evening. If the BBS was anything to go by, this change caught out quite a few people who'd already booked to return home on Sunday afternoon, including Safety and myself. We feared the worst, but it transpired that Monarch, our chosen airline, had a reasonable change fee. Other supporters were not so lucky and had to stick with their original arrangements.

After an early morning flight from Luton, we landed at Malaga airport around noon. After collecting a hire car, we set off in search of accommodation. After a mysterious knock-back from a near-empty campsite just around the corner from Chocky's place in Calahonda, we found a place a few miles down the coast, nearer to Marbella itself. The town of Cabopino looked vaguely familiar to us both, but we couldn't figure out why. Neither of us had travelled to this region before. We later learned that it was where the ill-fated BBC soap opera Eldorado had been filmed.

Chocky picked us up from the campsite, together with a couple of other mutual friends, Al and Trish, who we'd got to know via the BBS. They had booked the hotel the team were staying in at a fraction of the cost of the official trip and then discovered that the official trip, which it turned out had received no takers.

Chocky's previous recce proved invaluable as the place was some way out of Marbella itself, in quite a rural area past the town of San Pedro. Just as we had arrived at what appeared to be a small football stadium, Chocky told us to look further into the distance. About a mile away, across the fields we could see some more pitches with bleachers-style seats. This was Marpafut, not the stadium to our left, which belonged to the village team of San Pedro. Access to Marpafut was down a long unmade track and as we bumped along we all marvelled at how Chocky had worked this out given the complete absence of signage.

Palace's opposition turned out not to be Čakovec, as we had been expecting. Osijek had pulled out late on for reasons unknown, so we would now play Čakovec on Sunday. Today, Palace would be playing... San Pedro – the village team. Al was unimpressed:

"We haven't come all this way to watch a load of bus drivers and hairdressers!"

We assumed he was talking about the village side, although given the way Palace had played at times last season…

As Safety said: "You can only beat what is in front of you." And beat them we did, with goals from Jamie Smith, Steve Thomson, Gregg Berhalter and Wayne Carlisle, although the 4-0 scoreline was rather disappointing given the poor standard of the opposition. The main culprit for the low goal tally was Steve Kabba, who missed a hatful, including a couple of absolute sitters. We felt sorry for him and hung back to offer him some words of encouragement, which he appreciated, but he then managed to miss something else: a step on the way up to the changing rooms. Kabba collapsed in a heap in front of us.

There was no mercy from the onlooking Julian Gray and Clinton Morrison, who dissolved into fits of laughter. Even Vic Bettinelli got in on the act: "You better eat something light tonight, Kabs… 'cos you'll never finish it."

Around fifty fans were in attendance at the game. The club's much-vaulted 'spectator arrangements' appeared to involve simply leaving the main gate open. One group had arrived some 25 minutes late, covered in dust. They had been dropped off at the small stadium by a taxi. Eventually realising that they were in the wrong place, they set out across the fields, having to navigate a small creek and startling a local goat herder along the way.

With the next two days free, Safety and I explored the area with trips to the beach, the mountains and Gibraltar. Sadly, it was too windy for the cable car up to the Rock. Evenings were spent eating and drinking with Chocky, Trish and Al. We learned from the locals that Čakovec had trounced San Pedro 11-1 or was it 10-1, someone else mentioned 9-1. Whatever the actual score, it was certain that they had scored far more than Palace had managed. Nothing short of a win would see Palace lift the Marbella Cup.

Returning from a trip into the mountains on Sunday afternoon, we passed a luxury coach travelling through the main street in Marbella. The board at the front of the coach clearly said Osijek and it had a team onboard. So they were out there, but had clearly decided not to take part in the tournament. All very odd.

The game against Čakovec was an over-physical affair right from the off. Meaty challenges, illegal tackles and a large dose of Croatian play-acting rather soured the game. A friendly it was not, the referee's yellow card waving like a distress beacon. You could see why San Pedro had rolled over so easily, they must have been terrified. As early as the fifth minute, David Hopkin was cynically scythed down and retaliated fiercely. Although he was only booked, a furious Steve Bruce hauled him off straight away and proceeded to read the riot act forbidding any retaliation to the rest of the team at half-time. Palace went into the break leading by a Dougie Freeman goal that appeared to have more than a whiff of offside about it.

David Hopkin reappeared for the second half and converted a free kick, which squirmed under the keeper who grabbed it at the second attempt. Despite the ball being clearly over the line, as later confirmed by Palace Club Photographer Neil Everitt, the referee waved play on.

In the last ten minutes the game reached its boiling point. Freedman was kicked in the head whilst lying on the floor. After an almighty scuffle, the Croatian centre-half Skopljanic saw a red card that was long overdue. He initially refused to leave the field, protesting his innocence and claiming that someone had hit him. Čakovec went all out for revenge in the final minutes, with some filthy challenges. Some were so late, they thankfully didn't connect. It was especially sweet, therefore, when Wayne Carlisle skipped over a couple of reckless lunges, played in Steve Kabba, who unselfishly slotted the ball into the path of Julian Gray, who gleefully rammed it home.

The game finished 2-0, meaning Palace were the winners of the Marbella Cup. It was something of an anti-climax to find out there was no actual trophy.

"When Deano went up to lift the Marbella Cup, it wasn't there" came the chant from the stands, quite pointedly aimed at the Chairman, who simply shrugged.

Our last evening was spent in the company of the usual crew and Neil Everitt (a.k.a. Mr Cad) who had us in fits, recounting some previous pre-season tours. The next morning Safety and I flew home, happy with our Spanish adventure but both vowing never to camp again. After we collected our luggage at Luton Airport, a customs officer beckoned us both over. Maybe it was the sight of us both carrying a strap each of our large tent bag had aroused her suspicions.

"Open up this bag please, gents"

We said nothing as we unzipped the tent bag, which also contained two extremely pungent, sweaty sleeping bags. Just as we were about to unpack it further, an unbelievable stench rose from the bag and caught the officer full in the nostrils. Her face was a picture of disgust as she speechlessly waved us and the smell away from her.

The next day the Evening Standard ran a story about Palace planning to compete in a pre-season tournament in Florida the following year. It was light on detail and we concluded that it seemed rather unlikely. As predicted, we heard no more about it.

Palace started the season well and hit the top spot by mid-October, but things were not to last. After just three months at the helm, Steve Bruce decided his future lay at Birmingham City. Simon Jordan was dismayed and effectively put him on gardening leave until he was able to secure another Manager in early December. That was Trevor Francis – the man who Birmingham had sacked.

Francis failed to build on Bruce's groundwork, although the team was already faltering, as the impact of his departure appeared to be deeply felt by the players. It was clear from our patchy form in the early part of 2002 that the play-offs were not a realistic prospect and we ended the season with something of a whimper.

One bright note was that Palace announced that a return to Marpafut was scheduled for pre-season over the third weekend in July, with friendlies to be announced in due course. For once, we had plenty of time to plan a pre-season, so we booked flights and a villa for six. A proper grown-up holiday with our partners.

Palace versus 'the bus drivers and hairdressers' of San Pedro at Marpafut - July 2001

The inaugral winners of the Marbella Cup minus an actual trophy - July 2001

10

COMMUNITY SPIRIT (AND OTHER ALCOHOL)

The Championship season ended in late April to accommodate the 2002 FIFA World Cup. Palace's final reserve game was the day after the first team's season ended. The reserves were away at Bristol City and, having a spare afternoon, I decided to go and take some photos. The advances in digital cameras had awakened my interest in football photography and I needed pictures for the *Palace Echo* website as online photo content was now heavily regulated.

Whilst I was there, Palace surprised everyone by announcing that they would be competing in the post-season European Communities Trophy, to be held in Seville in three weeks time. Simon Jordan was keen to push Palace's brand internationally and explained at a fan forum later the same evening, that he regarded this competition as a good opportunity to do just that.

The competition would feature a team from each of the fifteen current members of the European Community. Palace were to be the United Kingdom representative. The tournament was intended to be an annual competition held in a different country each time. Seville were to be the first hosts and the event was being used to garner support for their 2012 Olympic bid. They had already built the centrepiece stadium, which was to stage the semi-finals and final of the straight knockout competition. The first two rounds were to be held at the grounds of Sevilla FC and Real Betis, both of whom were to compete, making the numbers up to a nice round sixteen.

I was straight on the phone from the car park at Ashton Gate to find out who was up for it. Safety and Andy Carey, now also known as "Hoover", were immediately on the firm, even before any discussion of likely cost. Mr Carey's nickname came about as a result of his habit of 'hoovering' his pre-match pints before anyone else was halfway down their glass.

Less enamoured with the prospect of a post-season tournament was the first team, whose season was now being extended by up to a month. A few players admitted that they had already booked holidays and Club Captain Dean Austin was one player who was particularly strident calling the competition 'Mickey Mouse' on his own website. He claimed he faced losing over £2,000 in holiday bookings. The Chairman responded, via a radio interview on *Talksport*, that Austin would be fully compensated.

In truth, we were also slightly puzzled as to why the club would head to Spain twice in a matter of three months, but simply put it down to our Chairman's connections in that region. After all, there were far worse places to go than Andalucia.

The cheapest route was via Luton to Malaga and then onwards by train to Seville. As it was a knockout tournament, we couldn't book the return or any more than one night's accommodation in advance. We decided to fly out on Saturday to give ourselves plenty of time to get to Seville for our first tie on Sunday evening.

Through the BBS, we had struck up a firm friendship with Michael and Mitch Copperwheat, who had moved to southern Spain just a month after Palace's tour the previous year. Michael, known as 'Biggus Mickus' on the BBS, invited us to stay overnight on his boat moored in Benalmadena harbour, close to Malaga. We gratefully accepted his kind hospitality, although I was slightly nervous as my track record on boats was, and indeed is still, not exactly stellar.

At 10am on the morning of our mid-afternoon flight, I was just getting ready to leave the house when my phone rang. It was Hoover:

"Where are you?" he demanded to know.

"Just leaving for the airport now, mate. See you there about noon"

"WHAT? I've been here in the bar since 8 o'clock. Bloody lightweight. Get a move on."

That was me told.

When Safety and I eventually arrived, Hoover was blowing the froth off his eighth pint.

"Did you get the time of the flight wrong?" I had to ask.

"Nope, just wanted to crack on, I can't believe you two are so late on parade."

My days of getting to the pub for opening time on a matchday were already well behind me, but not Hoover. No, he's still at it today. I was rather concerned that he might not be allowed on the flight, as he seemed in a rambunctious mood. However, when the time came to board he got his act together and promptly fell asleep as soon as we boarded the aircraft.

It was early evening when we touched down in Malaga. As we cleared customs, we could see an imposing chap who was built like a Norse God towering over everyone else in the arrivals hall. Six foot seven with a massive frame and a mane of untamed strawberry-blond hair cascading down his back. He was an awe-inspiring sight and he was wearing a Palace shirt.

This was Biggus Mickus, here to collect us. I began to relax about staying the night in the harbour, figuring a boat that was big enough for Mick should have ample room. In fact, he'd arranged for the three of us to stay on his mate's boat moored a few berths down. We went to dump our bags. The vessel had a huge onboard motor stowed along the deck of the main cabin. I barked my shin on an exposed blade of the propeller as I manoeuvred around it, realising just how sharp it was. We'd need to be careful of that later on, after a few beers.

It was an epic night. Chocky joined us and we hit the town going from bar to bar, numbers swelled by Mick and Mitch's local mates. Around 1am, we ended up playing pool in The Manor pub's basement. We had the games room to ourselves and discovered it had the most amazing acoustics. The Palace 'Glad All Over' CD appeared from somewhere and soon we were belting out Palace standards, with Chocky delighting everyone with his Vic Reeves Pub Singer doing 'Glad All Over' impression. Quite a few people back in England received a late-night phone call with nothing but raucous renditions of 'Flying High' or 'Power to the Palace' on the other end.

Amidst this unholy racket, Safety had found a corner of the bar to have a snooze in. Mickus was amazed, but I'd been on holiday with Safety before and knew it to be a habit of his. At least, on this occasion, I resisted the temptation to soak his shorts in beer, or draw all over him with cue chalk. It dawned on us after a while that Hoover was no longer with us. He'd certainly been there during the prank calls, as he'd phoned our friend Rick Ballantine. Rick had just moved into a new house that week, otherwise he'd have most likely been out there with us. Hoover took Rick's request to 'keep me informed' very seriously and would continue to phone him with updates throughout the trip, often in the dead of the night. I think Rick may have quickly come to regret his request as the only working phone in his new house was downstairs.

That was the last time anyone could remember seeing Hoover. Given his head-start on the beers, I thought he may have slipped out for some food. Half an hour later, he still wasn't back, so I headed out to look for him. I figured he might have decided to go back to the boat, not that he knew the lock code to get onto the pontoon.

As I approached the dock, I could hear someone drunkenly singing 'We are Sailing'. It was not Rod Stewart. There he was, stumbling up and down the jetty, tripping over mooring posts, almost launching himself into the briny.

"Come on, chap. Time for bed."

"Ah, there you are, I can't seem to find our boat."

I didn't mind, but he wasn't even close. A few minutes of 'manoeurves' later, we climbed aboard the correct vessel. Hoover promptly stripped naked and fell face down onto the long seat running down the side of the boat. I considered returning to the pub, but by now it was 3am and I was in quite an advanced state of refreshment myself. It suddenly seemed like such a long walk back to the bar. I texted Mickus to let him know all was well and that I'd see him in the morning. Hunkering down in the forward cabin, I tried to ignore the motion of the ocean. I had just drifted off when I heard a noise from outside the cabin door. I assumed it was Safety getting back, but then I heard the Hoover's plaintive voice:

"I need a wee…"

This was accompanied by frantic scrabbling at the door. Oh dear Lord, he thinks there's a loo on the boat and, worse still, that it's in my cabin! I sprung out of bed and opened the door to a butt-naked Hoover dancing on the spot clutching his manhood. Clearly the need was urgent. No time to get him dressed and across to the public washrooms on the quayside. He was also having a fair bit of difficulty keeping himself upright on the swaying boat. With one eye on that wicked prop blade, I steered him to the back of the boat and held him upright as he peed over the side.

With Pythonesque timing, an elderly Spanish couple were walking their poodle along the pontoon at half-past four in the morning. What must they have thought of the sight of me in nothing but boxer shorts, holding a completely naked man upright from behind while he urinated over the side of the dock? My mortification was only slightly diverted by the question that struck me: why on earth would you walk your dog at 4.30am? Maybe it too, was in urgent need of a wee. The Hoover's business completed, we retired immediately below decks. Hoover was back to sleep in moments, whereas I lay there awake, terrified that the geriatric dogwalkers had called the police to report an act of gross public indecency.

At some point I must have fallen asleep, as suddenly it was light outside. A larger boat was departing the harbour causing a bow wave that set off my nausea, time to get some fresh air above deck. I opened the cabin door to see Safety's head lying at my feet… just his head.

Oh my stars! The silly sod has only gone and chopped his head off on that bloody prop! Then he moved and mumbled something, which freaked me out even more. I was convinced I was having a nightmare. Slowly I realised that he must have been unable to figure out how to get into the other cabin. Instead, he had curled up in the footwell, pulled a sheet over the top of himself, leaving just his head exposed, resting on the deck. The man really can sleep anywhere.

This was all too much for me, I dashed to the quayside washroom where I was copiously sick. I'm not sure if it was motion sickness, the previous night's grog, or the shock of Safety's detached head that set me off. Returning to the pontoon, I spotted Mickus on his own boat enjoying a morning cuppa and chuckling at my frantic dash. His chuckles turned to gales of laughter as I recounted everything that had happened since I last saw him in the pub. At that precise moment, two rather sheepish faces appeared on the pontoon, which was enough to set him off again.

It would be fair to say none of the travelling party were in the peak of condition as we made our way to Malaga Station. Mickus was coming with us, but sadly Chocky – a graphic designer by trade – was bogged down with an urgent commission and would be watching on the box instead. None of us felt much like drinking on the train, but Hoover and Mickus put in a brave effort.

We had pre-booked a large room in a hotel close to the station. The temperature was touching forty degrees when we arrived in Seville and it seemed to take ages to walk what was really just a few blocks. We needed a beer to cool down. Revived, we hailed a cab to the Real Betis ground, but the taxi driver simply could not understand us. The pronunciation of Betis was our downfall. In the local accent, you drop the 's'. After some elaborate miming, he finally deposited us outside a large football ground, but we had no idea which one he'd taken us to. Thankfully it was Estadio Manual Ruiz de Lopera, home of Real Betis.

Our opponents that evening were Malmö FF, the Swedish team that had once reached the European Cup Final, where they were beaten by Nottingham Forest. A quick glance at the tournament programme revealed that most other countries had sent teams from their top flight and there were some quite famous clubs taking part, including Club Brugge, FC København and Eintracht Frankfurt.

The programmes were much-sought after. Hoover had taken a raft of 'orders' from back home and was looking to purchase around thirty. However. they were free with admission, so the person who also sold us our tickets was reluctant to part with more than one each. Hoover's entreaties of "Muchos programmos, por favor" buttered no parsnips with this ticket seller. Thus, the Great Programme Hunt began: Hoover was utterly relentless, begging locals for their copies and stealing any copies foolishly left unattended. Safety and I were rather more polite in the quest to fill our desired quotas.

We had met up with a few Palace fans in a nearby bar and a few more in the ground itself. Including ourselves, there were about twenty-five Eagles fans in attendance. Our number also included two English students, Lauren and Ellie, who were studying Spanish in Seville. They were appointed our official interpreters for the tour whether they liked it or not. Upon spotting our impressive pile of programmes and hearing how we'd amassed them, they dubbed us 'Jefe Anorakos' – Chief Anoraks. The name stuck for the whole tour.

Midway through the first half, we were joined by a familiar face: Simon Jordan. His opening gambit was to tell us that a fortnight ago he called off the forthcoming pre-season return to Marpafut.

"We need to get back to basics," was his reason.

No-one was impressed, especially Safety and I who had already booked our flights and a villa exactly two weeks previous. A shame he hadn't thought to make his decision public. Unlike Dean Austin, there would be no refund for us. We were even less impressed when Jordan's mobile phone rang and he proceeded to talk loudly to the caller for fifteen minutes. Once the call ended, he told us that he had been speaking to Geoffrey Richmond, Chairman of Bradford City, which had just gone into Administration the previous week:

"He was calling me for advice about being in Administration."

A still-seething Safety was straight onto the loose ball:

"What would you know about that? You didn't go through it, you just bought us out of it."

A fair point, indeed, and one to which the Chairman had no comeback.

It seemed to us that his 'back to basics' reasoning for cancelling Marpafut, coupled with his insistence on dragging the squad out to take part in this tournament, so long after the season had ended, was simply a way of punishing the players and management for our poor form at the rear end of the previous season.

Not feeling the love, Mr Chairman left us at half-time to go back to the Directors' Box. He did leave behind his programme, which Hoover was on like a flash.

On the pitch, Palace put up a decent showing, making light of the three week gap since their last competitive action. Club Captain Dean Austin had unsurprisingly not made the trip over, citing illness in his immediate family. A sweeping move down the wing on fifteen minutes found Danny Granville at the far post to head home. Malmö equalised, but almost immediately Steve Kabba, having discovered his Spanish shooting boots, lashed in an unstoppable drive.

Thanks to good work from Matt Clarke in goal and a ball cleared off the line by Curtis Fleming, Palace held on to win 2-1 and progressed into the quarter-finals in two days' time. Another game. Great news for the travelling fans, though the groundhopper in me was slightly disappointed that we wouldn't get to play at Sevilla's stadium. Admitting this out loud earned me a promotion me to 'Jefe Jefe Anorakos' for the rest of the night.

There was another game on straight after ours – Real Betis against FC Eztrella from Luxembourg – the winner of which would face Palace at the same ground. Safety and I stayed to watch the game, while most of our travelling support retired back to the bar. Despite the gulf in class, Betis made very hard work of disposing of the lesser team. The scoreline of 4-1 was total flattery, given gloss by two late goals. The home crowd was not best pleased and vented their disgust at the performance. We left feeling that the next round would be very winnable if the home side played like that again.

We headed back to the bar and then onwards to an Irish bar nearer to our hotel, having enrolled 'Pete the Pom' into our little gang. Pete's surname is also Lewis, although, as we quickly established, no relation to Dave 'Safety' Lewis. Pete had emigrated to Perth in Western Australia in his younger days and his nickname arose from there. The Irish Bar closed after serving us just one drink, despite the hours on the door suggesting it would be open until much later. The owner suddenly seemed extremely anxious for us to go, shoo-ing us towards the door within minutes of serving us. Mickus told him we would go when our drinks were finished. One glance at the height and breadth of our giant friend had the desired calming effect on him.

As we were contemplating heading back to the hotel, we heard some thumping bass appearing to come from within a large park across the road. Where there is music, there's usually drink, so we headed off in the direction of the beats. Unfortunately, the sound was emanating from a pimped-up Volkswagen Golf. But wait, in the dark depths of the park itself, a blue neon light could be seen through the trees. The fences were too high to scale, but we soon found an open entrance. Jackpot! The blue light led us to an open-air bar, which was still serving. With a DJ spinning blissed-out beats mixed with an occasional slice of punk and indie tuneage, it was one of the most agreeable late-night drinking spots I have ever encountered.

We made full use of extended drinking hours, inventing a rude song to the tune of 'Volare', about the local beer:

"Cruzcampo, woah-oh,

Cruzcampo, woah-oh,

We drank a lot of it,

A shame it tastes like shit."

In spite of our disrespect towards the local brew, the barkeep was delighted with his thirsty English customers and served us through until dawn

The hotel room had been a bit of a waste, we only had a couple of hours sleep before having to check out. Sadly, Mickus could not stay for the Real Betis game as he had some business to attend to back in Benalmadena, but he promised to be back for the later games, should we progress. He left early to catch a train back to Malaga, but not early enough as it turned out. He missed his train and was still mooching around the station when we got there to rebook a cheaper hotel at the Tourist Information kiosk.

We opted for the cheapest en suite room we could find in the centre of town, as we did not know how long the three of us would be staying for. The price was suspiciously low: only ten Euro a night each.

"Does it come with a roof for that price?" wondered Hoover aloud.

Indeed it did, but also came with a 2.30am curfew which we chose to ignore. Surely someone would still let us in, if we should happen to miss it? After checking-in, we headed into the centre of town and found an Irish Bar next to the Cathedral. Unsurprisingly, in there we bumped into the supporters of the tournament's Irish representatives, Bohemians.

They were here in good numbers for their tie against Sevilla, mostly young lads with easy Irish charm and blarney in good measure. They seemed particularly interested in Palace's hooligan firm, albeit in a completely non-threatening manner.

"What's the name of your firm? Is it the Dorty Thorty?" Their heavy north Dublin accents made us crack up.

"Don't worry lads, I don't think they are out here" I responded.

Whilst most of their fans appeared relieved, I did detect some slight disappointment from a few. After a few beers, we promised to lend them our support at their game against Sevilla, that evening. With what we had seen of the 'lenient' officiating towards the other local side, we reckoned they would need all the help they could get. The other thing they told us was that they had been guaranteed two games, so if they were knocked out in the first round, they'd be fixed up to play a friendly against one of the other eliminated sides, later in the week. They seemed surprised we knew nothing about this.

"Maybe it'll be against youse" suggested one.

"Nah! We are going all the way!" replied a confident Hoover.

As the day progressed, we learned that the organisation of I Torneo de Union Europea – otherwise known as the European Communities Trophy – was closer to Dean Austin's assessment than Mr Jordan might care to admit. Maybe it could not be helped that, of the sixteen original invited clubs, only fourteen actually showed up: Wüstenrot Salzburg from Austria and Greek side, Iraklis Sardonica were the no-shows. But what they did have control over was how they went about dealing with the loss of the two games. Iraklis' decision to pull out was known about a little in advance, so Sevilla's second team had been drafted in to make up the numbers and were due to play Portuguese side, CS Maritimo, that evening. In the event, Sevilla's second team did not appear.

Club Bruges had been scheduled to play the Austrians on the previous night but no game took place. Instead of giving both Club Brugge and Maritimo a bye into the next round, they were made to play each other. What we – and I suspect most other – spectators didn't know at the time was that both teams were going to progress anyway, regardless of the result. In effect, this absolutely pointless game was a friendly.

We took a cab to the ground and were again confused when we were dropped off in front of a shopping centre, with the Estadio Sanchez Pizjuan not visible.

The cab driver smiled and motioned for us to walk straight through the centre's main plaza. Sure enough, on the other side was an impressive tiled entrance to the stadium.

Unaware of its total insignificance, Safety and I elected to watch the early Club Brugge v Maritimo game, whilst Hoover and Pete headed off to a nearby bar, although not before another raft of programmes had been accumulated. They promised to be back for the Boh's game at 10pm.

We took our seats and were handed a team sheet by a friendly Club Brugge official. There was a name there that made us both giggle. The official assumed it was the Portuguese player named Eusebio.

"Not the real one" he explained helpfully.

"I hope not! He must be a pensioner now" replied Safety, but the joke was lost in translation.

Actually, the object of our merriment was one of the Maritimo substitutes: Fernando de Ornales – a Venezuelan journeyman who had played nine games for Palace upfront, in the depths of our administration crisis. He was absolutely hopeless for us. In those nine games, he contributed one assist and spanked the bar at Ewood Park, before his short-term contract was not renewed, very wisely in my eyes. As expected, he was completely anonymous when he came on. Club Brugge won the lifeless encounter 2-0.

The programme had led us to expect to see a couple of ex-Palace players in the competition: Sasa Curcic was featured in the Eintracht Frankfurt squad photo and Tony Folan was listed in the Bohemians squad. We'd already been informed that Folan had been released a couple of weeks before and later found out that Curcic hadn't travelled either.

It was time for the Sevilla v Bohemians game. The Irish fans numbered about fifty and were in fine voice. As the game kicked off, Hoover ambled in, clearly having blown the froth off more than a couple of beers. He lustily joined in with the "We are Boh's" chant that was echoing around the stadium at that point. Trouble was he thought they were singing "We are Bombs!" which drew a few sharp intakes of breath from some Dubliners. The noise being created led to a lot of staring from the young Sevilla fans and, sadly, also caused some of their older fans to subject us to a barrage of plastic bottles.

Although clear underdogs, Boh's put up a hell of a fight against the hosts, unluckily going down 2-1 and having a nailed-on penalty denied late-on by another partisan referee. It was becoming clear that anything other than a Sevilla v Real Betis final was not being countenanced locally. This didn't bode well for Palace the following evening.

We headed back to the Irish bar with our new friends, the Hoover's unwitting faux-pas forgotten about. Despite the defeat, they were out to enjoy themselves to the full, even when one of their Directors said that the tournament organisers were now denying any knowledge of the promise to stage a second game for them.

Also in the bar that evening were members of the Palace management team, including Steve Kember. You would imagine they would have preferred to keep a low profile, but Steve was up out of his seat leading a version of 'Glad All Over', exhorting us to join in. The Irish lads loved him for it, although maybe slightly less so when he started a chant of 'You'll be Home before your Postcards'.

When the management party left the bar, Steve waddled through the masses with his trademark bow-legged gait, earning cheers and applause from all sides. Even then, he couldn't resist a final cheeky dig at the Irish lads: "Going home, going home, going home."

It was another long night. The Irish bar shut around 4am, so we wandered the labyrinthine streets with a few Boh's boys, looking for the late bar they had found the previous night. We eventually found it, although it appeared to be shuttered up; the Irish lads knocked anyway. A spyhole on the door slid open and, after a brief exchange, the door was swung wide to reveal a cavernous cellar-like space, dimly lit and thick with smoke.

It was as local as you get, only the local dialect was spoken, so beers were ordered by pointing. Safety had the very devil of a job getting a vodka. The hard-drinking, chain-smoking locals barely gave us a second look. They were far more interested in a flamenco guitarist who was entertaining them with what seemed to us to be extremely tuneless wailing. An older lady got up to dance, scattering stools to create a makeshift dancefloor. We kept ourselves very much to ourselves.

When we staggered out, it was daylight and we found ourselves in the middle of the Seville rush-hour, navigating back to the Cathedral to find our way back to our hotel from there, for another scant amount of sleep.

We awoke at noon with the hotel cleaner demanding entry. We headed back to the Irish Bar for a late fry-up and to get into some sort of coherent matchday shape. After an easy afternoon, we headed back to a bar nearer the Real Betis stadium. Palace were again the 10pm kick-off, so we had plenty of time for tapas and to ease ourselves back into the drinking routine. Ellie and Lauren made a welcome reappearance, which also rather perked up the Boh's boys who we had persuaded to come and cheer us on.

We decided to forego most of the 8pm game, Maritimo v Helsinki. The thought of seeing Fernando again so soon was just too much to contemplate. We did catch the final stages and learned that he wasn't even in their squad for that game.

Boosted in numbers, the Palace support was much more boisterous than the first game. A rather portly steward in our enclosure was targeted with "Who ate all the tapas?" before a young Harry Potter look-alike a few rows in front of us became the target for our banter. Unlike the steward, he adored the attention and happily posed for photos with Hoover. More edgy chants like "You've only come to see the Palace" and "You'll never get the Olympics" brought forth a hail of missiles from the home fans above us, this time, however, it was only ice cubes. We decided we preferred the fans of Betis over Sevilla.

I would like to report that Palace were inspired by their noisy support, but nothing could be further from the truth. After falling behind early and with the refereeing firmly in the home side's pocket, Palace stuttered out of the competition. Not even the morale boost of Matt Clarke saving an extremely dubious penalty shortly after the opener could fire the team up. The performance in the first round had been a mirage, this was a continuation of our late season form. The Chairman was nowhere to be seen, no doubt devising further punishments for his under-performing charges.

When Betis sealed the game midway through the second half, no-one was the slightest bit surprised. We felt bad for the Irish lads who we'd dragged along to watch this lacklustre display. The hosts were hardly much better, which made the defeat even harder to take. Had we shown an ounce of the spirit that the fighting Irish had displayed the previous night, we might have progressed. Assuming, of course, the referee would have permitted that. It was a further embarrassment that hardly any of the Palace players could be bothered to applaud our fans, again in marked contrast to the post-match scenes after the Bohemians game. Something that did not go uncommented upon.

Then it was back to the local bar to enjoy our last night. Safety got chatting to a Palace fan from Beckenham. It turned out he hadn't been at the game and was totally shocked to find out that his team just played a couple of hundred yards away.

I scurried off to file my match report for the *Palace Echo* website and book flights home the next day in an all-night internet cafe, meeting back up with everyone else later. We treated the Irish lads to the delights of 'Party in the Park'. Sometime around 4am we decided to be a bit sensible and head back for an 'early' night. Arriving back in the city centre, we discovered that 'curfew' really does mean 'curfew'. No amount of hammering, hollering or stone-throwing could rouse anyone in our hotel to come and let us in. We tried phoning Pete, to see if we could sleep in his car, but his mobile was off.

Defeated, we headed for an all-night café close to the hotel. We ordered hot drinks and a ham roll. I tried in vain to engage the owner in conversation, whilst Safety and Hoover fell fast asleep at the bar, ignoring the fayre that I'd ordered for them. The owner was unimpressed and twice slammed his hand on the counter in front of them to wake them, as I eked out the ham rolls. Two local policeman entered the café and the owner made it plain that we were to leave immediately which, in the face of Johnny Law, we did.

Wandering aimlessly, we ran into another set of Irish lads chatting to a couple of familiar faces: Curtis Fleming and Tony Popovic. They knew of Curtis from the Republic of Ireland national team. Hoover thought it was a suitable time to instruct Curtis on the finer points of the full-back position. His tactical advice was not well met and both players promptly disappeared into the night.

At this point we found an open bar and gained a second wind, managing to stay awake until it was time to return to the hotel. Pete had kindly offered to give us a lift back to Malaga, so there was barely enough time to close our eyes. Upon settling our account with the hotel, we reflected that whilst it was cheap, we had, in effect, paid 45 Euro each for a daily shower and somewhere to store luggage.

We were in poor shape and fitfully dozed all the way home, which must have been rotten company for Pete. At one point, Hoover asked to pull over, where he was copiously sick, noting that the dark red matter present in his spew was either the remnants of that ham roll or blood. The last few days of hedonism had taken their toll on him and, if I'm honest, we weren't far behind him.

We met back up with Mickus, Mitch and Chocky in Benalmadena for a gentle, alcohol-lite afternoon, while the unwell Hoover slumbered in the boat, until it was time to leave for the midnight Easyjet flight back to Gatwick.

"If they don't get the Olympics then it's not our fault" was Hoover's final word on the trip. Of course, they didn't and it was an extremely short-lived dream. Early in 2003, Madrid was named Spanish candidate for the 2012 Summer Olympics. Despite the Spanish capital city being favourite, the games came to London. Seville's Olympic Stadium had to make do with a UEFA Cup Final in May 2003 and has hosted occasional Spanish international games since.

After the first two rounds, the tournament moved to the Olympic stadium, where Betis lost out on penalties to Maritimo in the semi-finals, meaning the 'required' final did not take place. Sevilla were the other finalists, after putting five past FC København without reply. The final itself was a bad-tempered affair with three players sent off. Seville won by a single goal in extra time, with only nine men on the field. Despite ambitious plans to become an annual tournament, the I Torneo de Union Europea was never competed for again.

Two months later, Safety and I returned with our partners for the holiday we had booked when we thought Palace would be on their pre-season tour. For me, however, the trip wasn't entirely football-free. When Palace announced their first pre-season friendly, away at Barnet on the Friday we were in Spain, I felt particularly cheated. So much so that, after careful negotiation with Sue, I flew back to the UK on a twenty hour round trip just to see the game. I figured that I had already spent over £500 to watch Palace in pre-season, so what's another £80 to ensure I actually caught a game? Budget airline deals have so much to answer for.

Palace flash a free-kick wide against Malmö at Real Betis - May 2002

Party in the Park! Biggus Mickus and Pete the Pom guard the beers, Safety and Hoover guard the Programmes. - May 2002

Ben Watson looks on as the Torremolinos players surround the referee again - July 2003

A half time cooler for the Torre troops. Chocky furthest on the right.- July 2003

11

SPAIN AGAIN

The Chairman's back-to-basics plan had little impact on the club's inconsistent form. That said, there were a few highlights: the goalscoring form of new signing Andrew 'AJ' Johnson, who had come to the club as part of the deal that took Clinton Morrison to Birmingham City; the 5-0 annihilation of rivals Brighton upon resumption of competitive hostilities after a twelve year break; and, two decent cup runs, which included beating Liverpool at Anfield.

I had been asked by the *South London Press* to cover occasional away games on their behalf. In addition to being the webmaster of the *Palace Echo* fanzine, in 2000 I had taken over as Editor and I guess, in their eyes, this gave me some 'currency' in the field of match reporting. I was getting a press pass into the games and a fee for the report, so I was more than happy.

Towards the end of the season, Trevor Francis was released and Steve Kember took over, initially on a temporary basis. He was then permanently appointed early in the close season and announced at a Fans Forum. It was also announced that the players would be required to report for training through the close season.

News on pre-season games was typically scarce. Unconfirmed rumours had been circulating since late April that Palace were looking to play Real Betis at home. This did not come to pass, though an exhibition game against PSV Eindhoven was eventually confirmed. Further rumours of another home friendly against Lille or Royal Antwerp also proved fruitless, though in the first international break we did play Brescia, as previously covered.

Hoover had discovered via the Marpafut website that Palace were booked in there for a week of pre-season training. He decided to book to go, despite the fact the club appeared to have no immediate plans to hold any friendlies out there. Middlesbrough were booked to be at Marpafut around the same time, so it was speculated that Palace might end up playing the Teesiders. Hardly the most exotic of opposition. For me, it was a case of 'once-bitten, twice-shy' and with the lack of any confirmation from Palace, I decided to bide my time.

On the eve of flying out to Spain, Palace finally confirmed that there would be one friendly out there, albeit not at Marpafut, as per 2001. The opposition would be Juventud de Torremolinos CF at their El Pozuelo ground. Anyone who has driven through the town on the main N-340 coastal road will have seen the prominent floodlights, although it's not entirely clear from the road that it is a football stadium.

Although this is an area in which I have many friends, I dithered about booking for just one game, only committing to it on the Wednesday night before the game on Friday. Nevertheless, the welcome from the ex-pats was as warm as ever, as I stepped off the plane into searing heat on the Friday lunchtime, having been up at 4am to catch the flight.

The afternoon was spent at Benalmadena Marina getting quietly unsober with the usual suspects, before heading off to the game, only a few miles up the road. Hoover, travelling with Darrell "Bourno" Bourne on this occasion, had scoped out the nearest bar to the ground the day before. He dubbed the bar "El Clifton Arms" and warned the owners that trade was likely to be brisk the following evening.

The main story of the trip was, for once, the game itself. This was one of the most bizarre first halves of football I have ever witnessed. It was clear from the off that the local side were not cut from the same cloth as the flimsy San Pedro lads of two years before. There were strong challenges flying in within seconds. The Palace side were not intimidated and gave as good as they got.

As early as the seventh minute, the young referee was pointing to the spot, after AJ was scythed down from behind. Dougie Freedman converted the penalty. The wild challenges kept coming, with Aki Riihilahti and Ben Watson going hard in return and earning a telling-off from the increasingly stressed referee. The first brawl broke out when Tommy Black had his legs taken away as he was surging towards the box. Even the coaching staff were getting involved with each other on the sidelines.

The next challenge from the home side brought forth an immediate red. The referee's patience had gone and he'd lost control. The game was barely fifteen minutes old. Given what had gone on before, it was by no means the worst tackle and both sides united to appeal to the ref to rescind the card. He was having absolutely none of it, even after both managers intervened.

Palace had most of the possession, dominating the middle of the park. The first breach saw Darren Powell sweep up with a firm but fair tackle. The Torremolinos forward reacted as though he had been shot, which led to another mass brawl. This was all too much for the rookie referee, who instead of getting involved, simply blew his whistle and gave a clear hand signal of "no more!" He then marched off the pitch with his fellow officials in tow. Confusion reigned.

Both teams trudged from the pitch to their respective dressing-rooms. With my reporter's hat on and perhaps emboldened by alcohol consumption, I jumped the fence, followed them down the tunnel and caught up with Steve Kember.

"What's happening, Steve?"

"Looks like he's abandoned it." said the gaffer, face like thunder.

"We are going to give it a few minutes and try and get him to restart."

I made my way back to the terrace and reported back to the thirty or so Palace fans who had made the game. We could hear shouting emanating from the dressing room area, but no-one knew enough Spanish to know what was being said, or to whom. After about ten minutes, with an early return to El Clifton looking increasingly likely, both sides reappeared as did the officials. The referee looked no less stressed than he had been before the stoppage.

Play re-commenced and we realised that the dismissed home player was now back on the field of play. As I wrote in my notes: "whether Torre had taken advantage of the referee's utter confusion and pulled a fast one, or this was something agreed upon by both teams, is a matter of conjecture."

Thankfully, the break in play had done much to calm tempers on all sides. Palace got on with playing the neat, short passing game that Kember had promised us at the Fans Forum. Just before half-time, Ben Watson let fly with a blistering drive for Palace's second.

At half-time, Palace took the unusual step of unveiling a new signing, or more accurately, a re-signing. Neil Shipperley emerged for the second half and confirmed to us that he had put pen to paper and signed a contract the previous Wednesday. It was something that hadn't been reported officially by the club, nor in any local or national newspapers. My first big journalistic scoop, or it would have been: sadly I was in no condition to update the *Palace Echo* website that evening.

Shipperley capped off his first game in his second spell at Palace with a goal and another header that was harshly adjudged to be offside. Palace should have added to the 3-0 scoreline many times, especially towards the end of the game as the hosts tired. Unfortunately, the demons that had haunted them in front of goal in the previous season had clearly not yet been fully exorcised.

At the final whistle, Kember made sure every Palace player shook the hand of each official, however the referee still had a face like a bulldog chewing a wasp. The Palace fans raced towards the bar, Hoover loudly complaining about the loss of drinking time, due to the first-half stoppage.

I had other ideas, having spotted a couple of young local children who had gone onto the pitch for a kickaround. I vaulted the fence once more, robbed the kids of their ball and set off towards goal to recreate Ben Watson's howitzer. The kids were not going to let me go that easily, harrying and tackling back. I managed to sidestep their tackles, with some skill I might add, considering the amount of booze inside me, before letting fly an unstoppable effort past the non-existent keeper. I wheeled away and celebrated with my shirt over my head, towards the laughing Palace fans heading to the exit at that end.

The reason for their laughter quickly became apparent. I had missed the goal. I prayed that no-one had videoed it. The kids thought it was hysterical too and demanded that they take penalties against the 'inglés gordo loco" (mad fat Englishman) until the groundsman eventually came to shoo us all off his pitch.

I caught up with everyone back at El Clifton and, over more beers, was relieved to discover that my glory run had only been captured in still photography, which did not show my ultimate embarrassment. The bar closed and we headed back into Benalmadena, I'd now been awake for over twenty hours, so it was no surprise that I crashed and burned at the first port of call, providing those with cameras another round of comedy shots of me drooling in my sleep outside the bar. I flew home on the Sunday after a very relaxed weekend in the company of friends.

Whilst I have returned to the area on countless occasions since, including the very sad occasion of dear Chocky's funeral in 2017, Crystal Palace have not. Despite many rumours since, sadly none have come to fruition. It is not just Palace ex-pats – whose numbers have swelled since those days – who feel frustrated by this, although my liver is grateful.

Indeed, our contact with Spanish sides since then has been limited to a single home friendly at Selhurst against Valencia in 2016, which Palace won 3-1 with a brace from Connor Wickham and a Mile Jedinak penalty. Palace's first encounter with Spanish opposition on 18th April 1962, however, is the stuff of legend.

Palace had installed expensive new floodlighting at Selhurst at the start of the season and the Chairman at the time, Arthur J. Wait, wanted to mark the occasion with a game against a marquee name in world football. The top flight English clubs wanted vast sums of appearance money. The Chairman is reported to have said "If that's what they're going to do to us, we might as well try to get Real Madrid." And so, that is exactly what he did.

Real were regarded as the very best team at the time, having won the European Cup five times since its inception seven years before and had already reached the final that year. They were current La Liga champions and were about to win it again, also adding the Copa del Rey later in the summer.

So it really was something of a coup to get the Spaniards, who had not played a game in London since the Second World War. Their one and only London experience had been against Tottenham Hotspur on a Thursday afternoon in September 1925 in front of just 170 people. Spurs fielded a reserve side and still won 4-2. The Palace programme for our game, however, decided this historic fixture was not worthy of any consideration and declared that this was the first time that Real Madrid had played in England anywhere south of Manchester.

Third Division Crystal Palace had paid £10,000 for the game and were expecting a sell-out crowd. The game commanded the whole of the front page in the *London Evening News & Star*. Then, as now, the Real Madrid line up boasted some of the world's finest players. Puskas, Di Stefano, Santamaria and Gento were amongst the best-known players in football and all made an appearance in the game. Palace's own star name, Johnny Byrne, had been transferred to West Ham in the weeks before the game, but he was allowed to return to the Palace line-up for this game.

Sadly the atrocious weather on the evening of the game meant the ground was far from sold-out, but the raised admission prices for the game, just about saw Palace turn a profit. Palace had been playing in a predominantly white jersey for many seasons, but deferred to their illustrious guests Los Blancos and wore a one-off claret and blue striped V-necked shirt instead.

John Carter, the father of my good friend and neighbour, Graham, was there to see the European giants grace Selhurst Park.

> "I couldn't quite believe it when I heard the best team in the world were coming to Selhurst Park. I recall having doubts that they would bring their superstars and, if they did, they would only play a few minutes. Ferenc Puskas was my idol, I watched him on TV when Hungary beat England 6-3. He was a short stocky man – a bit like Kenny Sansom – who didn't seem to run much but had a shot like a tracer bullet. I also liked Luis del Sol because his name meant Sunshine – he was also a great player.
>
> The higher admission prices were not a problem for me, I seem to remember that my father paid anyway. We stood behind the goal at the Whitehorse Lane end because it was cheaper than our usual place on the grassy bank – what is now the Arthur Wait stand. We had arranged to meet up with other friends."

Despite the conditions, Real Madrid got on the front foot early with two goals in the first ten minutes from Di Stefano and Gento. Ron Heckman briefly got Palace back into it, but by half time, Real were 4-1 up. Puskas and Sanchez hitting the third and fourth goals. As John Carter recalls, there seemed little hope for Palace:

> "I was a regular by then and had no expectation that Palace would rally as they did. I think the heavy ground conditions helped Palace, especially in the second half when they were playing towards our end. Goals from Andy Smillie and Terry Long brought Palace to within a goal of Madrid with twenty minutes left. My standout memories from the game were Terry Long's goal and the return of Johnny Byrne – one of our all-time greats."

The game finished 4-3 to the Spaniards, with Palace giving them a real scare towards the end of the game, sending 25,000 people, including the Carter family, home feeling their decision to brave the weather had paid huge dividends. Also in the crowd admiring the silky Spanish skills on show that night was a young Roy Hodgson who was a regular at Selhurst Park at that time.

It would be seven years before Palace would face another Spanish side. The club went on a post-season tour of the Costa Blanca – a reward to the players for promotion to the top flight for the first time in our history. They returned a season later for a fortnight post-season tour, one would imagine as a reward for retaining their top flight status. This time they played and won the Fisherman's Cup against San Paulo, then took on an Atletico Madrid XI and ended with a game against Mahon on Menorca. Ten years later in 1980, Palace faced Malaga in a one-off post season game in Spain. The Spanish encounters that followed have been covered in this book.

The Jersey Boys (and girl!). The dapper chap on the far left is Pete Bonthrone, standing next to Tony Woolley, Gerry Mansfield, Terry Venables, John Collins, Jim Kirk and his wife Pat. Sitting: Geoff Hayward - July 1977
[Photo: Neil Everitt]

12

HEY HO, LET'S GO!

Back to the 2003 pre-season and Palace were not yet done with foreign opposition. The game in late July against PSV Eindhoven was billed as the Philips Cup. The Dutch electronic firm was founded in Eindhoven and the football club began life as a Philips works' team in 1913. Their British Headquarters was in Croydon, although the operation was shortly to move to Guildford.

It was our first home game against overseas opposition since the Intertoto game in 1998. There had been resistance to allowing any home friendlies while we were ground-sharing, but with Wimbledon shortly off to Milton Keynes, many of the perceived obstacles melted away.

PSV Eindhoven had some highly-rated players on show, including Mark Van Bommel, Arjen Robben and Mateja Kežman. Over 10,000 people came, which seemed to confirm an appetite amongst fans for home friendlies against top European sides. Unfortunately, those present witnessed a fairly dour game, Palace never really at the races after an early Kežman goal and PSV were content to defend their lead. Palace's brightest, albeit brief, moment was Tony Popovic scoring from close range, although the equaliser was quickly ruled out for pushing.

The single goal was enough for PSV to lift the Philips Cup. There was initial talk of a return match in Eindhoven, the following pre-season, but nothing came of it.

Palace had played PSV twice before in the early seventies. When an early exit from the 1971 FA Cup left us with space on the fixture list, Manager Bert Head had arranged a home friendly and tantalised fans by announcing that Palace would field a mystery trialist. It turned out to be a player from Bolton called John Byrom, who very few had heard of and did not impress. He lasted until half-time before being subbed and was not seen in a Palace shirt again. Palace went down 4-2 on the day.

They gained revenge for this defeat during the club's pre-season later that year with a 3-2 away win. As part of a three game tour of the Netherlands, Palace also took on SC Feijenoord (now known simply as Feyenoord) and ADO Den Haag (The Hague), losing 1-0 and drawing 0-0 respectively. Palace had also played Den

Haag three weeks after the initial encounter with PSV in a midweek home friendly, again the game was goalless.

During the mid-sixties and seventies, the Netherlands proved a popular country for friendly opposition, both at home and away. Our first encounter with a Dutch club side was a 1-0 win over Alkamaar '54 (later AZ Alkamaar), who had come to Selhurst for a midweek friendly in March 1966. Palace then toured there five months later in pre-season, including a return leg and another win against Alkamaar, this time 2-0. The other games played on that tour were a 1-0 win against VW DOS (now FC Utrecht) and our first of three matches against SC Feijenoord, which ended in a 3-1 defeat.

The club returned to the country for the following pre-season, earning a 1-1 draw with SC Feijenoord, but were defeated in the other two games against MVV Maastricht and a team called Go Ahead. In an odd parallel with Palace's change of nickname in the seventies, Go Ahead changed their club name to Go Ahead Eagles, incorporating the bird on the crest of the town of Deventer where they are based.

Palace played a series of two friendlies against MVV Maastricht, home and away, over three months in 1972, the aggregate score being 2-2. The Dutch side could claim the overall win on away goals though.

Palace's last Dutch games before the Philips Cup came in 1976, as part of the pre-season tour of both Germany and The Netherlands. The first game was just over the border in Germany, a narrow 3-2 defeat to German club, Alemannia Aachen.

With Palace now being a third tier side, the opposition on offer was not of the calibre of sides faced in previous years. S.C. Heracles Almelo were the best known of the three Dutch sides played. Heracles have since risen into the top flight and have competed in the Europa League, thus are certainly more well-known now. Rijnsburgse Boys and WVV Wageningen provided the other Dutch opposition.

It was the first overseas trip with Palace for the club's long-standing official photographer, Neil Everitt, although he had to make his own way around the Lowlands, rather than travelling with the club:

"We found out about the trip from Harry Elsdon, who ran the supporters club bar. I went with Geoff Hayward. Our plan was to go by pushbike, because we had no money and what with Holland being flat. I didn't even own a bike, so I went and bought one from a bloke in Hampstead for twenty quid! We never used it in the end, because then we discovered a company called Trans-Alpino, who were based in George Street in Croydon. They were offering a cheap ferry ticket and ten days rail journeys on Dutch railways, so we went for that instead.

The thing that still astonishes me about those trips back then is how we found out any information about where the games were and how to get there. If you were going on holiday you used a travel agent. Even if you were just going on a ferry, you used a travel agent to book it. These days it's so easy in comparison. You can look on the internet and book everything. You can get a map up on your phone that will direct you straight to the place. There was nothing like that in 1976, I had a book at work called 'Train Travel in Europe' which wasn't very thick, but it had parts of the timetable and gave you an idea of where to change trains.

We got an early morning ferry from Harwich to the Hook of Holland and then had to get a couple of trains. We had chosen to stay in Simpelveld in Holland, close to the German border and Aachen, then go over for the game the next day. We got there about 10 o'clock in the evening and came across a B&B whilst wandering up the main street – it seemed like the middle of nowhere. There was a little bar downstairs from our room which had a few locals in, so we dumped off our bags at headed there.

'What are you doing here?' asked the owner. We explained about the game the next day.

'Oh, I know Crystal Palace' he said. 'Ian Evans, Peter Taylor...'

'How do you know all that?' we asked.

'I see them on the television.' He must have seen our run to the semi-finals of the FA Cup earlier that year. Nevertheless, we were staggered.

They brought forward the kick-off time of the Aachen game from the evening to the afternoon and we found out by a tannoy call over the station PA! It was very odd hearing an announcement in English to go to the station master for a message, while we were changing trains in Holland. We thought we were going to be deported!"

This was really the start of the era in which following Palace in Europe became popular among the diehard supporters. This tour saw a nucleus of fans coalesce that would go on to attend a great number of overseas trips. As well as Neil and Geoff: Chris Wright, Steve Carleton and Wiz were also on this tour.

Another regular of the group was Stanley Mann ('Stan the Man') who has previously recounted this trip in the *Eagle Eye* book, *We All Follow The Palace*. Stan recalled the story of managing to bunk in to the Aachen game after a chance encounter outside with the club's owner. Although they were seated in the Directors' Box, much beer had already been drunk. There was some questionable stereotypical behaviour exhibited towards their German hosts, which led to the owner's wife and Wiz having words. It did little to enhance our standing with the Club.

Neil takes up the tale after the game, upon the return to Dutch soil:

"Unfortunately, our B&B had no beds for the following night, but after the game we decided to head back to Simpelveld anyway. We were completely hammered and ended up sleeping in what we thought was a field. We woke up at 4am, freezing cold and realised we were in someone's back garden! We ended up sitting on the station platform for about three hours waiting for the first train.

Apart from the night in the field in Simpelveld, Geoff and I were staying apart from most of the Palace support. We were in B&Bs for a fiver a night, whereas the others were staying in a flophouse for down-and-outs in Arnhem for around a £1 a night. There was a mattress on the floor and that was it.

The team were based at a sports centre called Paapendal, outside of Arnhem. Some of the lads were invited to sleep in one of the players' rooms that night. Phil Holder had told them they could bunk down there, but Jim Cannon came in later and kicked them all out again. They ended up sleeping in rooms that had been reserved for Barcelona players, who were due there shortly.

After the second game in Almelo, we went to Leiden, near Den Haag to play Rijnsburgse Boys. Stan had his fedora on from the cup run, which some kids nicked off his head and threw onto the pitch. Stan had been drinking so he went onto the pitch to retrieve it and in doing so got in the way of play. I think I would have remembered if he'd prevented a Swindlehurst goal and more would have been made of it."

Perhaps unsurprisingly, Stan's recollection in the *Eagle Eye* book is somewhat different, claiming it was Wiz who had been messing around with these kids and that one of them deflected Swindlehurst's shot away, much to the particular chagrin of Palace midfielder Phil Holder. Neil remains unconvinced, however.

"You know how these stories can get embellished. It couldn't have been that bad, as I remember talking to a couple of the players in the bar afterwards, when just as an aside they asked what was going on with the pitch invasion."

There may still exist a video of the match that would resolve this memory difference, as this game was filmed by ITV. The footage was used in two documentaries; one about Palace and the other about our eye-catching young winger, Vince Hilaire. It seems unlikely, but somewhere in a dusty film archive the proof may be found to resolve this controversy.

"The last game of the tour was at WVV Wageningen, which has long since gone bust. It was an evening game, pissing down and horrible. Geoff and I couldn't find a B&B so we ended up staying at a hotel. It cost £7 a night, which we thought was bloody expensive."

The fun wasn't over though for the travelling fans, who were caught up in an incident on the overnight ferry home from The Hook.

"We ended up manning the lifeboat stations! It was very rough and I'm not usually great on boats. Initially I was OK and somehow got myself into the first class bar. There were a number of hooray henrys in there and one of them said: 'Ooh, I feel very hot, I'll take my jumper off.' I was thinking: 'Yeah, you feel sick, mate,' and that started me off. I was throwing up for the rest of the night. It got to four or five in the morning, I'd found somewhere to lay down across the seats in the restaurant area. It was nice and calm there and I felt much better.

The staff started to arrive to cook the breakfasts. One staff member came out the kitchen door followed by a puff of smoke. Another one goes in and a bit more smoke puffs out of the kitchen. The next thing, they get these trunks down out of the lockers and get asbestos suits out!

They opened the kitchen door and the whole place was on fire! Now I'm lying down and feeling great again, so I've decided I'm not going anywhere, just watching what is going on. Then they told everyone to go to the muster points and to get lifejackets on. I was one of the last people to move. Although I was sitting right by the incident, they hadn't actually spotted me. When they did, I had to go upstairs where the others were manning the lifeboat stations. In the end, the crew stood us down, but obviously there was no breakfast for anyone.

According to Stan, a couple of Italians had noticed the smoke and put lifebelts on before being asked and were wandering around the boat putting the wind up the other passengers before the alarm had gone off. After the voyage, the Italians guys were stopped from getting off as they were still wearing the lifebelts."

The following year, Palace had a two-game tour of Jersey, a destination they had visited once before, six years previously, when they beat a club side, First Tower United, 2-1 in mid-season. It proved a popular destination for the fans with a fair few making the journey, some of whom brought their wives and families over. Among the travellers was a dapper chap on his first Palace tour called Peter Bonthrone, who will feature regularly in later chapters.

"There was a chap called Jim Kirk, who didn't go to the first game but came over on the ferry afterwards. He said to his missus at the time:

"Pat, do you fancy going to Jersey for the week?"

"Sounds nice."

Pat only smelled a rat when we were all on the dockside waiting for Jim. She hadn't realised that football was involved and it's fair to say she wasn't best pleased. She dragged him off shopping that afternoon to make up for it.

I remember the first game against an Island U-23 side being at a very low level, albeit at a Jersey League team's ground. We got to St Helier in the afternoon, dumped our bags and four of us jumped a cab. Even the cab driver didn't know where the ground was. Eventually we arrived at a farm gate and this field, that's all it was, a field that was taped off and a shed. The shed was supposed to be the changing room, but you couldn't have got a whole team in it. Despite the primitive surroundings, Palace won 2-0. At least the second game against the senior Island side was in the Springfield Stadium, Jersey's biggest sporting arena. That second game was a rout – 9-3 and two missed penalties – I was sitting at one end taking photos and there was a Scottish holidaymaker who could not stop raving about Rachid Harkouk."

A couple of memories from the social side of that tour also stand out for Neil.

"It was the tour when many of our lads got into snuff (the tobacco product as opposed to the punk band). There was a lot of sneezing and strange brown stains down white t-shirts. It was horrible to be around.

The team were staying in the Hotel de France and opposite there was a nightclub we used to frequent called The Lido. We were all staying in different guest houses but none too far away, so we were in there every night. The staff got the impression that we were the team, even the larger members of our support. As a result, we were drinking for very little money. Then Ian Walsh and Neil Smillie, I think, turned up. They took one look at our lot and decided not to hang around.

Jim Kirk had an alternative theory about the cheapness of the drinks. He was in charge of the whip and believed it was because he was tipping our waitress very well. Even with the tip, it still wasn't costing very much. Then we spotted she was getting our drinks from behind a curtain, rather than the bar. We could have been drinking anything!"

Ultimately surviving the nightly dosage of dubious quality alcohol, Neil went on to cover the next two Scandinavian tours as the Club's official photographer.

"I went out with the team for the trips to Sweden in 1978 and Norway in 1979. On the Norway trip, I stayed apart from the team, who were based in the deep south of the country where, frankly, there was sod all to do. I stayed further north with the usual bunch of travellers. We went everywhere by bus, as I recall they didn't have much of a train system. Even when we played Viking and Lillestrom, which was quite a distance.

The game against FK Ørn was in the town of Horten towards the middle of the country. There was a bar called Saxon King that we used to frequent. Bars were generally in short supply in Norway then. They also had a youth hostel, which was some silly amount like a quid a night to stay. We'd been directed to it by a copper who was by the bus we'd just got off. There was a few of us checking in and we realised that Stan and Steve were already there ahead of us.

There was a long list of rules. Curfew was at 10.30pm, no smoking, eating or drinking in the rooms – it was all in Norwegian, but we were read the riot act as to what we could and couldn't do. We went to Stan's room only to find they had broken every rule in the book. There was a crate of beer on the floor, Stan was smoking a pipe and knocking out the ash on the side of the bunk bed. The place was a disaster zone.

After that, we were roystering around, staying at various ladies' houses but we used to turn up back at the youth hostel at about 7am. We would all be sitting outside when the bloke came to open the place back up again. He couldn't work out why we were paying money, but weren't actually staying there.

By the last night, we hadn't slept for so long and there was a guy called Charlie with us, who was in his sixties. We gave him the job of getting back before curfew and open the ground floor window, which happened to be in the ladies toilet – then we could come back a bit later and bunk in through the window. Come the evening he refused to do it, on the basis that he'd pulled. She was young enough to be his grand-daughter, but he was adamant. So we never actually got to sleep in there.

> There was one night where I hadn't got lucky. I got back to the hostel at two in the morning
> and found a shed with a boiler in it. It was warm, so I kipped down in there."

Aside from an infamous day trip to France in 1983, which will be covered later, Neil's next Palace trips abroad were not until after the Millennium, when he once again became a regular fixture on overseas tours.

Tucked in-between the Jersey excursion and the Swedish tour was a post-season trip out to Greece. Steve Carleton was the only fan to follow the team on that trip:

> "According to the Croydon Advertiser, we were supposed to be playing top flight Greek side
> Panathinaikos, but that got called off, so we ended going out to Corfu to play a Select XI
> there. It costs me £80 for the Athens flight and then a further £30 to get to Corfu.
> The reason I was told that the game was off was due to their arch-rivals AEK Athens playing
> in the Greek Cup quarter-final that night and they didn't want both clubs playing in Athens."

Here's where it gets a little intriguing. Upon researching the AEK game, it was in fact outside of Athens, albeit quite close by in a town called Eleusis. The team AEK played was Panelefsiniakos F.C. – they were a lower league team and perhaps more likely opposition for second division Palace. The close similarity in the name does lead to me to speculate whether they were the team that The Eagles were due to be playing, rather that the then-Greek champions. A case of cabbages and kings in *The Advertiser* press room, perhaps?

Steve's memory of the game on Corfu island, which Palace won 3-1, is dominated by a small bush fire that started next to the pitch. Another game was arranged two days later, back on the mainland, in a town called Ingoumentisa, which was connected to Corfu by a direct ferry service.

> "Me and a couple of the players boarded the ferry in the back of a pickup. Terry Venables
> bought me a beer on the ferry and I had a few beers with the players at their Corfu hotel and
> at the airport. I got back to Athens for the flight home and stayed overnight at a hostel. There
> I spotted a Palace scarf and therefore had to have a few beers with the owner that evening,
> who hailed from Shirley."

Motley Crue. L-R: the back of Paul James, Martin Young, Sue Witherow and Steve Carleton propping up the Crusaders Bar - July 2004

Even Glentoran's Oval Ground has something to say about the Gaddafi news - July 2004

13

DON'T DICTATE

The mid-seventies saw the start of a regular group of Palace fans travelling to overseas friendlies and it was the 2004 pre-season tour to Belfast that was the evolution of a new collective. The seasoned campaigners combined with returning veterans and new younger blood. The reasons for this resurgence were manifold: ease of travel, relatively early notice, and Palace's stock being particularly high.

The 2003/04 season was one of the most amazing rollercoasters that Palace have ever been on. Bottom just before Christmas and onto our third Manager, namely our ex-player Iain Dowie, the club then rose up the table all the way to the play-off places, before so nearly trashing it all on the final day by losing away at Coventry. Only a last-minute Brian Deane equaliser for West Ham United away at Wigan Athletic denied the Lancastrian side the final play-off berth. From there, Palace squeaked past Sunderland in the play-off semi-finals after a thrilling penalty shoot-out at the Stadium of Light.

The showdown final was at Cardiff's Millennium Stadium, while the new Wembley was being built. Palace's opponents on the day were West Ham – the architects of the almighty favour that carried The Eagles into the play-offs. Palace's mentality, however, was unstoppable. Buoyed by Dowie's catchphrases "Bouncebackability" and "One More Round' The Eagles edged the tense final by a single Neil Shipperley goal. Crystal Palace were back in the Premier League.

Early in April that year, when thoughts of promotion were still very much a pipe dream, reports appeared in the Northern Irish press announcing that Palace would be visiting Belfast for two pre-season games in mid-July. A testimonial for Gavin McArthur against his club side Crusaders on Wednesday 14th July and a regular friendly against Glentoran on the following Saturday, assuming their UEFA Cup commitments permitted. The choice of destination owed much to Dowie's Northern Irish family heritage and his links with the area; he had been a much-capped striker for the national side. Also, while he was Manager at third tier Oldham Athletic, it was a preferred pre-season destination.

The announcement generated a fair bit of excitement amongst the fans, although eyebrows were raised at the timing of the tour. Palace would be in Belfast during the twelfth fortnight, better known as the Loyalist 'marching season'. Local sectarian tensions are often elevated around this time and a number of fans questioned the wisdom of attending games during a time of heightened sensibilities.

The matter was discussed at some length on the BBS but the issue didn't ultimately appear to put many people off. Fans who lived in the city offered advice about personal conduct whilst there. Most city centre pubs had a football shirt ban in place as a matter of routine and, during the time we would be there, we were advised not to display club colours until we got to the grounds themselves. The local advice was well met and generally respected.

After the euphoria of the Cardiff triumph died down, there was growing disquiet that the Club had not actually confirmed the tour. They had announced other later friendlies and Glentoran's involvement in the UEFA Cup was no longer an issue. Many people, including our party, Sue, Safety and I, had booked flights and accommodation in advance to secure good prices. Surely they couldn't renege on pre-season plans for the second time in three years? Unofficial back channels to the club insisted all was well and our opponents were so sure that the games were going ahead they had started to sell tickets. But officially from Palace, an ominous silence reigned. With the club's newfound Premier League status, were they actively looking for more challenging opposition?

With three weeks to go, Palace finally allowed their inundated switchboard operators to officially confirm to callers that the tour was indeed going ahead. Not perhaps the most efficient use of the media at their disposal.

However, it seemed from the BBS that there would be at least a hundred fans travelling. Portadown were also at home in the UEFA Cup on the Thursday evening in-between the Palace games and that was also proving an attractive prospect for many travellers.

We knew a number of those reporting for duty on this tour. Hoover and his band of merry men had declared. The reprobates that we knew as 'Baldy's lot', including Paul 'Baldy' Withers himself, Dave Hynes, Mick 'Thirsty' Hersey, Glenn 'Colonel Britain' Bastin and his broodThe Palace Independent Sussex Travel club (known as 'PIST') had initially tried to arrange a coach trip, but it failed to garner enough critical mass, mainly because most people had already taken advantage of the cheap flights on offer before the coach was announced. Some of their members flew over anyway, amongst them the driving force behind PIST, Jake 'Billingshurst' Edsor and brothers Nick and Pete Redman, who we've known since they were young lads in the Palace Family Enclosure. A couple of the Orpington Pissheads, Paul James and Martin Young were also heading out, as was Dave London. A very healthy travelling posse.

On the Wednesday morning both Gatwick and Heathrow Airports were alive with the sound of Palace fans partaking of noisy liquid breakfasts. Our own party consisted of Sue, Safety and myself. We flew out early from Gatwick into Belfast International, where we hired a car for the tour. Things got off to a slippery start as we left the airport. The hire car had been upgraded to a Seat Ibiza with 'sports injection'.

The sales assistant pleaded with me to take it steady to begin with, as the up-rated engine was deceptively powerful and the car could be skittish in the rain. I smiled the blank smile of an experienced driver, deaf to such nannying advice. I was still within sight of the terminal building, fumbling with the windscreen wipers, when I found myself skidding sideways around the first roundabout; thankfully without connecting with anything or anyone. Okay then, I thought, as I untangled the steering wheel. Maybe I should take more notice.

The rest of the journey was spent feathering the throttle in the drizzly conditions. Our hotel was just outside the city centre itself, we dumped our luggage and the car and headed to the pub, which had been designated a meeting point for various fan groups. The pub's name had originally been mis-spelled as Birtles in the forum discussions, thus it had quickly become known as Garry's – after the Nottingham Forest striker – and was referred to as such in further discourse. When our cab drew up outside Bittles Bar, I was genuinely surprised that it was not actually called Garry's. It was the first time on a Palace tour that I was indebted to my wife's greater attention to the finer details. And it certainly won't be the last.

A fair mass of fan groups had gathered in the bar by early afternoon. The alcohol had begun to flow and vocal chords were loosened. The first strains of "The Famous Alan Mullery went to Rome to sign the Pope," brought forth sharp intakes of breath from the bar staff, even before the sweary part was reached. Their advice was firm and clear, but not delivered unkindly.

"Save the singing for the social club later, lads."

The day turned into a loose pub crawl around the inner city. We encountered all of the travelling groups we knew over the course of the afternoon, Baldy's lot leading the charge, with other groups drinking at a more leisurely pace and moving on as and when drinks were finished.

Hoover's crew were attracting some attention from the bar staff of the various establishments in which they were drinking, despite quietly keeping to themselves. Hoover was out there with Rick, Chris Plummer, Bourno, and Pete Bonthrone. I've previously mentioned that Pete was a snappy dresser and he was now in his sixties, but looked younger. He also had an uncanny likeness to Michael Caine, but for once that wasn't the cause of the extra attention. Instead, it was his dress sense. He was immaculately turned out in black from overcoat to his highly polished shoes. It seemed that bar staff worried he might be some form of senior military surveillance and would scurry off to alert their landlord, who would inevitably appear at some point for a 'wee chat' with the group.

After an extremely pleasant afternoon interacting not only with fellow Palace travellers, but very friendly and welcoming locals too, we headed off to Seaview – home of the Crusaders. We made our way to their social club, which was absolutely heaving, but we received the most astonishing welcome. Extra chairs and tables appeared from goodness knows where and somehow space magically appeared to squeeze us in alongside the locals. The previously aborted sing-songs began in earnest, although Alan Mullery now, and indeed for the rest of the trip, "went to Rome to sign… a man."

The game itself was a fairly gentle workout, as testimonials often are. Palace won 2-0 with both goals from Tommy Black, but also missed a whole host of good chances. With Palace having been promoted mostly using loan goalkeepers, there was some excitement to see our new goalkeeping prospects. Argentinian Julian Speroni had just signed from Dundee. In addition, we also had Hungarian Gabor Kiraly from Hertha Berlin on trial. Both keepers shared a half with Kiraly playing first. Sadly, neither saw any real action as Crusaders barely registered a shot on target, thus judgement had to be reserved. The initial thoughts on Speroni were that he appeared to be a little short and needed a haircut.

The next morning the hangovers were anything but gentle and it took until after lunch before we set off for Portadown's UEFA Cup tie against the Lithuanian side FK Žalgiris Vilnius. Martin Young and Paul James joined us in the car for the trip. Sue, being a good Irish Catholic, wanted to visit the grave of St Patrick, the patron saint of Ireland at Downpatrick Cathedral – about thirty miles from Portadown. The weather was miserable, so the rest of us stayed in the car making juvenile jokes about the town's rather literal name, while Sue went on her pilgrimage. When she returned, Sue informed us that Downpatrick actually means 'Patrick's stronghold' rather than the place where he was put down in the ground. That was us told.

UEFA restrictions meant the bars nearest to Portadown's Shamrock Park were closed, so we headed into the town for food and refreshment. We had been warned that the town wasn't regarded as particularly friendly, especially the area around the ground, but we encountered no problems. The green and white of the Žalgiris fans was much in evidence as they travelled in good numbers. Also well represented were several other Palace fans taking advantage of another game and, for most, a visit to a new ground.

The home side raced to a two goal lead, but the noisy away support was ultimately rewarded with two away goals to take back to Vilnius after an exciting 2-2 draw. The Lithuanian side progressed only as far as the next round where they were beaten 3-1 to Aalborg AB of Denmark. Also in UEFA Cup action in the country that evening were our opponents on Saturday, Glentoran, who earned a 2-2 draw against Finnish side Allianssi and later progressed to the second qualifying round, where they went out to Swedish side Elfsborg.

Friday was another day of sightseeing for us, this time further afield at the Giants Causeway. Sue had also spotted that Bob Geldof, who is a particular favourite of ours, was playing a gig just over the border in Letterkenny that evening. Over breakfast, the three of us decided to go, even if it would mean getting back to Belfast in the wee small hours. Also at breakfast, we noticed that the hotel was now occupied by a young national football side, and not just any national side, these were boys from Brazil. One of their coach staff bore an uncanny resemblance to Bebeto, one half of the Brazilian striking partnership with Romario, who had won the USA World Cup a decade previous.

He spotted us looking over and smiled cheerily. In return we cheekily gave a rendition of his famous 'baby-rocking' celebration from that tournament. His eyes lit up and he gave a thumbs-up, before joining in the trademark celebration. To this day, we have absolutely no idea if it was actually him and I can trace no record of him being involved with Brazil's coaching setup. But as far as I'm concerned, that morning we had breakfast with Bebeto.

The young Brazil side were in Northern Ireland to take part in the Milk Cup, a youth tournament of long standing, not to be confused with the English League Cup, which briefly went by the same name in the eighties, due to a sponsorship deal. This tournament, now known as SuperCup NI, involves national teams and club sides from all over the world at Under 19, Under 16 and Under 14 level. The elite tournament was starting on the Saturday and my inner ground-hopping geek was delighted to learn it would be possible to get two games and two new grounds in, either side of the Palace friendly.

The weather on the Friday was much better and it made for an enjoyable day visiting the main attractions on the north coast of the island. A few other Palace travellers had the same idea and we, quite literally, bumped into Hoover's gang while crossing the Carrick-a-Rede rope bridge. It was there that I received a strange text message from a number I didn't recognise that read:

"Make sure you buy the Guardian tomorrow for an explosive exclusive about the potential new owner of CPFC".

It wasn't particularly unusual for me to get that sort of message. Since I had taken over as Editor of *Palace Echo* and begun to do match reports for the local press, I was often asked to make 'informed' comment to the media. As a consequence, I would occasionally get the odd tip-off about a breaking Palace story. I did not take a lot of notice of it, other than to mention it to Hoover and co, who were generally quite well-connected at the club, but none had heard any whispers on that front.

After a superb gig, we travelled back across the Sperrin mountains in poor weather conditions, with the hire car twitching all the way back to Belfast on the rain-slicked roads. We arrived back at 2.30am and collapsed into bed, exhausted after a long day and gruelling drive back in the pitch dark.

I was fast asleep when, in my dream, my mobile rang. It was Sky Sports News on the other end telling me that Colonel Gaddafi has agreed to buy Palace and could I give them a comment? In my dream, I laughed at them and hung up. Moments later, I'm awoken by the mobile again. Still smirking about my dream-state interpretation of yesterday's text message, I glanced at the clock on the phone before answering. 7-bloody-a.m – blimey, someone's keen – better answer it in case it's urgent. It was the same person from my dream wondering why we'd just been cut off?

Suddenly I was wide awake with a cold, horrible feeling flip-flopping in my gut. I told them I would call them back in half an hour while I got my unexpectedly loosened shit together and rushed down to reception to find a copy of *The Guardian*. The story had been broken by Dom Fifield who was, by then, a trusted source of Palace news. Thankfully, it was rather more circumspect and measured than Sky had led me to believe, so I was in no particular hurry to call them back.

After a leisurely breakfast, I eventually returned their call and did a phone interview. I expressed what I felt was serious, relevant, but restrained concerns about Gaddafi's past and his country's alleged links to the Lockerbie terrorist bombing. I also tried hard to point out that the story still appeared to be quite tenuous, but the interviewer seemed less interested in that angle.

In the interview, I'd obviously said something that set the hares running. Throughout the morning, Sky began falling over themselves to repeat the interview to camera. I also received a text message from Hoover telling me that "Apparently there's a bloke on a camel with an AK47 riding down Bromley High Street looking for you." Oh very funny, mate.

Despite their initial vigour, Sky Sports blanched at the idea of sending an outside broadcast unit to East Belfast FC, where I was off to watch the eventual winners of the Milk Cup, Turkey U19, grind out a 2-1 win against Wales U19. They said, instead, they would catch up with me at the Glentoran game.

We received another extremely warm welcome at The Oval, home of Glentoran. A few of their fans actually lined up in a loose 'guard of honour' to shake our hands and thank us for coming over as we entered the gates of the ground. The number of Palace fans attending was greater than the Wednesday game, as people had come over from the weekend, something that clearly caught out Glens' programme editor, as they were completely sold out by 2.15pm.

The game started off at a cracking pace. Julian Speroni gave us a first glimpse of the talent that had led to his signing, with a string of world class saves. Midway through the half, Andrew 'AJ' Johnson opened the goalscoring floodgates, as Glentoran began to look rather leggy in the hot afternoon, after their UEFA encounter less than 48 hours before. Palace, on the other hand, made up for their profligacy in front of goal just across the Lagan on Wednesday evening and chased in another three goals by AJ, Tommy Black and Dougie Freedman.

It was at half-time that Sky Sports camera crew finally caught up with me. I duly gave them a repeat performance to camera. They asked me how I would react if it went through. Again, I told them I didn't think it would, but threw them a bone for a while saying I'd be absolutely disgusted, if we took, what was to my eyes, blood money. Then they asked whether I would still go to Palace? "Me and about 10,000 others once stopped going just because Alan Mullery was appointed Manager, so if Gaddafi ends up as Chairman, I think that's pretty much nailed on" was my reply.

None of this sounded particularly unreasonable to me. Apparently though, that still wasn't enough to sate the appetite of the ravenous Sky media beast. Sky News began to call asking for another on-camera interview. I ignored my phone to watch the second half in peace. Palace only managed one more goal with AJ completing his hat-trick. Despite this, he finished the match a frustrated figure having laid three good chances on a plate for Tyrone Berry, only for the youth team prospect to miss every one, including two open goals.

At the end of the game many of the Palace faithful took the short trip from the Oval to Belfast City Airport and, thanks to a conveniently-timed flight, were back in their own homes quicker than from an away game in the North of England.

Sue and I stayed on to visit her family in the south for a few days, so we made our way across the city to Windsor Park, home of Linfield FC and the national side, where Brazil U19 were taking on Israel U19. If we had not been quite so distracted over breakfast that morning, we could have probably scored free tickets from our mate Bebeto, or maybe from Sky News, who'd sent a crew there to conduct another interview with me.

As we entered the ground, we immediately spotted a Sky News truck, aerial aloft and a Sky employee scurrying over. Blimey, give us a moment here! The live interview took the form of me talking to their foreign affairs correspondent, back in their studio. The pompous sod was clearly more interested in trying to paint me as a stereotypical, xenophobic Englander, rather than a fan concerned for his club. His approach was not subtle, so I reverted to giving him monosyllabic replies and leaving long, pregnant silences instead of expanding on my answers. Sensing that I wasn't about to take his considerable bait, the correspondent wound up the interview quickly. Just as well, because the Brazil game had now kicked off.

I recently spoke to Dom Fifield, who exclusively broke the Gaddafi story. Dom still remembers the incident well:

"I was told that Simon Jordan had been approached by one of Colonel Gaddafi's sons. He had several sons: Al-Saadi was a footballer in Italy with Perugia at the time, but it was from another son, Saif-al-Islam Gaddafi, who headed the country's international investment portfolio, Libyan Arab Foreign Investment Company (LAFICO). It was Lafico that had the alleged interest in Palace. Basically, he had a bunch of money and he was meant to go and spread the word about how wonderful Libya was by investing in western institutions and companies and had taken a 31.5% stake in Juventus.

This Investment Fund, or figures purporting to be working on its behalf, had apparently approached the Chairman that summer, immediately after our promotion, tentatively suggesting that they might have an interest in buying Palace. I'm pretty sure it never reached the point of undertaking due diligence and I don't think Simon Jordan ever directly met the Libyans. I imagine they were using western lawyers and go-betweens to float the ideas and it came to nothing. However, at the time, for The Guardian it was an interesting story, with interest from those at the front and back of the book. I hadn't told the Sports Desk for a few weeks, so as to try and check out exactly what had happened, but on the eve of pre-season I finally mentioned it to them. They asked me to get Simon Jordan to comment before going any further.

I was working in the north-west at the time, covering Liverpool and Everton, so other than being a fan, didn't have much contact with the Club. However, Simon knew me and we got on quite well. He took my call on that Friday and we had a lengthy chat. He had always told me previously that anything he said to me was on-the-record and that he doesn't do off-the-record. We had a general chat about promotion and his disenchantment with being involved in football then. I casually enquired that I'd heard that the Libyans might want to buy in to the club and whether there's anything in that, privately expecting him to deny there was any truth in it. But he was very matter-of-fact about it. The following quotes are the ones I used verbatim in The Guardian:

'I've been told that Gadafy (sic) and his son are interested in acquiring Palace. If they did, I'd consider it. Gadafy is not a name which necessarily inspires enthusiasm from the British public, it comes with a degree of stigma but, if there is formal contact, we'd look to see if a deal could be best for the club. If Gadafy's money was able to progress Palace and allow them to compete at the top of the tree and be a successful football club, then one would have to take that under consideration.'

The paper ran with the story the next day in two forms. A front-page piece on Gaddafi wanting to buy Palace and then a double spread interview in the Sports section with Simon Jordan about his current feelings about football in general. Some of the other papers picked it up and Iain Dowie was asked about it after the Glens game. He said he had been given assurances that nothing was happening and the Chairman remained very committed to the club.

On Monday morning, I was on the receiving end of a long call from Simon, who began by saying he wasn't very happy with me. I could understand that given the story had generated something of a life of its own and had clearly impinged upon the first-team, given that the Manager had been asked about it. Perhaps in my naivety, I hadn't really seen that coming. We spoke and argued our respective cases. It transpired that he was particularly disappointed at the way Selhurst Park had been described as 'ramshackle' in the front-page piece – something I hadn't even written myself, but had been sub-edited in.

Then the Sports section had used an unflattering, dated picture of him in the bright red jacket he'd worn four years ago at his first press conference as Chairman of the club. Again, not something I had any input on. That said, my name was on the top of both pieces, so I understood his frustrations on those fronts. Although we parted on okay terms, he said he wasn't going to speak to The Guardian ever again. Within a year though, he'd started a well-received column in The Observer, effectively The Guardian's sister paper, which was trailed in The Guardian with a big interview by Michael Walker the previous day."

Leaving aside Wales, who have clubs competing in the English League system, Palace have visited the other Home Nations on relatively few occasions across our history. The Belfast tour was only the club's third visit to Northern Ireland in a hundred years and, at the time of writing, they have not been back since.

From the end of World War Two to the early seventies, Palace regularly faced Scottish opposition in home friendlies. Queen of the South, Clyde, Third Lanark, St. Mirren, Hamilton Academicals, Aberdeen, Dundee United, Morton and Partick Thistle, all appeared at Selhurst Park, sometimes twice.

However, Palace only made a handful of visits to Scotland, the first coming in a three game post-season tour in 1952. The tour opened with a charity match against Dundee United drawing 1-1, before facing the representative sides of Inverness and Moray. The second game was played in Inverness, the day after the game at Tannadice where Palace had travelled by bus for over an hour after the game to stay in Pitlochry, before another long journey the next morning.

Given all the travelling, it was perhaps understandable that this game ended in a 3-1 defeat, with the local press gleefully noting that if it had not have been for some heroics from Bob Anderson in the Palace goal, the score would have been much higher. Palace redeemed themselves two days later with a 2-1 win against the Moray side, in a game played at Elgin City's Borough Briggs ground.

Our three other visits north of the border came in the same 1972/73 season. A successful away pre-season 4-1 win against Dundee, having played their United neighbours at home the week prior. A two-legged tie against Heart of Midlothian in the Texaco Cup in the September and our final trip to date was against Aberdeen, coincidentally the very first Scottish visitors to Selhurst Park in 1948, who were soundly beaten 3-0. The Dons also lost 1-0 at Selhurst in the mid-sixties. This time however, our hosts gained their revenge in a midweek 2-0 defeat at a cold and raw Pittodrie, early in January 1973.

The Texaco International League Competition, to give the tournament its full name, ran for five seasons between 1970 and 1975. For the first two years, the competition invited teams from Northern Ireland and the Republic of Ireland. By the time Crystal Palace was invited to take part, the competition was solely for Anglo-Scottish teams. Palace's involvement against Hearts was short-lived, losing 1-0 in both legs. One of my early Palace memories is being allowed to go to the midweek home leg game and getting horribly confused about the concept of away goals counting double.

Since that season, there have only been two home games against Scottish opposition. First, a hastily-arranged friendly on a Saturday in February 1978 against Hibernian, when both clubs had already exited their respective FA Cups. The visitors winning by a single goal in a dire contest.

The second fixture was an altogether happier – and warmer – affair when we entertained Dundee for Julian Speroni's Testimonial post-season in 2015. Dundee fans relished their trip to South London and made a real night of it. Some firm friendships were formed that evening and if it had been up to the fans, there would have been a return game at Dens Park in the next pre-season.

The game finished 4-3 to Palace, although the Eagles had been 4-1 up going into the final stages of the game. Speroni started for Palace and played a half for each side. There was a story, probably apocryphal, that Dundee were supposed to be awarded a last minute penalty, which Julian Speroni would come upfield and duly dispatch. However, this piece of theatre was not communicated to the referee who blew for full time. Not sure I buy it, but it's a heart-warming tale nevertheless.

14

DEUTSCHLAND '05

After a poor start, Palace's 2004/05 Premier League campaign went right down to the wire. On the last day, no team had yet been relegated. Palace was one of the four teams that could fill the three relegation spots, the others being Norwich, West Brom and Southampton.

Palace had played Southampton at home in the penultimate game of the season. We were 2-1 up deep into injury-time; a result that would have relegated the Saints and put Palace in pole position to stay up. With the last kick of the game, Southampton equalised. Palace now needed to win away at Charlton to ensure staying up. The Addicks revelled in the fact that they earned a 2-2 draw, by virtue of another late equaliser, which relegated a club they saw as bitter rivals. In truth, Palace had been the architects of our own demise, the week previous. West Brom claimed the reprieve, though it was a brief stay of execution, as they dropped the following year.

Palace managed to retain the services of Iain Dowie as Manager post-relegation, meanwhile the club management was silent on pre-season plans. There had been a strong suggestion that we had been invited to play the inaugural game of TSV 1860 München's new stadium. The stadium that was being shared with Bayern München and was to be one of the 2006 World Cup stadia. Unfortunately, our relegation had thrown this into doubt.

A return to Northern Ireland seemed unlikely, if only because the standard of opposition was felt to be lacking last year. It was the end of June before Palace confirmed a two-game trip to southern Bavaria, though sadly not to play 1860, as newly-promoted West Ham had stepped in to take our place. Instead, the tour would take place in little-known villages to the south of Munich, taking on Czech Republic UEFA Qualifiers FK Teplice and German Bundesliga new boys, Eintracht Frankfurt.

Colonel Britain lived near Frankfurt at the time and he was able to provide a lot of helpful travel advice to prospective travellers, as well as being delighted that Palace would play in his own backyard. Well, almost.

Sue and I were out road-tripping in southern Turkey when the tour was finally confirmed, but by the end of the day she had managed to get inexpensive flights, hotels and hire car sorted out for this year's crew: Gibbo, his partner Tracy Peto and, of course, Safety. News of the tour destination did not go down well with Rob Ellis. He had been longing for Palace to tour Germany. Rob was, however, in the middle of a year-long trip around the Americas with Caroline. A cheeky weekend jaunt back to Europe was quietly researched, but tactfully never actually broached. Rob has still to reveal whether that was due to the cost or wanting to preserve his relationship. His sudden disappearance to Germany on the off-chance of seeing Palace back in 1998 remained a bit of an issue.

The proliferation of budget airlines gave us several options for scoring a cheap flight to southern Germany. Figuring we would need a hire car anyway, we elected to fly into the little-known Karlsruhe-Baden airport. From there, we drove down the autobahn to Munich on the Wednesday and, other than a minor hiccup, the plan ran smoothly. After rising at stupid o'clock for the 7:20am flight out of Stansted, we suffered a minor sweat when the M11 was closed, but we got there with about fifteen minutes left to check in. A closer shave than we'd planned, but nothing compared to the return trip.

A couple of years before, on a German football trip, Gibbo and I, together with Rob and Essex, had driven a route from Baden-Baden as far as Ulm. And what a stunning drive that was, through the Black Forest. Sadly, as we flew in on matchday, we didn't have time to take the same scenic route and so had to settle for the less well-featured autobahn. The flight and three-hour drive to Munich were uneventful and soporific.

However, we got a wake-up call on arriving in the city centre. We were greeted by blocked off roads and police with huge rifles cordoning off a German/Iraqi conference taking place close to our hotel. After checking in, we headed off to the main railway station to organise tickets for the 45 minute journey to Miesbach, where the Teplice game was taking place. At last, it was time to blow the considerable froth off our first beers of the trip, while we waited for the hourly train service.

On the train, the city quickly receded and the Alps drew enticingly close. Miesbach is a typical picture-postcard pretty Bavarian village. Upon arrival, we exchanged notes with various other groups of Palace fans milling around, as to the whereabouts of the ground. Hoover and his crew had decided to make tracks there with an hour and a half to go to the 6pm kick off time. What some people will do for a programme. We found a decent bar in the main square and got tucked into some more beers and some excellent local grub. Safety's quest for cider almost took a nasty turn when they tried to serve him with half a litre of apple juice topped up with beer.

At 5.15pm, we received a call from the advance party who had gone to recce the ground.

> "It's pretty basic but the good news is they've got a 'beer and sausage' tent. The bad news is that it's considerably further than it looks and it's all uphill, so you'd better leave now. There's no pavement in places and Hoover has managed to fall into a hedge. He's now really cross because, as well as being covered in cuts and scratches, there are no programmes."

We decided to do the only sensible thing: order another round and a large taxi, which duly deposited us at the ground in time for a quick pint before the action. The Palace turnout was admirable, over forty fans had made the game and were made very welcome by the locals. The turnout certainly seemed to catch some of our club officials out and, judging by their faces, they were less than pleased with the attention. Hoover pointed out to them: "If you could get us into Europe regularly we'd probably be less bothered about doing these sort of trips." He was lying through his teeth, of course, we live for these trips.

The game was a brutal affair, recalling memories of the 1991 Levski Sofia encounter in Gijon. A confetti of cards littered the game, including two reds in the first half. The first, a straight red for Teplice's Karel, who took out Dougie Freedman off the ball. Then our young defender Aaron Fray earned a second yellow for a rather innocuous tackle, although his first booking in immediate retaliation for the assault on Freedman should really have been a straight red. Just before the half ended, the referee stopped the game to read the riot act to both Managers. Although his sermon was delivered in German, both Managers understood his "cut it out!" instructions.

I was reporting on the game for the *South London Press* and taking photos on my new and expensive camera, though Mr Cad was also there in his official capacity. The combination of trying to write notes about the flow of the game, as well as taking pictures, meant I totally missed Fray's dismissal. It was only my grumbling at half-time about our lack of penetration against ten men that I was put straight. Embarrassment in print was narrowly avoided.

Palace were trailing 1-0 at the break to a very early goal from the Czech side and changed their entire line-up for the second half. In goal was Trinidad's Shaka Hislop, a surprise trialist, who was currently out of contract after three years at Portsmouth. Palace equalised early in the half after AJ was sent tumbling in the box from another crude challenge. He made no mistake from the spot.

A hospital pass across the middle just moments later led to Teplice's winner which, in fairness, was a fine strike from distance, leaving Hislop with no chance. Despite the referee's commandment, the rough-housery continued from the Czech side and AJ was eventually taken off for his own protection. His replacement was Ryan Hall, who should have by rights played for the whole second half, but for Fray's dismissal. Hall thought he had notched a late equaliser, only to see the offside flag cancel out the goal.

Knowing it was unlikely that we'd fancy the long walk back into town, 'our' cabbie came and found us after the game, returning us to our favourite bar. The landlord was delighted to see us again. More beer was sunk in fine company and we staggered off to catch the penultimate train back into Munich. It was raining back in the city, so we headed for the nearest bar outside the station and got stuck into more beer. Before long, the singing started and we were surprised to find the locals fairly tolerant of our behaviour. At least, they tolerated us right up to the official closing time of 1am, whereupon we were poured out of the bar with a firm: "The Bier is finished!"

The locals were, of course, all sat patiently around the horseshoe-shaped bar, waiting for the noisy Englanders to disappear so they could have a lock-in. We were just too tired and emotional to plead our case and staggered off to find our beds. The walk seemed to perk up one of our number – upon arrival at our hotel, Safety demanded to know if they had a bar. They did not and he couldn't quite get his head around the night porter's offer to serve him a vodka and lemonade in his room. That was probably for the best.

The next morning it was something of a surprise to find all five of us had just about made it down to breakfast, but one look at the faces around the table confirmed that the night before had been über-messy. Not quite as messy as the Hoover's night however, who was right now back in Miesbach, trying to retrieve his expensive sunglasses from the railway track, where he had dropped them as he stumbled onto the last train home to the city.

We eventually girded ourselves to take in the sights, but we were soon ensconced in an Aussie bar, gingerly sipping from our first beers of the day. After a trip to the architecturally freaky Olympiapark in the afternoon, we set off on the breathtaking drive to Innsbruck in Austria, and a fun-filled Friday was spent getting lost up in the mountains and discovering Safety's affinity with Alpine cows. Apparently they are *so* much cuter than the British varieties.

That evening, we drove west for an Austrian Second Division game, Austria Lustenau v FC Gratkorn. The standard was not high and the first half was deadly dull. The second period was enlivened by early goals, some bottle throwing and the most ineffective ejection ever. On the way over, we had been winding up the girls about how Lustenau were known as the 'Millwall of Austrian football'. When a full plastic bottle of beer was lobbed at a Gratkorn player, as Lustenau took the lead, we almost believed it ourselves. Within moments, Lustenau had made it two and we finally managed to work out what bizarre track the tannoy was playing as a goal celebration: 'Rama Lama Ding Dong' by Darts. That sort of cheese would only happen on the continent.

Gratkorn pulled one back with the goal of the game, a strike from range from their left back and shortly thereafter, another bottle sailed towards the Gratkorn keeper. This time the stewards waded into the throng behind the goal and, as I popped out for a wee, I spotted no less than eight security guards and stewards ushering away your typical meaty, tattooed skinhead, who proceeded to flick the vicky's at anyone who caught his eye. Less than five minutes later, he came striding back along the terrace with a fresh bottle in hand! His return was greeted like that of the prodigal son by the Lustenau massive.

The game finished 2-1 and we drove back into Germany to Füssen, the border town hosting the Eintracht Frankfurt game. Arriving two hours later, the town was in inky, rainy darkness, with street lighting appearing to be a rare commodity. Finally, we found our hotel in the hamlet of Bad Faulenbach. Our late arrival and lack of basic lighting saw us forgo the idea of exploring Füssen and we hit the hotel bar for a couple instead. The barmaid's name was Erni and she pulled the slowest Pils in the West.

In daylight, it became quickly apparent that our hotel was in some sort of financial administration, with many dusty and abandoned corridors and whole floors piled high with broken beds and dirty mattresses. Thanks to our late arrival and lack of a session the night before, we were up relatively early and in good shape to tackle the day. Getting out of the hotel was a priority, so we took a short stroll into town. Füssen is truly beautiful. A Hansel and Gretel fairytale town with gingerbread houses and an icing sugar castle. The sort of place you could imagine medieval knights and peasants roaming the streets. And, to our astonishment, that is exactly what we saw as we turned the corner onto the main street.

It turned out this weekend was the annual KaiserFest – an excuse for locals to dress in period costume and march around the cobbled streets for the whole weekend. Our game was to be a major part of the festival's events schedule. Roll up for Ye Olde Fussball.

Neuschwanstein is *the* iconic German castle pictured in a thousand dentist waiting rooms and of *Chitty Chitty Bang Bang* fame. Our morning was spent exploring there and, thanks to the lack of buses, which inconveniently stopped over lunchtime, rather more of the early afternoon than we would have liked.

Back into town, we had a chance meeting in the street with Peter Jordan and our fitness coach John Harbin, who promptly told us that we'd better not start any trouble – which was nice. Peter was not his usual chatty self either, looking harassed and pre-occupied. We soon guessed why, as the news arrived that the Centenary game against Inter Milan had been called off. The circumstances surrounding the on-off-on status of the fixture was covered in an earlier chapter.

It was my turn to go on the programme run, accompanied by a few hardy souls who also wanted to score their match tickets early. Despite the modest local ground being less than 10 minutes' walk away along the main road, we got hopelessly lost in the 'burbs, trying to locate the main entrance. At one stage, we even had to scale an allotment fence with several articles of clothing getting torn in the process.

Programmes secured, there was plenty of time to nip back into town via a more direct route and get back on the beer. By this time, our crowd had been befriended by some Eintracht supporters and the main square was awash with both sets of fans, toasting each other and singing each other's songs rather loudly. Handily, Eintracht Frankfurt are also known as 'The Eagles'. After a brief interruption by another flag-waving, medieval marching band, the beers and singing continued to flow at pace, until it was finally time to leave for the game. The atmosphere could not have been better, with almost a hundred Palace fans there. Again, several more fans had elected to travel out just for the weekend game.

Amongst our fans were a few that we recognised as being associated with Palace's hooligan firm, the Dirty 30. However, they made no trouble and appeared to be enjoying the atmosphere the same as everyone else. Later when writing about the trip in *Palace Echo*, I made what I felt was an innocuous punchline out of their presence by dubbing them 'the slightly grubby ten'. This throwaway joke – some silly wordplay on their moniker – did not go down well with their members, although it took a couple of years for the row to truly blow up.

The game kicked off at 5pm in the lengthening shadows of the gorgeous Alpine mountains and those hills were alive with the sound of Palace. The game was of much better quality, though less-incident packed than Wednesday's match. The first half was a quiet affair restricted mostly to the midfield areas. Palace, again fielding several substitutes, scored early in the second half through Jon Macken – his first goal in a Palace shirt. Something of a rarity as it turned out, given he only managed two goals in competitive first team action during his Palace career.

Frankfurt got themselves into gear after the goal and Hislop was called upon to make a string of saves. They thought they had finally made a breakthrough when Darren Ward gave away a penalty, but Hislop was equal to that too. The joy didn't last long though as Palace succumbed to a Van Lint header from a corner. Frankfurt went in search of a winner, but Palace managed to hold out for the draw.

With beers and shots available in copious amounts in the ground, the end of the game saw many fans in a very advanced state of over-refreshment. One of those was Sue, who had become separated from the others and, rather worryingly, had already wandered off in completely the wrong direction to the town. After walking along the river on her own, almost as far as the Austrian border, she finally managed to summon enough presence of mind to call us and admit she was lost – as was my patience by this stage. Gibbo managed to direct his sister to look for a road sign and then called a taxi to retrieve her. Back into town, several stiff black coffees were required before cordial relations were restored.

The need for food had the effect of dividing our support between several bars, rather than congregating in one place as we had before the game. We took the food option and re-emerged just in time to see yet another medieval march, this time by blazing torchlight. In one square, the marchers formed a circle whilst their chief rendered a lusty operatic number, completely unfazed by strains of 'Glad All Over' being belted out of a nearby bar.

We watched the fireworks, then found ourselves in a funky, punky bar where we drank until the wee hours in company of some genial local youths. Consequently, the next morning we were wrecked. Safety had hi-tailed it back to Munich early in pursuit of some speedway, however the rest of us were in poor fettle. Suddenly the planned trip to the FC Zurich v Grasshoppers derby had lost its appeal, as it would involve a total of six hours' driving. Our flight was at 9.40pm and a Zurich trip would also involve a tight deadline for check-in.

We narrowed our options down to two choices: mooch around the lovely town of Füssen, enjoying a nice lunch and more of the KaiserFest, before taking a leisurely afternoon drive back to Baden-Baden. Or drive an hour further away from the airport to Garmisch-Partenkirchen, then clamber around a mountain and explore a gorge recommended in the guidebooks. All I can say is, we must have still been drunk when we chose the latter.

By mid-afternoon we found ourselves – still feeling unwell – at the wrong end of Partnach Gorge, which we'd set out to explore, facing a locked gate. We'd ignored several 'Klamm Geschlossen' signs at points along the route, however, this time – and only now reinforced by said gate – did it dawn on us this meant 'gorge closed'. Our only means of return to the car now involved following paths up and over a steep hill. We had thought we'd be near to the car by this point and the hour and a half it took to get back there meant we would be seriously pushing it for our flight. On the plus side, the strenuous exercise meant the alcohol had finally left our systems.

Thank goodness there were few speed limits on the German autobahns back then. What there was, however, was a load of traffic and some appalling wet weather to contend with. Then we almost ran out of petrol ten miles from the airport. So our nerves were utterly shredded as we finally pulled into the airport at 9.10pm. There was no way they would let us on the flight that late. But then came the first slice of luck we'd had all day. Due to the German Grand Prix held that same afternoon, all flights had been extremely busy and long delays had accumulated. Our flight had not yet landed.

Ryanair were still able to check us in, while the plane was still airborne. An unscheduled stopover was avoided literally by seconds, as the plane thundered over to land, with me still sprinting from another part of the airport, after returning the hire car. Half an hour later, I was still shaking from the adrenaline rush, as we boarded the flight home. A bizarre, but ultimately happy ending to what our crew agreed was an excellent tour. And all the better for not having been held in a big city.

It was, perhaps, quite fitting that a tour of Germany took place in Palace's Centenary season. Although the professional Crystal Palace Football Club was formed in 1905, there had been an amateur side with the same name competing since 1861, albeit not continuously. The debate is still ongoing as to whether the club should claim to have been founded in 1861 rather than 1905. I suspect it will never be resolved to everyone's satisfaction. (Me? I'm an 1861 man.)

In 1896, the amateurs played an exhibition game at the Crystal Palace against a German FA representative side. The game was a complete mismatch, with Palace winning 13-0. This game had failed to attract much local interest, with an attendance of just 500 in an arena designed to hold 50,000 which, at the time, also hosted the FA Cup Final. The Club's committee decided to stick to attracting the bigger names in English football and not to invite overseas opposition again.

As you will discover in a later chapter, Palace almost played in Hamburg in 1914, but instead Palace's first footballing foray to Germany was, perhaps surprisingly, only two years after the end of World War Two. That tour did not involve games against German sides. Instead, the opposition was provided by British military sides: Combined Services and a British Army XI.

The players that formed the representative sides were all attached to professional clubs in England, Scotland and Wales, so it was no easy test for Palace. Many of the opposition players played in both games. The matches took place in Wuppertal and Bad Oeynhausen at opposite ends of the North Rhine Westphalia region, with the touring party being billeted at Army bases there.

The touring party left London on Monday 30th June and travelled on the overnight ferry from Harwich to the Hook of Holland. The next day was spent travelling across the Netherlands and West Germany on a train bound for Hamm, with lunch being taken in Bentheim. From Hamm, the squad travelled to Oberhausen where they were met that evening by the Games Secretary of the British Army Sports Board for onward travel to Wuppertal.

After a visit to the ground the following day, the players were free to see the local sights, doubtless including the Schwebebahn. This is the oldest electric elevated monorail with hanging cars in the world and is unique in Germany. The game against the Combined Services XI took place at 6pm that evening at the Zoo Stadium (now home to SV Wuppertaler) and resulted in a 2-2 draw. This was followed by a reception with dinner for both sides.

On Thursday morning, the party travelled over a hundred miles to Bad Oeynhausen, where they had the rest of the afternoon and the following day free, although you'd imagine that they would have trained at some point. On Saturday, the squad visited the ground in the morning and returned that afternoon for another 6pm kick off. This time, the opponents were drawn solely from the British Army and Palace were defeated by a single goal.

Another dinner reception followed the game at the NAAFI Club where such delights as celery soup, cold ham and tongue and apricot melba were served to both sides. The touring squad departed Bad Oeynhausen on Sunday afternoon, returning to London Liverpool Street Station around midday on Monday 7th July.

It was thirty-nine years before Palace first came up against a German side, Alemannia Aachen, as part of the 1976 pre-season tour, as previously covered. There was a much shorter gap until Palace's next visit to Germany in 1982 – a three game pre-season tour in Northern Germany. Dave Hynes was nineteen at the time and this was his first trip following Palace abroad:

"I was due to fly to Hamburg with Steve Carleton. He worked for British Caledonian at the time and was able to get a cheap fare by going standby. It turned out that the plane was full, so Steve was unable to get on. A stewardess gave me the news just before the plane took off. I arrived at Hamburg airport not knowing how to get to the hotel. It was my first time in the country and I spoke no German. I was approached by a couple of guys asking if I was a British builder looking for work. I went to the bus station and the first driver I spoke to was an older gentleman who spoke good English. He said he wasn't going to the hotel but would drop me close by with directions from there.

Steve eventually turned up the next day having had to fly into Düsseldorf and get a train north. We also met up with another Palace fan called John Bellars, whose Mum was German and he spoke the language. We met another guy who was on holiday with his wife in Baden Baden, but hating it. Although he was a Portsmouth fan, he had found out about the game and decided to jump on a train.

There was more travel trouble to follow when we arrived at the location for the first game. We rolled up close to kick-off time but there was hardly anyone about, only a few locals playing cards in the clubhouse. They told us the game had been moved elsewhere. They tried not to laugh and we learned the hard way the definition of 'schadenfreude'. To make matters worse we missed a goal fest, with Palace winning 4-3.

The next game was at SV Lurup. The previous season, the club had competed for the first time in the Oberliga Nord at the third tier of German Football. Unfortunately they had come straight back down into the Hamburg Regional League. Prior to our match, there was an exhibition game featuring former West Germany World Cup stars, including Uwe Seller and Wolfgang Overath. I'm not really sure what the locals thought when our players took to the field afterwards.

We ran into Palace's club secretary Alan Leather there and Steve asked him why the venue change for the previous game wasn't publicised anywhere. His response: 'Why would we?' didn't go down at all well. It wasn't the last encounter we would have with Mr Leather that day. The Lurup Chairman wanted a Palace shirt to get signed by the players and hang in the clubhouse. Alan Leather demanded that I give him the shirt I had on! I refused as I had nothing else to wear. It seemed like an odd request as the club could surely have donated a spare from the kitbag.

Before the game, we also had a frosty encounter with the Chairman, Ron Noades. We saw him walking on the pitch in shorts drinking a bottle of beer and said hello. He fixed us with a cold stare and said 'What the hell are you doing here? Are you here to cause trouble?' I was really disappointed by his unfriendly attitude.

Palace lost the game 3-1 but we managed to crash the reception afterwards in the clubhouse. They had laid on a band and David Giles got up telling everyone 'I'm from Wales, like Tom Jones' and proceeded to sing 'It's not Unusual' and 'Delilah'. The locals didn't know what to make of him.

I had my eye on some club desk flags as a little souvenir, but Alan Leather spotted me taking them. 'Put them back' he barked but the German Chairman came over and said I could have them. I walked away with the flags, smiling at Mr Leather as I went. The district of Lurup is quite close to the then German Champions Hamburger SV's Volksparkstadion. We were able to go in and take a photo on the centre spot; no-one was bothered back then.

The final game of the tour was the following day at SV Börnsen, who had just been promoted and would be playing in the same division as Lurup. The tiny Hamfeldroad ground was an eye opener. It felt like it was in the middle of a forest, I have a picture of Tommy Langley taking a corner, surrounded by nothing but trees, which still makes me smile. Along one side of the pitch was a disused old railway carriage, still on its rusted wheels, that the Manager and reserves used if the weather was bad.

Whoever designed the match ticket had over-excitedly described us as FA Cup Winners 1982 instead of quarter-finalists. Someone had then been given the thankless task of ruling through that line with black felt pen, however, the incorrect wording could still clearly be seen. The ticket also mentioned Palace having 'eight international players' – I've still no idea who they might have been.

Palace won that final game 4-2 and we finally had a nice interaction with a Palace official. The newly-appointed Manager, Alan Mullery offered us a lift back into the city. I sat next to Steve Galliers and opposite Henry Hughton and Kevin Mabbutt, listening to the lads planning their final night out in the city.

When Mullery boarded the coach, the players started barracking him: 'Mullers, Mullers, get the beers in' and, to his credit, he went back into the clubhouse and organised a couple of crates for the journey. I'm not sure what changed between this trip and the first game of the season. In his first set of programme notes, Mullery said he'd found the team ill-disciplined "but now they all wear suits and call me boss!"

The actual opposition for the first game of that tour is a matter of debate. Prior to the fixture, the *Croydon Advertiser* declared that Palace would be facing VfR Neumünster. However, a previous club history written by official historian, The Reverend Nigel Sands, listed the opponents as a Combined Flensburg XI, which also coincides with Dave Hynes' own memory.

It occurs to me that perhaps we were due to face Neumünster, but this game was called off and the game against Flensburg was hastily arranged, which might also explain the change in venue. In an effort to test this theory, I asked one of Palace's staunchest German fans and my good friend, Rüdiger Schwarz, for help. He happens to be a retired local journalist in that area.

VfB Lübeck fan, Rüdi travelled over to England in the seventies. While here, he visited Selhurst and fell in love with Palace. He has followed the club ever since and was one of the original BBS members. He came over to a game in 2000 with his wife and we became friends with him then. He still usually comes to Selhurst at least once a season.

Via the BBS, he would keep us informed about the fortunes of his local club VfB Lübeck. We knew it would only be a matter of time before we would pay him a visit at the Lohmühle Stadion on one of our German weekends. We first went there in December 2003 and have been back very many times since for both home and away games.

Unfortunately, Rüdi also drew a blank in the local archives. Second division Palace's tour against lowly German opposition was simply not seen as particularly newsworthy in 1982, even in the local papers. He had not gone to the games himself as he was studying at Stuttgart University in 1982. He has since shared the same bad luck as Rob in trying to see Palace in his home country. He did, however, tell me that it would not have been unusual for a team derived from players of the clubs based in Flensburg to play in such friendly games and the two biggest clubs in the region did eventually merge.

After that Hamburg tour it took 23 years to return to Germany for our adventure in southern Bavaria. Since then, there have been four further games against German opposition between 2014 and 2019, split equally home and away. Visits to FC Augsburg and Union Berlin, together with the home friendlies against Schalke 04 and Hertha Berlin, will be covered in later chapters.

Adler Freundschaft! Several Palace characters here, including Glenn 'Colonel Britain' Bastin, Jake 'Billingshurst' Edsor, Patrick Maw and the ladies either side of Sue on the right are: Jane "Skate" Vigus & Tracy Peto - July 2005

The Hills are alive with the sound of Palace. At Füssen - July 2005

15

AMERICANOS

The 2005/06 league season was, ultimately, one of disappointment. Palace had been favourites to bounce straight back to the Premier League. Many of these hopes were pinned on the retention of Andrew Johnson, who had agreed to stay at Selhurst. Shortly after a shaky start to the season, Clinton Morrison rejoined and hopes were renewed. Unfortunately, a couple of games later AJ sustained an injury, which meant he was sidelined for a good while.

Palace milled around the play-off positions without ever really threatening the automatic promotion places, eventually finishing sixth. The play-off semi-final pitted the club against the division's form team, Watford. The tie was effectively over after a 3-1 defeat in the first home leg. A goal-less draw at Vicarage Road sealed our fate and our Manager, Iain Dowie, decided that a move further north was in his and his family's best interests. A few days later, when he was unveiled as Charlton's new Manager; eyebrows and court injunctions were raised. He'd not even made it north of the Thames, never mind back to his family in Bolton.

Palace appointed old player favourite Peter Taylor to the helm. Taylor had made his name at Palace in the 1975/76 cup run as a lively winger, before a prestigious move to Spurs. His managerial career had encompassed many league and non-league clubs and included a spell in the England coaching set-up, leading to a one game caretaker appointment to the Senior side, between Kevin Keegan and Sven Goran Eriksson.

Shortly before that home tie, Palace had announced their 2006 pre-season tour to the United States, together with an ambitious plan to launch a franchise club in Maryland. The full story of CPFC USA is told in a later chapter.

The tour, as originally announced, was a three-game affair, opening with the inaugural game of CPFC USA in Annapolis. The second game was an exhibition against the current Major League Soccer (MLS) Champions, LA Galaxy, in Richmond, Virginia. Although David Beckham was a year away from joining the Californian club, they did boast one of the USA's best-known players in striker Landon Donovan.

The final game was to be against Virginia Beach Mariners of the third tier of American football. However, it never happened. Less than a month before the match was due to take place, the club changed ownership. The new owners had no interest in fulfilling the fixture, even though tickets were already on sale at that point.

At the time of the tour announcement, the fans had been prepared for an expensive transatlantic trip. The same source who'd leaked news of the Northern Irish and Germany tours in the previous two years had let slip that Vancouver was our most likely destination. Thus, the tour on the east coast of the States, with its multiple options of less costly flights, came as a relief.

A small number of the regular travelling groups declared their intent to attend. The Stateside fans were similarly excited to have the opportunity to see Palace in action first-hand. Plans were hatched on the BBS for pre-match bars and meet-ups.

When news of the Virginia Beach Mariners postponement finally came through, the travellers were handed a double whammy. Most people had already made plans to travel there and booked expensive hotels, but Palace had now arranged a friendly at Swindon on the Sunday, the day when most travellers had booked to fly back. In addition to the two of us, Sue also took charge of the flight bookings for Hoover and Pete Bonthrone. She managed to change the flights to the Saturday evening without too much extra expense, although we all lost a night's pre-booked accommodation in Virginia Beach. This would give us enough time for a dash down the M4 to the County Ground, providing, of course, the flight was on time.

With no official press officer or photographer making this tour, the club asked me to step in and provide match reports and photographs from the games. The *South London Press* had already asked me to provide both, so I was more than happy to oblige. It was also a World Cup year and it seemed no sooner had we got home from an amazing adventure in Germany, than we were off again.

We arrived in Washington DC on Friday afternoon, with the first game scheduled for the Saturday evening. Pete and Hoover were staying at a different hotel to Sue and I, so our cab dropped them there. The hotel looked nice enough, but it was away from the centre out in the 'burbs, near a major freeway interchange. It is fair to say that my wife has a taste for the finer things in life and is an absolute demon when it comes to getting the best value out of hotel and airline loyalty schemes. Sue had secured us a night at the Hilton, just two blocks from the White House. As you will discover, our experience of Washington DC was somewhat different to that of Pete and Hoover.

Due to jetlag, Sue and I were up very early and so we headed out for a whistle-stop walking tour of the Nation's Capital, before picking up a hire car at noon. We headed down to Annapolis, via a quick pitstop at the impressive 35,000 capacity

Navy-Marine Corps Memorial Stadium, where we had initially thought the game would be staged. No such luck, though the actual venue was certainly unique. We had decided to stay over in Annapolis for a couple of nights, whereas most fans, including Pete and Hoover, had chosen to head back to Washington after the match.

The game was played at the US Naval Academy, which was also Palace's training camp for the tour. It is a working naval area that requires photo ID before you are allowed to set foot on the grounds. Non-natives such as ourselves were required to show their passports. The pitch area was a little underwhelming compared to the stadium we had visited on the outskirts of town. Just a couple of bleachers on two sides, a hastily arranged merchandise area and a bar. The grass on the pitch also seemed overly long, but least the there was a scenic view across the Severn River. Even that became a double-edged sword, as biting insects emerged in the murky, humid evening air.

This did not dampen the spirits of the travelling faithful, who were in fine voice. In mid-June, Sue had spoken to Jim Cherneski, the Sporting Director of CPFC USA, to try and clarify the situation with the Virginia Beach game. While in conversation, he said the thing he was most looking forward to was English fans coming to show the locals how vocal support was done. They are a bit quiet here, he admitted. He would not have been disappointed by the Red and Blue Army that assembled for duty that evening. Richard from the Gijon trip came over along with his compadre Graham Attaway. The late Graham Maskell, someone who ran Palace coaches all over England in the seventies, accompanied by well-known local referee, Michael O'Keefe were out there too.

Baldy, The Colonel, Dave Hynes and Thirsty had come together to make the trip and, along with the Hoover, led the singing, backed by a number of ex-pat Palace fans and BBS alumni, including Phil Manning (Palace fan From Alabama), Will Block (Winston the Dog), John O'Connor (Big Bad John) and a chap seemingly only known as The Vicar. They had travelled from all points of the United States to attend the game. There was even a Palace fan on honeymoon with his new wife, who literally stumbled across Palace on tour on the day.

The Colonel spied a couple of young American boys wearing Manchester United kits. He strode off purposefully in their direction and appeared to be having words with their mother. A few moments later, the two boys reappeared wearing brand new Palace shirts. The Colonel had been asking whether he could buy them both Palace shirts, on the condition that they would immediately replace their United jerseys, which they were very happy to do.

The CPFC USA team had been drawn from the best players from local universities and colleges who were not already signed to a team. Amongst them was Maurice Edu, who went onto play for Glasgow Rangers. Palace UK were also sporting some new faces, including a high profile trialist: striker Jay Bothroyd, who had been released by Charlton. It was Bothroyd who opened the scoring on eleven minutes, although the goal was credited to Lewis Grabban. Bothroyd shot from the left side of the box and Grabban raced in to see the ball home. He was credited with the goal by the PA announcer, but I was taking photos right by the goal and I can assure you that he did not get a final touch.

The Americans responded to going behind with some tough tackling, which resulted in a cruciate injury for promising young left back Rhoys Wiggins. I managed to capture the challenge on camera, and it was widely used in the local press back home. Wiggins said in a later interview, that he had that picture pinned up at home to motivate his recovery.

Edu was the culprit, with an awful challenge from behind. At home, it would have been a straight red, friendly or not. So instead it was Palace who were down to 10 men, while an unplanned substitute was readied. USA made the most of this and scored their first ever goal through Rade Kokovic. Palace regained the lead quickly through Grabban and sealed the deal straight after half-time when Tommy Black headed home. Palace should have scored many more, but for the fine goalkeeping of Chris Seitz, who made a string of quality saves, including a Dougie Freedman penalty.

The local crowd of about 500 seemed to enjoy the occasion and the singing, although at times they didn't seem to be paying an awful lot of attention to the game. Joining me pitch-side on photo duties that night was James Calder, an ex-pat Palace fan originally from West Norwood who was now resident in Washington DC. James was someone I would get to know much better on subsequent tours.

After grabbing a word with Peter Taylor, for the match report, we headed to The Ram's Head pub, where post-match revelry was in full swing in the downstairs bar. The area had been effectively annexed by Palace fans. The walls were covered in Palace flags.

Crystal Palace branded vodka and gin had been discovered behind the bar and Phil from Alabama was dishing out shots of Woodford Reserve bourbon. Hardly anyone seemed that impressed with it, though. However, there is always one idiot who decides not only to down his shot but to 'minesweep' the leftovers. Yes, the idiot was me. The singing and conga lines continued into the small hours, it was a fantastic night and, judging by the comments of the locals, a little different to what they were used to. They loved it just the same.

As soon as I stepped out into the fresh air, I knew I was in trouble. One of those ubiquitous American newspaper vending machines nearby the pub received an unexpected early delivery. Quite how I made it back to the hotel, I'm not sure, as my legs had gone. The next day was probably my worst trip hangover since Italy

1990. Luckily, this time we didn't have anywhere to be the next day, so I slept in, pretty much the whole day.

Back in Washington, Hoover and Pete had some bother of an entirely different kind, as Hoover recalls.

"During the afternoon we had a meet up on a static boat for drinks with some of the other Palace fans out there. Most began to drift away after 9pm, but Pete and I stayed on for a night-cap. We headed back to the hotel around 10pm. Pete and I disagreed as to which way it was. In the end, he agreed that I was probably right and off we went. We walked up a side street on a hill and the streetlights weren't up to much, so it just got darker and darker until we were in this housing estate. I didn't remember coming down this way and thought maybe I have got it wrong, but my pride was not ready to admit it yet. I was just praying there would be a right turn that I would recognise.

I remember passing a guy who was sitting outside his house on the path, he had a dirty old string vest on and looked like a tramp. It was a sticky, hot, humid night. Pete started to question whether we had got this right, but before I could answer another character materialised. I don't know where he'd come from, whether he'd come out of one of the houses or a side-turning and I got the feeling he was deliberately following us. We kept our cool, not wanting to panic. It was a fairly straight road with no turnings and we wanted to stay on, what appeared to us to be the main drag. Thus, we couldn't really lose him, but the road was taking us further into the estate.

It became pretty clear that he was, indeed, following us, he got right up behind us and pulled a little knife. I remember thinking 'Oh my Christ, here we go – we are in real trouble here.' I mean I could hazard a guess at what he was after, but just what can we do here? I'm completely lost and with Pete, who was in his late sixties then, options were limited. Do I peg it? But I'd easily outrun Pete and I can't leave him on his own. So I decided to front the guy up, shouting angrily "What do you want?" There was a bit of umming and ahhing and posturing, but no actual fisticuffs. I quickly glanced back to Pete, but he wasn't there! He'd already legged it up the road.

I turned back to face the bloke and thought 'well, I better run too' and set off after Pete. After 400 yards I was knackered, but we both kept going, our aggressor half-heartedly gave chase but ceased pretty quickly. We stopped eventually but we were still in the dimly-lit project and totally lost. We didn't fancy knocking on any doors for help. Then, like a scene from Starsky And Hutch, this police car came roaring over the crest of the hill – actually in the air – and slammed to a screaming halt in front of us.

The officers practically manhandled us into the back of their car and angrily demanded to know what we were doing in that area at this time of night? They made it quite clear it was a complete no-go zone. They calmed down when we explained we were simply lost tourists.

> *After we'd been dropped off and had a cup of tea in the room, the whole incident seemed quite unbelievable. In fact, Pete suggested we go back out for another beer, but I made it clear I wasn't going to move from the hotel until the morning!"*

The downtime between the games saw the different travelling parties go their separate ways to explore the multitude of tourist attractions in the area. These included the Smithsonian museums in Washington DC, Shenandoah National Park and the battlegrounds and monuments of the Civil War, before gathering again in Richmond, Virginia for the second, and now final, game of the tour. And only half a game at that.

The Richmond Tap House was the nearest bar to the University of Richmond's Sports Field, where the game would take place. This became the focal point for both the Palace overseas travellers and the North American fans, including ex-pat Trevor Weldon, who I first met in St Vincent. He had driven forty hours from Nova Scotia, picking up Chas, a native New York Palace fan, en route.

The normally sleepy, suburban, side-street bar was completely taken over, much to the delight of both the bar owner and the small band of Wednesday regulars. The Palace 'Glad All Over' CD was played on repeat and the singing got louder each time around as the fans gathered, lubricated by ever-increasing amounts of booze. Baldy and The Colonel managed to down thirteen Long Island Iced Tea cocktails, each one containing five shots, before the game.

Eventually, under ominously darkening skies, it was time to move onto the ground. The antics didn't stop there, with Baldy trying to gate-crash the official Palace team photograph on the pitch. Although not successful, he did end up in a play fight with Kickeroo, Richmond Kickers' kangaroo mascot, much to the delight of the spectators. Kickaroo, who initially appeared sporting an LA Galaxy jersey, was extremely taken with the Palace fans. He ditched his yellow shirt for Palace's gunmetal grey and white away number and spent a good portion of the first half having photos taken with the Palace contingent. There seemed to be more Palace fans at this game than at Saturday's match, but there appeared to be no Galaxy fans present.

Palace started well and were quickly in front after Jon Macken had followed up a rasping long-range Tommy Black shot, which the keeper could only parry. Galaxy equalised through Nagamura after a poor Michael Hughes back pass. Not that Hughes was entirely to blame, the spongey, uneven pitch was causing control issues for both sides.

All through the half, a spectacular thunderstorm could be seen and heard to the east, but the rain only started as the players trooped off for half time. Within a couple of minutes, the downpour had become torrential, defeating Kickeroo's attempt at half-time entertainment, in the form of a game of musical chairs.

As the thunderstorm moved right overhead, the Americans deserted the open terraces for shelter. The Palace fans, however, stood defiantly on. In typical fashion, Pete Bonthrone was sartorially geared up for anything the American weather might have in store. From his shoulder-bag, he produced a large transparent poncho and proceeded to clamber into it. Unfortunately, the pictures of the Red & Blue Army taken during half-time make it look like we're being led by a man inside a giant condom.

There was no sign that the storm was going to move away, so after about 25 minutes the game was officially abandoned under Virginia State safety directives. Both teams were going to field a different line-up in the second half, so those players were understandably frustrated, as was Peter Taylor. Our German winger Marco Reich reacted to the news by slipping off for a crafty smoke under the shelter of the stand, while others came out to meet with the fans.

The fans were denied another chance to see Jay Bothroyd in action, or indeed, the much-vaunted Landon Donovan for Galaxy. We did, however, get to see the now-veteran US midfielder Cobi Jones, still sporting his pineapple-shaped hairdo that had been a talking point during his time in England with Coventry.

After the game, most fans headed back to the Tap House where the party restarted right where it had left off. The daughter of one of the bar's more grouchy regulars was in there that evening. She said that he was always complaining that nothing ever happened in his local, he happened to be out of town that week, so she felt compelled to ring him.

"Daddy, Daddy, there's a load of drunk Crystal Palace soccer fans singing and having a party here tonight". His exact reply to her was not disclosed, but she intimated that he simply refused to believe it.

Dave Hynes remembers that night very well.

"The bar owner had assumed we were there following an English college soccer team and had looked Palace up on the internet. He was surprised and impressed to find out that we were such a big deal, 'You guys have your own website and everything.'

It wasn't just the bar owner who was confused by our friendly invasion. A local lady in the bar asked me 'Why are you all chanting?' I replied 'We aren't chanting, we are singing.' 'Oh honey' she said, 'That ain't singing.'

There was table of around ten local students by the toilets. They weren't exactly scared, but seemed a bit wary and intrigued. I walked past them and said: 'I'd like to apologise on behalf of Her Majesty's Government for our behaviour.' One of them went 'No way man, this is the best night we've had in here for years!'

A bit later, I broke out into the pre-chorus refrain from 'Can't Take My Eyes Off Of You', "Dah, da, dah, da, dah, da-da-da-Dah..." I spotted the barmaid moving her legs to it and she said 'Oooh, I know this one.' Of course, then the chorus started: 'We love you Palace, we f'ing *hate Man U' and she laughed. 'All the time swearing, what's with all the swearing?' She really thought we were going to sing the Frankie Valli song."*

Sadly, I missed out on all this fun. With a print deadline looming, I had to return to the hotel room to pad out a half-match report and process my photos. I returned at closing time to pour Hoover, Pete and my wife into the hire car for the journey back to the hotel. The next morning there were some extremely sore heads and delicate tummies on the trip across to Virginia Beach. At least mine wasn't one. This time.

Our game-turned-beach weekend on the east coast had already been curtailed by the Swindon friendly, but we made the most of our time there. On the Friday, a fans' meet-up had been arranged, which included Pete Redman, who was now living in Bermuda. He had arranged to fly across for business, also expecting to catch a game. Sorrows were duly drowned long into the night, but not before a few of us had headed over to check out the Virginia Beach Mariners stadium, on the off-chance of catching a competitive game at some lower level.

It was not clear exactly what the Mariners' new owner had planned instead. All I can tell you was that when we arrived, they were in the middle of erecting a bouncy castle on the middle of the pitch. In fact, this was to be the last competitive season for the Mariners, as the club was wound up the following March. After a couple of quick snaps we headed off to the meet. The next day, Pete, Hoover, Sue and I were up early for a five-hour drive back to Dulles airport.

Our hopes of getting back home in time for the Swindon game took a dent when we were sat at the end of the runway, waiting for another huge thunderstorm to pass over. After a delay of an hour, we finally took off but, thanks to a tailwind across the Atlantic, we arrived back to Heathrow on schedule – set for a tiring drive down the M4. It was not only the fans who arrived at the County Ground jetlagged as Palace fell behind to two first-half goals, before finally finding their stride and grinding out a 2-2 draw.

The pre-season campaign also featured a midweek home friendly against Portuguese top flight side Boavista. Their squad included new signing Peter Jehle, the Liechtenstein international goalkeeper who had been on trial at Palace as a teenager. Palace opened the scoring with a powerful drive from a new signing of their own, winger Mark Kennedy.

Wholesale changes in the Palace line-up at half-time saw Senegalese international Fary Faye equalise for the club from Porto just a minute into the second half, while most of the crowd – and it appeared the team – were trying to work out who was now playing and in what position. Palace retook the lead from a Jon Macken header midway through the half and were rarely troubled thereafter. It was a rather disappointing showing from the European visitors and Palace's 2-1 victory was more comfortable than the result might suggest.

The tackle that resulted in cruciate ligament damage for Rhoys Wiggins. In Annapolis - July 2006

Paul 'Baldy' Withers kicking off with Kickeroo, the Richmond mascot - July 2006

Under stormy skies. Baldy, Colonel Britain, Hoover and Winston the Dog are singing in the rain, whilst Pete Bonthrone keeps dry. At Richmond - July 2006.

Terry Venables, Steve Kember and Ernie Walley appear thrilled to be in Memphis - May 1979
[Photo: Ian Weller]

Team-mates in opposition: Steve Kember and Neil Smillie, on loan at Memphis. Note the
Delta Airlines sponsorship on the back of the Palace shirt - May 1979
[Photo: Ian Weller]

16

ATLANTIC CROSSINGS

The Stateside trip in 2006 was Palace's second tour in the USA. The first had come in May 1979. A post-season tour had been arranged at the invitation of the North American Soccer League (NASL). The league was keen to enhance its image in the eyes of the American public, who generally had little interest in the original brand of football. Several other English clubs also took up the invitation around that time.

The rise (and fall) of the NASL is well documented elsewhere. The clubs paid top dollar for World stars of the game, such as Pele, George Best and Franz Beckenbauer, giving them a final huge payday in the twilight of their careers. As it was a summer league, several British professionals would ply their trade out there in the British close season. Our own Steve Kember played three of four seasons for the Vancouver Whitecaps, missing only the 1979 season. Sadly for him, that was the one when Vancouver won the title. Other Palace alumni – John Craven, Derek Possee and Ray Lewington – were, however, part of that Championship-winning team.

Palace's league season had ended the week before with a Friday night game against Burnley. The match had originally been scheduled back in the winter but had been postponed due to the weather. It had been re-scheduled after the regular season was due to have ended. Back then, no-one cared if the final round of games were not all played on the exact same date and time. The match set an attendance record for Selhurst Park of 51,482 (although 51,801 was announced on the night). Those who were there attest that several thousand more were actually inside the ground.

The reason for the interest was that Palace were in with a chance of winning their first Championship since their inaugural league season in 1920/21. Such was the fine balance of the table, a Palace win guaranteed the Championship, a draw would still see Palace promoted, however a defeat would mean Palace would finish outside the promotion places.

The huge crowd were beginning to get a little nervous when the game was still goal-less deep into the second half. Palace had only lost four times all season, but one of those games was away at mid-table Burnley. The explosion of noise and relief that greeted Ian Walsh's 76th minute opener is still the loudest crowd noise I have heard at Selhurst. David Swindlehurst added another before full time and Palace were crowned Champions. Steve Kember was ensured a Champions medal, after all.

The team that Palace overtook at the top was, coincidentally, flying across the Atlantic for a post-season tour at the very moment our game was being played. The final score from Selhurst was relayed by the pilot to the team onboard. That team just happened to be our most deadly rivals, Brighton & Hove Albion, managed at the time by Alan Mullery. To add insult to injury, when they landed they also discovered that one of their tour games had been called off, due to the 1979 oil crisis.

Palace's American adventure was out of the price range of most regular travellers of the time, who were keeping their powder dry for the forthcoming pre-season Scandinavian tour. However, Ian Weller did make it out there.

"The first I heard about this tour was in the Croydon Advertiser of 20th April and the following week there was a piece on the tour where Terry Venables invited the fans to join them, staying at the same hotel as the team. Further details were available from Marlar Payne Sports International Limited. I duly sent off for details and the full package costs came to £565 as detailed on the information sent to me. Interesting to note one of the Directors of Marlar Payne listed was a certain 'T Venables'.

It was going to be my first trip to the USA, so I did not want to just be based in Florida, as I wanted to also visit New York and Washington, where a friend of mine worked at the British Embassy. Having decided that I would make my own way to see the proposed three games and with only two weeks to prepare, it was a race against time to get my visa for the trip and organise a flight over the pond. Back in 1979, the cheapest flight to New York was £50 one way, on Freddie Laker's DC10 Skytrain. You did not book up in advance, just turned up on the day of your flight and off you went. My father, who took me to the airport, could not believe how cheap it was, saying it cost more to get to Scotland.

We were due to play our first game against Atlanta Chiefs, where Palace's ex-striker Jeff Bourne was now plying his trade. On reaching Atlanta I found out the game had been cancelled. The reason wasn't clear to me, it may have been linked to the oil crisis, although that had no personal impact on my chosen transport, as I was either travelling by plane or greyhound bus, neither of which were affected.

The remaining two games of the tour against Memphis Rogues and Fort Lauderdale Strikers were scheduled consecutively on 23rd and 24th May. The game in Memphis was held at the Liberty Bowl Memorial Stadium, home of Memphis Tigers, the University of Memphis

American Football Team. Its capacity, back then, was in the region of 50,000 spectators, so the crowd of 2,850 looked lost in the vast bowl. I think the majority of spectators were curious soccer fans rather than supporters of the Rogues.

I turned up at the stadium about an hour before kick-off, not knowing what sort of crowd they were expecting. I was one of the first spectators to arrive. I went looking for a programme seller with not one in sight, maybe it was too early for them, however, I didn't see a single seller before entering the ground.

Memphis Rogues had three Palace connections: Charlie Cooke as Coach, along with young players Steve Lovell and Neil Smillie, both actually on loan from Palace. The standard of football played by the Rogues was probably around the Southern League standard and Palace ran out easy 3-1 winners on the night, with first half goals from Dave Swindlehurst and a brace from Ian Walsh.

The second half soured when George Graham suffered a broken leg – the injury that ultimately ended his playing career. It looked like an accidental challenge to me, no bad intent, just one of those things that can occur. According to the press report I picked up the next day, the injury hit the team hard. Terry Venables said 'All our kids were very upset. We're a very close team and we felt pretty low after what happened. We weren't really up to playing after that.' Moments later, Rogues scored a consolation and then, in the closing stages, Palace's Tony Sealy and Rogues' Hugh O'Neill clashed, which resulted in a multi-player scuffle. Both players were dismissed amidst heavy tensions. The teams made up at a postgame party in Overton Square.

After the game I went to the main offices to enquire whether a programme had been printed for the game. I was advised they had, but they had arrived at the stadium after kick-off, leaving them with a large box of unwanted programmes. They said I could help myself to as many as I liked, which I duly did, asking for a large plastic sack so that I could carry them back to my hotel.

I was able to take a photo of Terry Venables, Steve Kember and Ernie Walley on the pitch prior to the Memphis game, but the only other time I was in contact with the players was the next day on the flight from Memphis to Fort Lauderdale, which had a stopover in Miami to drop passengers off. While still on the plane at Miami, I was able to have a chat with the players and staff and get my Memphis programme signed by them all.

The game against Fort Lauderdale Strikers took place at the Lockhart Stadium, where David Beckham's Inter Miami would begin their MLS journey forty years later. The attendance was 7,121 and benefitted by being played in a more compact ground, with a capacity of around 17,000. It felt much more like a lower division English ground, with a good atmosphere. Before the game, some home spectators held a BBQ, their cheerleaders added a touch of glamour and, at one point during the game, their band suddenly struck up.

The Strikers had former Palace player Ron Newman as Coach and also had international stars George Best, Gerd Muller (West Germany) and Teofilo Cubillas (Peru) in their ranks. All three took part in the game against Palace, although Best and Muller were clearly well past their prime, Cubillas was still playing international football for Peru. The Strikers played to a standard more to a level of the lower division of the football league, but despite playing the day before, Palace went on to win the game 2-0 with goals from Vince Hilaire and Dave Swindlehurst.

Fortunately from my point of view, there was no in-game PA commentary at either game. The Memphis players were announced and individually introduced to the crowd but I can't remember if this was also the case at the Fort Lauderdale game.

I did not meet any US based or ex-pat Palace fans at either game – had the internet been around then that might have been different. An interesting aspect from both games is that the Palace shirts and shorts were sponsored by Delta Airlines, a first, I believe, for Palace, in respect of kit sponsorship.

Despite the tour taking place with the backdrop of the oil shortage, the biggest impact on my travel plans in the whole trip came the day after the tour ended. A DC10 plane crashed soon after take-off from Chicago, which instantly grounded all DC10 planes, including Freddie Laker's Skytrain. I only found out about this at Kennedy Airport, where I spent the next 25 hours, before getting a standby ticket to get me home."

Although these 1979 games were the first Palace matches to be held on the US mainland, Palace had twice crossed the Atlantic for post-season tours in 1962 and 1964. Palace won all eleven games across the two tours. The first tour was based solely in Bermuda, with three games against Bermudian Football League and FA representative sides, plus a further game against a Canadian club side also touring on the island.

The tour appears to have been planned for some time with mentions of Palace's visit to the island appearing in the Bermudian local press from the turn of the year.

It was a festival of goals for Palace, who racked up 25 goals in the official games. In the second game of the tour, Palace were awarded six penalties, although only three were scored.

The final official game of the trip was an exhibition game against Toronto City, a Canadian side who had topped their league table in the inaugural season, but had lost in the post-season play-offs. In that season, they were able to obtain the services of high profile loan players from England, including Sir Stanley Matthews and Danny Blanchflower. The side that faced Palace included Tom Finney, although the local press noted "the Palace defence did a fine job of isolating Finney from most of the action and his team-mates added insult to injury with a game-full of faulty passes." Palace ran out 5-0 winners. The 17-strong tour party also found time to enjoy sightseeing, golf and deep-sea fishing on the island.

After the official tour games, Palace also played an impromptu friendly against Bermudian club side West End Rovers, where they ran in another eleven goals. One local commented "I thought Crystal Palace was a football team but when I heard the score, I had to look to see who was hitting the sixes."

That game came about after some local controversy. At the reception after the second game against the Bermuda Combination XI, Palace Manager Arthur Rowe challenged the League and Cup Holders, Pembroke Hamilton Club to a game. The committee of the double winners, however, felt that the costs to stage such a game would result in a loss to the club and, after some deliberation, declined the challenge, Instead, losing Cup finalists, West End Rovers stepped up to the plate. Pembroke Hamilton were on the receiving end of some sharp criticism from the local press and a war of words was conducted in the Letters page for some time after Palace had left the island.

The Bermuda Recorder sports correspondents' summation of Palace was rather double-edged: "Crystal Palace, apart from some dubious tactics employed by several of its players, has pleased local fans and players, with its brand of football on the field and the conduct off the field." The tour was, however, deemed a success by the islanders, who turned out in their thousands.

Two years later, a similar post-season tour to Bermuda was arranged. Given the previous local issues with costs, Palace had agreed to cover their travel expenses so, as a result, the tour was dependent on promotion from the third tier. This was duly achieved in the final game of the season, which was a home match against Oldham. Palace's centre forward at the time, Peter Burridge, recalled the game in an interview for the *Palace Echo* fanzine:

> "That was probably the worst we played all season. If a neutral had watched the game, he'd have thought they were Champions. We'd come out throwing bunches of flowers into the crowd and we were all looking forward to the trip to Bermuda arranged upon our promotion.
>
> If we'd won we would have been Champions. A draw was good enough to get us up, however we lost 1-3 and if Watford had won 5-1 or something then they would have gone up instead. Luckily they also lost on the day, but it was a bit near the knuckle, with the Bermuda trip in the balance. I have very fond memories of that trip, but none that I can tell you!"

The maxim 'what goes on tour, stays on tour' was clearly alive and kicking in 1964! On this trip, Palace first flew into Montreal to face Montreal Italia. It seemed initially as if the free-scoring exploits of the 1962 tour were not to be repeated, as Palace only won by a solitary goal. However, the scoring groove was revived in Ontario with a seven-goal thrashing of Hamilton Steelers. The players and club staff also managed to squeeze in a sightseeing visit to Niagara Falls during their time in Canada.

The goals continued to flow once in Bermuda, with a further four games: three against various Bermuda representative sides and one against the current League and Cup winners: Young Men's Social Club, netting a total of 21 goals and only conceding twice. Unlike the first tour, this time all the games were played at one location: Devonshire Recreation Club. Again, this decision seemed to have its roots in the desire to keep costs down, although it was noted that one of the other venues who were invited to tender had recently installed a long jump sand pit by one of the goals!

The Bermuda FA used the tour to formulate their National side, who had a forthcoming international tour to Iceland in August. They selected a total of 36 local players to be used across the games with Palace. As such, Palace's tour was keenly anticipated with one gentleman writing to *The Bermuda Recorder* to declare that "of all the sides the Bermuda FA have brought here in recent years, Crystal Palace have not only shown how to play football, but they were far above all other teams in their sportsmanship on the field of play." A slightly different take from the one expressed by that paper's own sportswriter at the time.

However, after the tour, the decision to use such a large squad attracted a great deal of criticism in the local press. The take was that it would have been better to have selected a smaller squad to play in all games. The Iceland tour was, however, regarded as a relative success following a win, draw and defeat across the three games which resulted in a level record for the tourists.

The three Canadian teams that Palace played on these tours competed in the Eastern Canada Professional Soccer League. The league ran for six summers from 1961 to 1966 before it was subsumed into the National Soccer League. The clubs were predominantly made up of European immigrants although, as we have already seen, the teams were augmented by some of the stars of English football.

This practice had been banned by the time Palace played against Toronto City in 1962 – Tom Finney had actually come out of retirement and signed for the Canadian side, although only made a single goalscoring league appearance. Two years after that, on the eve of the 1964 tour, Toronto City signed Palace's inside-half and former England international Johnny Brooks, alongside a certain Malcolm Allison, who was then appointed as Player-Manager. That season, Toronto finished second in the league, but were crowned champions after winning the play-offs. None of the club sides that Palace faced across these two tours now exist, though both Montreal and Toronto host clubs in the MLS. Palace would eventually return to Canada in 2016, which will be detailed in a later chapter.

Palace have also played three games against American opposition at Selhurst Park. The first came when Palace hosted Dallas Tornadoes in a mid-season game in October 1969, in front of just over 3,000 fans. The team that Palace fielded was made up almost entirely of reserves as, due to a League Cup replay, the first team was away on the same night to Derby. This led to a compensation payment being made to the American team. To add insult to financial injury, the cup replay was eventually abandoned in the 85th minute with the score at 1-1.

The friendly finished 2-0 to Palace, with goals from Ron Harland and also Per Bartram, who had got married earlier in the day. The other notable thing about the game was the match programme, which opened out in the middle and featured a strange hand-drawn cover featuring a gun-toting cowboy and a gushing oil well. The Tornadoes coach was Ron Newman, who you may remember played for Palace and was the head coach of Fort Lauderdale Strikers when we played them ten years later.

In March 1981, Palace entertained Minnesota Kicks in midweek. Les Carter opening the scoring, but Palace were pegged back late on and the game finished 1-1. The attendance was a disappointing 1,490 but the team were on the point of being relegated from the top flight and had just appointed Dario Gradi our fourth Manager of the campaign.

The notable feature of this game was an NASL-style shoot-out to decide the game. This involved a player dribbling from 35 yards out and trying to beat the keeper within five seconds. Jerry Murphy was Palace's only scorer. Minnesota won the shoot-out with a strike from former Palace striker, Stewart Jump. Our most recent game was against CPFC USA in September 2007, which is detailed in the following chapter.

In 1990, a few days after the FA Cup Final replay, the club took the players away to the Caribbean for an informal tour and holiday. They played four games while there against various representative sides from the region.

The first two games were played in Trinidad & Tobago against many players from the national side, who had narrowly failed to qualify for that year's World Cup. After a 2-2 draw in the first game, Palace fielded mostly youth players in the second game, which was reflected in the final score – a 4-0 defeat.

The final games were played in Jamaica (won 2-0) and the Cayman Islands (won 4-0). The game in the Caymans had a false start as Palace's Kit Manager, Spike Hill, recalls:

> "We originally travelled to the Caymans but the game was called off due to a monsoon and
> flooded pitch. If I remember correctly, the tour was extended to accommodate a return to
> Cayman [from Jamaica] to play the match."

CPFC USA Co-Managers Pete Medd and Jim Cherneski - July 2006

Rade Kokovic celebrates scoring CPFC USA's first ever goal - July 2006

17

FRANCHISE F.C.

On 4th May 2006, Palace announced an innovative plan to create a brand new Academy and Developmental Soccer Club development in the United States, to be called CPFC USA. This scheme was part of Simon Jordan's vision to increase the 'footprint' of Crystal Palace around the world, which we'd had already glimpsed with the club's entry into the European Communities Tournament back in 2002.

It was envisioned that the new club would have a system for identifying and developing the best young talent in the US and run junior teams from Under 9 to Under 18 levels. It was intended that the senior team would compete in the United Soccer Leagues (USL).

At the time the USL served as FIFA-affiliated second and third divisions in the US, underneath the Major League Soccer division, although in common with many other American sporting leagues, there was no automatic promotion or relegation. The club was to be based in Baltimore, Maryland. It was proclaimed would "train and play in the finest facilities in the Mid-Atlantic region".

In the initial press release, Bob Dowie, Crystal Palace's then-Director of Football and brother to Manager Iain, expanded on the Chairman's vision:

"It was one of the key briefs given to me when I came on board. To establish a presence in developing football countries to give Palace access to their best and brightest, up-and-coming young talent, as well as their current star players. The club have been working hard over the last eight months or so to define the US Based Academy set-up. We have visited Baltimore and Annapolis area in late-April to personally validate the facilities and the people who will run the US venture."

Dominic Jordan, Palace's Vice Chairman and brother to Chairman Simon, also had this to say:

"We see this as a vital extension of our already growing recruitment network. The facilities and the people involved in the CPFC USA are first class and just as importantly, represent a true extension of the Palace way of doing things. We continue to make investments in the Club's future and are excited by the prospect of our investment giving us access to the top US youth talent, in what is without doubt, one of the fastest growing football nations."

The guys at the helm in America were Jim Cherneski and Pete Medd, both in their early thirties. Jim and Pete had met at Towson University in their playing days, where they both went on to have spells as assistant coaches. Both went on to play in the USL and indoor football sides along the East Coast.

Jim Cherneski was appointed Sporting Director of CPFC USA and Pete Medd became the Club President, though both men were also the joint coaches of the senior side. Pete's parents, Randall and Cathie, also became involved with the launch of the club, providing financial and moral support.

Both Randall (known to his friends as Randy) and Cathie were huge soccer fans and Cathie had been involved in the MLS side Columbus Crew. They would come over to England to watch Palace as guests of the Chairman and also take in other top flight matches while here.

Cherneski, who'd had unsuccessful trials with Brighton in his youth, was in England on a soccer tour and had a chance meeting with a Palace club official, thought to be Bob Dowie. The official expressed interest in setting up a new team and stayed in touch with Jim when he returned home. That chance meeting was the genesis of this venture. The enthusiasm for the new club was evident in Cherneski's Stateside press release:

> "It is very exciting to launch this Academy and PDL club in the Baltimore area. I played in the last season of USL professional soccer with the Baltimore Bays in 1997 and it was sad to see the professional outdoor game leave the area. We are excited to bring it back with true quality and professionalism. This is a real opportunity for young players in our area to get recognized and develop under the Crystal Palace FC developmental system. This is a 100-year-old club with a rich history in player development and their expansion of the Academy into the United States is just another example of their commitment to nurture young talent. Last season in the English Premier League, Crystal Palace were one of the few teams to field five players which came through their Academy into the first team."

The USL Vice President, Tim Holt was similarly enthused by the new club:

> "We are very excited about Crystal Palace joining us. USL, and the PDL in particular, are excellent vehicles for player development and scouting at the international level. We are confident Crystal Palace, as pioneers in a movement we feel could expand to other clubs, will find this venture to be very successful given the number of talented players in this country. Jim Cherneski deserves a great deal of credit for making this project a reality."

The move failed to capture very much press attention on either side of the pond, however the plan received a cautious thumbs-up from the Palace support, which was more pre-occupied with the upcoming play-off games against Watford. The announcement of the pre-season tour to launch the new club Stateside was the main focus of certain fans' excitement.

Buried away within the programme article was mention of the first fruits of the partnership: "one of the outstanding USA youth players is likely to be coming to Palace in the coming season." This was assumed to be Neven Subotić, who arrived in London for trials at that time on the recommendation of Jim Cherneski.

The young centre-half had been born in the former Yugoslavia, then his parents had relocated to southern Germany early in his life, to escape the Bosnian War raging around them. When the family's permission to stay in Germany expired, they moved to the United States, where the young defender ended up playing internationally for the US U17 and U20 sides.

He came over to Palace with his father and the official line is that he turned down Palace and moved to Jurgen Klopp's Mainz 05 side, back in Germany. It was inferred, however, that Palace had taken too long to decide whether to offer him a professional contract and he'd decided to look elsewhere. Whatever the truth, the club missed out on a player who later followed Klopp to Borussia Dortmund and went on to pick up two German championships and played in the Champions League Final at Wembley in 2013.

The first task for the new club was to put together an amateur side to play the inaugural friendly against CPFC UK. The side was comprised of younger players, currently playing for college sides, graduates and former professionals. The fact that the senior side only managed a 3-1 win was a source of pride to the nascent American offshoot.

Over the course of the next ten months, in addition to their commitment to scouting young talent, Jim Cherneski and Pete Medd set about putting together a squad to compete in the USL. It had originally been envisaged that the club would play in the USL Premier Development League, but ended up in the 10-team USL Second Division. An open trial was held and the pair were overwhelmed with interest. Over a hundred players turned up for the trial held in freezing conditions, coming from as far away as Japan.

CPFC USA's first league fixture took place on 20th April 2007, an away game at Charlotte Eagles in North Carolina, over seven hours journey by coach. It was an inauspicious start, with CPFC USA conceding three times in the first twenty minutes. The game was played on a minimum-width high school pitch in front of a noisy 2,000 strong home crowd, who showed their derision of the new side. Behind the pitch there was an equally noisy funfair. Cherneski remembers being completely bewildered by this and at half time wondered out loud 'what have we got ourselves into?' The final score was 4-1, which after the disaster of the opening minutes, could have been a lot worse. Ibrahim Kante scored the first competitive goal for the new team.

In their first home game against Cleveland City Stars things got worse, with a 0-4 reverse and changes were made. The centre-backs and goalkeeper were replaced and although the next two games at home were lost, the scoreline was only 1-0. Progress of sorts.

The progress was confirmed with a 3-0 away win at Wilmington Hammerheads, the following week. That win kicked off a seven-game unbeaten league run, though there was a disappointing 1-0 Open Cup defeat to lower-level Ocean City Barons, in the midst of this run. The streak launched the club from the foot to mid-table, yet they couldn't quite claw themselves into the top four and a place in the play-offs, finishing fifth. The best result of their inaugural season was an 8-1 thrashing of Bermuda Hogges, owned by former Manchester City favourite Shaun Goater. The Hogges' home ground was one that Palace had played on during their 1962 tour.

Palace themselves had initially lent a couple of their young professionals to gain competitive experience, midfielder Lewwis Spence and striker Charlie Sheringham, son of former England striker Teddy. However, neither featured in the season much, due to injury. No further Palace players were loaned thereafter.

The 2007 USL season ended in August, but the US team came over to England and fulfilled a return friendly fixture against Palace at Selhurst Park, during the September international weekend. This was a dull affair, with Peter Taylor electing for a line-up that could generously be called experimental; with Dougie Freedman captaining the side from a central midfield role alongside Danny Butterfield. The game was settled by a single goal in the 28th minute from an unlikely source, right-back Matt Lawrence, who met a Butterfield corner perfectly.

The following 2008 season was CPFC USA's most successful campaign. Not only did they qualify for the play-offs by virtue of finishing fourth in the league, they also had their best run in the US Open Cup. After disposing of Los Angeles Legends in the first round and then squeaking past the team considered to be our league rivals, Harrisburg City Islanders, winning 3-1 on penalties after a 2-2 draw, the prize was a third round tie at home to MLS side, New York Red Bulls.

Palace put the moneyed New Yorkers to the sword 2-0 to set up a quarter-final tie away at New England Revolution, another big MLS club. Palace pushed them all the way to penalties, where they unfortunately succumbed 5-3.

The league play-offs commenced with a home tie against Harrisburg City Islanders and once again it finished 2-2 after extra time. Much to the chagrin of our rivals, Palace won again 7-6 on penalties. The following week they faced an away game with Charlotte Eagles, who had finished at the top of the table. The regular season champions proved too strong for Palace, narrowly winning the tie 2-1. The club also got three players into the league's Team of the Year.

By now, the Stateside club had taken on further personnel. An Academy Director, a General Manager and a Director of Communications had all been hired. That latter role was filled by James Calder, who you may remember was the other photographer I became friendly with back at that inaugural game in 2006.

James recalls how he got the position and what the role actually entailed:

"I was hired at the beginning of January 2008, in the middle of the off-season between the first and second seasons. I had ingratiated myself with Jim Cherneski and Pete Medd by donating my photos from the 2006 inaugural friendly to the club. I hoped that it would give me a chance to be closely involved with the organization moving forward.

Photography was a serious hobby for me up to that point, so I had no professional experience shooting football. When the club used some of my images on their website, I was obviously thrilled, and asked if they might be interested in using me as their official photographer when their debut season kicked off. They told me to get back in touch nearer the time.

As the season opener approached, I called and offered them a per-match fee that was less than half the going rate. The response was very non-committal. They told me I should call back again, closer to the date. This happened a few more times, until it was now the day before the match. When I called this time, they rather unenthusiastically agreed to my offer. After providing them with photos from the opener, they asked me to call again before the next home fixture and they'd let me know if I would be needed again. I did, they said yes again, and after the third home match, finally they said I should just keep showing up, unless they told me otherwise.

At the final home game of the 2007 season, Pete Medd came up to me soon after the final whistle, shook my hand and thanked me for my work. He then asked if I'd be interested in a full-time job with the club. This came as a total surprise, and I quickly responded with an enthusiastic 'yes'. After calming down a bit, I then asked Pete exactly what kind of job he was picturing, pointing out that there was no way the club needed a full-time photographer.

He told me he was thinking about a Communications/Marketing Director position, to which I replied 'Great, but I don't actually have any relevant experience'. Pete countered 'Right, but we love the captions you provide with your photographs, you're a smart guy, and most importantly you're a fan!'

Two months later, I left the IT job I'd had for nearly twenty years to start at Palace Baltimore, taking a 50% pay cut in the process. Though I was so unhappy in tech at that point, the mental health benefit far outweighed the drop in remuneration. At least initially.

I wore many hats while working under the title Director of Communications. The obvious stuff was writing and disseminating all press releases, handling press enquiries, as well as designing and publishing the matchday programme. I also had to find and manage the matchday announcer.

Beyond the obvious, I also retained my role as matchday photographer for the 2008 season, which was quite the challenge as I was also keeping notes via voice recording to enable me to write the match report press releases, as soon as possible after the final whistle. Due to my IT background, I also managed all technology for the club. That included designing and managing the website, including building an online shop for merchandise and ticket sales from the ground up. Ticket and merchandising sales, both on matchdays and at regional coaching clinics for kids by Palace Baltimore players, were also my domain.

I also took on some marketing and graphic design responsibilities, despite no previous experience: designing adverts for the club to use in print and online; designing adverts for smaller club sponsors to use in the programme and on our website; designing, printing and constructing matchday advertising hoardings for sponsors.

As for the most random job I was given, early on Jim asked me to figure out how to affordably get player names and numbers onto players' shirts and shorts. Once I'd done the research, I ordered a heat press and supplies of custom numbers and letters for the club, and it was then my job to get them onto the kit.

I often had an intern or two on matchdays to help with ticket and merch sales, but everything else I did basically by myself. It was absolutely knackering, but I didn't care. I was assigned this wide range of roles in the interests of helping reduce the cost of running the club.

A lot of those first two seasons is a blur. At the beginning, I was just absolutely thrilled to be working for the club I'd supported since my childhood. I was born in Bromley and grew up in West Norwood. Basically, this was my dream job. I think initially, my wife was really happy that I was now doing something I loved at last. However that started to wear off for her, once the scope of my job became clear and the amount of time I was spending at work. I did travel with the club for some of the away fixtures in the first season, and then almost all of them in the second season.

The first season was such an emotional rollercoaster, with that disastrous start and then eventually turning things around. Though I suppose that is the Palace way.

The second season was when the job started to turn sour. I saw cracks appearing in the foundations of the American club. We failed to make any real progress in either growing our fanbase or on getting agreement for a permanent stadium. The global economic crisis made it clear there wasn't going to be a magic influx of money from ownership on either side of the Atlantic to solve these problems. The emotional highlight of that season was our brilliant victory over the New York Red Bulls on a suburban high school field, in front of a couple of thousand delirious local supporters and some very upset travelling fans from New York! Apart from the massive thrill of such an amazing upset, that was the one moment when I thought maybe, just maybe, we were turning a corner, and that the club would start to gain recognition and popularity organically.

Of course the visits by the London club each off-season were enormous fun, getting to meet the players, staff and travelling support. Sadly, I never got to see Palace Baltimore play in London, although I did get to feel very important whenever I did come back to London. I would just have to let Jim Cherneski know if I wanted to go to a particular match with my Dad and he would get it sorted for me. I'd go to the main receptionist at Selhurst Park to pick up the tickets under my name and the envelope would say 'From Simon Jordan'."

Although things were looking up on the pitch and the club was now well-regarded within US Soccer, the finances were not so rosy. It's not uncommon for US clubs to operate at a loss. The key to making money from professional soccer is to own your own stadium and stage events that bring in more money than the soccer games. The club went to the City of Baltimore with expensively-drawn plans for a 15,000 capacity stadium downtown.

On the other side of the Atlantic, Palace's financials were beginning to cause some concern among supporters. Palace had again been eliminated from the play-offs at the semi-final stage and we had recently secured funding from a Cayman Islands hedge fund, Agilo, which described itself as specialising in 'distressed companies'. The Chairman laughed off the idea that Palace fell into that bracket at the time, yet the fans remained unconvinced and, other than kit provision, there was little financial assistance being directed across to the US arm's ambitious plans for a stadium.

The 2009 season saw the US club unable to recreate the highs of the previous one. The division had been reduced to nine teams and Palace could only finish sixth. This was particularly galling as not only was this one place outside the play-offs, but the fifth spot was taken by neighbours Real Maryland Monarchs. This club who, after a disastrous first season in 2008, had proclaimed themselves as the 'real' football club of the region, seemingly trying to stoke up a local rivalry.

Palace USA regarded themselves as already having something of a rivalry with Harrisburg City Islanders and had mostly ignored the trash talk. Palace history seemed to be repeating itself Stateside, with the club preferring to maintain a rivalry with a team some distance away, rather than mouthy next-door neighbours.

James points out that the location of the new club was perhaps the most significant reason behind the discord:

"The Real Maryland rivalry existed because of a couple of things, as far as I recall. One was the clash of egos between respective coaches and owners. However from our perspective, the more significant cause was the fact that suddenly this other franchise had been approved by our league, in a location that overlapped with our supposedly guaranteed catchment and marketing area.

> I never knew the details from a legal or contractual perspective, but basically Pete and Jim
> felt they had been betrayed by the USL. As I understood it, the league was supposed to keep
> teams separated geographically, so that they didn't take business away from each other."

After an ill-tempered home game against the Monarchs, which the visitors won by a single goal, they then proceeded to trash the dressing room. The Palace USA officials were not impressed. But ultimately it was the three defeats by the Monarchs that meant they would finish above CPFC USA. In the Open Cup, Palace returned to Ocean City Barons but there was no revenge to be had there, with the Barons winning 3-0.

The season did bring forth another encounter with the parent club, when Crystal Palace went to the United States as part of our 2009 pre-season schedule, playing both CPFC USA and Harrisburg City Islanders in two friendlies. More on those games can be found in a later chapter. The tour did give a few English Palace fans, including myself, the opportunity to attend a CPFC USA home league game, coincidentally also against Harrisburg City Islanders. The extra transatlantic support brought them some luck, as CPFC USA won 2-0. The English travellers were treated as honoured guests and given VIP treatment by Randy and Cathie Medd.

Another season passed. There had been no visible progress with the City of Baltimore over the proposed stadium. Worse still, the financial property crash of 2008/09 had taken its toll on both the Jordan and Medd families. Back in England, in January 2010, Palace was placed into administration, which meant there could be no further assistance, financial or otherwise, heading across the Atlantic. However, the US club was confident that they would get their stadium, so decided to move ahead with the 2010 season.

James recalls how one of his favourite moments in his role also foreshadowed the impending financial crash:

> "At Christmas 2009, I was over visiting my family and I interviewed Neil Warnock in person,
> in his office at the training ground. I really enjoyed talking to him, and he came across as a
> genuinely warm and caring person, despite his reputation. This wasn't too long before the
> London club went into administration. I remember having to end the interview a bit early,
> when the Manager had to take an urgent phone call from Simon Jordan. As I slowly exited
> his office, I distinctly recall the unhappy look on Warnock's face as he listened to whatever it
> was Jordan was telling him."

The Jordans had reassured CPFC USA that the American club would be part of any rescue deal. As it turned out, that was not the case, so the US Club, now renamed Crystal Palace Baltimore, was cut adrift. That said, Pete Medd has since gone on record to say that the Jordans were pioneers who were fantastic to work with.

To make matters worse, the club moved into the temporary USSF Division 2 Professional League. This twelve-team league was formed as a compromise between the feuding USL and North American Soccer League (NASL). This league was supposedly the second tier of the American and Canadian soccer pyramids and therefore a step up from USL Division 2. Palace Baltimore was entered into the NASL Conference half of that division and, predictably, the decimated club finished last in both that and the combined table. They also fell at the first hurdle in the Open Cup, losing 1-0 after extra time to Richmond Kickers. Now heavily in the red, players' wages were being paid out by the US Soccer Federation.

James left the club two months into that third and, ultimately, final season:

"It was an amicable parting. During that off-season my dream job had begun to turn into a nightmare. When talk about 'self promoting' to this new league started around the club, after the second season, I was highly sceptical, to say the least. As the new season approached, I could see pretty quickly that the higher costs associated with playing at the next level, including air travel and live video streaming of home matches, would be unsustainable without additional funding.

There was no magic pill to fix the attendance problem, while the financial crisis meant the owners couldn't help. So I knew that without some sort of miracle the club was doomed. After just two home games, I knew I had to get out, so I started looking for another job and resigned at the beginning of June. To save money, I didn't go to any away games.

My responsibilities were all handed off to an intern. I checked the results over the remainder of the season, but didn't go any deeper than that. It was too painful. After Palace Baltimore, I worked for my friend's small tech company for seven years, doing a combination of IT and marketing functions. I now work as a manager at Trader Joe's speciality supermarket in Washington DC. I've supported my other home team, DC United since their inception in 1996, though my emotional attachment to Palace is still the stronger of the two, despite the distance."

The hand-to-mouth aspect of the season saw the club play at several different home grounds and often struggle to field a team, with Cherneski even coming out of retirement himself to make up the numbers.

The club did not re-emerge for the 2011 season, officially going 'on hiatus' in an announcement on 3rd December 2010. This coincided with the 'official' termination of the four-year relationship with Crystal Palace. The announcement stated that the club intended to join the North American Soccer league in 2012 after an extensive rebranding, including a name change. At the centre of the reorganisation was actively progressing the downtown soccer-specific stadium. After that day, nothing more was heard from the club.

It wasn't the end of soccer in Baltimore though. In 2012 a brand new club was founded in the city called Baltimore Bohemians, which competed in USL Premier

Development League. After their first season, the club partnered with Republic of Ireland club Bohemians, with the agreement that the club would trade talent (sound familiar?). They also moved into one of CP Baltimore's old grounds. They lasted four more seasons before also 'going on hiatus'.

The dissolution of CP Baltimore ended up in the American courts, when seven coaches from the Youth Academy setup sued over unpaid wages and won their case, putting further financial strain on the remaining club officials. The story has a happier ending for Jim Cherneski. Whilst at the club, Jim had been developing and refining a new type of non-slip football sock, working with former squad players while they searched for new clubs. The demise of the club left him in serious financial straits, however he managed to get backing for his patent and TruSox was born.

Former Palace winger Victor Moses was one of the first Premier League players to try out Jim's socks and gave them a huge public thumbs-up. The recognisable design is visible above the boot-line. Soon players everywhere were wearing them, much to the annoyance of many kit manufacturers. It was an ongoing battle against the multi-national sportswear brands, which will often pressure players and clubs not to use them. Ultimately though, TruSox has become a multi-million dollar brand. Cherneski later returned to football management, this time in England, with Cheshire League side, Egerton FC. Many entrepreneurs achieve success when they pull their socks up. Few can claim to have been pulled up by their socks.

Pete Medd started M Power Education in Maryland, a massage therapy education school, which is now encompassing a broader education career direction.

The story of Crystal Palace USA is a fascinating tale: a bold experiment that ultimately failed. Leaving aside the financial issues, James reflects on why that was:

"I think interest in outdoor soccer at this level in this region was pretty underwhelming. Indoor soccer was much more established and popular. I do think the added entertainment aspects that are part and parcel of all major professional sports in the US, things like exhilarating musical cues and PA announcements throughout games, cheerleaders, promotional activities, these things make traditional soccer seem pretty unexciting, except to first generation immigrants from soccer-loving countries and their friends and family, on whom enthusiasm for the sport might have rubbed off.

I'm really not sure if the lack of travelling supporters is a major factor in the flat atmosphere at many games. I think it has more to do with how relatively young the sport is here, the lack of appreciation for the game, the lack of intense rivalries. But that's changing with time, I think. Looking at some of the newer clubs and the bigger crowds they're getting – Seattle, Atlanta, Nashville, Cincinnati, as long as Major League Soccer can keep itself going – unlike the original NASL – I think things will keep improving.

I'm not sure I understand why soccer works in one American city but not another. Maybe Baltimore is not the right city for football. Or maybe it's just a sign of a well-run or poorly-run business."

CPFC USA Director of Communications, James Calder - July 2009

Cliiftop view of the IFK Göteborg game at Grebbestad - July 2007

Colonel Britain and 'Sheriff Fatsuit' lead the singing outside the pub in Grebbestad - July 2007

OPERATOR, GET ME SWEDEN

18

OPERATOR, GET ME SWEDEN

The 2006/07 league season was, for me at least, one of the most forgettable in all my years of watching Palace. It started brightly enough with three straight wins, then the wheels quickly came off. The style of football under Peter Taylor attracted increasing derision as the season progressed. Palace bumbled along, never in any real danger of relegation, yet similarly never really mounting a serious challenge for the play-offs. With Millwall and Brighton both relegated the previous season, there was not even much local derby action to get excited about.

At least the tail end of the season was brightened for some by the early announcement of the club's 2007 pre-season plans in early March. A return to Gothenburg in Sweden for a two-game tour against local sides, between 21st and 28th of July. The devil, however, proved to be in the lack of detail.

Palace chose Playhard Sports, a specialist sports tour organiser based in West Yorkshire, to co-ordinate the team's schedule and also offer various 'official' packages to supporters. With the plentiful availability of budget flights, the pricing of these packages did not find much favour with the fans, who preferred, by and large, to make our own arrangements. This led to a scaling back of planned activities, including the cancellation of the party night with the players, for those nine supporters who did decide to travel on the official tours.

Their initial advertisement in the Palace programme and website carried the badges of IFK Göteborg and BK Häcken but stated that the exact dates of the two proposed fixtures and opposition were subject to change. Early indications from Playhard were that the games were likely to be on Tuesday 24th July and Thursday 26th July. It was always unlikely that we would play Häcken, as they were involved in the UEFA Cup and our tour fell in the middle of the first qualification round, where they were drawn to play Icelandic side KR Reykjavik.

More than a month trickled by without confirmation of the fixtures. With those budget flight prices rising, many fans elected to take a chance on the indicated dates. Finally, some seven weeks after the tour had been announced, fixtures were confirmed as IFK Göteborg on the Tuesday and Second Division regional league side IK Oddevald from the city of Uddevalla on Friday 27th July. The match date change caught out some fans, one of whom was Wags, who had booked a midweek break with his wife Jen, around the football, then found his budget wouldn't stretch to the expensive flight changes and accommodation that they'd need to stay for the second game.

Another unwelcome nugget of information revealed was that the game against IFK was to be played in the tiny coastal resort of Grebbestad, some 160 kilometres north of Gothenburg and, judging by the Swedish transport websites, a three hour trip at the very least. Even more concerning, there appeared to be no football ground, nor very much local accommodation. Sue got on the case early and managed to secure a bunk house on the harbour. But most fans ended up in a Swedish holiday camp about five miles away.

It might have all been very different, however, had there been some substance to the internet rumours stemming from a report on the Egyptian football website gopharoahs.com, whereby Palace were looking at taking part in the inaugural El Ettehad International Football Tournament, being staged at the new 80,000 capacity Borg El Arab Stadium, fifty kilometres west of Alexandria in late July. Other teams mentioned as possible participants in the proposed eight team tournament included Wolves and Aberdeen.

At a supporters' question and answer evening in mid-March, Palace Managing Director Phil Alexander categorically denied there had been any contact or discussion about this tournament, which came as some relief to fans who were faced with spending over £600 in airfares alone, before having to think about the twin difficulties of travelling within Egypt to the remote stadium and, more crucially, getting a drink in a strict Muslim region of the country.

Having nothing to do with this tournament turned out to be a blessing, given the experiences of the only eventual British participant, Aberdeen, who suffered a complete nightmare in Alexandria. Even before they set foot in Egypt, their participation was called into question by many Dons fans, who were angry that a possible Intertoto place would have to be sacrificed in order to take part. Aberdeen eventually finished third in the Scottish Premier League and thus qualified for the second qualifying stage of the UEFA Cup itself.

Once there, losing the first two games in searing heat immediately ended the Dons' hopes of winning the tournament, but that was just the thin end of the wedge. Players' luggage was lost; two players escaped, thankfully uninjured, from a head-on car crash; they found the crowds to be extremely partisan and during one match, a protest by local supporters had to be quelled by riot police. The local press was also hostile towards the Scots, due to their disappointing showing in the first games and perceived unfitness within the squad. The officiating was not up to much either – they had a player sent off for checking if a punched team-mate was alright!

The Dons' Manager, Jimmy Calderwood, ended up gathering the players together on the eve of their return home and apologising for bringing them on such a shambles of a trip. But even then the woes were to continue: their flight home from Alexandria was cancelled because the plane suffered a cracked windscreen at the start of its journey from Ethiopia, causing them a delay of over 24 hours. The tournament was eventually won by the other European guest, Maritimo of Portugal.

Whilst Aberdeen were having a calamitous time in Egypt, Palace's own tour was proceeding in an altogether more ordered fashion in Scandinavia, well, for the players anyway. The supporters certainly weren't going to let a small thing like the astronomically high Swedish beer prices diminish their enthusiasm for the trip and were in loud and boisterous form throughout the week.

It was an impressive turnout across the two games with an estimated 150 supporters travelling from overseas. Most of the tour regulars were present, as well as a number of groups making their first forays following Palace abroad, including an all-girl trio from the BBS: Janet Gates (Lightweight), Jane Vigus (Skate) and Samantha Caplan (Miss Chief). The red and blue numbers at each game were also bolstered impressively by Palace's Scandinavian supporter groups, revelling in their first opportunity in almost ten years to see Palace in action on local turf.

Travelling fans began to descend on Gothenburg over the weekend, with the majority arriving on Monday and Tuesday. The red-eye flight from London Stansted to Gothenburg City airport proved the most popular option. Our party of four, Sue, Gibbo, Tracy and I, opted for that route to lessen the potential for problems in getting to Grebbestad the following day. Our foresight was almost scuppered before we got to the airport when a crash occurred right in front of us on the M11, however we got there in the nick of time for our flight.

Just after 11am local time, we found ourselves abroad on the streets of Gothenburg, looking for a bar. The first one we came across was the aptly-named 'Palace' bar and, after a bit of door-rattling persuasion, they opened early to accommodate us. Within an hour, more than fifteen fans had found their way to this bar and a lively opening session ensued, followed by a light lunch. Napkins bearing the bar's name were secreted away with the intention of hanging them alongside our flags on the fences at the first match. This minor comedy was eventually thwarted on two counts: first we completely forgot to take them to the game and secondly, anyway, there were few surround fences at Grebbestad.

The rest of the day was spent wandering the streets of Gothenburg, investigating various bars and cafés, while bumping into some of the recently arrived players, who were taking coffee on Avenyn, the main strip. Paul's Billiard Bar proved a popular venue and strains of 'Red & Blue Army' could be clearly heard for several surrounding streets through the early evening. We elected to finish the evening by returning to The Dubliners, an old haunt from Palace's last encounter in Gothenburg ten years previous.

The next morning we were up bright and early for the 10am train to Tanum, the closest railway station to Grebbestad. Hopes of some traditional tinnies on the train where dashed when the shop assistant in the train station declared, with a wicked glint in her eye, "This is Sweden, we do not sell beer before 11am." The more intelligent – or alcoholic – fans, depending on your point of view, had anticipated this and purchased suitable supplies the previous day.

We arrived in postcard-pretty Grebbestad Marina after an onward bus journey from Tanum, at around 1pm. After lunch we headed off to what was to become 'base camp' in Grebbestad – the Pub Hörnet. Numbers were soon swelled by another busload from the noon train, as flags were gradually plastered across the pub wall. The flags, sing-songs and general good humour attracted the attention of local people, who drove up and down past the pub taking photographs of the friendly invasion.

Even the occasional unofficial traffic hold-ups for the purposes of photographs were taken in very good part by the Swedes. It was good to see so many faces from the Scandinavian supporters' group, anxious to make friends with their travelling brethren. It was particularly great to catch our old friend Inge Lauritzen, the editor of *Ørne Blikket*, the Norwegian version of *Eagle Eye* and the longest-running Palace fanzine.

Soon it was time to leave for the game. We headed uphill for the short journey to the stadium – I use the word 'stadium' extremely loosely here. Siljevi Idrottsplats, home of Grebbestads IF, is basically a park pitch with a few benches and picnic tables scattered around it and one tiny stand. That said, the ground was very attractive, nestled in a pine forest, with a high rock face running along one side. The weather was less alluring. A steady shower fell through the game and without floodlights, the light was extremely poor. The match had been well promoted within the town and a fair few IFK fans had also travelled up, which led to an officially declared attendance of 1,300, although you could not help thinking that quite a few locals had simply wandered in through the forest.

The programme for the game was a simple black and white four-page A5 size affair, given away free upon entry. But it soon became apparent that there were actually two versions of the team sheet: one with completely incorrect squad numbers and a much shorter players' roster for Palace. This sent the collectors into something of a frenzy as they tried to round up copies of the misprinted edition.

The game itself started very brightly for Palace, as Paul Ifill latched onto James Scowcroft's cushioned knock-down header, before swiveling and drilling it into the roof of the net within 90 seconds. Ifill suffered a nasty injury midway through the half, however Palace responded to the setback in fine style. Scowcroft received a long ball from defence and powered home an absolute worldie from 25 yards. Or so I'm told.

At the precise moment Scowie's vicious volley was ripping out the net pegs, I was somewhere in the forest, caught upside down in a vicious patch of bramble. As Mr Cad was on this tour, doing the official club photography, I had decided to 'get creative' with my own pictures. I'd discovered a route to the top of the cliff, where I could take some interesting aerial-style photos of the game from high above. So far so good. Unfortunately on the way back down the steep, rain-slicked path, I lost my footing and overbalanced. The weight of my camera back-pack sent me headfirst into the thicket. Aside from scratches and bruises, no serious damage was done and my camera lenses survived the tumble unscathed. Predictably, our gang found my misadventure hysterically funny.

Late on, IFK pulled one back, but it was too little, too late, especially when their Swedish international, Pontus Wernbloom, was sent off. There had been fears that IFK would only send a reserve side, but the starting eleven showed only three changes from the team that contested their last competitive first team game. As such, the win represented something of a scalp for Palace, whose pre-season games in England prior to the tour had generally been against low standard opposition.

The rest of the night was spent frequenting the bars and kebab shops of Grebbestad, with Pub Hörnet again a very popular choice amongst the Palace faithful. As the beer flowed, so did the songs, with The Colonel leading the choristers. Many old classics were dusted off, including lusty renditions of 'Two Little Boys' (back in a more innocent time), the FA Cup standard 'She Wore a Yellow Ribbon' (all five verses) and a particularly spirited version of 'We've got the Best Team in the Land' with the entire chorus rising to its feet to emotionally acclaim the 'Geoff Thomas, number eight' line. The highlight of the night was when the Colonel's German pal Nils, who is a trained opera singer, gave us "I Found an Old Handbag" in full operatic style. The pub gave him a deserved standing ovation.

The following morning, we made our hungover way back to Gothenburg, eschewing the train for a bus ride, which seemed to be slightly quicker. The previous day, we'd been told that there was a Champions League qualifier on Wednesday, an hour east of Gothenburg in the city of Borås. This involved Swedish Champions and current league leaders Elfsborg playing Northern Ireland double winners

Linfield. The tie was well poised at 0-0 from the first leg and there was some Palace interest in the tie, with our former centre-forward Matthias Svensson now leading the line for Elfsborg.

So barely two hours after arriving back in Gothenburg, a party of fifteen Palace fans headed east on another bus. After a walk through the town and a reasonably warm reception from the Linfield fans congregating in the main square, we headed to the recently built Borås Arena. We had been told that the home stands were sold out, but provided we got there early we should have no trouble getting into the away end. And so it proved.

The game was a fairly drab affair, with Matthias Svensson being credited with the lone goal that sent the Swedes through, though his meatball header did rebound off the crossbar and back onto the keeper's outstretched arm before actually finding the net. Svensson managed to enrage the very vocal Linfield contingent with a range of dives and play-acting that brought memories of his time in a Palace shirt back into sharp focus. Linfield only made a proper go of it in the last few minutes, but were eventually denied the away goal that would have seen them through as one of the shocks of the round. The consensus was that a bit less caution earlier in the half might have paid dividends.

The bus was packed to the rafters for the return journey to Gothenburg, where the evening was finished back in Dubliners, which was absolutely heaving with very drunk Swedes. We'd been told that it was payday in Sweden but we hadn't expected such enriching displays of public inebriation.

Although there was a small programme of Swedish football scheduled for the Thursday evening, none was within a reasonable travelling distance of Gothenburg, so we made the most of a day off. Swimming in the hotel pool, enjoying river and sea cruises, as well as visiting the local theme park, Liseberg, which is purportedly the biggest in Scandinavia. Others tracked down the 'Chrystal Palace' in Tradgardsforeningen Park built in 1878 – an exact replica of our Crystal Palace, however their version is still standing and blooming as a Roseutium. Some decided to head for Uddevalla a day early to scout the bars there, with Harry's Bar being noted as 'the place' to be.

The match in Uddevalla coincided with the city's annual Fjord Festival and accommodation was at a premium. The advance guard pitched up in the City Square at 11am and occupied a large area of the outdoor bar, set up especially for the festival. Between heavy showers, the Palace fans enjoyed the local entertainment, joining in with the band and the afternoon's pop quiz, despite it being entirely in Swedish. Our answer to every question: ABBA. Don't knock it, we got quite a few right.

The rain showers became heavier and more prolonged, so when Harry's Bar opened at 3pm, most of our support decided to congregate there to continue the pre-match beers and sing-song. Midway through the afternoon, the atmosphere soured somewhat, when members of the Dirty 30, who had travelled out for the Friday game, arrived in the bar. Unlike Germany in 2005, this time they were mob-handed. There had been some rumblings in the Dubliners the previous day that they wanted 'a word' with me about my little joke in the fanzine piece about that tour.

We were in the company of Baldy and Hoover's respective crews, when our tables were approached by a dozen or so gentlemen intent on airing their grievance. Now I'm not usually one to hang around in these situations but I was emboldened by a couple of drinks at this stage and there wasn't really anywhere to run to. In fact, I remember feeling more incredulous than frightened that my daft two-year old pun had come to this.

An elder statesman emerged from their massing ranks to act as their spokesperson and a frank exchange of views ensued. Unbeknownst to me, Hoover, The Colonel and Baldy had also closed in around our table, should it kick off. I, however, was completely oblivious to this even being a possibility, not least because Sue was standing right beside me. I really could not understand how a silly little joke had supposedly caused this much upset and I stood my ground on that.

Thankfully, the discussion ended without violence, when they felt I had accepted their point that no Palace fan should be making a punchline out of other Palace fans and that I would not do it again. What none of them appeared to realise was that I'd already stopped producing the fanzine at the end of the previous season.

Shortly after that I had to leave to retrieve my camera gear from the hotel and collect my press pass from the ground, so I left Sue and our gang drinking in the bar.

Oddevold's Rimnersvallen stadium has the air of a 1960s municipal sports track. Nevertheless, it's a tidy little ground with a main stand on one side, a covered terrace on the other and fairly shallow open terracing behind each goal. It had rained heavily during the day and the pitch was particularly stodgy in places, which led Peter Taylor to use almost a completely different team in each half and some unusual player positioning. Palace took the lead on 25 minutes when winger James Dayton scored his first senior goal with a low, bobbling shot.

At half-time, an impromptu game of football broke out between Palace fans and Swedish youngsters on the running track behind one of the goal lines. This appeared to unduly alarm the stewards, who had no success in trying to usher fans back to the terrace, until the teams re-appeared. According to the local press, a recent pitch invasion at a Sweden v Denmark international game, which saw the referee being struck and the game abandoned, had left the stadium officials unnecessarily twitchy. Amidst this friendly kickabout, The Colonel had a brief contretemps with the long-jump pit and had to retire early to the terraces, somewhat battered and bruised.

Fifteen minutes into the second half, Oddevald equalised. Goalkeeper Scott Flinders could only parry a speculative but strong long-range drive from Marcus Larsson, before the rebound was finished off by David Engelbrektsson. In the end, fitness levels played a part, as Palace steamrollered their part-time opponents in the final twenty minutes. A goal from Clinton Morrison on 72 minutes was quickly followed by a tap-in from David Martin, after good work from Stuart Green. Ben Watson rounded out the score with a scintillating strike from a 25 yard free kick, in the dying minutes.

After the game, some headed straight back to Gothenburg by bus to catch the early flight on Saturday morning. For those staying, it was back to party time at Harry's, before winding their way back to Gothenburg and then home over the course of the weekend, accompanied by memories of a mostly satisfying tour on and off the pitch.

The players' own take on the tour was captured by Matt Lawrence in *The London Paper* the following Monday.

"We'd arrived in Gothenburg on Monday afternoon and were all looking forward to a relaxing evening before the following day's training, and the game against IFK. Our fitness coach, Mark Hulse, had other ideas. He decided that after 12 hours travelling it would be of a psychological benefit to run our proverbial butts off. The science behind this was never revealed and, with a knowing nod from the gaffer, the lads launched him into a nearby river. I'm sure we paid the consequence for our actions in the following day's gym session, but it brought a smile to our faces at the time.

The game against IFK was going to be our sternest test of pre-season so far. The hosts are regular participants in European competition and, more importantly, were mid-season in their respective league campaign.

With Sweden having received as much rainfall as us this summer, the game had to be played out on a bog of a pitch. This was conducive to a number of flying tackles, and IFK made sure we were acclimatised to the rigours of competitive football once again. The game proved to be an entertaining one, with us just running out worthy winners.

After a single session on the Wednesday, we had a double session on the Thursday, with a coach taking us to the training ground. We thought everyone was on board as the clock ticked round to leaving time, and then ambled on a late arrival (if there's one thing the gaffer hates it's poor punctuality; especially from the younger pros).

'Dartford' Dave Martin felt the wrath of the gaffer and had to run around the track that encircled the training pitch while everyone else enjoyed the football session.

Our penultimate day of the trip saw us train in the morning, followed by another game in the evening. To be honest, I'm not sure who we played but we beat them 4-1 on an even worse pitch than before. The only notable part of the evening was the remarkably large number of inebriated Palace fans in the crowd. I think that tells you all you need to know about the game."

This tour was markedly different from the pre-season jaunts to Scandinavia that took place from the mid-seventies through to the early nineties, not least in the number of games played. In this book, I haven't gone into any great detail about these tours for a few reasons which will become apparent.

Palace's first post war trip to Sweden took place in 1973 as part of Malcolm Allison's first pre-season. Palace played three games in the Juli Cupen (July Cup). This was an international tournament hosted by Västerhaninge IF, which had been running since 1970. In previous years, Partick Thistle, Manchester City and Hull City had been invited to take part, with the latter teams lifting the Cup in 1971 and 1972 respectively.

In 1973, it was a six-team tournament with four Swedish sides and two from England; Sheffield Wednesday was the other English team. The six clubs were split into two groups and each team in the group played each other once. Then a third game was played against a team from the other group depending on the final positions. The winners of each group met in the final which was played at Hammerby IF's Söderstadion in Johanneshov, near Stockholm.

Palace's first game was against IK Sirius and they won 3-2 with goals from Derek Possee, Charlie Cooke and Don Rogers. The other group game against Sandvikens IF finished 1-1 with Bobby Tambling the Palace scorer. With Sandvikens only beating Sirius by a single goal, Palace qualified for the final by virtue of number of goals scored.

The final was against the hosts, Västerhaninge IF and Palace won 3-0 with goals from Possee, Rogers and Tambling. The day after the final, Palace played a friendly against Degerfors IF and notched a 1-0 win to end the tour on a further high.

Palace returned to Sweden a year later for a further three games and Steve Carleton travelled out for his first Palace tour abroad:

"It was an Interrail trip. After 38 hours travelling, we arrived in Helsingborg where the first game was being played and slept in the Customs Hall. We moved on to Linköping where we played IF Saab and saw our only win of the tour. The other two games ended in draws. The final game was against IFK Norrköping. After that game we were refused entry to a pub in Stockholm, not because we were wearing colours or looked yobbish, simply because our hair was too long!"

Four years later, Palace returned to Sweden and the following year toured in Norway for the first time as covered in an earlier chapter. In 1980, the club returned to Sweden for their overseas pre-season tour.

In 1982, Palace played their first – and to date only – home game against Swedish opposition. Our old friends IFK Göteburg were the visitors to Selhurst. Although it was a mid-season game for Palace, it was a pre-season game for IFK and their young Manager, Sven Goran Eriksson, who went on to make quite a name for himself in England. In fact, the game was more a warm-up for the resumption of their UEFA Cup campaign; a quarter-final against Valencia, the following Wednesday.

The Swedes won 3-1 at Selhurst and remain the only Swedish side to have beaten Palace. The friendly saw them on their way to winning not only a domestic league and cup double that year, but also to lift their first UEFA Cup against hot favourites SV Hamburger.

The Scandinavian pre-season tours resumed under Steve Coppell in 1987 with a six-game tour of Sweden. That trip was mired in controversy as, shortly after the club returned home, *The Voice*, Britain's only national Afro-Caribbean newspaper, alleged that on the tour there had been a late night racially-motivated confrontation between the young black players at the club and some of the senior white professionals, who had been drinking. The club refused to comment on the specifics of the allegation, other than saying that the matter was being dealt with internally.

The following season, Palace toured in the northern reaches of Norway, Sweden and Finland. The game in Norway against FK Mjølner was notable for two reasons. First was the location; it took place in Narvik within the Arctic Circle and to date remains the furthest north that Palace have played a game. Secondly, Palace lost the game 3-1; their only defeat in all of the post-war Scandinavian and Finnish pre-season tours. In perspective, that is one single defeat in 15 tours and 68 games.

Such was the low quality of the opposition, many of the games were extremely high-scoring encounters. One unfortunate Swedish team, Bankeryds SK, shipped nineteen goals in two successive years, only replying twice. With so many games and so many goals, it becomes tricky for the players and club staff to be able to make anything other than very general recollections about these tours, hence the difficulty in documenting them in any great detail.

Back to 2007, the following Tuesday after returning from Sweden, Palace continued their pre-season with a home game against RSC Anderlecht. This game had been tentatively planned for some weeks, but was dependent on the Brussels side winning the Belgian Jupiler League, which they duly wrapped up in mid-May. An official announcement of the match was made shortly thereafter. However, due to Anderlecht's appearance in the Belgian SuperCoupe and the proximity of the game to the start of their league season, they decided to send a fairly weak squad across to Selhurst on the day. Indeed none of the players who started against Club Brugge in the SuperCoupe were selected to travel.

The Belgians then proceeded to turn up late, forcing a kick-off delay of 15 minutes. However, when the game finally did get underway, Palace quickly realised that this under-strength side was going to be no pushover. It was their new signing French striker Cyril Thereau, who opened the scoring on 26 minutes, when he managed to turn and fire home all in one movement, despite being closely marked.

Palace had plenty of decent chances themselves in the first half, including a Clinton Morrison 'van Basten-style' volley, which drew an equally world-class save. Half-time changes meant Palace looked a more cohesive proposition in the second half. Ben Watson equalised from the penalty spot following an extremely dubious handball decision on 50 minutes. From there on in, Palace generally had the better of the play, especially when teenage sensation Victor Moses came on for the final third of the game and wowed the crowd, despite a rough ride from his markers. The game finished honours even, in front of 5,232, with Anderlecht bringing at least 150 vocal fans across for the game.

There were also three Palace fans decked out in Anderlecht colours in the Upper Holmesdale, which almost caused an incident before the game. Long before the days of those extremely dubious 'half and half' scarves, Rob, Graham Carter and myself had dug out our Anderlecht shirts from the footie trips we'd taken to watch 'Les Mauves' in years previous. We were happily waving to the away fans, who having spotted us, were delightedly waving back.

This prompted the Upper Tier stewards to surround us. In the comically loud tone of an Englishman speaking to a foreigner, we were asked:

"DO YOU WANT TO GO AND JOIN YOUR FRIENDS?"

They appeared mystified by our perfectly south London-accented response:

"No mate, our season ticket seats are right here".

At first, they would not have it and threatened again to move us, but finally accepted a made-up tale of having just swapped shirts in the pub with some Belgians.

"Look, just behave yourselves" came the muttered parting shot.

A few weeks later, Palace had one further game facing overseas opposition at Selhurst, against their American partnership club CPFC USA, which was detailed in the previous chapter. After a relatively poor start to the season, Peter Taylor had been dismissed to be replaced by a controversial choice, Neil Warnock. He took most of the autumn to turn the team around, but following two long unbeaten streaks between November and mid-January, then again in March and April, Palace made it into the play-offs.

They faced Bristol City in the semi-finals, where a poor performance in the first leg at Selhurst resulted in a home defeat. The team rallied away at Ashton Gate, never usually a happy hunting ground. And so it proved again, as Palace were denied after extra time, with Ben Watson missing a penalty that would have sent us through in normal time.

19

BOHEMIAN RHAPSODY

There was no foreign pre-season tour in 2008 and not even a sniff of a home friendly against overseas opposition either. Instead, Neil Warnock preferred to take the whole squad down to the West Country, where three first team friendlies were arranged and the youth players took part in the Errea South Western Challenge.

Our touring clan was not to be denied, though. Ten of us took over a house in Port Isaac for the week. We were joined by others lodging in the pub next door and a great time was had by all. Due to the arcane point-scoring rules of the Errea tournament, Palace Youths somehow managed to qualify for the weekend finals. However, this eventuality had not been foreseen, so the youth team had to withdraw. The club had not obtained the requisite parental permission or insurance to stay for longer than five days.

The lack of a foreign tour in 2008 was rather a shame, as it was exactly a hundred years since Palace's very first foray abroad. After a good 1908 season finishing fourth in the Southern League, the club toured Bohemia (in the area that is now the Czech Republic) playing six fixtures there. The tour was cost-free to the club, with all expenses being paid by recently formed clubs to gain experience against English sides. Manchester United and Middlesbrough were also there at the same time.

There is a record of the trip in the club's handbook for the following season. 'Our Tour in Bohemia' was written by an unnamed member of the party. The report is certainly 'of its time':

"With a view of giving the players an enjoyable holiday trip after their arduous season, the Directors accepted an invitation to play a series of matches in Bohemia, and Mr. Goodman arranged (in conjunction with Mr G Payne, of Prague) all the details.

Messrs. Cook & Son, in whose hands the whole of the travelling and hotel arrangements were placed, did everything possible for the comfort of the team and our thanks are due to them for their courteous attention to all requirements.

A merry party consisting of Mr Sydney Bourne (Chairman of Directors), Mr E. F. Goodman (Secretary-Manager), Mr Birch (trainer), and Johnson, Collyer, Walker, Innerd, Ryan, Brearley, Lewis, Garratt, Swann, Bauchop, Woodger, Roberts and Needham, left

Holborn Viaduct on May 14th, and by the time we reached Queenborough, Birch, by his display of German money and his command of the German language, fully convinced us that he was quite prepared for anything that might happen in Germany, But he was not quite sure of what might happen on the ocean!

However, we had a "mill-pond" passage to Flushing. The only incident there was an enormous purchase of picture postcards by Ryan. After a few minutes stay we got into our through carriage for Prague, a journey which occupied 22½ hours. The country we passed through was flat and uninteresting until we reached Dresden, and then, right along the banks of the Elbe, through the Saxonian Switzerland, the scenery was so glorious.

I forgot to mention that we were awakened in the middle of the night at Gooch, the German frontier station for Customs purposes. Goodman and Collyer were painfully aware of this fact! Well, we were heartily glad to reach Prague, about 4 o'clock on Friday afternoon. We were met at the station by the captain and many members of the Slavia F.C. and Mr G.Payne, who arranged our list of matches, and who acted as our agent for the tour and accompanied us to all our matches. His offices as interpreter were of the greatest use to us.

Carriages were on hand to take us to the Hotel Cheval Noir (Black Horse), which was to be our headquarters during the whole stay in Bohemia. And splendid quarters we found them! It is probably the best hotel in Prague, and evidently boasts a chef of the very best class, for we found the cooking beyond a fault. We also met with every attention and courtesy from all the staff there. There is a most enticing café-garden, where we had all our meals.

Just as we were sitting down to our first dinner the band struck up our National Anthem – a very pretty compliment which we much appreciated, and for which Birch thanked them in his best German. Early to bed, for we were all fatigued after our long journey.

Next day, a little sight-seeing, and as we were getting ready to start for the Slavia F.C. ground, for our first match, a violent storm burst over the town. The ground was saturated, and being of a clayey nature, it was in a wretched state, and our players found the greatest difficulty in keeping their feet. However, they performed well enough by 5 goals to 4, and took things fairly easy.

The next day we played them in a return match, and the ground, under a baking sun, had become very hard. We put up the best game of the tour and won 4 to 1. Woodger had a field day on his own, and delighted the crowd with his clever play. Indeed, the whole team showed really fine form, and Johnson's goalkeeping was a popular feature of the game."

This game was notable in Palace's history as it was a first time that the club played a game on a Sunday. A first for Palace, as back in Britain, no games were allowed to be played on the Lord's Day at the time.

"Monday and Tuesday were free days, devoted to seeing the many historic and deeply interesting places in the City, I may mention that Prague has a population, including the suburbs, of over half a million, and there are about 50 football clubs there. I should think there were about 100 tennis courts around the Slavia F.C. and Sparta F.C. grounds.

Wednesday evening we played Smichov F.C., a students' team, and had a most enjoyable game, winning comfortably by 7 to 1. Thursday, through an arranged match (with Novometsky) falling through, we had, as opponents, a mixed team of Slavia F.C., which included several reserves, and we found them a very tough lot. We beat them 2 goals to 0. Friday was free, and we still had plenty of sights which were well worth seeing, and we enjoyed them immensely.

On Saturday we had to journey to Konnigratz. The University Students provided the opposition, and played a most gentlemanly game, but were no match for us, as we defeated them by 10 goals to 1. We had to stay the night there and get up at five o'clock the next morning to catch the only train that was any use to us.

We got back to the "Black Horse" about 9.30, just as people were returning from early Mass, and felt that we had really earned our breakfast. After lunch we were on the move again and took the train to Kladno, a mining centre up in the mountains. Great preparations had been made for our visit and about 4,000 people were round the ground when the kick-off took place. They expected many more, but a heavy thunderstorm was banging about all day and soon after the game started it burst right over the ground. It was not a half-hearted storm either. The thunder was deafening, the lightning blinding and the rain a perfect deluge. Players and spectators were equally relieved when the whistle blew for time. We won 6 goals to 1. Thus, in a playing sense, ended our tour.

Although we won every match pretty easily, it must not be assumed that the teams we met were all of a very poor order. Far from it. The Slavia F.C. is one of the best, or possibly the best on the Continent and they would put up a real good game against many a league club. They are trained and coached by I.Madden, the old Celtic and Scotch International, and play a fast, hard game right up to the finish. They know every trick in the game, but their weakness is that they cannot do them so well as our English players.

The other teams came a good bit below this one in footballing ability, but all have the making of good sides. All our matches were contested in the very best of spirit, and we met with every courtesy from all our opponents, their club officials and spectators. Our lads played clever and gentlemanly football all through, and the Bohemian Press and football public were loud in their praises of our team.

A special compliment was paid to us, when, at the railway station, just before we started for home Mr R.H.Schwarz, the secretary to the British Consulate, and from whom we received many kind attentions during our stay, arrived with a formal invitation from the Slavia F.C. to visit them again next year. We believe this is the first time any team has been invited two successive years.

The refereeing is the worst part of the game out there. It is extraordinary! It would be amusing if it were not so intensely irritating. I refrain from going deeply into details, but would suggest that if one of the referees we met should ever be ambitious enough to 'hold the Whistle' in a league match over here he should bring his own Coroner along. He'll want one! I'm not sure, but I believe Brearley and Bauchop are going to collaborate in a book on 'Bohemian Refereeing: from a Crystal Palace F.C. point of view.'

Anyhow, everyone thoroughly enjoyed the tour, and after the first day or two were quite at home with the language and the coinage. Indeed, during one of the games, Walker's comments on the play, in fluent (Black Country) German, filled us with amazement! Birch, too, towards the end was beginning to speak Bohemian like a native (of Sydenham), but some of his experiments in strange foods were decidedly risky, especially for a trainer.

We must have met nearly every Britisher and Colonial in Prague, and found them all good fellows, who helped considerably towards our enjoyment. One of the most pleasing incidents of our trip was that, of Captain Wentworth-Forbes, His Majesty's Consul for Bohemia, dining and spending an evening with us, an honour we greatly esteemed.

On Monday May 25th we were due to leave Prague at 3pm, and a host of opponents and friends turned up to wish us "good-bye" and "bon voyage", and to ask us to come again. Three cheers from us and three more from them, and we were off! About 27 hours rail and boat journey, and we landed on our dear shores at Queenborough, and another 1½ hours and we were back in London.

One word more; on Mr Goodman's shoulders rested all the responsibilities of a novel undertaking, and right well he met them. To his untiring work and unfailing good temper, the greater part of the success and enjoyment of the tour was due."

Why Palace did not return to Bohemia is lost to us now. Perhaps the relatively poor showing, 16th in the League the following season, meant the players were not to be rewarded in the same manner. It would be another six years before Palace would venture overseas again, although they did undertake two friendlies on consecutive days in Wales in October 1909 against Ton Pentre and Cardiff City. The latter game was held at Cardiff Arms Park. This was an attempt to challenge rugby's dominance in the Welsh valleys, or 'missionary work' as the press of the day described it.

On the very eve of the First World War, the Club undertook a six game post-season tour to Scandinavia, playing two games each in Denmark, Sweden and Norway.

Steve Martyniuk, in his highly-recommended series of books *The Origin of Crystal Palace FC*, has researched this tour in impressive detail. Thanks to his fourth volume, we know that Palace was also scheduled to play in Hamburg at the start of the tour and, indeed, stopped briefly in that city after travelling up through Belgium on the train, before heading onwards to Denmark. What happened to that game is not known. Steve noted that there was no indication that this might have been down to the increasing political tensions and rhetoric between the UK and Germany.

In Denmark, Palace faced a Danish Select Team chosen from four Copenhagen clubs. The match took place on a site that is now occupied by the Telia Parken: the home ground of FC København and the current Danish National side. Palace lost both games: 2-1 and two days later, 4-2.

In Sweden, we played twice in Gothenburg, first against Örgryte IS and then IFK Göteburg, at the Walhalla stadium. There is still a football ground on that site, which is less than a mile as the crow flies from the Ullevi Stadium where Safety and I attended the 1997 friendly against IFK. Although it was not the one we passed on the walk to the ground, which is where Örgryte now play, albeit in a newer stadium than the one we saw. Palace won both games: 3-1 and 4-1 respectively.

The final games of the tour were held in Norway against local regional select XIs, in the capital city of Oslo, although it was known at the time as Kristiania, before reverting to the ancient name of Oslo some ten years later. The games were staged at the newly-relocated Frogner Stadium, indeed, the first of the two games, against a Grenland Select XI was the inaugural game at the new gravel-surfaced arena. Palace ran in six goals without reply, with Ernie York scoring a hat-trick.

The final tour game, two days later, was against an Oslo/Kristiania select side which resulted in a 4-1 win. Two different adverts for the game carried two different names for the same team, however I guess the locals would have been used to this descriptive convention. The stadium is still in use today as the home ground of Frigg FC. Is it too childish of me to hope that their team runs out to a certain Sex Pistols b-side? The gravel of old has been replaced by an artificial grass surface, while the arena is still used for ice skating in the winter, just as it had been in 1914.

Palace would not play abroad again until February 1937, when they were invited to travel to Rotterdam to play a Dutch National XI. The game was held at Sparta Rotterdam's ground on a Wednesday afternoon, where 10,000 spectators enjoyed a 2-2 draw. Palace led twice through two Jacks, Palethorpe and Blackman, but were pegged level with seven minutes to go. There was a growing trend for European national sides to play 'unofficial' international friendlies against English clubs based in the south east around this period. Southend, Gillingham and Reading all took part in such games.

Just over a year later, the invitational fixture was repeated at the same ground, with the Dutch team now being billed with the grander title of Royal Netherlands FB. Palace lost this encounter 3-2 with Albert Dawes and Trevor Smith on the scoresheet for Palace.

Four days into 1939, Palace accepted an invitation to play the Belgian national side at Stade Joseph Marien in Brussels, which remains the home of Royale Union Saint-Gilloise today.

The game against Diables Rouges (Red Devils) as they were – and still are – known, was notable for taking place under floodlights, a novelty for most English clubs at the time. Palace players were further unsettled by a rough sea crossing via Ostend, which ruled Fred Gregory out of the game with acute seasickness. It was so bad that on the return home the club opted for a shorter crossing via Calais. To add to the woes, it was a foggy evening and the pitch was slippery. Depending on which press report you choose to believe, the game was watched by 5,000, 8,000 or 9,000 spectators.

Despite all these obstacles, Palace gave a great account of themselves, losing narrowly 5-4 with goals from Albert Dawes, George Daniels and a brace from Albert Robson. The Belgian press was effusive in its praise:

> "The compact formation of Crystal Palace, in spite of a rough crossing, in spite of the defeat they suffered, upheld the honour of British football. It was a defeat that was by no means dishonourable for two reasons. Firstly it was undeserved, and secondly, it was inflicted by an almost international team. The Crystal Palace team gave us once more a brilliant demonstration of the possibilities of English Football, our rivals that evening taught us many new things."

Palace was immediately invited back for another fixture, but the club was focused on promotion that season, albeit unsuccessfully. Just like the Scandinavian tour in 1914, the political situation in Europe was again quickly deteriorating, spiralling towards a Second World War which would preclude further opportunities to play.

That remains, at the time of writing, Palace's only ever senior fixture in Belgium, though the country does hold the distinction of supplying Palace's first foreign-born player. In 1947, Belgian winger Marcel Gaillard signed for the club. That is not to imply, however, that Palace had developed an international scouting network – he was signed from Tonbridge.

Palace have faced Belgian opposition twice more, both at home. In 1971, RFC Bruges (shortly before they changed their name to Club Brugge) provided the opposition for John Sewell's testimonial and, in 2007, we saw the visit of RSC Anderlecht, as detailed in the previous chapter.

There was a strong rumour that Palace would be hosting Royal Antwerp in early August 2009, but that came to nought. Our home friendlies that season turned out to be Norwich, who had just been relegated from the second tier and Gillingham, who had just returned to the third level after promotion, when a previously announced game against AS Nancy fell through, due to the French side's concern over the swine flu epidemic. To make matters worse, Palace contrived to lose both 1-0.

Although there were no Palace games against international opposition in the 1920s, Selhurst Park was the venue for a full England international on Monday 1st March 1926. 23,000 people crowded into Palace's recently-opened stadium. The

FA had promised Palace a full international upon completion of their new ground and almost eighteen months after the club's inaugural game against Sheffield Wednesday, they made good on that promise.

Appropriately for St David's Day, England's opposition was Wales and it was the visitors who triumphed 3-1 on the day, after England were reduced to ten men for much of the game due to injury. Substitutes were not a feature of the game back then. Selhurst Park has since hosted several England amateur and U23 internationals.

When the Olympics came to London in 1948, Selhurst Park was chosen as the venue for early rounds of the football tournament. One of these games entered the Olympic record books as the highest scoring game in the finals, when eventual gold medalists Sweden smashed a dozen goals without reply past South Korea in the quarter-finals. At the time of writing that record still stands. The other game between Denmark and Egypt finished 3-1 to the Danes after extra-time.

It was the advent of floodlights at Selhurst that opened the floodgates for international friendlies at home. Although floodlighting had been installed at a few grounds in the thirties, the Football League had been initially reluctant to approve its use for competitive games. In the early fifties, the tide was turning in favour of their use and in the summer of 1953, Selhurst also became a floodlit venue, with an inaugural floodlit friendly against Chelsea that resulted in a 1-1 draw on Monday 28th September.

Thereafter, every Tuesday in October became 'Floodlight Football' night with a series of friendly games, mostly against other league teams in higher divisions than Palace. However, they saved the best until last. The final one in the series was against top flight Parisian side, Stade Français. The sports club is better known these days for its highly successful rugby union club, not least their crazy strips. The football team still exists, but now competes in local leagues.

Palace won the fixture 4-2, our only victory in that initial series. In the matchday programme, the Board reported their delight at the great success of their trial venture, promising that the series would return in the future. The midweek floodlit friendly became an integral part of Palace's calendar for many years to come.

Over the next few seasons, a host of different Scottish League teams visited Selhurst, together with Danish side Esbjerg fB and Austrian clubs FC Vienna and Wiener AC. Another popular friendly game was against an International Managers XI, which saw veteran stars and football managers of the period come together to form an exhibition side. In 1959, Palace hosted a Caribbean XI and ran out 11-1 winners; at that time, the biggest-ever margin of victory against an overseas team.

We have already seen that Real Madrid visited in April 1962 to open our revamped floodlights. A couple of months before, CHZJD Slovan Bratislava from Czechoslovakia (now Slovakia) had been narrowly defeated 3-2 at Selhurst. Bratislava returned to South London five years later but went down again to a single Palace strike. The mid-season home friendlies against foreign opposition continued until the mid-eighties, before they fell out of favour.

Pitch imperfect. Turf laid over the base plate at Waldorf - July 2009

Presentation of the Medd Cup.
L-R: Pete and Randy Medd, Val Teixeira, Danny Butterfield & Neil Warnock - July 2009

20

TAKE ME OUT TO THE BALL GAME

The 2008/09 season failed to live up to the expectations set by the incredible run from the relegation places to the play-offs in the previous season. With increasing money problems, Palace were unable to compete with the sides around them in the transfer market and this was often reflected in the performances. Never in real danger of relegation, Palace eventually finished in 14th place, but were docked a point for fielding an ineligible player after the season ended and subsequently dropped a position.

The circumstances surrounding that deduction can be filed in the bulging archive labelled 'Typical Palace'. In the final minutes of the final game of the season, Palace brought on Portuguese winger Rui Fonte – the teenage younger brother of Jose, our regular centre-half. Rui came on loan from Arsenal on transfer deadline day the previous January but failed to make much of an impression. That final game was against Sheffield United and had been moved to the Sunday for television coverage, as the Blades were in with a chance of automatic promotion.

The game finished goal-less which left the Yorkshiremen in third place and in the play-offs, where they lost in the final to Burnley. Palace's hard-won point was then snatched away, after it was discovered that Fonte's loan period had expired at midnight on the Saturday, therefore he was ineligible by a few hours, due to the game being selected for TV. To add insult for injury, no-one can recall him even touching the ball in the short time he was on the pitch.

With Neil Warnock's expressed preference for a pre-season in the West Country, eyebrows were raised when it was announced that Palace would return to the US for a one-week tour. Typically though, the club failed to confirm what fixtures were planned. A chance meeting with Warnock revealed the team would be based in the Washington DC area and that friendly matches would form part of the tour. It was assumed, correctly, that one would be against our USA partner club, however the venue came as something of a surprise.

The game was to take place at the home of South Maryland Blue Crabs – a minor league baseball side in a small town called Waldorf, 25 miles south of the

Capitol. A first for Palace, playing football in a baseball stadium – unless you count Derby County's former home, which once hosted the sport long before Palace ever played there. Like buses, the second opportunity to take in Palace at a Ball Park was announced just a week later with the news that they would be facing Harrisburg City Islanders at the home of the Lancaster Barnstormers, deep within Amish country, in Pennsylvania.

After our experiences in recent years, Sue had been nominated to take charge of the travel arrangements. Her services became jokingly known as Eden Park Tours. Hoover came up with a rather more unflattering, actually downright rude nickname for our travel agent but to immortalise it here would lead to an instant loss of my marital privileges.

We had decided to take the plunge on booking flights early, on the basis of our conversation with Mr Warnock, as the prices were starting to rise alarmingly. Given that Lancaster was around 125 miles from Washington in the opposite direction to Waldorf, it was clear we would need to hire a mini-van for our crew. In addition to Sue and I, the party consisted of Hoover, Mr Cad, Pete Bonthrone and a new recruit to our crew, Chris Plummer, who was one of the key figures in organising Palace away travel for many years.

Though Palace would be playing on a Monday and Thursday, the best flight deals were to be had for a Friday to Friday trip, even taking into account the extra accommodation costs. We arrived in time to attend one of CPFC USA's home USL games, coincidentally against Harrisburg. The game was taking place on a Friday evening at University of Maryland Baltimore County Stadium, just outside Baltimore itself, where we would be spending the weekend, before moving back south to Waldorf.

It proved to be an eventful couple of days in Charm City. We were mindful of the City's reputation as the Murder Capital of America, as gruesomely depicted in the television drama *The Wire*. We were warned to stick to the Inner Harbor area where we were staying and not to venture too many blocks back from the waterside. Hoover and Pete certainly did not need telling twice after their experience in 2006.

Saturday morning was spent sightseeing, I decided to get another game in and drove to see Real Maryland v Pittsburgh Riverhounds. Strangely, I was not able to tempt any of the others to accompany me, not even Sue. They preferred instead the bars around the iconic Camden Yards baseball arena, where the Baltimore Orioles were hosting the Toronto Blue Jays.

That evening, our gang decided to head to Slainte – an Irish Bar that sponsored CPFC USA on Thames Street. I got back from the match, dumped the car at the hotel and headed out to join the others at the bar. My cab could not reach Slainte as the street was closed to traffic for the night, so he let me out at the start of the strip.

As I walked along, bar after bar was heaving with the bright and beautiful people of the city, enjoying cocktails soundtracked by fine soul music. My spirits soared in anticipation of a party night, but then I reached Slainte.

I've seen more life in a tramp's vest. Our gang of five, who made up most of the clientele, were sitting around watching the baseball. I excitedly told them about the more happening joints along the street, but I couldn't get anyone to move – they were settled in for the night. The baseball finished and the music started. It's fair to say traditional Irish is not among my most favourite musical genres and my increasingly desperate entreaties to go somewhere else were ignored.

Chris and Pete headed off around midnight, but we were there until the bitter end – the very bitter end in my case. All of the bars kicked out at the same time and getting a cab proved tricky. Eventually we piled into one. It became quickly evident that our driver was not the sharpest tool in the box. He had never of heard of our hotel, The Hampton Inn, a very well-known hotel chain in the States. Neither did he seem to know the street when we told him. Eventually, after cruising around the main streets of Inner Harbor, we spotted the road. Unfortunately it was a one-way street and with the meter spinning suspiciously fast, we decided to cut our losses and take a short walk down the side street, instead of getting him to find the right end to drop us right outside the hotel door.

As the four of us stumbled along the street, two jet black pick-up trucks with tinted windows screamed to a halt blocking the road around fifty yards ahead, between us and the hotel entrance. Two gangs of young lads piled out and, to our absolute horror, drew guns and began firing at each other. *The Wire* was coming to life before our eyes.

Hoover pulled Sue into a side alley and hid behind some trash cans, whereas I stood rooted to the spot, unable to comprehend what was going on. Mr Cad, however, just kept on walking towards the hotel, the unflappably cool dude that he is. Suddenly, the two gangs started to whoop and holler, screaming with laughter and slapping each other on the back.

We had not stumbled into the crossfire of gang warfare after all; just some extreme high jinks between mates and mercifully no casualties at all. Well, I say no casualties, but there was some underwear that wouldn't making it home to the UK. We slunk past the back-slapping youths, still really shaken up and followed Mr Cad into the hotel. In the lift, we asked him why he'd not reacted? "I knew that they were blanks, they sounded just like toy cap guns."

After the long Saturday session, Sunday morning was a struggle for some of the party. So much so that we had completely forgotten about the incident the night before. As we were heading out for our pre-booked City sightseeing tour at noon, Sue piped up: "Hang on, did we get shot at last night?" And the memories and the shakes came flooding back, though the shakes might well have had as much to do with our hangovers.

The mode of transport of our sightseeing tour was a 'duck'; more precisely a DKW American ex-military amphibious personnel carrier, repainted bright yellow and repurposed as a tour bus, which travelled both on road and water. Duck Tours even operated in England for a while, until the crafts were deemed unsuitable.

As you know by now, I'm not in my best form on boats. Added to that, I had a hangover that refused to abate. I was just hoping that this tour would prove to be more 'on road' than 'water-based'. Sadly not – the tone was set when the guide came along the craft giving out duck quackers and we were encouraged to quack along with the 'Birdie Song' being blasted out of the speakers as we set off. This whoop-ass was all too-American for Mr Cad. His face was a picture. Indeed, his whole being radiated his utter disgust for the proceedings. This was not what he'd signed up for. Mr Cad's grim demeanour simply egged on Sue, Hoover, Chris and Pete to quack even more enthusiastically but he remained stoic in his distain. Such was my hangover, I just wanted the ungodly racket to stop.

My face, at first just ghostly, turned a whiter shade of pale, as the captain of the duck slalomed his vessel around the mooring posts at speed. Had I been able to face breakfast, it would have made a reappearance at this point.

Suddenly the Captain's breezy, brash tone changed to a worried mutter, then into a cry: "Oh jeez... turn, baby, turn!" We were heading straight for the corner of the dock. The antique craft finally turned away but a fraction too late and we crunched into it. His starboard brake lights met a watery end, while we were jolted out of our seats. The Captain was not quite so full of himself thereafter. The tour concluded at a much more sedate pace. At least my stomach was grateful.

Next morning, we were up early for the journey down to Waldorf, amidst a vanload of poor Basil Fawlty impressions and even poorer puns about salad and nuts. We were able to check-in early at our motel and by noon were on a recce of the stadium and the town. The Regency Furniture Stadium was easy enough to find, with a huge electronic billboard pointing the way off the main road. The game was up in lights, so we stopped for photos, before proceeding to the ground. The gate was open with no-one around, so we had a look inside.

Since the games were announced, we'd been curious to see to just how a football pitch would be laid out on a diamond-shaped baseball field. It wasn't immediately obvious to us on entering the ground as, with only six hours to kick off, the turf was still being laid and the goals and pitch markings were absent. Hoover remarked, "Warnock will do his nut if he sees the state of this."

The stadium itself was almost brand new. It had opened a year before with an inaugural game, coincidentally against Lancaster Barnstormers. The main stand was behind the pitching plate with open seating off to the left. The right side was mostly open, but incorporated a children's adventure playground and a swimming pool. The far end was taken up by the scoreboard and billboard advertising.

We headed back to explore the town and discovered that there wasn't very much of one. It seemed that a generic shopping mall was the epicentre of Waldorf. At least there was a large sports bar at the mall, which was designated our pre-match watering hole.

The game attracted a modest crowd of just over 2,000, around half the actual capacity of the stadium, but a big jump up for the USA side, who had managed only 400 at their previous league game. In addition to our travelling party, we met up with three young lads who we recognised as regulars from The Cherry Trees in South Norwood, also 'Rich the Eagle' Bamber – now resident in the US – and his pal Sam Burch, over from the UK.

In all, I counted ten other Palace fans that had made the trip from the UK. Sam was already a familiar figure to Palace travellers, having been in Sweden in 2007. He has cerebral palsy and is confined to a wheelchair. Sam's steadfast refusal to let his disability prevent him following The Eagles home, away and abroad, remains a true inspiration. It was a real pleasure getting to know him better on this trip.

The match was billed locally as the Medd Cup and the Palace website claimed that the game at Selhurst had been the inaugural encounter, although there was no apparent mention of this back in 2007. Those who made the game enjoyed a goal-fest. Alan Lee opened the scoring with a header inside 15 minutes, but our American counterparts equalised quickly through their captain Val Teixeira and then struck the woodwork with their next attack.

Palace thought they had regained the lead on twenty minutes but Neil Danns' header was ruled out for offside. As half time approached, CPFC USA man Zack Flores spectacularly volleyed home. Unfortunately though, it was into his own net to restore the visitors' lead.

The second half saw an early goal, when Palace's new recruits Darren Ambrose and Freddie Sears, on loan from West Ham, combined well and Sears slotted home. Just as after the first goal, CPFC USA responded quickly through Jordan Seabrook. But as the Americans began to tire, Alassane N'Diaye added a fourth and the luckless Flores managed another crazy own goal on full time. Palace had comfortably retained the Medd Cup, although the CPFC USA Chairman, Randy Medd, jokingly claimed that they should be awarded the Cup on the basis that they had scored more goals than the English team.

Although Mr Cad was on the trip as Official Photographer, I'd been commissioned by the *South London Press* to write match reports and more candid entries for their online football blog, as well as updating the Palace Echo website. It would have made more sense for me to be in the press box, but I could not pass up the opportunity to get pitch-side to take some photographs. Also, I was curious to find out whether the turf had bedded down safely. As it turned out, the hastily-laid pitch was anything but stable underfoot and I feared the worst.

During the game it was interesting to hear the CPFC USA subs chatting about the high quality of professionalism and discipline of their English counterparts. They seemed completely in awe of Palace. The score-line was an irrelevance to them; they felt very privileged to have the chance to play against players who they clearly regarded as being near the pinnacle of footballing excellence.

After the game, the crowd was invited down onto the pitch to mingle with the players and the Palace travellers made good use of the opportunity to grab photos and autographs with our lads, who were happy to oblige. Sam made it down onto the pitch, his wheels carving deep trenches through the unstable turf.

With my reporter's hat on, I took the opportunity to grab a few words with Neil Warnock, who was surprisingly complimentary about the pitch:

"It was just what I wanted – a nice temperature, a lovely surface and no injuries. Everybody had a good run out which is what we set out to do. The hotel and facilities here are really good and we are enjoying ourselves."

Beer had been available throughout the game and drinking was permitted in sight of the pitch, so it's fair to say our party had been making full use of the facilities. Nevertheless, Hoover made loud demands to the mini-van driver that a return to the sports bar was required. I didn't actually mind, but he was barely onto his second pint at the bar before he fell fast asleep, perfectly balanced upon an upright bar stool.

We had decided to spend the two days between games visiting Philadelphia, a new city for many of us, although in the years to come we were to become quite familiar with it. Rich and Sam were also heading there, so we agreed to meet up and we all spent a most enjoyable couple of days sightseeing, including another Duck Tour.

Though no further shootings occurred in our presence, my underwear barely escaped unscathed from a close encounter with the local delicacy, the Philly Cheese Steak. One of these greasy beasts was responsible for that 'Duck Tour' almost being rechristened the 'Dump Tour'. For some in our party, it was the highlight of the whole trip, watching my face turn puce as we rattled over the cobbled streets and onto the Delaware river. I daresay even Neil Warnock would have admired my turn of pace at the end of the tour, as I sprinted for the restrooms after an hour of sheer intestinal torture. Thankfully, by the evening, I had recovered sufficiently to enjoy a curry at 'Palace at the Ben' – a restaurant so appropriately named, we were hardly going to go anywhere else.

Arriving in Lancaster, Pennsylvania, for the encounter with Harrisburg City Islanders, we were greeted with signs boldly proclaiming 'A World Class Soccer Match'. Our party wondered aloud what other team might playing here, because they could not possibly be talking about Palace. Apparently though, they were. The American talent for unconscious hyperbole went beyond the posters. The local cable TV station ran news items and adverts that had to be seen to be believed, proclaiming Palace to be 'One of the Most Famous Soccer Clubs in the World!'

One of these adverts took the biscuit. It featured 'World Class Soccer' clips of Palace in their pomp, however this was rather undermined by a short segment of an all-American 'tough guy' scoring a penalty past the Lancaster mascot and then celebrating by ripping off his baseball shirt to reveal a girlie sports bra, whilst squealing 'Goal' in a really high-pitched voice.

Still, it appeared to work. On the back of such promotion, advance ticket sales were over 5,000 already – double the number that came to the first game. Not everyone was taken in by the hype though, one guy in the box office when we turned up for an early afternoon nose around, was a bit disgruntled. "You'd have sold right out straight away, if you'd have got Arsenal here."

The chap behind the counter fixed him with a steely grin but said nothing. I doubt it was the first time he had heard something similar in the past few weeks. After an awkward pause, the punter bought tickets anyway. The Lancaster Barnstormers stadium had a major advantage over the Waldorf arena, in that it is right in the centre of a decent-sized town and they were hoping for a significant walk-up on the night that would push it close to the 7,500 capacity. This game also proved more popular with the Palace ex-pat contingent who came across in greater numbers for this game: Big Bad John, the Vicar and Winston the Dog with young family in tow, were all present and correct.

After the stadium recce, we settled down in the local brewery to enjoy a pre-match meal and a few handcrafted ales. On the way to The Brickyard – the hostelry closest to the stadium – we came across Lombardo's restaurant. This was just begging to be photographed and our pictures were accompanied by a rousing chorus of 'Just One Lombardo!' bellowed out on their doorstep. The staff and their early evening trade were suitably confused by these antics. I was all for venturing in to explain ourselves and to find out whether they might have a familial connection to the great man. I was quickly dissuaded by my companions, who had worked up something of a thirst walking the half-mile between bars in the oppressive heat.

Once at the game, we had to suffer the indignity of our national anthem being drowned out by a helicopter landing on the pitch delivering the mascot and the match ball. The players were not the only ones having difficulty in keeping a straight face at this point. Unsurprisingly there were no such interruptions for 'The

Star-Spangled Banner' – indeed, the PA announcer solemnly instructed us all to stand and respect the flag, which the US servicemen had borne aloft.

The first half hour of the game was spent wishing we had stayed in the pub: World Class Entertainment it was not. Then suddenly Palace came to life, after a truly excellent finish by Freddie Sears and rattled in two more superbly executed goals before the break: a swirling free-kick from Darren Ambrose and thunderous Neil Danns header converting an inch-perfect Danny Butterfield cross. It felt like Palace had finally delivered on the 'World Class' promise, if only in a short burst. With the job effectively done, the second half saw wholesale personnel changes and Palace never looked like recapturing the form during those devastating fifteen minutes. Harrisburg even managed a consolation goal of some quality themselves.

The reaction from the local crowd as they flooded the pitch looking for autographs after the game reflected the view that, never mind the weary cynicism from the UK contingent, Palace were truly a class act. I even spotted the Arsenal punter, beaming with delight, whilst chatting animatedly to Paddy McCarthy. The official attendance was announced as 5,099. The hoped-for walk-up had not materialised, but no-one seemed to mind very much.

A post-match session ensued back in The Brickyard, where an increasingly merry band of travellers and Palace ex-pats treated the locals and Harrisburg fans alike, to loud renditions of Palace terrace favourites – accompanied at one point by the ubiquitous CD of Palace standards. Despite the racket, we became aware that there was competition from the front bar, in the form of a karaoke night. Not to be outdone, our brave lads entered the fray with a lusty rendition of 'Glad All Over' that turned several female heads. Sadly, the single chaps amongst our happy throng were in no condition to establish any meaningful transatlantic relations.

The next day we gathered ourselves for the late evening flight home from Dulles. The day was spent sightseeing out at a traditional Amish village and a whistle-stop tour of the US Civil War battleground of Gettysburg, where we beat to death an already weak joke about needing the address for our SatNav. Back at the airport, we reflected on a most enjoyable tour in relaxed company. What we did not know then was that it would be a whole five years before we'd be following Palace again on a proper overseas tour.

The mascot and matchball arrive by helicopter at Lancaster - July 2009

Players and fans pose together post-match at Lancaster. Sam Burch and Richard Bamber in the centre. John O'Connor is just behind Sue. - July 2009
[Photo: Neil Everitt]

It's Waterford Crystal! - August 2013
[Photo: Neil Everitt]

A warm Irish welcome awaited Palace on their first visit to the Republic - August 2013
[Photo: Neil Everitt]

21

ONE HIT WONDERS

The next time Palace played overseas it was as a top flight club, although this occasion was only a one-off game, rather than a full tour. The four seasons in-between were a real rollercoaster, with a total of seven different managers, both full-time and caretaker, at the helm. It also saw Palace descend into financial Administration for the second time in eleven years.

Back in 1998, there was no points deduction penalty for entering Administration, however in January 2010, ten points were immediately taken from the club. At the time, Palace were on the fringes of the play-off positions, but tumbled into the relegation dogfight as a result. The fire sale of integral players like Victor Moses and Jose Fonte saw the on-pitch form nose-dive too. The season came down to the final game against Sheffield Wednesday at a sold-out Hillsborough to decide which of the two clubs would be relegated. Palace needed at least a draw to survive.

In a thrilling last day, Palace took the lead twice only to be pegged back both times. Deep into injury time, Palace broke away in a two-on-one situation. Darren Ambrose fed striker Stern John expecting a return pass that would leave him with an open goal, however John decided to shoot himself. The keeper parried and the ball was hacked clear off the line. The pressure was back on Palace and the referee seemed content to play on well passed the five minutes of injury time that had been initially displayed. Just as the Owls were about to launch in another corner, the final whistle finally sounded and Palace were safe. The result protected the club's status as one of only a dozen clubs not to have been outside the top two divisions in thirty-three years.

A month later, a new consortium known as CPFC 2010, took both the club and Selhurst Park out of the hands of Administrators and a new chapter was about to begin for Crystal Palace FC. The consortium consisted of four local businessmen: Steve Browett, chairman of Farr Vintners wine merchants; Martin Long, former head of Churchill Insurance; Jeremy Hosking, a city financier and headed by Steve Parish, Managing Director of TAG Worldwide marketing firm.

I was particularly pleased that Steve Browett was involved, as I knew him to be a proper home and away fan and an all-round lovely fella. Sue and I had met him briefly a couple of years before, in an upscale Wandsworth restaurant, where he'd spotted me as a fellow Palace fan. We chatted for a few minutes as he was leaving the restaurant and our Australian relatives, who were treating us that night, were mightily impressed that it was me who'd been recognised, in a restaurant with a reputation as a celebrity hangout.

As we joked about my newfound celebrity status, the Sommelier brought an expensive bottle of Champagne to the table – a present from Steve – with the message "EAGLES!". It wasn't just the Aussies who were gobsmacked now. I eventually managed to track Steve down after a few days to thank him properly and later learned he was also very good friends with Pete Bonthrone. I knew the club was going to be in very good hands.

The new owners set about improving the club from the ground up, but there were to be no quick fixes on the pitch and pre-season plans were confined to a West Country training trip, incorporating friendlies with Dorchester Town and Exeter City, which was played at Tiverton Town FC. Many of the regular travellers enjoyed a short break in Dorset and Devon. Our own crew was boosted by the welcome addition of Biggus Mickus and Mitch, who flew over from Spain, although my liver was less impressed by this.

The first season saw Palace flirt with relegation again. Former Scotland international boss George Burley had been initially appointed as Manager. His managerial career highlight had been getting Ipswich Town into Europe in their first season back in the top flight and he came to Palace after his stint as Scotland's Manager.

He failed to inspire a team that had lost even more key personnel prior to the resolution of the Administration. He was sacked mid-season, with Dougie Freedman given a chance to make a name for himself as a manager, after Bournemouth's Eddie Howe had turned down the job. Palace eventually secured their divisional status with a late equalising goal from debutant Ibra Sekajja in the penultimate game of the season away at Hull City.

The close season held little joy on the pre-season front for fans or the club. The Club's West Country training camp was flooded out, which meant the squad returned home early. This meant the cancellation of a friendly game against Bath City on a Friday evening, which should have formed part of the journey home. Instead, a hastily arranged game at Basingstoke took its place.

The 2011/12 season had brighter notes, as Dougie Freedman got the team off to a solid start and inflicted a 3-1 away reverse on rivals Brighton, their first defeat at their shiny new stadium at Falmer. The win sparked a six-game undefeated run that saw Palace rise as high as third place in the league. The emerging talent of winger Wilfried Zaha was also a major factor.

Sadly, Palace could only manage another six wins all season and a dreadful run-in saw Palace slip from mid-table at Easter to the eventual 17th, though not in any real danger of demotion.

The season is best remembered for a run all the way to the League Cup semi-final, including a 2-1 extra time win at Old Trafford. Despite Palace taking a slender 1-0 lead over Cardiff in the first leg at Selhurst, they fell behind quickly in the away leg to an own goal. They managed to hold the tie all the way to penalties, where they were ultimately defeated.

The 2012 pre-season fayre was as unexciting as the previous year, though the first friendly down at Lewes on a Friday evening was preceded by a mammoth pub crawl, led by Steve Browett himself. The following Friday, a game at Margate also saw a fair few fans booking B&Bs for an overnighter by the seaside.

The first round of the League Cup was actually Palace's first competitive fixture that season and the draw threw us an away tie against Exeter City. The regulars took this as an opportunity to re-visit old haunts from their 2010 Devon excursion.

The season that followed was one that defines the Crystal Palace Football Club experience. A narrow 2-3 opening day defeat to Watford seemed to indicate that neither side would be bothering the top end of the table, given the porous nature of both defences. Indeed, after two more league defeats and a League Cup shellacking at Preston North End, Palace sat at the bottom of the table.

Yet by early November, Palace were sitting on top of the league. They were, however, already on their fourth manager of the campaign. Despite Dougie Freedman appearing to have gathered some momentum, he decided that 18th-placed Bolton Wanderers were a better long-term bet and left to join them. First senior coach Lennie Lawrence was put in temporary charge, but then he elected to join Freedman at Bolton. Next it was the turn of Curtis Fleming to get an unexpected promotion, even though it seemed he too would shortly be heading to Bolton. Finally, Palace announced Ian Holloway as their permanent Manager.

From that point on, Palace were never out of the top six and, despite a late wobble, finished fifth. There were several reasons for this. Arguably the biggest was the electric form of Wilfried Zaha, who earned a couple of England Caps and a £15m move to Manchester United in the January transfer window, only to be immediately loaned back to Palace for the rest of the season. The thirty-goal tally from Glenn Murray and some canny acquisitions in the transfer market also proved to be massive for the club's eventual promotion. The club had signed the likes of Joel Ward, Peter Ramage, Damian Delaney, Danny Gabbidon, Yannick

Bolasie and veteran goalscorer Kevin Phillips, a perennial pain-in-the-proverbial when playing against us in the past.

It's fair to say that going into the play-offs, Palace's form was fairly dire, with only one win in ten and that being a last-minute winner against Peterborough in the final game, which condemned the Posh to relegation on a staggeringly high 54 points, but also secured Palace's place in the play-offs. Dougie Freedman's Bolton finished in seventh, just one place outside the play-offs.

Palace had to face Brighton in the play-off semi-final over two legs, possibly the biggest games ever between the two sides. Palace were at home in the first leg and ground out a goal-less draw, although the loss of Glenn Murray to a long-term cruciate ligament injury was a devastating blow. At the end of the game, the Brighton fans celebrated like they were already at Wembley.

Enter Wilf Zaha, whose second-half brace five days later down on the south coast sent Palace to Wembley instead. There, the Eagles were to face Watford, the team that had finished third in the league. The two clubs that contested that poor opening game of the season were now to face-off for the greatest prize. As games go, it was not a lot different to that first encounter, although clearly both defences had improved immeasurably. The game remained goal-less after ninety minutes. The deadlock was finally broken when Zaha, in what we believed at the time would be his final game in a Palace shirt, was upended in the box with six minutes left of extra-time. In one sweet strike from the penalty spot, Kevin Phillips repaid Palace for all those heart-breaking goals against us. Palace were back in wonderland, after eight seasons in the second tier.

With a late end to the season and not knowing what division the club would be in, the options for a pre-season tour were fast receding. Bordeaux had been approached for a home friendly on the weekend prior to the season starting, but their involvement in the French equivalent of the Charity Shield put paid to that. There was some short-lived excitement when Inter Milan were rumoured to have accepted the date, but they mysteriously seemed to prefer a friendly against Real Madrid on that day instead. As covered in an earlier chapter, Lazio ended up providing the opposition for our marquee home friendly.

Palace elected for a training camp in Portugal in early July, but no friendlies were arranged. Palace fans' four year wait for another taste of international football was finally ended by a one-off game in the Republic of Ireland, against Waterford United.

The announcement of a single game overseas against a second tier Irish club on the first weekend in August was met with a lukewarm reception. But for the overseas regulars, starved of anything, it was descended upon like manna from Heaven. Sue got to spend time with her Irish relatives, whilst I was determined to wring as much football out of the weekend as possible and had eyed up several Irish League grounds to tick off, over what was an Irish Bank Holiday weekend. While researching these fixtures, I spotted that Waterford were due to play in a league game the previous night, some 150 miles away in Galway, bringing the value of the friendly in terms of an on-field test for Palace further into question.

The Spraoi Festival was also happening that weekend in Waterford, with up to 100,000 people expected to be in the city, which meant the accommodation costs were already stratospheric. A lot of the travellers offset this cost by finding the cheapest Ryanair flights available to Dublin and Cork and headed back there after the game, though the kick-off time of 6pm didn't make this an easy proposition either.

Added to that, Waterford appeared to be in some severe financial difficulties, with a former Manager trying to get the club wound up before the game. The court case rumbled on and the game appeared to be in serious doubt, which caused plenty of worry amongst the Palace fans. It was eventually settled in the week before the friendly. Game on.

The Friday morning Aer Lingus flight from Gatwick to Dublin was a sell-out, not least because this was also the squad route out to the Emerald Isle. Sue was particularly happy after spotting her favourite player, Damian Delaney, airside in the South Terminal. Her excitement increased when she realised the only spare seat on our full flight was next to her and he was the only Palace player not yet onboard. As you will discover later in the book, this would not be the only time that the Irish centre-half left it to the last minute to board a flight.

As he advanced down the aisle, he clocked both the empty seat and Sue's over-eager face. With that he turned on his heel and spoke to the cabin crew who found someone willing to swop seats with him nearer the front of the plane. Sue was not best pleased, whereas I found it utterly hilarious.

Friday evening brought forth a game at red-and-blue-shirted St Patrick's Athletic for me and a night on the sauce for Sue with her family in Kildare. On Saturday morning, after a visit to Marlay parkrun, we pointed the hire car south for the two-hour drive to Waterford. Despite some heavy traffic in the city, due to the festival, we got out in plenty of time for pre-match liveners and to meet up with some familiar faces, including Andy, Tracy, Wags, Safety, Hoover, Rick and Skate. We also ran into Steve Browett and his gang. In every bar, Palace supporters were in evidence. The turnout was impressive, considering the initial apparent apathy towards the game.

I was covering the game for the *South London Press* and left early to get to the ground, via our hotel, which should've been around a twenty minute walk. At this point in the afternoon, the narrow pavements were becoming dangerously overcrowded. The crush got so bad that at one point I was completely stationary for over ten minutes. Despite having left the pub two hours ahead, I began to think that I might miss kick-off.

Eventually I escaped the crowds and made it to the Royal Showgrounds in plenty of time, securing a couple of programmes that were already in very short supply. It was clear that, though the court case had been settled, this club was still in extreme financial difficulties. I phoned back to the pub to relay my experience of getting to the ground and advise them to leave a bit earlier than they'd planned. As usual, my advice fell on deaf ears and more than a few missed both kick-off and the chance of a programme.

The home side started brightly, showing no signs that they had played the previous night and not got to bed before the wee small hours. Slowly Palace got on top and opened the scoring on the half-hour mark through Stephen Dobbie. Soon after the break, it was clear that Waterford were wilting, but a series of crazy misses from Palace players kept the score-line stubbornly at 1-0. It took Palace until the 77th minute to claim another goal, a first in club colours for new signing Dwight Gayle. Palace added two more before the finish, through Ibra Sekajja and trialist Osman Sow.

The official attendance was 1,159 and it seemed that Palace supporters outnumbered the home fans, despite the club claiming only 200 tickets had been sold to Palace fans. The crowd was around half of what Waterford had drawn for the visit of a Manchester United XI a couple of weeks before. The Waterford Club Officials were, however, full of praise for Palace fielding a strong side, whereas the Red Devils had inevitably brought over a squad of mostly under 18s, something the Irish club felt they had been seriously misled about.

The love-in was reciprocated by Ian Holloway, who declared the trip to be a huge success in his post-match interview and he was already looking to return to the area next year. That news went down well back in the pub when I finally made it back there, where a huge night was had. Although I must confess, I remember very little of the detail. Memories of my hangover the next morning are in somewhat sharper focus.

The journey back to Kildare seemed to take ages and suddenly my plans for the first half of the Shamrock Rovers v Aston Villa friendly, at their new ground, then onwards to a league match at Bray Wanderers, seemed foolhardy. In the end, I compromised and settled just for the Bray game. The bracing sea air dispelled my lingering headache, but it also meant I was bloody freezing in just a t-shirt.

The following day, after stopping to buy a hoodie, I headed back down south to take in the FAI Cup game at Cork City. Their opponents were a non-league side from north Dublin by the name of Kilbarrick United. Their grand plan to execute a giant-killing appeared to be 'kick Cork off the park'. The Cork City fans I was standing near renamed their opponents 'Kill-Cork'. I would normally favour the underdog in such circumstances, but their foul play made it impossible. And, besides that, any club that plays the Sultans of Ping and The Frank and Walters over their PA will always get my vote. Cork rode the storm and won the tie 3-1, but went out in the next round to eventual cup winners, Sligo Rovers.

Given its proximity, it seems amazing to me that this match was Palace's first, and to date, only game in the Republic of Ireland. There have been few other single country encounters in Palace's history and most of those were home games. In the sixties, Bangu of Brazil and Ghanian club Asante Kotoko (which translates as Asante Porcupine!) visited Selhurst. The South Americans came away with a 2-0 victory, whereas the Africans went home on the wrong end of a 3-1 scoreline.

In the early seventies, Zenit Leningrad (now Zenit St Petersburg) of Russia came to London in mid-season and played out a 1-1 draw. In the eighties, Palace hosted a Japanese national side and the visitors came away with a 2-1 win. Palace received an unusual mid-season invitation to take on the Qatari U21 international side in the Middle East, which they accepted, although the game finished goal-less.

As recorded earlier in this book, Palace have also played a Bulgarian and a Croatian club. Bringing the list of one-hit wonders up to date, a month after the Waterford game, Palace ran out 2-0 winners against the Oman national side at Selhurst during the September international break. Stephen Dobbie and Kyle Da Silva got the second half goals for Palace. The game was poorly attended as it was scheduled at the same time as an England World Cup qualifier in Ukraine.

Aside from Qatar and Oman, Palace have opposed sides from two other countries in the Middle East region. In the early seventies, while Palace were a top flight club they faced two Iranian clubs: Pakyaan at home and Persepolis in Tehran. Both games resulted in handsome victories.

The trip to Tehran in November 1972 merited a full report by Manager Bert Head in his column in the matchday programme for the following league game at home to Leeds. It was a fascinating insight into the nature of the midweek friendlies that he seemed so keen on, whilst many were questioning the value of a club mired in the relegation positions taking up most of its time in-between Saturdays to travel to far-flung places for a friendly.

It was, perhaps, little different to the teams involved in the European competitions, but the journey alone was a different level to what any other English team would face that week. Sky-jacking was a prevalent threat at the time which resulted in lengthy baggage searches. There were areas of the Middle East that were no-fly zones for commercial aircraft, which involved a lay-over in Tel Aviv before flying back out across the Mediterranean before finally turning back towards Iran.

Once there, however, the squad received excellent hospitality and the temperature was not as hot as some had feared it might be. The party enjoyed various sightseeing trips and also a cabaret evening featuring Norman Wisdom, who had travelled on the BOAC flight over with the club.

Although Persepolis were the current Champions, the club had just turned professional. As such, they were unable to compete in their national league and thus were finding international opposition to play against. They had previously faced a top Yugoslavian side and were about to travel to play Bayern München.

A crowd of 32,000 enjoyed the game and Head noted that the way those fans supported the home team when they were attacked was both 'eye-opening and ear-shattering, especially to the younger lads'. Elsewhere in the Leeds programme, the players had been quoted as saying that the home side had 'not much bottle' and Palace romped to a 5-1 win.

Head declared the trip to be largely 'trouble-free' and a success on several levels: financial, team-bonding, acquiring a huge trophy for the club's cabinet and, most importantly, setting the team up to earn a point at Derby on the following Saturday. That said, he did note that the round trip to the Stadium on the overcrowded Tehran roads was unbelievably chaotic, counting nine near-misses with their coach. The long journey home was also described as 'tiring' with touch downs in Rome and Paris for further baggage searches.

Encouraged by the success of this venture, Head noted that there might well be another similar trip in January. The club did, indeed, make another midweek excursion for a friendly early in the New Year, although one imagines the eventual trip to Aberdeen was not in the Manager's thoughts when he dropped that hint.

Four friendlies against various Israeli sides were held. The first game, a mid-season away friendly against a national side in January 1971, ended goalless. In the August of the same year, Maccabi Netanya visited Selhurst in pre-season and were soundly beaten 4-1.

In August 1984, the final friendly of the pre-season campaign was a 3-0 win over Hapoel Tel Aviv. Four years later, almost to the day, Palace hosted a side listed only as 'Tel Aviv' in the record books in a behind closed doors friendly at Selhurst. No-one missed much though, Palace won the game by a single goal. Despite some research, I have not been able to ascertain which of the several Tel Aviv clubs it was, although it seems unlikely that it was Hapoel again, as their senior players were on strike around that time.

22

FRIENDS WILL BE FRIENDS

After the years of tour famine, Palace surprised everyone by announcing a feast of trips in 2014. Not only a three-game tour to the USA, but also two one-off trips to Austria and Germany.

This largesse owed much to Palace securing their Premier League status for another season. Ian Holloway's managerial reign did not quite last the year, having only secured three points in a single win in the first eight games. Head Coach – and lifelong Palace fan – Keith Millen, took over on a caretaker basis and steadied the ship, gaining four points in as many games, yet still the club was mired at the foot of the table.

When Tony Pulis took over the helm permanently, Palace began to slowly cruise up the table to safety. In mid-January the club left the relegation zone for the final time and safety was achieved relatively early in mid-April, following a five-game winning streak. In the penultimate game of the season, Palace managed to totally derail Liverpool's title challenge, coming back from three goals down at home on 75 minutes with a late rally that robbed Liverpool of all three points.

Footage from that game was beamed around the world and was dubbed: 'Crystanbul' – a reference to Liverpool's own fightback from three down in the 2005 Champions League final out in Turkey. Palace's stock was riding high, not least in terms of global 'brand awareness'. Initially strong rumours abounded of a game against a Hungarian side in Budapest, which would have been a new country for Palace.

The first to be announced was a full tour to the States, where Palace would face MLS teams Columbus Crew and Philadelphia Union, plus a final game against USL side Richmond Kickers – the site of the abandoned friendly against L.A. Galaxy back in 2006. Continuing the mid-naughties vibe, Palace would also be returning to southern Germany for their final pre-season encounter against FC Augsburg, though the timing of that announcement – less than a month before the game – had the internet forums howling in disgust at the lack of cheap flights to Bavaria.

Palace's first foreign encounter, indeed their first friendly of the pre-season, would be in Austria. An early training camp in the mountains was a regular feature of Stoke City's pre-season preparations under Tony Pulis, usually with a game thrown in at the end, although occasionally these were billed as 'behind closed doors'. At the end of June, it was confirmed that Palace would play GAK Graz at the end of the training week and that fans would be welcome to attend. The 'GAK' stands for Grazer Athletiksport Klub, if you're wondering.

The timing of the game was bad news for me. It would be the first overseas Palace game I'd miss in thirteen years. Unknowingly my fate was sealed way back in 2007, when it was announced that the 2014 World Cup would be held in Brazil. Like many people of my age, the World Cup was the first time I took a serious interest in football. The grainy images from Mexico seemed totally exotic and the winners Brazil captured my heart. Although our television set was black and white, I knew exactly what colours they played in, due to my much-prized my sticker album – and what an iconic strip it was!

Ever since then, the World Cup has been a special event for me. The German World Cup in 2006 was one of the best times of my life, especially the fortnight I spent out there. So, when the tournament went to Brazil, I wanted so badly to go that I put aside any thoughts of the South African tournament and started saving for 2014. Around 2010, it dawned on me that the only way we could realistically afford to go was if I could trade in my self-employment for an employed job with a reliable monthly income. It just so happened that I had an offer from a company, where I had been contracting.

Even then it was not straightforward. To enable me to spend a month out there, I had to negotiate an unpaid sabbatical with my employer. Then the American tour was scheduled for the week after I returned from South America. I had managed to wangle a week's holiday for that – but there was no way I could now ask for further time off, the first week I was supposed to be back at my desk. In fact, I didn't even bother to ask. The truth was that, despite all our saving, our World Cup adventure – as brilliant as it was – had hit me hard in the wallet and I would still need that regular income for a while yet.

That is how I came to miss out, not only on Palace's first game in Austria but also one that turned out to be a landmark game. I seem to have this uncanny knack of missing the wrong ones.

Of our regulars, Hoover and Mr Cad made the trip travelling out together. Another of my friends, Derek "Del Boy" Collison was on one of the two mini-buses that travelled. He recalls a truly amazing trip that spawned a much greater friendship.

"I'd been to Waterford by minibus the previous year and got the taste for overseas games. When I heard, through my good mate Lou Arnold, that there was going to be a minibus to Austria, I jumped at the chance. Not a moment too soon, as it turned out they only had one seat left. I didn't know many of the others onboard but after that trip nearly all of us are still firm friends. There were nine spaces on the bus and the travel and accommodation came to £430, excluding spends.

It was a very long drive. I left Croydon and met the minibus at Chislehurst at 8am and we arrived at Dover around 10am. Once across the Channel we ran into some navigational issues. Our driver, Ricky, who was a chauffeur by trade, knew the roads well and decided to skirt around Paris rather than take the most direct route. However, this did add on a lot of time and when night fell we were only just in Germany. Also, Lou our designated navigator hadn't been very specific about our intended destination when using online maps, so had picked up the wrong destination. As a result, we were actually much further away that we thought. The decision was made to stop for the night around the Nürburgring.

I quickly googled places to stay and, as it was now so late, we ended up at hostel in Aachen. We knocked on the door and it was answered by someone who was the absolute spitting image of the recently-incarcerated Rolf Harris. Somehow we kept a straight face. Turns out 'Rolf' was a guest there, but he could speak good English. He managed to find the Manager and between them, they found room for us.

I had a few beers with me and there was a beer vending machine too, so we had a nightcap in the dorm. This didn't go down well with a couple of Libyans, who were trying to sleep and begged us to keep the noise down. We decided to head off to get a kebab and when we got back there was a load of police with dogs, sniffing around our minibus. Not sure what they thought of us, but it passed off without incident.

Around nine in the morning we set off and had an easy drive from there, with a couple of stops, eventually arriving in Graz mid-afternoon and headed off to our respective hotels to check-in. We met up again at Flann O'Briens, which had been identified as having good range of ales and beers, not just Pils. There we met up with Wiz, who'd flown over for what was effectively a day trip. That's dedication right there. After a few beers, we grabbed cabs to the match. There was some confusion as to where the ground was, with some of our crew being taken to the Merkure Arena, which was shared by Sturm and Grazer AK before the latter went bust and was dissolved. Another person in our gang ended up at a different ground entirely. We all made it eventually, though.

The side that Palace were facing was the new phoenix club, now known as GAK Graz, who were starting again at the eighth tier of Austrian football. Their previous ground, known as the Casino Stadium, had been sold many years previously for housing, so that was unavailable to the reformed club, thus they had a new home.

The ground was a council-owned sports arena, south of the city centre, which was also home to SC Kalsdorf. It was a nice little arena with food and beer readily available. Another minibus had travelled over, run by John Duthie, while a few supporters had flown over. There were a couple of ex-pats too. We didn't know everyone, but they were wearing Palace colours so we did have a chat. All in all, I'd estimate about 30 to 35 fans travelled – the total gate was around 1,800."

It was historic, record-breaking game for Palace. Of course it was – I wasn't there. The sides were totally mismatched and Palace ran in goal after goal against the newly-formed team. The Eagles opened their account on five minutes through Joe Ledley with a shot off the crossbar. Then followed a Yannick Bolasie penalty, a Glenn Murray route one rasper, followed up by him driving a shot on the angle for the fourth. A fine solo goal from Jerome Thomas rounded off the first half.

An entirely different Palace team took the field for the second half and conceded early. Sacher headed home for GAK to the loudest cheer of the day and sporting applause from the Palace contingent. This stung Palace Mk2 into action and the floodgates were quickly prised open. Stephen Dobbie regained the upper hand three minutes later, the first of four goals for him, including a five-minute hat-trick! Youngster Jake Gray and Marouanne Chamakh both nabbed one and a Johnny Williams brace completed the Palace rout.

The game ended 13-1. It was Palace's biggest victory against foreign opposition in the professional club's history. Not every Palace fan there remembers the goal-fest. A drunken Hoover spent much of the game chatting to a home fan. When he woke up the next morning, after having spent most of the night asleep on the toilet, he thought the final score was 3-0. Mr Cad, who'd been denied use of their shared room's facilities, took much delight in correcting him.

What happened after the game was every bit as remarkable and heart-warming as the amazing score-line, as a lasting 'freundschaft' (friendship between two clubs) was founded. As Del explains:

"We walked in behind one of the goals and there were crates of beer everywhere. One of our lot thought they were free and helped himself! He was soon put straight. We headed for the bar and sausage stand, which had become a bit of a meeting point for the Palace fans who had travelled.

We started singing songs and during the game attracted the interest of their younger ultras, smartly dressed in mod and Lambretta gear. They began moving towards us, singing their own songs louder and louder. We were a bit uneasy, but then they started singing our songs as well. I wasn't sure if it was a wind-up at the time and went off to get some more food and beers. There I ran into a huge police sergeant, who for all the world looked like the gendarme from 'Allo 'Allo with his enormous moustache and pill-box hat. He spoke some English, so I explained my concern and he seemed to take it on board. I went to rejoin the others and Wiz started laughing as, unbeknownst to me, four of their armed officers had followed me back to ensure there was no bother.

Palace didn't let the players come over to talk to us at any time before, during or after the game. But Frazier Campbell and Jerome Thomas did run over to shake hands at half-time. They were swiftly told off by our coaches and ushered away.

We did get on to the pitch at the end of the game, as we were invited on by the GAK fans. We were initially reluctant and explained to them that doing that in England would get you a ban, even at friendlies, but they seemed very insistent. So we went on the pitch, which was just as well, as it would have been regarded as an insult if we hadn't. We ended up clapping each other and singing each other's songs. While we were on the pitch, we were able to see Damien Delaney, Johnny Williams and James McArthur in the tunnel to say 'well done'. Later, we saw the players and Tony Pulis getting on to the coach in the car park. We stood around the front of it singing Palace songs. Pulis was right at the front with a beaming smile and one of my mates, Richard Egan, managed to jump on the coach and sit beside Paddy McCarthy to offer congratulations on the fine win, before being told to get off.

After the players' send-off, we returned to the club bar to drink and socialise with the GAK fans, who seemed genuinely pleased to have us there. It would be fair to say that their 'Red Firm' and the older 'Road Crew' had something of reputation for violence within Austrian football, prior to the club's bankruptcy. This group continued to follow the new club and it turns out that they'd heard of Palace's ultras and thought there might be some 'action' to be had. However, they quickly realised we were just regular fans and they joined us for a drink too. Indeed, they've become some of our firmest friends amongst the GAK support.

We went back in the end of their first season, when they won the title and promotion. We even got on the pitch with their fans and were holding up the Trophy! After that game, Lou and I were offered a lift back to Flanns from a gentlemen with a nice Jag. We'd been getting on with everyone at the club well, so couple of us went with him and my mate, Huggy, went with another guy.

It turns out our driver was Harald Ranenegger, the Club President. We asked him 'Why did you pick Crystal Palace for your first game?' He explained that they had looked at the way AFC Wimbledon and FC United of Manchester had established themselves again, but they really wanted to play a Premiership team from London – either us or Fulham. Turns out Palace were cheaper, even though Fulham had just been relegated! Fulham had asked for 12,000 Euros, whereas Palace wanted 8,000, presumably because the club already knew they would be in Austria for Pulis's bootcamp.

In the other car, Huggy was having a similar conversation with his driver.

'So do you support Graz?'

'Ja'

'Do you live in Graz?'

'Ja'

'So why do you support GAK?'

'I am Heinz, I am the first team Manager.'

This became a regular trip for Palace fans. Every season since, GAK have been promoted. They are now in the second tier and back at the Merkure Arena, having outgrown the municipal sports arena. We usually go back at least three or four times a season, for home and away games. I can't begin to fathom how many beers get sunk on these trips but it does get messy. On one occasion, I was so drunk I got wheeled out of the ground on a trolley. I didn't believe it, until I saw the pictures.

Some of the fans that we have become friendly with also come over to watch Palace. Markus and his missus came to FA Cup semi-final in 2016 and Diddy was with us at the Cup Final itself. A trio also came over at an away game in Liverpool, drinking in the iconic Arkles pub. This game proved something of an eye-opener for them:

'All we see on the telly is the scarves and singing before the game, but during the game they are so quiet and boring!'

When I fell ill and wasn't able to go over for a year, they made me a 'Get Well Soon, Derek' banner which they held up at the games. After our first trip, they'd made a banner 'GAK and Crystal Palace: Rockin' all over the World' which was hung at the top of the terrace. We've been featured in the local press and media. The connection has become so well-known now that supporters of their biggest and oldest rivals Sturm Graz admitted in their programme that they hate GAK and Crystal Palace. Just beware if you ever go to a Sturm game and decide to wear your Palace shirt.

Even during the Coronavirus lockdowns, the friendship has continued to flourish and I still speak to them on video-chat most weeks."

Although this was Palace's first game in Austria, the club has faced Austrian opposition on two, almost three, other occasions. The first two games took place in 1954 as part of the 'Floodlight Football' series at Selhurst. First, FC Vienna visited in the February for an exciting encounter which finished 4-3 to Palace. Now known as First Vienna FC, they are the oldest football team in Austria and, as such, are still known by their English name, rather than 'Ersten Wien FK' which would be the literal German translation. The following season, they won the Austrian Championship. Like GAK, they have suffered huge financial difficulties in the last decade resulting in a demotion to the fifth tier.

Eight months later, it was the turn of 'WAS Vienna' to visit and play out a 2-2 draw. The apostrophes are deliberate as it turns out WAS Vienna was Palace's anglicised version of their proper name which was Wiener AC (Atheliksport Club). This club merged with Austria Wien in 1973 to form FK Austria WAC Wien, however that club has since reverted to Austria Wien. A phoenix club was founded in 1983 under the original name, which lasted until the early 2000s. Although the sports club still exists, competitive football is no longer a part of their curriculum.

The almost game was scheduled to happen in February 1985. Palace were due to face Austrian Champions, FK Austria Wien at Selhurst as part of the Austrians warm-up tour of England, before their European Champions Cup quarter final with Liverpool, later that month. The Viennese club were on a midwinter break and the English weather, that year, had caused a huge disruption to the fixtures with Palace going a month between League fixtures.

Ironically it was the thaw rather than the snow that caused the late postponement of the game. A pool of water appeared at the Holmesdale Road end of the ground, which froze over that night. The club decided it was too risky to proceed with the evening fixture has it was likely to freeze over again. The Austrians had already played Southend and Fulham, so at least they got some game time on of the trip. Not that it helped against Liverpool where they lost 5-2 on aggregate.

Del (centre) with the GAK boys, Robert & Gille (seated) on a visit to Selhurst Park
[Photo: Derek Collison]

Glenn Murray equalises at Columbus Crew - July 2014

The Palace end at Philadephia Union in the shadow of the Commodore Barry Bridge
- July 2014

23

NEW KIDS ON THE BLOCK

Just five days after the GAK Graz game, most of our touring party assembled at Heathrow for a now familiar flight out to Washington Dulles. Our travelling party comprised of Hoover, Pete Bonthrone, Chris Plummer and Wags, plus Sue and me. Mr Cad was launching a new work venture and decided that a week in the States would be too much of a strain on his nascent business. This meant that I was, once again, asked to take photos for the club.

Sue had organised flights and accommodation for our crew and, once again, I was designated mini-van driver. Eden Park Tours was back in business. However, due to the sad passing of one of our best friends, Sue and Wags were not with us at the airport, as the funeral was on that same day.

Sue had figured out that she and Wags could change their transatlantic flights to the following day, grab an internal flight to Columbus and, assuming there were no delays, would get to the football ground an hour before kick-off. This was not a cheap rearrangement, however, and it would have been unfair to ask all of our party to delay their travel and potentially miss the opening game. Sue was very understanding about me missing the funeral. While I was very uncomfortable about it, this did mean that I could drive the mini-van and the party from Dulles to Columbus, so not everyone would have to change their plans and incur extra expense.

This also meant, just for once, that I was in charge for the first leg of the journey. What could possibly go wrong? Needless to say, Hoover was already ensconced in the airside bar with Chris by the time I arrived and he was well on it. Pete was elsewhere, enjoying airline lounge hospitality. As usual, he had chosen to fly first class. An uneventful flight arrived a little early – Hello Dulles, my old friend. By the time we had boarded those peculiar high-rise transit trams they have there and got through to the customs hall, it was later in the afternoon than I hoped, given the long drive ahead.

Picking up the car seemed to take an age, not least due to the confusion of Sue – the second named driver – not actually being present, despite me presenting her driving license. It was around 3.30pm by the time we hit the road for a five-hour drive to Wheeling in West Virginia, our designated overnight layover. It was now close to rush hour and previous negative experiences with the Washington Beltway meant I took an executive decision to head cross-country on smaller roads, to cut some time and mileage from our trip. Huge mistake.

About half-hour later, we were stationary on a state road, unable to turn around, following a collision between two large farm vehicles just ahead of us. The road was totally blocked and it took around an hour before we could move again, after being diverted across farmland. Due to the time difference, although it was 5pm where we were, it felt much later. I'd already been awake over fifteen hours and was feeling the effects. Yet, we still had more than four hours driving ahead of us.

We discussed our options as we pressed on, the wonderful scenery on the Historic National Road – America's oldest highway – keeping me alert. We decided to try and make it all the way to Wheeling. We stopped briefly in Cumberland for a planned food stop, only to find the eatery Sue had previously scoped out was closed for a week of redecoration. Our luck was truly out.

We redefined the meaning of fast food, grabbed some pizza slices and got back on the road, dining on the hoof. We still had two-and-a-half hours to go, with the light fast fading. I'm not sure how I kept driving. I certainly don't remember a lot about that leg. I'm pretty sure Hoover and Chris kept me awake by talking all sorts of nonsense. Although we were now on an Interstate, the road was dark and practically deserted, aside from the occasional articulated monster truck, lit up like a Christmas tree. It felt like we were in a remake of the film *Duel* as these gargantuan vehicles thundered up behind us.

The West Virginia state line was a welcome sight and couple of miles up the road we turned off to our Holiday Inn lodgings. Although the hotel was described as being in Wheeling, the town itself was ten miles up the road. It was a typical travellers' stop on an Interstate junction, with not much else around and nothing remotely resembling a hotel bar.

At this point I'd almost been awake for 24 hours and was long overdue for bed, but when Hoover discovered there was an Applebees open for drinks just on the other side of the intersection, suddenly I gained a second (or was it third) wind. We dumped our bags and reconvened in the lobby, although Chris sensibly decided to hit the hay.

The receptionist stopped us as we were about to set off and enquired whether we wanted a cab.

"You said it was only over there" Hoover said, gesticulating back towards the freeway.

"Sure is, but you can't go on foot, there's no sidewalk. I can get a cab for you. It'll take about half an hour to get here."

"We'll take out chances" replied Hoover striding out the door, leaving the receptionist open-mouthed.

It took all of five minutes to walk. Yes, it was pitch black and we had to cross a couple of the Interstate's on-off ramps, but the lack of traffic meant this presented no problems. Soon we were in the bar area of the chain restaurant and, upon confirming they were still open, settled down for a couple of beers to decompress from our mammoth journey. A server approached our table.

"What can I get you folks?"

"Three Yuenglings, please" came our eager reply.

"Coming right up, can I just see some IDs when I get back with your drinks please?"

Although our ages visibly ranged from early to late middle-age, servers in the States can get personally fined if they don't check, so caution now overrides the desire to make a sale. As a result, I do not go anywhere without my passport when I'm in the US and, it transpired, neither did Pete. The look on Hoover's face, however, was a picture – he'd left his ID back in the room. I slipped him Sue's driving licence and told him to make out he'd picked his wife's up by mistake. He was still most unhappy at the possibility of that long-awaited beer being cruelly dashed from his lips.

Upon returning with our drinks, the server noticed three official documents on the table and didn't bother to actually inspect them. Hoover sucked up all of his beer before the server left the table, in case he suddenly decided to look a bit closer and confiscated it. With perfect comic timing, the doors swung open and two police officers walked in, sending him into a further panic. The cops were off-duty and only there for an after-work beer, but Hoover still couldn't completely relax. After two more beers, the jetlag kicked back in and we headed back to the hotel.

The next morning, refreshed, we headed out for the remaining 130 miles to Columbus. As it was matchday, Hoover was champing at the bit to get the journey done and settled into a bar for a session. Sue and Wags had sent a text to confirm their first flight was on time. It seemed like our luck might be finally on the turn.

After a recce of the ground around noon, we were pulling into our hotel between the German and Brewery districts of the city. Despite the inviting location, not much appeared to be open locally and so after check-in, Hoover led the charge towards the main street, falling into the first bar that was open. As I would be driving everyone to the game, I left after lunch and spent the afternoon sightseeing in the city with Chris. The news from our duo in transit continued to be good, they had landed and cleared customs in the States and were now waiting at the gates for their internal flight.

As well as driving and taking photos, I was filing match reports for the *South London Press* so we headed to the stadium early. The ground was next door to the Ohio State Fair, which was also now in full swing. This made parking a bit of an issue, but a combination of Pete's VIP ticket and my press credentials meant we were able to park inside the stadium itself.

The Crew Stadium was the first MLS soccer-specific stadium to open, back in 1999. There was a significant Palace connection with Columbus at the time. Palace's former centre-half, Gregg Berhalter, was their Head Coach. Berhalter became the first Palace player to represent his country at the FIFA World Cup in 2002 and later went on to become the Head Coach for the USA international side.

As I settled into the press room, chatting with Palace's social media team, a text came through from Wags. They were stuck on the runway at Dulles while a thunderstorm was raging overhead and no prospective departure time. So close, but yet so far.

Right on kick-off, I received a call from Sue. They were in a cab leaving Columbus Airport and should arrive in about twenty minutes. Their delay had been almost an hour. The stadium was about half-full and the Palace section appeared to be heaving. Around a hundred American Palace fans, including a coach-load from the Detroit area over four hours away, had made the game. The home fans were in good voice in the north corner of the ground, taunting their opposite numbers with a peculiarly tuneless chant that claimed "Crystal Palace: it's a really dumb name for a soccer team" which they appeared to find hysterically funny. Later, I learned that 'Crystal Palace' was the name of an infamous Wild West brothel.

Those fans, known as the 'Nordecke' (North Corner in German), were further delighted when their side took the lead on fifteen minutes converting a free header in the six-yard box. As I was snapping away pitch-side, hoping the action might swing up towards the end Palace were attacking, I heard my phone ringing; it was Sue. Although they had made it to the ground, the security guards would not allow them into the ground with their flight bags. No amount of pleading or cajoling was working, so could I possibly bring the van keys to the gate and they would stow the bags there. A good plan, except for the small detail of the van being parked inside the stadium.

In the end, I got them to run around to the media entrance where I was able to get their bags into the press room, after a chat with a far more understanding club official. With the light fast fading, making sports photography difficult, I was running out of time to get enough pictures and now was at the wrong end of the ground. Of course, this was the moment that Glenn Murray chose to equalise. My long-range photo of his finish will never win any awards.

The second half was typical of an early pre-season friendly, in that Palace made a host of changes. Our hosts were in the middle of their league season and made somewhat fewer changes. However, it was Palace who took the lead midway through the half, when Jake Gray jinked the keeper to score, adding to his goal out in Austria. Ten minutes from time, Palace were hit with a sucker punch following some poor marking and the score was tied at 2-2 where it finished. Not before Palace contrived to miss a host of late chances, however.

After the game, I attended the post-match press conference. Tony Pulis could not have been less interested in talking about the game, he trotted out bland soundbites about how nothing could be read into the game as it was too early in the season. He also referred to tiredness amongst the squad after the Austrian training camp. It came across as though he really didn't want to be there. I found his demeanour quite odd at the time: he was never one to give lengthy press conferences, often standing rather than sitting to take questions, but even for him this seemed brusque.

After the formalities were over, we headed back into town for a nightcap and the next day headed back east towards Philadelphia for Friday's game. Having spent time in Philly between games in 2009, we elected to break the scenic journey up with an overnight stop in rural Pennsylvania. Sue had picked up a recommendation for a steak restaurant in a small town called Chambersburg, so that became our destination.

The restaurant was indeed a good find, but such is the American way of eating out early, it was almost deserted by the time we arrived for our 7.30pm dinner reservation. By the end of the mains, we were the only customers left, with the staff watching us from the kitchen, fervently hoping we'd clear off without ordering dessert. We gave them a break and headed across the road to an equally sleepy bar.

The next day we rolled into Philadelphia more than ready for that night's game. Sue's research had come up trumps once again: she had identified a bar that regularly ran private buses to Union's stadium, known back then as 'ppl Park'. The purpose-built ground was located 15 miles south-west of the city, near a town called Chester. We'd been warned that it was not a particularly safe area, so I was pleased not to have had to park our hired van there. Sue had been assured that 'away' fans would be most welcome, both at the bar and on the bus.

It was early afternoon when we arrived at Brauhaus Schmitz and settled in for a pre-match session, marking our first drink with a 'team photo'. We were joined through the afternoon by more Palace fans, both UK and US residents, including Wiz, Kev Mason, Rich the Eagle and Big Bad John. As the big steins of beer went down, the Palace flags and the noise levels went up.

When our transport to the ground arrived, we were delighted to find that it was one of those iconic yellow American school buses. Better still, it was loaded up with beer. We piled on and claimed the back seats as 'our territory', with Rich erecting his flag across the back window. The Palace songs commenced, as we got stuck into the complimentary beer. Our Palace chants were interspersed with Wags and I singing snatches the Sultans of Ping's classic indie anthem 'Where's me Jumper?' as it contains a lyrical reference to the 'People's Park'… ppl park… geddit? No, neither did the locals.

Our excitement at travelling on the school bus was tempered when we realised they don't feature air-conditioning and as a result are as hot as hell inside. Every window was opened to get some air into the bus, creating a wind tunnel inside as we trundled along the freeway. I felt something whip sharply across my face as Rich's flag came loose and was sucked out of one of the open windows. Rich was sitting further down the bus chatting to a home fan, blissfully unaware that his prized Play Off flag was now adorning a gutter on the I-95. Even when the Sultans' lyric had been amended to "Where's the flag gone?" he still didn't cotton on.

Another drawback of our chosen mode of transport was a complete absence of onboard toilet facilities. The Friday rush-hour traffic out of the City slowed our progress towards the game. The beer consumption dramatically decreased. Soon, our bladders were bursting. It took another half-hour to get to the stadium, by which time we were in agony.

Matters took a further turn when Rich came to retrieve his flag and was informed of its fate. We fled the bus, trying desperately not to wet ourselves laughing at Rich's sorrowful face. We finally found relief against a nearby freeway support, much to the bemusement of the local traffic cops. Poor Sue had to wait until she was inside the stadium.

I left the gang for my media duties and it turned out that I had been allocated a seat in the press box, rather than pitch-side access. Probably just as well. I really needed to sit down at this point. I started to take long-range shots of the stadium from my seat in the press box, but Palace's own media team were quick to ask me not to take any pictures of any Palace officials I might spot in the stands. I thought this a little curious, at the time, but did not give it too much thought. I wasn't capable of much rational thought at this point and guessed it was, perhaps, a potential new signing.

I finally managed to get pitch-side access to take photos, however the game itself did little to engage my interest. It was settled in Palace's favour by a single goal which came midway through the first half, when Union defender Ethan White inexplicably misplaced a clearing header back over his own keeper. A familiar face on the opposing side was Maurice Edu, who played for CPFC USA in that very first game against us.

Philadelphia Union are a relatively new side. They were formed in 2008 and took their place in the MLS in 2010. Strangely, Palace had previously encountered their main supporters group, The Sons of Ben, on the 2009 tour, a season before the team actually started playing. Some of the group had started to follow Harrisburg City Islanders, in preparation for the launch of their own team. It seemed to us to be a rather bizarre concept, but now, as back then, the group showed little interest in engaging with Palace fans, preferring to keep to themselves.

There was an increased number of Palace fans at this game, housed in an open stand in the shadow of the Commodore Barry road bridge, spanning the Delaware River. Palace's promotion to the Premier League had meant that the club had gained a new legion of fans Stateside and there was an impressive amount of red and blue on display. The New York Eagles supporters club were represented in good number and Trevor Weldon had once again made the long trip down from Nova Scotia, accompanied by his young daughter this time.

As I was on the bus, I was not able to hang around for the post-match press conference. I rejoined the gang for a somewhat more subdued journey back to Brauhaus Schmitz. Back in the bar, the party started once more and carried on right through the rest of the evening. Mindful of a long morning drive ahead of us, Sue and I retired at around midnight.

The next day, we headed south on the I-95 keeping half-an-eye out for Rich's flag. Not that we would have wanted to retrieve it; the rain was torrential. Our plan was to spend Saturday night in Washington D.C. after a nostalgic afternoon in Annapolis. On Sunday, after lunch in the Capital, we headed down through Virginia for Monday's encounter with Richmond Kickers.

Whilst we tried hard to recreate the party atmosphere of 2006 by revisiting the Richmond Tap House, it just did not have quite the same magic. The bar was deserted and only a few weeks away from being sold for development. At least we got to see a full game this time, though. Palace rounded off their US Tour in fine style, with goals from Peter Ramage, Glenn Murray and Marouanne Chamakh, against a side who were on a long unbeaten run in the USL at the time.

It was an interesting game for Murray, as injuries elsewhere in the squad meant he was asked to play at centre-half. In the press conference afterwards, Tony Pulis said – rather mischievously – that he thought it was Murray's best showing of late. The players came and mixed with the fans afterwards, signing autographs and happily posing for photographs.

The next day was back to the airport and, for me at least, another transatlantic night flight from which I would have to go straight to work – just as I had a fortnight before after returning from the World Cup. This did not get any easier with practice.

It was only twelve days later that we found ourselves back at an airport, travelling abroad to see Palace again. Our destination was Stuttgart airport, although the game was in Ausgburg. The lack of any reasonably priced flights to anywhere nearer to the city meant we would also need a two-and-a-half hour train journey. Eden Park Tours had done a fine job in organising a reasonably-priced trip and our party of five consisted of Hoover (who'd managed to get to all three 2014 trips), Mr Cad, Wags, Sue and me. Poor old Rob. This was yet another Palace trip to Germany that he had to miss out on. The late announcement of the fixture had meant he was already committed to a family holiday in Dorset.

The train trip was no hardship as German trains are fantastic and generally very punctual. Happily ensconced next to the bar in the restaurant carriage, the journey seemed to take no time at all. I had visited Augsburg a couple of times before: I stayed there during the 2006 World Cup for a game in Munich and also for a spot of ground-hopping in 2010. Wags and I took in an U23 game at their former home, the Rosenaustadion. The city itself was pleasant enough, mostly modern, but with an older centre and main square.

I had identified some extra games to squeeze in while we were in the region. No sooner than we had checked in, Wags and I were heading off for a Friday evening lower league game at TSV Dachau. It was a further hour and a half on the train and there were no other takers in our party, the rest preferring to have a relaxed evening, eating and drinking in the main square. We arrived back from our game around eleven to find that our gang had met up with other Palace fans, including The Colonel and Dave Hynes.

A pleasant evening of drinking and reminiscing about trips of old turned slightly sour just after midnight when a 'Ten German Bombers' chant started behind us. We turned to see two drunk blokes in their mid-fifties, exhorting us to join in. I declined their invitation rather sharply, which led to a vocal stand-off that looked at one point as if it might turn physical. Thankfully, calmer heads than mine in our party prevailed and everyone returned to their seats.

The waiter who had witnessed the argument told us that he would not serve any of us again, but as soon as the two older guys had slunk off, he was happy to continue to serve our party. The next morning the pair made an unexpected reappearance at breakfast. They were staying in the same hotel as us.

"Don't say anything" warned Sue, but before I could confirm that I had no intention of doing so, they shuffled off to eat elsewhere. Their body language radiated embarrassment about their behaviour the previous evening.

Our German friends Patrick Kovacic and Christiane Rhefus were arriving that morning, so we headed to the main railway station to meet them. Conveniently there was a large Brauhaus in the station itself and it became the pre-match focal point for Palace fans to meet. This, in turn, attracted a fairly sizeable police presence.

It was all good-natured though and I had a little grin to myself when I overheard The Colonel telling someone not to start singing about German Bombers because 'Neil doesn't like it'. It became increasingly busy, so we decided to head off and find somewhere a little quieter to chat with our friends, before boarding a tram to the match.

The SGL Arena opened in 2009, a little way south of the city at the end of a tram line, close to the University. The fixture had not captured the locals' interest and the Palace end seemed also quite sparse, due to the late announcement and relatively high travel costs. The stadium catering outlets only took their own pre-pay cards, which had to be purchased first. It was only when we had loaded a sizeable number of Euros onto our card that it became apparent that the beer on offer in our end was effectively alcohol-free. This did not go down at all well, especially when the club initially refused to refund money on the cards. Luckily the Augsburg officials saw sense and allowed it.

The Holmesdale Fanatics had travelled over for the game on a coach, but even they could not rouse a performance from either side, who played out the most forgettable of goalless draws. At half-time, several Palace fans fell asleep on the terrace and remained that way for much of the second half. We could only apologise to our German mates for the poor quality of footballing fayre, though they were happy enough to have ticked off a new Bundesliga ground.

The next day we headed back to Stuttgart early. As it was another city I had visited during the World Cup, my mind was on ground-hopping rather than sight-seeing and Stuttgart Kickers amateurs were at home in a lunchtime kick off. Wags, as ever, was my trusted companion, while the others went to do the sights and a spot of lunch. It so happened that Hull City were also in town for a friendly against VfB Stuttgart that afternoon. To my surprise, everyone was up for this game, even though we would need to leave before the end to get our flight home.

After some fuss getting tickets, we arrived after ten minutes to be greeted by the sight of former Palace loanee Tom Ince. After a bright start to his loan spell, he had faded somewhat, but it was still thought that we might sign him permanently, so it was a bit of a surprise when he elected to join Hull instead. The 'Palace reject' chant we struck up confused everyone in the ground, not least the player himself, who dribbled the ball out of play in front of us and looked totally bewildered.

It was the performance of another of Hull's new signings that had us all drooling. Left back Andrew Robertson was a class above anyone on the pitch and we longed for a player of such composed stature to fill what had become a problem position for Palace. It was no surprise when he joined Liverpool for big money following Hull's relegation and became an integral part of Jurgen Klopp's side.

This had been a decent pre-season campaign for Palace and the regular travellers were delighted with the number of games abroad. However, there was to be a sting in the tail. Just two days before the season started Tony Pulis walked away from the club, having previously negotiated to take his bonus for keeping Palace up earlier than it was due. His general disinterest at those American games suddenly made sense.

Despite a very narrow away defeat at Arsenal on the opening weekend under the caretaker guidance of Keith Millen, it was clear the club was in turmoil. Neil Warnock was appointed as Manager for a second spell and, on the same day, Wilfried Zaha returned to the fold, initially on loan.

Aside from a couple of notable victories against the Merseyside clubs, Palace struggled through the first half of the season, sculling around the relegation places. Over Christmas, Neil Warnock was relieved and former Palace Talisman, Alan Pardew took over the reins as Manager. He steered Palace to mid-table relatively quickly and an equal-second best finish of tenth place in the top flight.

There were also changes in the club's ownership mid-season, with most of the CPFC 2010 consortium selling the majority of their personal stakes to an American duo, Josh Harris and David Blitzer. The pair were private equity investors with stakes in sports franchises based in New York and Philadelphia. It was revealed that talks had been ongoing for some time. The US investors had progressed negotiations with Steve Parish, who would be staying on as Chairman, during the pre-season US tour. The reason for my photo 'embargo' at the game in Philadelphia finally became clear.

The infamous 'Tap House' in Richmond. Virginia - July 2014

The only highlights at Augsburg were the ones on the stand roof - August 2014

The late, great Bourno at Union Berlin - July 2015

The sparsely attended Cape Town Cup Final - July 2105

24

CAPE CRUSADERS

Whilst the 2015 overseas pre-season schedule did not scale the same heights as 2014, in terms of the number of trips or games, the cities visited were absolutely world class: Berlin and Cape Town.

Rumours started in earnest at the end of the previous season at the annual Palace Beer festival. A potential trip back to Germany was mentioned by Steve Browett, perhaps to be held over the third weekend of July, somewhat earlier in the pre-season than last year. Hamburg or Berlin were in the frame as the possible venue, although no indication of which club. Also around that time, rumour of a tournament in South Africa began to do the rounds, with a possible rematch with Kaizer Chiefs.

As has become the norm, fans were kept on tenterhooks for actual confirmed details and we constantly bemoaned the rising cost of flights on the BBS. Palace insisted that they were bound to wait until the home club was ready to formally announce the game. However, the news leaked out, both about a Germany game against 1.FC Union Berlin from the Bundesliga second tier and Palace's participation in the Cape Town Cup, early in the second week in June. Official club confirmation came a couple of days later. A four-team tournament where Palace would play South African side SuperSport United and then one of Ajax Cape Town or Sporting Clube de Portugal (better known here as Sporting Lisbon).

At the time, Sue and I were on holiday in the US with Wags and Jen, travelling down the Music Road in the Deep South. Nevertheless, Sue swung into action and both trips were booked while we were on the road. There would be six in our party going to Cape Town: Hoover, Mr Cad, Safety, Wags, Sue and me. For Germany, Sue booked up a weekend for eight, with Wags and Gibbo travelling to meet us later in the day.

The Berlin trip had a new member on our firm. After years of teutonic disappointment, Rob was finally able to make a Palace friendly in Germany. Like me, he was particularly excited about the opposition. On our numerous German football trips, we had encountered Union Berlin and their characterful ground, Stadion An der Alten Försterei, a few times before.

Rob had been to a Union game with the lads on a footie trip that I had missed. Their main memories of their first visit was that it was the coldest they had ever been at a game, but the welcome they received was one of the warmest. Ever since then, it was one of the clubs that they would look out for. The history of 'Einsern Union' since they were founded in 1966 is a fascinating tale that I cannot do any justice to here, but I commend you to explore it further.

On my stag weekend in 2007, we ended up there when a game at Tennis Borussia Berlin was called off at short notice, leading to a frantic dash across the City. Two weeks later, Wags and I were back in Berlin for a gig and had already planned to take in their home game against VfB Lübeck. We ended up seeing two successive home games which earned a nod of recognition at the beer stall on the second visit.

In contrast to Rob's first visit to Union, the Lübeck game was the hottest I have ever been at a football game. The temperature was well over forty degrees centigrade. I had to buy a Union white retro shirt just to wind around my head to keep the sun off. I must have looked a proper sight, but I really did not care. The seventy or so Lubeck fans in the away end were subject to the full glare of the sun and even got hosed down by the ground staff watering the pitch at half time. On another day, this might have sparked a riot, but the VfB fans were simply grateful for the respite.

Similar to the previous year, the most cost-effective travel plan was to fly into a different city and take a train to our final destination. We flew into Hamburg on the Friday and then took a train to Berlin. In addition to Sue and me, our travelling party consisted of Hoover, Rick, Bourno, Mr Cad, Safety and Rob. This meant we were able to squeeze in a visit to the Hamburg station-side bar called Capri – a favourite from our regular footie trips. Some morning refreshment was partaken while we waited for the train to Berlin.

This being early pre-season, opportunities to squeeze in extra games were limited but Rob came up trumps with a Friday night friendly in Brandenburg and then a tournament back in Hamburg on the Sunday, involving Concordia Hamburg; yet another German club we have developed a soft spot for.

As the rest of the party was settling down to Friday evening dinner and drinks in the German capital, Rob and I headed west to Brandenburg SC05 Sud, around an hour away. Although a committed groundhopper, Safety had little interest in these neutral friendlies, or indeed Sunday's games. Try as we might, he could not be persuaded to join us.

It was their first home friendly of the new season and the game had attracted very little local interest. However, those that did make it were absolutely fascinated by us. They could not get their heads around why Palace fans would come to this meaningless game. We tried to explain the concept of ground-hopping, but they simply would not have it. We felt like minor celebrities as their fans lined up to have selfies with us.

One of their burly fans invited us to inspect his Millwall hooligan tattoos. Once he felt he had sufficiently impressed us with his credentials, he was friendly enough and he seemed not to care about the south London rivalry. He even bought us a beer.

Matchday dawned bright and warm. Once more, our ranks were swelled by Patrick and Christiane. The game was a 2pm kick-off, so we headed off early to Köpenick, where the stadium was located about 25 minutes south of the city on the train. We exited the station and almost immediately fell into an open-air bar that had been designated mainly for use by Palace fans. There were also plenty of home fans happy to mingle and chat with us, including a chap called Sebastian Schalow, who was proudly wearing a Carter the Unstoppable Sex Machine t-shirt.

I should take a moment to explain why this was a huge deal for me. As well as being one of my all-time favourite bands, Carter USM are also very good friends of mine. I got to know both Jim (Jim Bob) Morrison and Les (Fruit Bat) Carter by following their subsequent musical projects, after the initial break-up of the band in 1997. After I went self-employed in 2001, I did a fair bit of driving and website work for them, also I somehow fell into lighting and roadie jobs. When Carter USM reformed in 2007, I became a fully-fledged 'Crazy Carter Crew' member. I still drive (and operate a bubble machine onstage) for Jim today, although he foolishly refuses to allow me to accompany him on my ukulele. Jim is a Palace fan who occasionally comes along and was with me at the 2013 play-off final. (I'll gloss over Fruity's Millwall sympathies here.)

To see a t-shirt of 'my band' worn by a local was just a little bit special and, better still, Sebastian recognised me from Jim's solo gigs in Berlin. At home, I do, very occasionally, get recognised as 'Mr Spoons' – my Carter Crew name – however, this was the first time it had happened abroad, which was a wonderful ego boost. Selfies and beers all round.

The Palace turnout was impressive, it was the largest contingent of overseas travelling fans I had seen. We had already met up with our good Skate and also Jason Axell and Danny Whitmarsh, veterans of the St. Vincent trip in 1990. We bumped into all the usual suspects from past trips: Wiz and Kev Mason; Baldy and Dave Hynes; Dave London with his family and scores of others that I will be in trouble for forgetting.

The total should have been even higher; the Holmesdale Fanatics had organised a coach, which Derek Collison was also booked on, but it simply never turned up at the meeting point. Undaunted, many of them decided to get down to Dover, cross on the ferry and then took trains. Others piled into cars. Del made it as far as Victoria Station before deciding to 'sack it off' in his own words. A few of the Fanatics did make it to Berlin, fair play to them for their efforts, but they were understandably pissed off at the turn of events.

There was an expectant buzz in the air as we supped those pre-match pints. Palace had just made a big-name signing in French international midfielder, Yohan Cabaye. At the time, it felt on a par with the excitement generated by the capture of Attilio Lombardo in the nineties. It had been confirmed that Yohan would be getting some game time here.

We made our way to the ground in a happy mood and took our places in the away end. The stadium was very different to how I remembered it, with much more seating. It was also now covered on all sides, which we were grateful for as it was a very warm day. Thankfully, nothing like the 2007 temperature though. The forest setting does make it one of the most attractive German grounds I have visited.

I would like to say the game lived up to our expectations, but that would be a lie. Both sets of fans created an atmosphere, but aside for the briefest of moments in the first half, when a Glenn Murray header found the net before the referee ruled it out for climbing on his marker, there was little joy.

Yohan Cabaye was amongst several substitutes that came on for the second half, but it was an unremarkable debut from him and, indeed, his team-mates. Palace fell behind on the hour and gave away a second late on.

After the game, a few of us tried to get into Union's main supporters bar, to relive the hospitality we had been shown on previous visits, but we were advised that we would not be made welcome today, which was a bit of a shame. We returned to the 'Gäste' bar near the station and continued the party with the locals there. The defeat was quickly forgotten as the beers and the songs flowed. Hoover indulged in a bit of shirt-swapping with an elderly local, ending up with a rather battered Union t-shirt, in exchange for a pristine away shirt. He spent the rest of the day complaining about the smell of his newly-acquired souvenir.

After a couple of hours, the crowd began to thin out and we took that as our cue to head back to the city centre for dinner in the Hackescher Markt area and riverside drinks on the deckchairs at the Ampfelmann Bar. Passing tourist boats were regaled with Palace songs long into the evening.

Like last year, we were up early to head back to Hamburg, as Rob and I had games to get to there. Due to its proximity to Lübeck and our friendship with Concordia, Hamburg was a city that we had both visited countless times before.

The tournament, deep in the northern suburbs, was actually at a ground that Rob and I had visited before. Indeed, it would probably be more unusual to find a ground in Hamburg that we have *not* seen a game at.

SV Halstenbek-Rellingen were the tournament hosts, but the game we were there to see involved Concordia Hamburg against SV Rugenbergen. Luckily this was the first game, as we wouldn't be able to see all of the later game. Concordia was no longer the same club whose hospitality Rob, Gibbo and others had enjoyed on several occasions. They had lost their famous old Hamburg ground, the Marienthal, to development and the club had merged with another. Consequently, none of the people or committee members that Rob knew from ten years ago still followed the club.

It seemed no-one was that bothered about any of the clubs taking part. From memory, the attendance was about twenty people, and that included Rob and myself. Rob hung his Palace flag with the Corcordia Hamburg badge in the one corner and the team did us proud with a 9-2 victory. The goal-fest made our trip worthwhile. We left midway through the second game and caught a cab direct to the airport to rejoin the others. Even a game involving the hosts themselves could not draw a crowd.

It was a mere three days later that Eden Park Tours swung back into action to organise the long trip down to Cape Town. The first leg of the journey to Johannesburg was with Virgin Atlantic and, thanks to air miles, Sue and I were able to upgrade to first class. The flat bed was much appreciated on the turbulent overnight flight.

Wags was travelling on a staff deal for a ridiculously cheap price as some of his family work for Virgin. The slight issue was his place was 'standby'. When we got to the airport, it seemed the flight was already overbooked and that he might not be able to travel on that evening's flight. He was still fretting at the gate with other standby passengers, while we were onboard being served pre-flight drinks. It seemed appropriate to send him some less-than-supportive texts at this point riffing on the lyric of the Ronan Keating song 'Life is a Rollercoaster' – "Wags on a standby ticket, he's been denied it!"

Just as they announced they were closing the aircraft doors, a sweating Wags appeared in the aisle. He had been given the last seat on a full flight. We gave him a rousing chorus of "Wags on a Standby ticket, he's been supplied it", which immediately attracted stares of disapproval from the cabin crew.

Landing at Tambo Airport in Johannesburg, the plane was taken to a remote stand and, after some delay, we were bussed to the terminal. This was bad news for us, as time was already tight for our connecting flight. Thankfully, there were no issues with customs, even with Mr Cad's working visa, so after a brisk trot through to the domestic terminal, we were at the gate ready for the relatively short hop down to Cape Town.

When the Cape Town Cup was first announced it would be fair to say there was a few moments of consideration given to its location, before we booked up. We had heard anecdotal evidence from people who had been to South Africa and Cape Town for both the 2010 World Cup and for Test Cricket that it wasn't the safest place to spend time. Others said that it was one of their favourite cities in the world, certainly no more dangerous than London and we should not hesitate to go.

Our mate Andy 'Puttsy' Puttock had confirmed that he had been mugged on an England Cricket Tour, just a few hundred yards from the hotel we would be staying in, which reawakened our unease. However, he also insisted that if he had not been very drunk there is no way he would have wandered down that dark side-alley, thinking it was a short cut.

His tale did serve to reinforce our approach to our personal safety, but Cape Town and indeed, the friendliness of the South African people we met, proved to be a delightful revelation. We absolutely adored everything about the place, so much so that Sue and I went back there on holiday the following year.

Another chap we got to know on this tour was Dan Weir. He is a young professional photographer who is also a Palace fan and had started taking photos at Palace in recent years. As a result, he had got to know Mr Cad very well. He combined the tour with a holiday to the region and became friendly with a local driver and tour guide called Mansur Enus, who was happy to also take our group under his wing and show us the sights.

We were staying near the popular Waterside area. Our first night was spent enjoying a fine feast at Balthazar restaurant, followed by a few pints at The Ferrymans Inn, which became our base for the trip. The Ferrymans had live music and a cheesy disco in the adjoining marquee. Safety and I decided to bust out some eighties moves on the dancefloor to the likes of Depeche Mode and the Human League and he quickly garnered the attention of some attractive local ladies. I left him to it and back at the table, we began crow-barring Palace players names and puns into every song lyric, much to the puzzlement of the other patrons. As a result of that evening, I can no longer hear the earworm chorus of The Killers' song 'Human' without mentally substituting:

"You gotta let me know... Ricky Newman... or Andy Ansah?

And I'm down on my knees, looking for the answer

Ricky Newman... or Andy Ansah?"

And now you can't either. You're welcome.

During the next day before the game, Mansur took us on a driving tour of the city, though unfortunately the cable car up to the top of Table Mountain was closed due to high winds. In the afternoon we regrouped at the Waterside and met up with the rest of the travelling Palace fans out in Cape Town. They had occupied Mitchells – the bar next door to Ferrymans – decorating its outside area with Palace flags. Out of an odd sense of loyalty, we continued to get our drinks in Ferrymans and popped next door to socialise with our fellow fans.

Around 25 fans had travelled out from the UK and there were a few ex-pats from other corners of Southern Africa. The Palace contingent in full cry attracted a lot of passing attention and photography from the locals. Amongst the happy throng were veteran Palace tourists Wiz and Kev Mason, who had taken a circuitous route, transiting in Dubai, then Botswana. Also out there, Adrian "Agey Boy" McCulloch and Damo Farino - my season-ticket neighbours from the Holmesdale Upper Tier.

Our game kicked off at 5.45pm and was the first of two that evening. Our opponents, SuperSport United, were a top flight side from the Pretoria region of South Africa. The club was originally known as Pretoria City, but was bought out and renamed by SuperSport, the group of national television channels. If that was allowed in the UK, the equivalent would be SkySports United FC competing in the Premier League.

The tournament had been heavily promoted throughout South Africa, but it was clear from the lack of any crowd on the walk up to the stadium that attendances would not be what organisers had hoped or budgeted for. Later research on the local football forums suggested that the choice of teams had not helped. Even though the tournament was being held in Cape Town, the lack of South Africa's heavyweight clubs, Kaizer Chiefs and Orlando Pirates, had drawn a lot of criticism. Likewise, the invitation of Crystal Palace was met with online scorn. That familiar cry, "why not Liverpool, Arsenal or Manchester United?"

With Pretoria over 900 miles away, the number of SuperSport fans was also small and only the lower tier was open. The Green Point stadium is an impressive arena, with a capacity of 55,000, built for the 2010 World Cup. It hosted the semi-final, but will be more familiar to anyone who watched the BBC daily coverage, as this stadium was their studio backdrop.

Upon kick-off, there were probably less than a thousand people in the stadium. The organisers did not declare official attendances through the tournament, out of embarrassment one assumes. Palace fans congregated on the halfway line, whilst the SuperSport 'Swanky Boys' collected behind the goal. Both sets of supporters made a reasonable amount of noise, but it was lost in the vast arena. Even though the crowd was miniscule, the vuvuzelas were much in evidence.

Palace took hold of the game from the off and raced into a four goal lead. Mile Jedinak opened the scoring after just three minutes and Chung Yong Lee, Jordan Mutch and Fraizer Campbell all got on the scoresheet, before the game was half an hour old. At that point, Palace decided to step right off the gas with a place in Sunday's final assured and the game finished 4-0.

After the game went off the boil, the Palace fans amused themselves by gently winding up the plethora of persistent refreshment hawkers patrolling walkways. Part of the fayre on offer were doughnuts, iced with either blue and white, or red and white icing. The sellers, who had the most annoying habit of getting in the way of the action, had to contend with repeated demands for only red and blue iced doughnuts. This silliness culminated in the whole Palace section chanting "We want Red & Blue doughnuts!" to the tune of 'Seven Nation Army'.

After the game, Hoover sought out the SuperSport fans to indulge his new passion for swopping shirts. He didn't manage to get a shirt, but instead came away with a comedy miner's helmet bedecked in SuperSport insignia and beer can holders. Most people returned to the Waterside, however Wags and I stayed for Ajax Cape Town against Sporting Lisbon. Despite the local side's involvement, the crowd was barely much greater than for our game.

We lasted until half-time. Though we'd allowed for the fact it was the middle of winter in the southern hemisphere, neither of us were properly dressed for it. A strong sea breeze brought in freezing winds and the temperature swiftly dropped to around zero. We headed off back to the bar with the home team a goal up at the break. Outside the ground we were both almost knocked off our feet by the strength of the icy gale; the stadium creating a strong wind tunnel effect.

We weren't the only ones to have had trouble leaving the ground. Poor lighting outside the ground had earlier caused Hoover to disappear down a large hole in the pavement. He was not a happy camper when we caught up with him, although it was not just his sore leg that was responsible for his mood. He had booked the trip knowing that he would only be able to do the first game, due to a pre-booked family holiday. The realisation that he would miss Palace play in an all-too-rare final was beginning to sink in. He cheered up a little over a burger supper in the nearby shopping centre, where he took some delight in annoying unsuspecting passers-by with loud blasts on his newly purchased vuvuzela.

We were up early the next morning for a 5K parkrun. The British Saturday morning institution is also massively popular in South Africa. Sue and I were already parkrun regulars back home and had completed one in Dublin before the Waterford game two years before. On this occasion, we persuaded Wags and Safety to join us. Although Safety walked all the way, he only finished a couple of minutes behind a hungover Wags who was 'running'.

After parkrun, we had a full day of sightseeing lined up. It began with a trip to Robben Island, where Nelson Mandela was incarcerated. The stretch of water between the island and the mainland is notoriously rough and, as previously noted,

I am a notoriously bad sailor. I had been dreading this and took a double dose of anti-seasickness pills before the trip. I survived the boat trip across without disgracing myself, but when we were loaded up onto coaches to tour the Island, I fell fast asleep and remained that way for most of the time there.

On the way back we were herded on to the smallest seagoing vessel I had ever seen and the wind had got up again, ensuring a choppy crossing. The only way I could cope was to take another pill, go on the top deck and pretend I was driving the boat. I looked utterly ridiculous but it worked. Of course, it did mean that once back on terra firma, I crashed out again and remember little of Mansur's trip to show us the penguins at Boulders Beach, or the whales sighted en route.

I awoke back in Cape Town in time to seize the evening and wave goodbye to Hoover as he headed off to the airport. His departure was marked with a song in the hotel bar to the tune of 'The Lion Sleeps Tonight':

"He's the Hoover, the flighty Hoover, the Hoover flies tonight...

He's in the air, He's in the air..." (repeat to fade).

Sunday was the afternoon of the Cape Town Cup Final, where we would face Sporting Lisbon, who had scraped past the locals on penalties after a 2-2 draw in normal time. Palace had played the Portuguese giants once before, in a midweek pre-season game at Selhurst back in 2004, where Palace striker Gareth Williams had scored the only goal of a dull game.

In the morning on the day of the final, first we had an appointment with the top of Table Mountain, now its cable car was reopened. When we got there, the queue was immense. It had not run in the previous days and it was scheduled to be closed again for a fortnight for maintenance. This would be our only chance to get up there, but the size of the queue meant cutting it fine for a pre-match lunch.

Had the Hoover been with us, there was no way he would have gone up the mountain, preferring his pre-match pints instead. We decided to go for it and the queue suddenly seemed to move a lot faster. When we ascended, we expected to find the summit overflowing with people, yet it felt as if there was hardly anyone there. It was a glorious morning: the views are absolutely stunning in all directions, certainly worth missing out on pre-match liveners.

Back at the Waterside, Safety and I dashed over to the stadium, still hopeful of catching a few minutes of Ajax Cape Town v SuperSport. We would have probably caught Ajax's last-minute equaliser had we not been waylaid outside the ground by a group of exuberant Congolese youths who hero-worshipped Yannick Bolasie. They were so excited to meet us and wanted to show off the Bolasie match-worn shirt, which they'd acquired after Friday's game. After several rounds of group photos, we heard a cheer from inside the stadium, for the late goal, followed quickly by the final whistle as we entered the Stadium itself. Ah well, it was not to be.

Onto the main event; more of a damp squib as it turned out. The potential excitement of seeing Palace lift a trophy quickly dissipated as Palace were dominated by Sporting in every department, apart from the actual scoreline. Cue more silly songs about doughnuts, but without any vocal opposition fans to compete with, well, it all seemed a bit forced.

Though the game remained goal-less until the last fifteen minutes, Palace never looked likely to snatch a winner. The coup-de-grace was delivered by Sporting substitute Fredy Montero. Just before full-time, he added a second, making the final score a truer reflection of the game. No cup glory for Palace today, but it was nice to at least get to a final.

Most of the Palace fans hung around for a while and some of the players reappeared to throw their shirts to the travellers. Sue was particularly pleased to nab big Brede Hangeland's shirt, although less thrilled when she realised it fitted her perfectly.

We headed for home the following day, again transiting through Johannesburg, this time without the need to scurry between flights. We were surprised to run into the Palace team at the airport, assuming they had flown home directly from Cape Town. The club appeared to be travelling on British Airways and their departure was an hour earlier than our Virgin flight.

We were enjoying a drink in an upstairs lounge, getting ready to head to our gate, when we were surprised to see Damian Delaney and Marouanne Chamakh racing through the concourse below, with the BA gate already showing as 'closed'.

"That's the fastest they've moved all weekend" I sarcastically commented.

We already knew from the Ireland tour a couple of years before that Mr Delaney seemed to like cutting it fine when boarding a flight. Now he had gained a partner-in-crime. It was only years later that Delaney admitted via Twitter, that they actually missed the flight that night and copped a right earful from management when they finally got home.

The following weekend, many Palace fans took to the water again, this time for a short boat trip down the Thames for a friendly at Fulham. Strangely though, I was back in Berlin for the German SuperCup as a guest of Fox Sports, who had just acquired the rights to televise the Bundesliga outside of Europe. Earlier in the previous season, I'd helped my pal Marc Ollington who, as well as being Carter USM's manager was also a highly ranked television exec at Fox. I'd provided him with some informal, anecdotal marketing research about the attraction of German football for his channel, when they were making their pitch. Including me on this press junket was a lovely way to thank me for my help.

By recent standards, Palace got out the blocks very quickly when the season started. They got up as high as second and were consistently in the European placings for the first half of the season. At the turn of the year, Palace were lying fifth with the other surprise package, Leicester City, in third. As the bigger clubs struggled to gain momentum, Leicester capitalised and incredibly ended up winning the Premier League, by contrast Palace's league form nose-dived and we went three months without a win.

By the time of the next victory in April, at home against a struggling Norwich City, Palace had also been dragged into the relegation mire. Survival was only guaranteed at the penultimate game of the season with a home win over Stoke City. The saving grace was an FA Cup run that took us all the way to another final, just proving the old adage 'you wait for ages then two come along together'. Sadly, just like the Cape Town Cup, the FA Cup one ended in disappointment too, as we lost 2-1 to Manchester United in extra-time.

The poor league form in the second half of the season had led to some calls to replace Alan Pardew as Manager in the close season, but the Board decided to keep faith with him.

Congo boys are mad for Bolaise
- Cape Town, July 2015

A pint for Pete. Brauhaus Schmitz, Philadephia 2014 & 2016

All aboard! Palace on a booze cruise down the Ohio River, Cincinnati - July 2016 [Photo: Dan Weir]

"When Fraizer scores we're on the pitch..." Me on a Glory Run at Vancouver Whitecaps - July 2016 [Photo: Dan Weir]

25

COAST TO COAST

During the season, there were strong rumours that Palace had been offered some prestigious pre-season matches out in Sydney, Australia. Our declining form meant we were unable to commit to the tour, as it was dependent on retaining our Premier League status.

Towards the end of the season, the word on the street was that another transatlantic trip seemed to be the club's favoured option. Just days before the FA Cup Final, this was confirmed as a three-game tour starting in Philadelphia with a rematch against Union. From there onwards to new club FC Cincinnati, a ULS team with big ambitions to move up to the MLS. The last game involved a trip over to the West Coast and up into Canada for a friendly against MLS side Vancouver Whitecaps.

The cost of the travel alone was not for the faint-hearted. At that stage, however, everything still depended on the result of the Cup Final. If Palace had won, then the club would have qualified for the group stages of the Europa League, starting in September.

Once we knew that, sadly, no European adventure awaited us, we began to make plans for the Stateside trip. A number of fans said they would pick and choose which games to attend rather than commit to the whole thing. There would be five travelling under the Eden Park Tours umbrella for the whole tour: Hoover, Mr Cad, Dan Weir, Sue and me. Having been to the Philadelphia Union friendly two years before, Wags decided he would just go to Canada.

It was confirmed in June that there would be no European excursion in this pre-season, when the previously covered home friendly against Valencia was confirmed for the last free weekend. This came as a disappointment for many but from a selfish point of view, my wallet was glad not to have that extra expense.

One of the good things about travelling to the States for pre-season was the chance to take in some competitive games, as their leagues operate in summer. Sue and I decided to head out a few days earlier than the rest of our party to take in some soccer on the East Coast. First, a game at New England Revolution in

Boston, followed by New York Red Bulls at home the following day. Big Bad John very kindly put us up when we were in the Big Apple. Puttsy also decided to fly across early and came along to the game in New York.

The others flew out to New York a couple of days later and together we took a train down to Philly the night before the game. Despite getting in quite late, we found a decent watering hole just around the corner from our hotel in Penn's Landing. It is a lovely part of the city right on the Delaware River, which is the natural border with the State of New Jersey. The team hotel was just down from our own hotel on the dockside. Sue and I had a good view of the players enjoying breakfast on the sun terrace as we jogged down the river path.

The Union matchday was very much a repeat of two years previous, with one very sad exception. Our friend and regular travelling companion Pete Bonthrone had passed away a month earlier. First order of the day upon arriving in Brauhaus Schmitz was to recreate the 'team photo' we'd taken in 2014. Pete's space at the head of the table was left empty with just his pint and Palace baseball cap sitting there, as we raised our glasses to his memory. He is still a very much-missed member of our party. At his funeral, we presented his family with an album of our favourite photos of Pete on tour. Mr Cad had even managed to unearth one going right back to his first overseas trip to Jersey in 1978.

Although it was mid-week, a good number of the East Coast-based Eagles were in town for the game and the Palace fanbase divided between the Brauhaus and Tir na nÓg for pre-match drinks. There was, however, no swerving of our loyalties to the Brauhaus and their beer-laden School Bus.

With my press days now long behind me and two photographers on hand to capture the action, I was free to join the rest of the Palace faithful in Block 134 of the now-renamed Talen Energy Stadium. The home attendance was noticeably smaller than the previous game and it was not just down to the fact this was a midweek game. The Union fans were not particularly enamoured to see us again and vented on their fan forums bemoaning a lack of ambition from their club. The all-too-familiar question: 'Why not Man Utd or Liverpool?' was given a thorough airing. It struck me as slightly cheeky to be moaning about our perceived lack of quality, seeing as the only overseas club to have beaten them in their short history was Palace two years before.

It did seem as if the stay-aways had the right idea, as the game was a fairly awful 0-0. The game in New York had also finished goal-less and Puttsy was less-than-impressed at having been to two games without seeing a goal. At least Sue and I had seen some goals up in Boston. Still, we had a chance to mingle with the American fans and familiar faces from recent tours.

Back in the Brauhaus, I got chatting to a car-load of Palace fans who had driven up from Pittsburgh. We had booked up to stay in that city the next evening as we road-tripped our way down to Cincinnati. Pittsburgh had been chosen on the basis that none of us had previously been there and that USL side Pittsburgh Riverhounds happened to be at home to Richmond Kickers that evening. Obviously, I had a lot of input into this decision. As designated driver, this was only fair.

The guys we met in the Brauhaus often watched Riverhounds and promised to meet me there the next day. I have to say I had my doubts, given the state that we left them in. The now-familiar road trip west from Philadelphia is one I will never tire of; the scenery is stunning. We had arranged a surprise lunch-stop for Mr Cad in his almost-namesake town of Everett, just off the interstate. I say town, it was more like a village. We stopped at Kelly's Scenic View Restaurant for lunch, fearing that it might be the only place to eat.

On closer inspection the Restaurant looked like just an ordinary house with all the blinds pulled down and the entrance unlit. Had it not been for a few other vehicles in the car park, we would have assumed it was shut. We tried the door and found it open, we walked into a deserted eatery. Goodness only knows who owned all the cars in the car park.

Eventually a lady appeared, who seemed slightly inconvenienced by our presence. Moreso when we told her we wanted to eat in. She led us to a table in a dimly-lit dining room at the back of the building where the blinds were again pulled firmly down. We asked why and were told it was too bright and hot when the sun shone through the windows. There would be no Scenic View for us. The food wasn't up to much either.

Mr Cad had recently passed a significant birthday milestone and had spent the trip regaling us with morose predictions of his imminent age-related demise. As we left, we asked about all the cars out-front and we were informed, quite crossly, that people used it as parking for the Cemetery next door. This was an open goal for Mr Cad, who responded:

"You might as well just dig a hole and leave me here."

We rolled into Pittsburgh in late afternoon, wondering aloud why their bridges appeared to be painted yellow. Predictably, it was just me who fancied going to the football and I set off alone, across yet another yellow bridge. What followed was one of the most extraordinary games I have ever attended as a neutral.

The Highmark Stadium was situated on a riverbank almost on the confluence of the Allegheny and Monongahela rivers. There was a railroad running along one side of the stadium and the main open-air bleachers commanded a perfect view of the imposing City skyline, together with the boats on the river and trains on the tracks.

I had worn my Palace shirt to be easily spotted, but my newfound friends were nowhere to be seen. When we caught up with them later in Cincinnati, it turned out that they had arrived home still feeling rough from the night before and were promptly banned from going out again by their other halves. They had, however, given me the useful tip of only paying for General Admission, then going wherever you want in the ground as no-one checks.

I took my place close to the halfway line and the game was only minutes old when a young lady approached me and said I was sitting in "Row of the Week", took my photo and handed me a giant cookie. If I looked mildly panicked in the photo that appeared on the club's website, it is because I thought she might want to see my ticket.

As the game progressed it became quite dark and not just due to the onset of evening. I looked up to see jet-black 'mothership' storm clouds emerging from over the hill behind the ground. We were about to get soaked, the city skyline suddenly looked like something out of the original *Ghostbusters* movie. And then the rain came.

I say rain, it was a Biblical torrent. The absolute maelstrom of thunder and lightning that accompanied the downpour stopped the game in its tracks and everyone in the ground scurried for cover. Sheltering under metal bleachers was not perhaps the wisest course of action, especially as the rain was pouring through them, but really there was nowhere else to go. A blinding and ear-splitting instantaneous flash-bang confirmed that the storm was right overhead.

The storm went on for around twenty minutes until, as abruptly as it came, it stopped. The crowd ventured out from under the stands and dried our seats as best we could, as emergency services sirens wailed all around. A steward mentioned that something had been struck by lightning in Station Square Mall, next door to the stadium. Forty minutes later, the game had still not restarted and the only lights on in the stadium appeared to be of the emergency variety. I could not even get any food as the outlets were all without power.

Whilst we waited, I chatted to nearby Pittsburgh fans and asked the question that had been on my mind since arriving in the city:

"Why are your bridges painted yellow?"

"They are not yellow" came the rather abrupt reply. "They are Aztec Gold!"

Suitably chastened, I ended my line of enquiry there. There seems to be a number of different explanations on Google, so to this day, I am still none the wiser. They all mention Aztec Gold, though.

The lightning had taken out the area's sub-station and they were waiting for urgent repairs by the electrical company. Not that the club was able to communicate this effectively without a functioning PA system, we were relying on word-of-mouth and Twitter. I was aware – from previous visits to weather-interrupted games in the States – that the game could be restarted up to two-and-a-half hours later. At nine o'clock, with my stomach rumbling like the earlier thunder, I gave up and headed off. That cookie was just not cutting it. The others were enjoying dinner in a large sports bar by the baseball stadium. I joined them and managed to grab myself a late bite.

After my meal, I idly glanced at Twitter and noticed the game had just re-commenced and Richmond had gone one-up with a penalty. To the amazement of the rest of the gang, I simply hopped back in the van to go and catch the rest of the game. The stadium now had fewer than seventy people left in the stands and the elapsed game-time was showing as sixty minutes when I got there. I was quickly rewarded for my efforts with another Richmond goal.

With ten minutes left, I decided to do a circuit of the ground. Just as I was walking past the changing room area, a young player in Riverhounds squad gear spotted my shirt and came over:

"Crystal Palace! My uncle played for them."

"Oh nice, when was that."

"Last season."

"Oh, err, right. What's his name?"

"Emmanuel Adebayor!"

I wasn't entirely sure I believed him at this point, but thought I'd be polite.

"Oh yeah, he did quite well for us."

He began laughing: "Nah, not really, he only scored one goal,"

"Yep, against Watford I think."

"Nah, it was Swansea."

Blimey, he was right too. My doubts vanished and he introduced himself as Alex Harlley. He asked for a selfie to send to his famous uncle. When the final whistle sounded it was nearly midnight, for a game that had kicked off at 7pm.

The next day we headed down to Cincinnati arriving in time to watch Palace conduct an open training session at the U-shaped Nippert Stadium in the grounds of the University of Cincinnati. There were probably more people watching that training session than had attended the Union game two nights ago. The southern Ohio public had really taken to soccer and the team had an average of over 20,000 in their first USL season – a previously unheard-of level of support in that league. If Union fans had been under-whelmed by our game, the absolute reverse was true of Cincinnati fans, the game was already completely sold out.

On matchday, the Stateside Palace fans had arranged a midday meet up on a pleasure boat cruise along the Ohio River. Given my track record on water, I was reluctant to go, but when I heard I could tick off another state as the trip left from the Kentucky bank, I decided to go. Given the trouble, I had gotten myself into in Cape Town, I dare not risk falling asleep with a game to get to, so travel-sickness pills were not an option, so I turned to a tried and trusted sailors' remedy instead. I plundered the grog rations.

By the time we cast off under the Taylor-Southgate Bridge (two ex-Palace players for the price of one), I was plastered. The midday sun beat down on the boat and only more beer could cool us all down. The trip quickly became a raucous sing-song, with fans taking it in turn to distract the Captain, so they could sound his horn in time with 'Glad All Over' belting out from the decks.

After two hours of good-natured chanting and the bar drunk dry, I suspect the Captain and his crew were pleased to see the back of us. The FC Cincinnati fans had invited Palace travellers to join them at their usual pre-match watering-hole, a German-style beer garden called Mecklenburg Gardens. From there they would march, en masse, to the ground. We were also invited on that, although typically most Palace fans opted to stay drinking. I went along on the march with the 'Nati' fans simply because, by this point, I really needed some fresh air.

The buzz in the ground was incredible. There was genuine, palpable excitement amongst the locals for the game and their fans wanted selfies with any Palace fans they came across. It was akin to being rock stars. The game passed in an alcoholic blur. The Palace contingent were in fine voice having been inspired early on by a Jordon Mutch worldie from 25 yards.

FC Cincinnati were no pushover, however and gave the Palace defence some anxious moments. Midway through the second half, Wilfried Zaha – by far and away the most popular player with the 'Nati fans – added to the score with a trademark dribble and powerful finish into the opposite corner from the edge of the box. Both sets of supporters exploded in appreciation of both the move and the finish. At the end of the game, we were treated to a huge firework display.

The attendance was announced as 35,061, which was a little surprising as the official attendance for soccer was 33,800. One assumes that because there was no need for any fan segregation for this game, seats that were normally roped off were made available. It smashed the Ohio State attendance record for a soccer match.

The drinking continued long into the evening at a Pizzeria Pub between the stadium and our hotel. It must be said we were in a proper state by the time we made it back to the Holiday Inn. Luckily, we did not have to be up early for our flight to Vancouver the next day, or that would have been a struggle.

The Delta flight to Canada was routed via Chicago O'Hare Airport and there was about three-quarters of an hour between the flights. After a slightly late take-off and a diversion around a thunderstorm, we landed with around fifteen minutes to spare to get to the international departure gate. Despite pleading with Delta staff to request briefly holding the plane, we ended up sprinting through the airport only to find the aircraft doors had closed. Lucky for us, there was another flight to Vancouver later that day, but with the time difference it meant we did not get to our hotel much before 10pm.

Although it was a Sunday evening, we were told there would still be places open for a drink and to try Doolins, about half a mile away. The bouncers on the door of the Irish bar eyed us with some suspicion and insisted on seeing ID. This time, it was the oldest member of our party who was found wanting. After some negotiation, Mr Cad was eventually allowed in without having to return to the hotel to get documents.

Wags was flying in that evening. Just before midnight we received a text to say he had landed and was on his way. We warned him about the ID situation, but when he arrived the bouncers decided they now required two forms of photo ID. Again, after some discussion, he got in. It was particularly mystifying as the joint was not exactly jumping.

The next morning, we threw back the curtains in our room to realise just how close our hotel was to the stadium, with a perfect view of its roof just across the street. We had the whole of Monday free and spent the morning on a hop-on-hop-off sightseeing bus tour, before heading to enjoy the sunny afternoon in Stanley Park.

Tuesday was matchday and we had a new addition to the gang in the form of Hoover's mate, Andy 'Tippo' Tipping, who'd also flown in from the UK for this game. The previous night, Hoover had scoped out a suitable pre-match drinking establishment just around the corner called The Shark Bar, where a good proportion of the afternoon was spent. It became the focal point for most Palace fans congregating before the game, including several West Coast-based Palace fans who'd flown north for the match.

At the stadium in BC Place, we had a quick look around their Hall of Fame. As mentioned previously, both teams have shared many personnel down the years, especially in the heady days of the NASL, back in the late seventies. Also, Jordon Mutch, who played for Palace in this friendly, subsequently joined Whitecaps on loan in 2018. We did spot a huge picture of Steve Kember, which brought pride and joy.

Moving on to the bar in the Palace section and, once again, we fell foul of licensing regulations. Sue ordered up a round of drinks, but they would only serve two at a time and refused to serve her the second beer until I was present. During the game, there were beer sellers walking the aisles, but again, they would not serve you until you could demonstrate the beer you had been drinking was completely finished. Whoever thought this would slow people's drinking had clearly not encountered the mentality of English football fans, who regard such nonsense as a challenge. We were completely smashed by half-time.

There was nothing on the field to keep us otherwise occupied. Palace fell behind early in the second half, but we were not worried because our striker Fraizer Campbell was now on the pitch. It's fair to say his goalscoring record for Palace was less-than-prolific and the rather sarcastic chant "When Fraizer scores, we're on the pitch" was often heard over the previous season. Desperate times call for desperate measures and we wheeled out the chant again. Surprisingly, it worked almost immediately.

Fuelled by beer and bravado, we led a charge towards the pitch, leaving the confused Vancouver stewards trailing in our wake. It was only when we reached the barrier that we realised it was at least an eight-foot drop to the pitch. Somehow sense prevailed in our alcohol-befuddled brains. We trooped back to our seats, winking at the puffing stewards as we passed.

Just as they began to scold us, Fraizer scored again and we were off on another glory run, leaving the stewards in our wake again. Sue said it was like a scene from the *Benny Hill* show, with only the Yakety Sax theme tune missing. When we finally made it back to our seats, the stewards had decided that discretion was the better part of valour and left us alone.

Whitecaps worked hard to get back into the game and got their equaliser fifteen minutes from time. They should have probably gone on to win it but for some fine work from Julian Speroni. Not being able to face going straight back to the Shark Bar, after the game, I hung around for the second game between two local Chinese sides, but the standard was so poor, I lasted about twenty minutes.

Back in the Shark Bar, Hoover had been indulging his habit of trying to swop shirts, except there was no-one willing to swop a Whitecaps shirt with him. Undeterred, he found a young lady who was more than happy to exchange her blouse for his shirt. We would not let him swop back, so he ended up wearing it for the rest of the evening. After the miner's hat and the smelly T-Shirt, this was a new low.

We had booked an early morning excursion to breakfast with Grizzly Gears by their enclosure at the top of Grouse Mountain. There were several sore and grizzly heads as we headed north, but the mountain air seemed to help. My dislike of boats is equally matched by Sue and Hoover's fear of cable cars, so for once, I was able to have a laugh at their expense.

The final ascent to the bear enclosure was on an open ski-lift. Unfortunately, I ended up with both of them on my chairlift, whimpering with fear and refusing to look at the spectacular views. Hoover was sweating and fidgeting so much on the vinyl seat, he almost slid right underneath the safety rail. When we finally got to the top, his seat was soaking wet and the operator actually had to towel the seat dry. I reminded them, with an evil grin, that they still had to go back down.

We were heading home on an evening flight and spent the rest of the day back in the city mooching around the Chinatown area. We concluded that Vancouver is very easy to like, even if the application of their licensing laws seemed rather more miss than hit. We flew overnight to New York, where we had to clear customs before boarding our onward flight back to Heathrow. Normally two and a half hours would be adequate but we'd suffered long customs delays previously in JFK airport, so were a little nervous.

The customs process has been streamlined by partial computerisation, but it still took the best part of an hour to get through. Mr Cad had to go through to the manual line, as he had a working visa. An hour later, he was still not through. We waited for him as long as we could, but they began calling our flight, leading to our second airport dash in four days. We just made it to the gate and so, by the skin of his teeth, did Mr Cad, as we tried our best to keep the gate staff from closing the flight. He was heard to remark that such strenuous exercise at his time of life would only serve to hasten his inevitable demise.

Palace went on to win all but one of their pre-season fixtures on home soil but then suffered a poor start to the season. Three straight league victories hauled them back up the table in September, before another awful run saw Alan Pardew's tenure as Manager come to an abrupt end. Sam Allardyce took up the reigns just before Christmas, but he started slowly. A run of four straight wins, beginning in mid-February, hauled Palace out of the relegation mire. Another ten points in the final eight games secured Premier League status for another season, although it was only made mathematically certain by beating Hull City 4-0 in the penultimate game and relegating them in the process.

There appeared to be grounds for cautious optimism going into the close season, but this did not last very long as Sam Allardyce decided to move on unexpectedly. In a departure from recent managerial appointments, Frank de Boer was installed as Manager in early June. The former Ajax and Inter Milan manager had been successful in Amsterdam but had lasted only 85 days in Italy. The move away from appointing someone with a proven track record of managing in the Premier League was greeted with reservations by the fanbase. Quite rightly as it turned out.

Wilfried Zaha and Julian Speroni in the Dog House, Wan Chai - July 2017

Wags has an unfortunate encounter on the Stadium Concourse - July 2017

Palace & Liverpool emerge from the Tunnel at Hong Kong Stadium - July 2017

26

EAST IS EAST

Rumours regarding the 2017 per-season campaign had started relatively early. Around March, there was a story emanating from Hong Kong that Palace were being considered for the Premier League Asia Trophy. This was, of course, dependent on Palace retaining their Premier League status.

In mid-April, another rumour emerged that Palace would be travelling back to the Republic of Ireland for a game against Limerick – the club where Sam Allardyce began his managerial career. This one seemed to have legs, but was ultimately scuppered when Allardyce left the club. Ireland was not entirely Palace-free that summer, as a youth squad visited the north, to lose 4-0 to Glenavon.

In late May, Palace confirmed their participation in the Premier League Asia Trophy, alongside Liverpool, who they would play in the first game, together with Leicester City and West Bromwich Albion.

The Tournament was founded in 2003, running every two years thereafter. Initially, it involved Premier League teams and a team from the host country, but in 2017 that changed to just four English sides. It is the only official Premier League competition played outside of England and Wales.

The tournament had previously taken place all over the Far East: Malaysia, Thailand, China, Singapore and Hong Kong. The competition was returning to the National Stadium in Hong Kong for the 2017 tournament, although it was originally rumoured the games would be split between Hong Kong and Shanghai's Hong Kou Stadium.

There was a lot of fan interest in going out to Hong Kong, despite flight prices alone being in the region of a thousand pounds. By the time the tickets went on sale the following week, around a hundred fans had already booked, mostly from England, but also a fair number of Australian Eagles. That's when the hassle started.

The English Premier League had made no provision for travellers from England to follow their teams, leaving it up to the clubs. Palace maintained that there was nothing they could do about this and fans would have to book via the official online ticket site, Citylink, based in Hong Kong. With huge local interest in the competition (or, more accurately, Liverpool) coupled with the Citylink site not being particularly reliable, Palace fans faced some anxious hours trying to obtain tickets, with all the best seats seemingly snapped up within a few minutes.

There was no question of being able to organise tickets in the same area, you just had to grab what you could on the open seats behind each goal. One of the problems was that the four games were across two days and a ticket covered both games on that day, thus anyone with a ticket was guaranteed a Liverpool game. Most Palace fans managed to get themselves sorted, although some ended up paying over-the-odds on ticket reseller websites. The club eventually said they would try and assist anyone who had missed out. It was a bit galling to discover, at the first game, that West Brom fans had been given their own block of Upper Tier seats on the side, organised via their club.

Sue had organised our travelling party of eight, the others being: Hoover, Safety, Tippo, Wags, Mr Cad and Dan. We stayed at the Excelsior Hotel in Causeway Bay on Hong Kong Island which was within walking distance of the stadium where the Tournament was taking place. This was also the ground upon which Palace played Happy Valley in 1995.

We flew in late afternoon on the day prior to the first game on the Wednesday. We landed in very heavy rain and, from the look of the completely flooded airport aprons, it looked like it must have been raining for days. Further unease arose once we regained internet access and the talk from home was that the first set of games were now apparently in some doubt. This was compounded when we got to the hotel and met up with a chap who worked for Liverpool's shirt sponsors, Standard Chartered Bank.

He told us that it had indeed been raining constantly over the past few days and Liverpool had not been able to train on the pitch that evening, mentioning that the organisers were looking at back-up plans. He alleged that the most favoured was to play one-off games on the Friday rather than a knockout format. He said that it was still the intention that Palace would play Liverpool. Again, this depended on the rain clearing up, which it was forecast to do.

By the time we left the hotel to go to a fans meet-up at the Dog House Bar in Wan Chai, the rain had eased considerably. We were tired and jet-lagged, with every intention of just going out for a couple of drinks. So of course the evening turned into a proper session. The bar was already heaving with Palace fans when we got there at around 9pm. Shortly after, many of the players showed up, accompanied by Messrs Parish and Browett, together with the Palace Media team. It was well after midnight when we finally staggered out of the bar, clutching our free commemorative t-shirts and looking for some supper. That night set the tone and I do not think any of us went to bed sober for the rest of the trip.

The weather on matchday was much improved and we got an early indication that both games would thankfully be going ahead. We found a small bar that was about halfway between our hotel and the stadium and settled in for the afternoon. Wags and I headed out to watch the first game: West Brom against Leicester. After a lively start, with the Baggies taking the lead on 10 minutes and the Foxes equalising, the game rather petered out, ending in a 1-1 draw that was settled on penalties in favour of Leicester.

When we got into the stadium it was already full of local fans decked out in Liverpool shirts and scarves. The Reds even had their own dedicated club shop under the main stand, with the queue stretching back the length of the pitch. In the other stand was another shop selling merchandise for all four clubs. Both West Brom and Leicester had their new season shirts on sale, whereas Palace could only muster a plain white t-Shirt with a large badge in the middle. The black t-shirts that had been given away for free in the Dog House were altogether better.

As mentioned, there was a small group of West Brom fans present, but no Leicester supporters were in evidence, aside from the odd local, daring to swim against the red tide.

Hong Kong's 40,000 capacity National Stadium was reminiscent in some ways to Huddersfield's ground, with two crescent shaped stands down the sides, however the seats behind the goals were open and fairly shallow. We quickly discovered the delights of two-litre glasses of beer on sale from vendors patrolling the aisles, with barrels strapped to their backs.

Although most people had tickets in different blocks, Palace fans congregated in two areas: in the seats vacated by the West Brom fans in the stand and in a small block of open seats behind the corner. During the first game it became apparent that there was a pretty lax attitude to sitting in specific seats and locals seemed okay with swopping seats to accommodate the Palace group. There also appeared to be no issue with simply standing on the walkway above the seating to watch the game, which is what Wags and I ended up doing.

The chap who had served us beer during the first game had sensed he was onto a good thing, so he came and stood behind us, no longer bothering to patrol the aisles. When the others arrived, they were amused to find we had our own personal barman and he was clearly delighted at the arrival of even more thirsty customers.

The game itself was a bit of a non-event. Palace simply were not at the races, mustering only a single shot on target. The only surprise, aside from Liverpool's all-tangerine kit, was that they took so long to capitalise on their dominance. The first goal from Solanke came on the hour, followed up by an Origi tap-in ten minutes from time. Palace never looked settled in a new formation and, despite admirable vocal support throughout the game, appeared almost disinterested.

After the game, some rather inebriated Palace fans spotted former Republic of Ireland midfielder turned TV pundit Andy Townsend doing a piece to camera in front of the block. This led to a spell of good-natured piss-taking about him being dropped from ITV. It was clear from his stony face that he was not at all happy with the banter and he moved elsewhere to finish his piece.

We headed back into town for more beers and then for a nightcap in our hotel's famous Dickens Bar. There we bumped into an English TV producer, who was covering the games. He realised, after a while, that we were Palace fans and asked us, quite seriously, if we would please lay off Andy Townsend as he had apparently taken the barracking very personally.

The time between the games was spent doing tourist things as, thankfully, the weather stayed good. By day, we went up to Victoria Peak on Hong Kong Island and went on a hilarious guided food tour. By night, we watched the sun go down from the rooftop terrace in our hotel before heading off to a real ale bar for an evening generously hosted by Steve Browett.

The next evening we headed for the highest bar in the world: Ozone on the 118th floor of Ritz-Carlton in Kowloon, to see the nightly 'Symphony of Lights' across the harbour. This was also the hotel that Liverpool were staying at. When we pulled up at the entrance, we were astounded by the sheer numbers of local Liverpool fans waiting behind a barrier hoping for a glimpse of the team. A small cheer went up as we got out the cab and it was as much as we could do not to go over and pretend to be their players. Given the price of drinks in the high-rise bar, we ended up wishing we were.

As we'd lost in the semi-final, our game against West Brom – billed as the Third Place Play-Off – was the first game on the Saturday evening. The pre-match pattern followed that of the previous game. Wags and I decided to go to the opposite end of the ground for the first half, to get a different perspective of the stadium. It proved to be a good move as we were directly behind Luka Milivojevic as he curled home an early free kick from 25 yards. West Brom tried to counter but seemed as lacklustre as Palace had in the first game. They had far more shots than Palace but very few caused any danger.

Palace again struggled with what was being asked of them by their new Manager. But just before the break, Luka Milivojevic, who was playing centre-half, found Bakary Sako, who let fly from thirty yards. His shot deflected twice on the way into the goal, leaving Baggies' keeper Ben Foster with no chance.

At half time, we left our seats to rejoin the others at the other end of the pitch. On the way around we saw a young local lad wearing a Brighton shirt. He looked absolutely terrified when he realised the two burly six-foot Palace fans wanted a word with him. We quickly reassured him all we wanted was for him to pose for a comedy photo with Wags pretending to strangle him. It was a good job he understood some English.

The second half, what I remember of it, was a typical friendly; multiple substitutions constantly disrupting play. The game descended into petulance as it wore on, not the great advert for Premier League Football that the FA would have hoped for.

A few Palace fans stayed on for the final, although some, I suspect, were just hoping for another chance to wind up Andy Townsend. Just before the teams came out, a huge Liverpool flag was passed over the heads of the lower tier. It was naive to think there would not be a reaction when it reached the Palace section and, sure enough, the flag was quickly hauled down. The locals realised this was happening and a good-natured tug of war with the flag began over the fence. Surrounded by locals behind us, we were quickly outnumbered as they tugged at our arms. Overwhelmed, we eventually let go, although not before my Fitbit went flying off, never to be seen again. A fitting penalty for my drunken tomfoolery.

I lasted the first half of the final and saw all the goals in the game. One time Palace transfer target Islam Slimani gave Leicester the lead, but they were quickly levelled by Mo Salah's first goal in a Liverpool shirt, more traditionally clad in all red for the final. Just before half time, Phillippe Coutinho grabbed what would prove to be the winner.

I wandered back to the bar, bumping into some English ex-pats on the way. Just as well, because my sense of direction was shot to bits. We had a friendly chat, even with the Millwall fan in their number, before they pointed me to the right bar, telling me to come down to the Dog House later. I rejoined the others, but before long our matchday bar was closing. I decided to go and meet my new pals back at the Dog House, whereas everyone else favoured the Dickens Bar in the hotel.

I tried for a cab, but it was extremely busy at that time of night, so I set off on foot. I really should have realised that navigation while under the influence was not my forte. I'd headed off in completely the wrong direction. After walking through increasingly dimly-lit streets I found myself back at the now deserted and dark stadium. Out of the gloom, an empty taxi miraculously appeared and I hi-tailed it back to the safety of the hotel bar.

What was supposed to be a quick drink extended long into the night and we crawled up to bed around 3am. A few hours later we were woken by the sound of lashing rain on the window and a note under the door telling us there was a Grade 8 typhoon on the way. We were told to keep the curtains shut and advised that the whole island was locked down. We tried to negotiate a later checkout, not least because I was suffering with a monster hangover, but there was nothing doing.

We shambled down to the basement bar and holed up there for the afternoon. The smell of the roast dinner carvery was making me incredibly nauseous, so, for once, a drink was out of the question. The typhoon never actually got over Grade 3 and the island opened up mid-afternoon. Some of our gang headed off to see the large Buddha, as they had originally planned, albeit by bus as the cable car was not running. Sue and I stayed in the hotel and I finally managed to force down some food.

That evening, we were on the midnight flight home. We arrived to find the West Brom Manager, a certain Tony Pulis, in the check-in queue. In similar style to Andy Townsend, he was reminded of his abrupt departure and that Palace had successfully sued him for breach of contract. The chant "Oh, Tony Pulis, we're having your house!" rang out loudly across the terminal.

Following the return from Hong Kong, the squad was off on another trip, not quite so far east this time but a one-off game against Metz in France. As the game was announced with less than three weeks' notice, quite a few of the regulars had already made other plans and missed out. This included Wags, Gibbo and I, who were already booked to fly to Hamburg for Rob's stag weekend.

We quickly discovered that Metz is not the easiest place to get to, either from the UK or on a cheeky day trip from Hamburg. The best UK options were to drive, or take a flight to Luxembourg followed by a train. As I was not there, I asked Carl Davies for his memories of the trip and, yet again, I appear to have missed another eventful one:

"The late confirmation of the game was the reason I chose to go out on the morning of the game, rather than the day before, like the rest of my mates. I had to be at a work meeting in Holland on the Friday, so my lad, Luke and I were on the first flight out to Luxembourg on the Saturday morning. There was a train that went from there to Metz every thirty minutes.

We grabbed some breakfast and a few cans, then boarded the train. The funny thing was seeing all the battered, hungover Palace fans who had also decided to go via Luxembourg, but had gone the day before and clearly had a big night out there. Luke and I were pretty fresh, but there were people throwing up on the train. There was a couple of away regulars sat close by, one of whom got back off the train saying: 'I can't do this' and I never saw him again for the rest of the day. I'm convinced he just stayed in Luxembourg all day!

We were into Metz by eleven o'clock and did what you should never do: it was a beautiful, sunny day but we couldn't check into our hotel until later, so we sat in the nearest bar. Within about half an hour, there was around twenty of us, mostly guys, a couple of women and my lad, sat outside the nearest bar to the station. We were all-too-visible and before too long the police had well and truly clocked us. You knew there was going to be trouble, probably a good three hours before kick off. You could see it, feel it and the French police definitely fancied it.

We all decided to move on to another bar and chuck our bags into the hotel on the way. From that moment on we had police riot vans following us, front and back, as well as down every side road. We were following Google maps towards the general direction of the ground and turned one corner to find the vans parked across the street and the police brandishing their shields. They told us 'You are not going this way, you cannot pass'. We were searched and told we weren't going to be allowed to go to the ground.

One of the guys had a snood, which was enough for the police to say 'It's very hot, this is to cover your face, you aren't allowed to do that in a French ground. You are not going in.' They tried to take him away in the van, people tried to pull him out and so we said: 'Look we've come here in peace, we've got women and kids with us' but they were insistent that we were 'the Ultras'.

They told us that we could not drink and to go to the ground. You can drink in the ground, they said, but we are not letting you into any bars. They gave us the route they wanted us to follow to the stadium. It was to set us up, not for trouble, but just to make it hard work. When you looked back at the route to the ground, versus what they'd given us, there was a lovely little walk along the river that took you right to the away end. But no, they sent us on a route where they could follow us and it took us down a steep grass bank, where they could watch and film us the whole way down. When we got down there were a load of little bars that were all blocked to us.

We were shepherded into the away end a good hour and a half before kick off, which wasn't where we wanted to be. We quickly found out it had nothing on sale inside, other than bottles of water. We'd had four or five pints beforehand, but it must be the most sober I've been at a Palace pre-season friendly. Looking back now, it just added to the fun of watching football in France and a European trip.

The Holmesdale Fanatics coach finally arrived and it was funny watching the French police realise that these were the ones they'd been told about and trying to contain them, then get them in the ground. The HF had turned up just about on time, having come over on a coach and they were absolutely battered and knackered. They got in, set their flags up and climbed up onto the barriers at the front to orchestrate their singing.

Out of the home end came a teenager, who sprinted down the side of the pitch, climbed up, pulled one of the flags down and off he went. Ultras culture demands that should you lose your flag, you have to disband. The HF went berserk and tried to get over the fence, but realised they couldn't. The police had come down with batons drawn. They only way they could do it was to get out the back and go round into the home end. They all piled out to the exit, the police realised what was going on, got around the back themselves and tear-gassed them!

As a result, the whole of the away end just filled up with tear gas. The police tried to calm things down and realised what the catalyst was. Halfway through the second half, some poor sod was dragged out of the home end, carried the flag back accompanied by two stewards and returned it to the HF. Honour was restored. I can only imagine the words that the police had with this Herbert who'd stolen the flag.

'It WILL be returned and you are going to return it yourself and say sorry!"

A Wilfried Zaha volley gave Palace the lead 10 minutes into the second half. Palace had been on top at this point, hitting the woodwork three times before scoring. Ten minutes from time, Metz grabbed an unlikely equaliser with a worldie from Niane and the game finished 1-1.

I reckon the total Palace crowd in the ground was 250-300 that day. It was made all ticket and that, coupled with the late notice, meant quite a few people I know decided it had become too much hassle and not to bother. It certainly put off those who had mates of other clubs, who might fancy the weekend, given they were talking about needing Club ID and names printed on tickets.

There were rumours going around all night that there was going to be trouble, but in fact it was the complete opposite afterwards. The Fanatics got back on their coach and left. The Metz city centre and river, once we finally got to see it, was beautiful. It was a lovely summer evening and there were people sat outside the bars wearing Palace shirts. There was not a hint of trouble, we had a bite to eat and the only problem we had was getting eaten alive by the mozzies!

Local people were coming over and, upon seeing our shirts, stopped to thank us for coming. They even bought us a round of drinks. All the feelings of antagonism and fear of trouble beforehand had completely gone by 7.30pm in the evening. We had a really lovely time in the end. It had all the ingredients of a good little Palace trip: a fair few stories and giggles, a nice bit of sun, the nervous energy of being abroad and the chance to squeeze in a random game.

The next day was the Luxembourg Super Cup Final. I worked out we had just about time to get there for a 4pm kick off, see the game and get back to the airport for our evening flight. The trouble was it turned out to be all-ticket. We went along anyway and saw what we thought might be the players going in. No harm in asking and, after a couple of false starts, I had ten 'billets' thrust at me. We took out two and went in, leaving the others attached to the fence by the entrance, in the hope that someone might be able to use them.

A couple of weeks later, a friend sent me a photo of the away end at Metz, just before kick-off, where you can clearly see Luke sitting on his own looking a bit disconsolate. I reckon I must have been in the loo at the time. My wife Lisa went mad at me for "Leaving our son all on his own!"

The Metz game was not the only occasion a flag caused a disturbance at a Palace match in France. Possibly one of the most famous and talked-about incidents took place 34 years before, at a friendly against Calais Racing Union FC. Allegedly, one caused the abandonment of the game with two minutes to go.

I have already alluded to this incident elsewhere and it even made the national news, with one of the tabloids running with a back page story along the lines of 'They are at it again' — the 'they' being English Football Hooligans. The truth, unsurprisingly, was a lot less hyperbolic than the paper made out.

The games took place in early August 1983 in towns in the Nord Des Pas Calais region, in the northernmost tip of France. As such, it was very accessible for Palace fans to travel across by ferry. Regular travellers Mr Cad, Ian Weller and Steve Carleton were among those who travelled over.

Palace played on the Thursday against US Gravelinoise (Gravelines) at their ground and won 5-1 in front of a dozen or so fans. The second game was held on Saturday in a town called Guînes around fifteen kilometres away from the ferry terminal. There were two games held that day, of which Calais v Palace was the second. This timing gave many of the travellers a bit of a problem, as Mr Cad remembers:

"We thought it was being played in Calais itself, so when we found out it was some way out, we knew we'd have to leave a few minutes before the end of the game to get the last ferry back. It's a shame I wasn't there to see what happened."

Ian Weller, who was at the other end of the ground, was unaware anything untoward had gone on:

"We were not aware the match had been abandoned, we just thought it was full time. We wanted to get away pronto so that we made sure we were able to get on the ferry to Dover."

So, what did actually happen that made national news back in England? Over to Steve Carleton, who was there to the bitter end:

"The story was wildly exaggerated by The Sun, which claimed that Palace fans had tied the Calais goalkeeper to the goalpost. Someone just dragged a flag in front of him during the game, from which the photographer took an out-of-context picture.

Although there was only around a dozen of us at Thursday's game, well over a hundred came across for Saturday's game. Every bar in Calais seemed crowded with fans from various South London pubs. You had to take a bus or cab to the ground, passing by the perfectly adequate Calais home ground.

Once we got to the ground at Guînes, there was a huge beer tent with wine or beer for around 10 pence for a small glass. Towards the end of the game, the trouble started with youths from the estate next door. Until that happened there was no police around. All I can remember is dipping under a barrier and getting kicked in the chin. One of my lot was hit by a bottle and ended up getting stitched up by the Palace physio, Bob Woolnough. Me and three others got a lift back to Calais on the team coach. Ron Noades moaned at us all the way."

Steve is a member of *Palace 'Til I Die (PTID)* Facebook group. Upon sharing his tale of this and his many other trips abroad to that group, one of the 'flag invaders' came forward to back up Steve's memories. The reply reads: '[we] got into the goalmouth and I slung the flag over the 'keeper and pulled him towards me. He bent into me and and I went over his shoulder. We were all so pissed, I just laughed and the keeper shook his head'.

The *Croydon Advertiser* reporting also detailed some conflicting stories about the incident. Manager Alan Mullery, who did not actually travel to France, was quoted as saying that "someone on the radio said there was a pitched battle between 150 Palace supporters and 150 French supporters. What actually happened was that three spectators came onto the pitch and tried to pinch the Calais goalkeeper's jersey and then wrapped a Union Jack around him. No one defends this sort of thing. All the while it happens, people tend to stay away from football."

Palace captain Jim Cannon, who was there and played in the game, was also dismissive of the radio report. "To say there were 300 people fighting is ridiculous, there was not 300 there. Most of the time the Palace supporters seemed to be fighting amongst themselves. These people are a disgrace and they let us and themselves down."

In the week after the game, someone purporting to be a 'Palace spokesman' went on *LBC* radio to talk about the trouble, presumably as a result of the national press coverage. Ron Noades was apoplectic and threatened to sue the radio station as this was not an official spokesman of the club. *LBC* quickly issued on-air apologies.

The chairman also issued a statement condemning the trouble and those involved saying that any further trouble from that group would result in an injunction preventing them from entering Selhurst Park. That statement was printed, without specific reference to the Calais game, in the first couple of matchday programmes of the season.

It does seem likely, from all the evidence above, that the game was abandoned for the crowd disturbances rather than just the flag incident with the goalie, but that is the tale that has passed into Palace folklore.

Palace returned to take part in the post-season Gravelines invitational tournament in the four years following. The games were not pre-publicised and the first that most fans knew of them was when the local press reported the scores. From what I have been able to establish, the squads we took each year comprised mostly of youth team players, with the inclusion of a senior first-teamer or two. The squads were managed by the youth coaches.

In 1984, Palace finished runners-up to the hosts, having lost on penalties in the final. In 1985, with Henry Hughton captaining the side, they went one better. After defeating Olympique Grande-Synthe 1-0, in their opening group match, they defeated Dunkirk-based USF Coudekerque 3-0. This set up a rematch with Gravelines which Palace won 4-2 on penalties after a 2-2 draw. In 1986, Palace beat Villerupt 1-0, before losing by the odd goal in seven to Sélection Maritime. The final game against Gravelines resulted in a 7-1 thrashing for the hosts.

The following year, our first game was against an Austrian side named in the *Croydon Advertiser* as 'SV Sparkasse'. However, Sparkasse literally means 'savings bank' and is the name of a large European financial institution. They have sponsored many teams in Germany and Austria and often integrate their brand into the club's own name. It seems that there were no programmes for that tournament, so it is difficult to establish which club it was that Palace beat 2-0. The other games on that tour were similarly victorious, 6-4 against Olympique Grande-Synthe and a 1-0 win over Gravelines.

Aside from the 1983 friendlies and those Gravelines youth tournaments, Palace had only played in mainland France once before and that was also against Metz, at the same Stade Saint-Symphorien venue, back in April 1967. Palace ran out 3-1 winners that day. As covered previously, in 2001 Palace played SC Bastia on the French island of Corsica.

There have also been relatively few games against French opposition at home, though the country did provide the first non-British opposition to Selhurst Park, when AS Nancy visited as part of the Festival Of Britain celebrations in May 1951. Not much celebration for the home fans, as the visitors won 2-1. Stade Français came over two years later, as part of the 'Floodlight Football' series.

In 2018, Palace entertained Toulouse, newly-promoted to the French top flight that season and with an ex-player amongst their ranks. John Bostock broke the record for Palace's youngest-ever senior player at 15 years and 287 days when he made his debut against Watford in October 2007. However, things turned sour at the end of that season when he was snapped up by Spurs. The fee went to the transfer tribunal and Palace received what was regarded to be a paltry fee of £750,000 with add-ons, which would amount to a further £1.5 million, dependent on appearances.

A decade later, the homecoming was not a happy one for the errant midfielder. The fans didn't give him too much of a hard time but the Palace team certainly did. Although Toulouse took the lead, goals from Christian Benteke, Jeffrey Schlupp and a penalty from Luka Milivojevic put the game beyond them by half time. Wilfried Zaha then added a fourth late in the game.

Briefly rewinding back a year, to our final pre-season game at home to Bundesliga side Schalke 04. Ironically, this was the first pre-season game to be confirmed. Our German friends Patrick and Christiane travelled over for the game, as Patrick is a huge Schalke fan. He was doubly pleased to add Selhurst Park to his long list of British grounds. It is a friendship that has flourished in spite of the passion my mates and I have for his arch-nemesis, Borussia Dortmund. Patrick even sat in the Holmesdale with us, though it was for the best that he was out of earshot of Rob.

Despite the fast-emerging doubts about Frank de Boer's strange team selections and formations, Palace came from a goal down at half time to equalise on the hour with a Christian Benteke header after a weak punch from the German keeper.

Those fears proved to be well-founded and Palace lost their opening four league games without scoring. This led to Frank de Boer being shown the door. In came septuagenarian Roy Hodgson as Manager, bringing with him Ray Lewington as Head Coach, a familiar face at Selhurst. Despite losing the next three league games, again without scoring, Roy slowly turned the sinking ship around starting with a memorable home victory against champions Chelsea in October.

Palace moved out of the relegation zone in mid-December and only briefly dropped back in for a couple of games in March, after a run of tough games. Palace went unbeaten in the final six games and finished a very respectable eleventh in the table.

Palace fans bask in the sun at Metz prior to the incident with the HF flag - July 2017
[Photo: Dan Weir]

Carl & Luke Davies explain to Sue how they ended up on the wrong side of the tracks in
Helsingør - July 2018

Hodgson's homecoming. At Halmstads BK - July 2018

Some of the crowd are on the pitch... well it was all over. At FC Bern - July 2019

27

ALL HAIL TO THE CHIEF

Palace's survival in the Premier League owed much to Roy Hodgson's vast depth of managerial experience, both at club and international level, spanning over forty years. Over the course of the next two pre-seasons, the fans began to suspect that Mr Hodgson was rather fond of a curtain call on his former stomping grounds. Palace ended up playing friendlies in Denmark, Sweden and Switzerland; all countries where Roy had enjoyed managerial success.

It was very nearly a different story in 2018, though. Going into the last couple of games, the word on the grapevine was that Palace would tour the west coast of the United States and return to Canada. As days passed, details became firmer and we began to get excited. A midweek friendly against San Jose Earthquakes in northern California, followed by a weekend game against Cardiff City in Edmonton, Alberta.

It was at the penultimate game of the season – co-incidentally in Cardiff – that our usual sources all but confirmed the details, right down to actual dates and kick-off times. The tour would take place during the final week of the 2018 Russia World Cup, which was rather off-putting for those regular Palace travellers who also follow England.

Flights were researched, accommodation provisionally booked and other potential games investigated, including an absolute corker: Seattle Sounders v Borussia Dortmund. This game was taking place the day after the San Jose match in the very city we would need to change planes in, to get to Edmonton. It all seemed too good to be true and, sadly, it was.

The announcement that we'd been led to expect imminently simply never came. Instead it was replaced by different rumours of a Scandinavian tour. It took until the start of June for that tour to be confirmed. One game in Denmark and one in Sweden, both against second tier opposition in their respective countries.

The opening game in Denmark, against Helsingør, was to be Palace's first game in the country in 104 years and our first game against a Danish side in 54 years when we had faced Esbjerg fB at Selhurst. The Swedish opposition was to be Halmstads BK, which had been the first club to appoint Roy Hodgson as their

Manager. He rewarded them by winning the title in his first season and again in 1979. In contrast to Denmark, Palace had last played in Sweden just eleven years ago at Oddevold – another of Roy's former clubs.

It was hard not to feel disappointed by this relatively low-key tour, having had the prospect of another transatlantic adventure dashed. A few days later, the knife was twisted again when San Jose announced that La Liga side Real Valladolid would be fulfilling the friendly fixture on the same date we had been advised. The Spanish club would then be travelling up to Edmonton to face Cardiff City in an exhibition game. Ah well, at least the Scandinavian games would be a cheaper trip and more Palace fans were likely to go.

I said cheaper but it was certainly not cheap. Food and beer prices in Scandinavia are, frankly, shocking and accommodation costs are also high. At least flight prices into Copenhagen were more reasonable. We had identified a Swedish league game in Malmo, just across the famous Øresund Bridge, for the Saturday evening between Palace games, so Copenhagen was the best place to base ourselves. Helsingor was a little over an hour away by train, Halmstad around two hours and Malmo a mere thirty minutes.

For the non-matchdays, Sue ended up booking a house, via AirB&B, in Utterslev, one of the posher suburbs of Denmark's capital city. This was a much cheaper option for our party of six, as we were able to cater ourselves for three days and take advantage of supermarket prices for food and drink. It also gave us a base from which to enjoy a barbeque and watch the World Cup Final on the Sunday afternoon, without having to find an expensive bar. With us this time was Hoover, Mr Cad, Tippo and Dan.

The first game was the day after the second World Cup semi-final in Moscow, which as it turned out, involved England against Croatia. As the rest of the party flew into Copenhagen from Gatwick, I was arriving from Moscow on a Manchester United branded Aeroflot plane.

My Mum had been taken ill and hospitalised in late June. We'd had a fraught couple of weeks waiting for her to have a relatively minor operation, which kept getting needlessly delayed. As a result, my stress levels were through the roof and I hadn't been able to watch many of the World Cup matches live.

When the host nation was knocked out in the quarter-finals by Croatia, suddenly a deluge of tickets became available for the semi-final, as the Russian public sold theirs back to FIFA. Unbeknownst to me, Sue managed to get a ticket for me, which had the desired effect of replacing my stress levels with excitement. The result wasn't what we'd hoped for, but I had an absolutely amazing, if exhausting time. When I finally met with the rest of the gang, I could have quite cheerfully gone straight to sleep instead of out to the game.

The town of Helsingor is most famous for its castle, Elsinore, which is the setting for Shakespeare's play *Hamlet*. Sue and I had a quick look round the outside, while the others decided that pre-match drinking was more important than sight-seeing.

Hoover also had other things on his mind. Somewhere between the airport and the hotel, he'd lost his passport. Terrified that he would not be let into Sweden for the second game, he contacted the British Embassy to request a replacement and was given an appointment early the next day, together with online forms to fill in. He set about completing these in the pub before the game. Initially, they were stumped by the requirement for a photo against a white background, but eventually found the only white wall in the bar. In the gents.

It must have been a disturbing sight for the other patrons when he and Tippo rushed to the toilet brandishing a camera-phone. They would have been similarly bemused had they tried to follow them in, as Hoover had his foot wedged up against the door whilst the impromptu photo session took place.

It was about fifteen minutes to the ground, pretty much a straight walk out from the town square. As we arrived at the ground, the first Palace people we saw were Carl and Luke Davies, who were looking rather hot and bothered. Carl recalls that their journey to the Stadium was rather less straightforward:

"Luke and I were staying just outside the town in a Hotel with a load of other Palace fans. We dumped our bags, looked on Googlemaps and the ground seemed to be right by us. We thought we've got loads of time to wander down there and get a drink and a bite on the way.

We got there and went through the gates, but there was no-one there. We weren't expecting many, but it was deserted. We sat in the main stand, still nobody. Turns out we'd gone to the Elsinore stadium, where the Danish National team often trains. I did find out that Helsingor sometimes used the ground for pre-season friendlies, which may have caused the confusion. We worked out where Helsingor's actual ground was from the phone, so set off for the right ground.

The trouble was it was the other side of a railway line. Talk about setting a bad example to the lad! We had to climb a fence, cross the tracks, then tramped through someone's back garden to get onto the main road by the ground. Had we stopped for a drink before going to that first ground, I reckon we would have missed the first half."

The game was an early evening kick-off. The home side, just a week away from their league season starting, raced into an early lead. After being stung, Palace came to life and after a spell of pressure, Alexander Sørloth, back in the country where he had made his name, equalised. Palace kept up the intensity, but couldn't find a goal to take a lead into the break.

During half time, for reasons mired in excess alcohol consumption, Hoover busted out his best dance moves to 2Unlimited's 'Get Ready for This', which was being pumped through the club PA at ear-splitting volume.

Straight after half-time, a much-changed Palace side responded with some nifty footwork of their own, as Mamadou Sakho slotted home a flicked-on corner. Palace seemed to be heading for victory, but James Tompkins turned a cross into his own net with seven minutes left. A late flurry by the Danes almost saw them claim victory at the death, but Tompkins redeemed himself with a goal-line clearance.

The next day, Hoover and Tippo were up early and away to the capital to organise the temporary passport. The rest of the party were able to take their time and allow hangovers to clear, before heading to the AirB&B house. Hoover and Tippo rejoined us and we learned that the new passport was only good for the return trip to the UK, which was not the news he'd been hoping for. However, he was also told that there were unlikely to be border checks between Denmark and Sweden when travelling by train. Shortly after his Embassy visit, he also learned that his original passport had been found on the train serving the airport, though by then it had already been cancelled.

The house we had booked turned out to be a family home. The occupants had gone on holiday to France. They had, however, left Buster the cat behind and pretty much all their belongings were in situ. Although Buster (pronounced 'Booster') was supposed to be fed by the neighbours, this didn't stop him constantly pestering us for food. We laid in some beer and provisions for the weekend at the local supermarket and made the most of the afternoon sun, drinking on the terrace. The evening was spent at a local pizza restaurant.

Early on Saturday, Sue and I borrowed the family bikes and rode off to do a parkrun at Fælledparken, in the shadow of FC København's Telia Parken Stadium. If that ground name sounds familiar, it's because this was the site where Palace had played a Copenhagen Select XI twice on their 1914 tour, although the stadium has been completely rebuilt since then.

That afternoon, we headed off to Malmö FF for their early evening league game against Östersunds FK. Hoover decided to risk it and made the journey. As we'd been led to expect, there was no passport inspection. We had been made aware that there had been some recent racial tension simmering in the city, so we stuck to the centre. Close to the main station, we found an agreeable bar overlooking the canal, to while away a couple of hours.

We took a cab out to Malmö's new 22,500 capacity stadium, located right next door to their former ground, which they vacated in 2009. Upon entering the ground, we heard that the honoured guest for the match was none other than Roy Hodgson. He is still regarded as a legend by Malmö fans. He masterminded five Allsvenskan titles in a row whilst there. There was even a part of the ground unofficially designated as 'Hodgson's corner'. When the camera picked out Mr

Hodgson watching from an executive box, midway through the first half, the ground erupted and he received a standing ovation.

The game was not a thriller, Malmö took the lead in the first half, but their increasingly sloppy play in the second period led to an equaliser for the most northerly club in the Allsvenskan. After the game we got another cab back to the central station, which turned out to be one of the most hair-raising rides I've ever had. Our driver was not content to sit passively in the matchday traffic, he sped down pavements and the wrong-way down one-way streets at the most ridiculous speeds, laughing maniacally the whole time. It took most of the train ride back to Copenhagen for us to calm down.

On Sunday morning, I received a text from Wags: "Are you going to the game today?" – to my shame, I had not even checked to see if anything might be on, assuming the World Cup Final would take precedence over all other football that day. In fact, FC Nordsjælland had a noon kick-off against Esbjerg fB at the engagingly-named Right To Dream Park. The game was taking place only ten miles north of where we were staying but there were no trains or buses that could get me there in time. Sue was out getting stuff for our World Cup Final barbeque, so I had no access to an Uber. I contemplated taking the bike again but I had no means of locking it, it was twice as far as the parkrun and, in truth, I was still saddle-sore from yesterday's ride. I resigned myself to missing it, although I kicked myself for the rest of the day.

The weather was glorious that afternoon, if anything rather too hot, as we prepped food and fired up the charcoal. In addition to the double helpings that Buster was getting, he decided that all the raw meat we had lined up on the kitchen worktops would make a nice snack and, whenever our backs were turned, he jumped up trying to 'boost' our burgers and steaks.

We also ran into trouble with the neighbours. Our barbeque was sending huge plumes of smoke across the other gardens. The English-speaking, cat-feeding neighbours came rushing over to inform us that outdoor grilling had been banned a fortnight ago in the city region, due to the dry, hot weather and danger of grass fires. Although we tried to quickly extinguish the grills, we only succeeded in creating bigger clouds of smoke and steam, causing further disapproval and curtain-twitching among our temporary neighbours.

The next morning, we set off for Halmstad leaving behind a cat that was twice the size as when we arrived and some relieved residents. The train across to Sweden was again without any form of border inspection, so Hoover was finally able to relax, knowing he would see the game. The passengers on the train were intrigued by the 'beer tower' of empty cans that grew during the journey. They began to ooh-and-ahh whenever a jolt threatened to down our structure.

We arrived in Halmstad in the early afternoon, checked in and headed into the city centre. Although the port has city status, it was more of a town. It was understandably quiet for a Monday but there were a number of temporary pop-up bars in the middle of the town square. They served as a base for Palace fans to congregate. After an afternoon session, we headed up the bank of the Nissan River towards Örjans Vall – the home of Halmstads BK.

Before the game, there was a ceremony to induct Roy Hodgson into the Halmstads Hall of Fame which prompted another standing ovation. Palace looked far more up for the game than they had the previous Thursday, even without Wilfried Zaha, who had returned home to attend to a family matter. Christian Benteke opened the scoring on twelve minutes but the Swedes hit back immediately to equalise. Despite the heat, Palace moved up through the gears and scored three in five minutes towards the end of the half. Goals two and three came from Patrick van Aanholt, whilst Sulley KaiKai grabbed the fourth.

The second half saw Palace take a while to get back into their stride, but the home side offered little in response. On the hour Palace moved further ahead when James MacArthur curled a sweet strike home. Five minutes later, Jason Puncheon hit the sixth and final goal of the game with his first touch. Despite the heavy defeat, the Halmstads fans were happy to chat on the walk back into the centre and a few stayed to share a drink with us back in the main square.

Palace's success on tour translated into an unbeaten pre-season once back at home, concluding with the emphatic win against Toulouse, covered in the previous chapter. The season itself started well with an away win against newly promoted Fulham. Then Palace stumbled badly, with just one win in eleven, however, not once did we fall into the relegation zone. Palace's season took an upturn just before Christmas, with an astonishing 3-2 away win at champions Manchester City. The Etihad Stadium had never been happy hunting ground for Palace. The team had never previously won there and were usually also on the receiving end of a netful. Palace finished the season in twelfth place with 49 points – the highest total since returning to the top flight in 2013.

Expectations for an exotic, far-flung 2019 pre-season tour were quite muted. After the Scandinavian tour, Roy Hodgson had made clear his preference for staying closer to home. Palace's participation in the UhrenCup in Switzerland was announced within a fortnight of the end of the season. Although, it cannot be described as exotic or far-flung, Switzerland was a new country for Palace to visit, with clubs of a new nationality to play against.

The UhrenCup is a long-established tournament held in the Biel region of Switzerland, organised by the watchmaking industry. The first competition was held back in 1962 and featured international teams, although for a long period it was only open to Swiss sides. The tournament has been held in some form most years since 1962. Palace became the fifth English side to take part: Ipswich Town (1963), West Ham United (2011), Stoke City (2017) and Wolverhampton Wanderers (2018) having preceded the Eagles. To add to the pressure, all but West Ham had lifted the trophy.

The format of the competition saw Palace pitted against two Swiss sides: FC Luzern in Biel and Young Boys Berne in Berne, although not at their Wankdorf stadium. The ground of lower league side, FC Bern, was to be used for the game. Many fans were disappointed by this news, I was not quite so unhappy, as I had seen Holland play Italy at the Wankdorf in Euro 2008. FC Bern would be a new ground for me!

The other side in the four-team Tournament was our old friends: Eintracht Frankfurt, however due to the nature of the competition we would not face them. They would also be playing the two Swiss sides, with the final positions being worked out across the four games. Any draws being resolved by a penalty shootout, the winners of which would gain an extra point.

The timing of the tour was at the start of the club's pre-season, as per the previous year. With Palace having already announced two games on the two weekends preceding the start of the season, it seemed unlikely there would be further overseas trips. Just as well, because as we found out, Switzerland is one expensive country to stay in. Everything from flights, trains, accommodation and of course food and drink came as a shock to our wallets.

Our party on this trip consisted of Hoover, Cad, Tippo, Dan, Wags, Sue and me. The most cost-effective route was to fly into Geneva and get a train up to Biel. Although it is an expensive country, the scenery is superb. The train ride up from Geneva was wondrous. We enjoyed the lakes and mountain vistas, accompanied by our first beers of the trip. No beer towers this time, though, in deference to the steward in the buffet car, who was something of a character.

We arrived on the day before the game and, after a meal, toured the bars of Biel/Bienne. We learned that the town has a dual name, as it is on the border of the German and French speaking areas of the country, although most people we encountered spoke Swiss German. The town is located at the head of the Bielersee lake, in the first foothills of the Jura Mountain range. The first night we didn't venture into the old town, preferring the bars around the centre. It was not the most lively of places and we soon ended up in the one bar that was open late, along with other Palace travellers. Even that place kicked out at midnight.

We noted from the posters in the town advertising the tournament that the perceived selling-point of Crystal Palace was, again, Roy Hodgson. He had been the national Manager of Switzerland and is credited with reviving their fortunes in the early nineties, gaining qualification to both the 1994 World Cup and 1996 European Championships. Under his tenure, they also achieved a FIFA ranking of 3 – the highest position the country had ever reached.

Matchday saw Hoover following his established first game of the season routine. He was out early with Tippo to scope out the ground and prospective watering holes close by, before hitting a bar for opening time. We were already aware that the newly-built ground was a bus ride away at the far edge of town, a couple of miles from our hotel. Hoover reported back that there was nothing open at the ground, which was effectively part of an entertainment complex. There was one bar in there that would be opened late-afternoon for the game.

We spent the day sight-seeing around the old town and grabbing some lunch before taking a slow amble out towards the ground. Hoover and Tippo had found themselves an Asian restaurant about a mile from the ground, but by the time we got there it was closed and they had moved on to the bar at the ground. We eventually met up in the bar at the ground where a young, overly-refreshed Palace fan was trying, without success, to get a sing-song going. He was with a group of three other young lads, who seemed a little embarrassed by his antics. It transpired that they had only just run into him and were now trying to keep their distance.

We got chatting to them; they were decent lads on their first Palace tour abroad. It became clear that they had been really caught out by the high prices and were wondering how their money was going to last until the weekend game. We stood them a couple of rounds – it was the least we could do.

Soon it was game-time and, on police advice, the Palace fans were only sold tickets in the small away end, with dire warnings about being found anywhere else in the ground. This was complete overkill. If there were any FC Luzern fans in the ground, they did nothing to make their presence felt or heard. Neither had the game captured the imagination of the local public, with only around 800 people in attendance, in the 5,000 capacity Tissot Arena. Over a hundred of these were Palace supporters crammed into one tiny corner. No amount of friendly discussion with the club officials or the police could alleviate the situation, despite the swathes of empty seats either side of the enclosure.

There were a fair few people who missed Palace's goal, as there was barely a minute on the clock when an unmarked Christian Benteke rose to meet a Max Meyer cross. The Swiss side struck back quickly and equalised within five minutes. And that was it for the scoring. The early promise died away and the game became bogged down in midfield, with chances at a premium for either side.

The game was settled on penalties. All five were scored by both sides with James McArthur, Joel Ward, Martin Kelly, Jeff Schlupp and Alexander Sørloth netting for Palace. Young midfielder Nya Kirby notched the sixth for Palace, then Wayne

Hennessey saved Luzern's first sudden death penalty and Palace had gained the extra point.

After the game we headed back to the bar, to let the meagre crowd go on their way. By the time we got back into town on the bus, in search of a late night bite, everything was closed. The following day we decided to head out to ramble through Taubenloch, a scenic gorge in the hills behind the town. Upon arriving we almost immediately encountered a group of exhausted Palace fans coming the other way. They'd gone out much earlier in the day and got lost, missing most of the picturesque gorge itself.

That evening, Young Boys played Eintracht Frankfurt back at the Tissot Arena. Wags and I wanted to go but the game was supposedly sold out, so we had a fancy meal out instead. Carl Davies did go and reported back that the stadium was nowhere near full. The Swiss club ran riot against the German side, winning 5-1. Now nothing less than a win against Young Boys would be enough for Palace to lift the UhrenCup, in a game that had effectively become a final.

We moved on to Bern the next day and spent a couple of days sightseeing, including a visit to see the bears of Bern – the animal species from which the city takes its name. Our hotel was almost overlooking the Wankdorf stadium, which was frustrating for Wags who had not already seen a game there. But soon afterwards we discovered that Young Boys reserve team would be playing a game there on the Saturday morning, so Wags would get this ground ticked off after all.

On the Friday afternoon, I hired a car so that Sue and I could go and do our now traditional tour parkrun. Switzerland is not a country that has yet embraced parkrun, so we needed to drive into France to find one. The car also came in handy for Wags and I to head back to Biel for the dead rubber that was FC Luzern versus Eintracht Frankfurt, that evening.

We got into town early, ordered grilled chicken and chips from a kebab shop with outside tables, washed down with a couple of Diet Cokes. The cost of which came to over thirty pounds each for this humble meal which really drove home the ridiculously high price of everything in Switzerland. This game at least provided some goals, with the Germans winning 3-1 quite comfortably. Given the thrashing they had been on the receiving end of from Young Boys and our draw with Luzern, we began to think that tomorrow was going to be a big ask of Palace.

Sue and I were up early on matchday to get to our parkrun and, thanks to light traffic, I even managed to get back in time to join Wags for the final stages of Young Boys' reserve team game. At lunchtime, we headed off to the Palace game, which was on the other side of the city. Changing from the tram to a bus, we passed Mr Pickwick, the English pub which seemed packed with Palace fans, flags proudly on display.

We decided to meet up with Hoover and Tippo, who'd found a pizza restaurant around ten minutes walk from Stadion Neufeld, where the game was taking place. After some pre-match beers, we headed off to the ground. Again the police presence seemed unduly heavy and we were subject to very thorough searches. Palace supporters were again confined to one part of the stadium behind the goal. Thankfully however, this time we were given the whole end. It was a shallow terrace and, as the ground was also used for athletics, the sightlines were poor.

On the plus side, they were serving beer.

We quickly made friends with the FC Bern guys in charge of the beer stall at the far end of the terrace. They looked after us very well. By the end of the game, they were telling us we had to come back and watch the real team in Bern, as we like a good drink. They even handed us club pennants of their team. However, Derek Collison recalls a less happy experience with the catering inside the ground:

"We drove all night and hadn't eaten before we got to the ground.

I'd had about three pints and it had gone straight to my head. I went to the bratwurst bar and bought one. As is the norm in that part of the world, it came with a small bread roll. I asked them to cut the bread in half for me, but was told that they weren't allowed to. I said 'well, you've got a knife there', but he repeated that this wasn't permitted. With that, he handed me the knife to cut it myself.

We had all been thoroughly searched for anything resembling a weapon on the way in and the bar inside was using plastic glasses. I thought that handing me a knife seemed completely ironic. I started to cut the bread but, being rather under the influence, I managed to cut the top of my thumb off!

The stewards took me to the first aid post around the back of the main stand, where I ran into Dougie Freedman, Mamadou Sakho and Steve Parish. I went to shake hands with Steve, but he saw all the blood and refused. The first aiders sorted me out and I went back to watch the game. Although by then my sausage was cold."

Palace had a decent turnout, almost trebling the number who had been at the game in Biel. The glorious summer weather coupled with the prospect of Palace lifting some silverware had clearly enticed a few to jump in the car and make a weekend of it. We met up with Dave Hynes and Colonel Britain on the terrace and spent the game catching up with them, fondly reminiscing about our other trips abroad.

One of the reasons we spent too much time drinking and chatting was the game was dreadful. Palace fell behind in the fifth minute after Vicente Guaita came racing out of his box to clear a ball he never looked like getting to first, leaving the Young Boys forward with the simplest of shots into an unguarded net. On the half hour, the rest of the Palace defence went AWOL and the game was effectively over at 2-0.

Despite a brief flurry of chances at the start of the second half, Palace never really looked like getting back into the match and Young Boys seemed content to see out the game without going for the jugular. The result meant not only did Palace lose on the day, but they ended up finishing third in the table. Only Palace could enter a two-horse race and end up in third place.

Although the result was not what Palace fans had come to see, fans remained in good spirits and not long after the final whistle we came out of the terrace and onto the running track to greet the players who were warming down. Round after round of selfies were taken as the players and staff happily posed with the fans. All the while, most Young Boys fans remained in their stands, patiently waiting for the Cup to be presented, seeming bemused by the friendly pitch invasion. A few did also come onto the pitch to mingle with the Palace fans in convivial fashion.

It was with one such fan that Hoover finally managed to arrange an actual shirt swop; rewarded at last with an authentic replica top after all his years of trying. We headed back to the pizza place for some food and then onwards to Mr Pickwick's, which was a lot quieter. Our evening session there led to Dave and the Colonel missing the last train back to their hotel in Biel. They had to cab it back which came to an eye-watering 150 Euros.

After a matchday that had turned into a major drinking session, Sunday afternoon was spent up a nearby mountain trying to clear our heads before the journey home. It was the day of the Cricket World Cup Final, involving England and New Zealand, so the cricket fans in our party were also trying to follow the game on the train back to Geneva.

Our flight was delayed and the airport's wi-fi was shonky, at best. This meant we ended up boarding the flight with the game tied and into its historic 'Super Over' decider. The full nature of England's amazing win only became apparent after we'd landed back at Gatwick.

The rest of the pre-season was an unusually miserable experience, save for a 5-0 thrashing of Bristol City at Ashton Gate, as previously noted an absolute bogey ground for Palace.

The final friendly at home against Hertha Berlin saw Palace go down 4-0 – equalling the biggest margin of defeat to an overseas side. After that, it came as a surprise when Palace had managed to climb to fourth place in the first four games of the season, although the Champions League form did not last. Palace settled in mid-table, enjoying some unbeaten runs along the way.

And then the virus struck.

In Mr Pickwick's after the Young Boys game looking forward to our next trip, little did we know…
L-R: Hoover, Mr Cad, a yawning author, Tippo, Sue, Col.Britain, Wags, Dave Hynes, Dan Weir
- July 2019

A 'Gentleman of the Press' once more. CPFC v Brøndby - September 2020

EPILOGUE

FULL DISCLOSURE

When I started writing this book in 2005, I had a theme and a title, but no real idea of style or tone for the book. I had trip diaries, fanzine articles and research, yet binding them together into a cohesive narrative proved to be a huge challenge. It got to the stage where I was continually rewriting and re-editing to fit my ever-changing ideas of how to present the book, without any form of version control. A couple of fruitless and frustrating years later, I simply gave up on the project.

It was a combination of things that made me resurrect the idea. During the coronavirus lockdown, Cris Lehmann restarted his own long-gestated book about the origins of his *One More Point* fanzine and had been in contact about providing some pictures. Whilst we were chatting, he encouraged me to dust off my own work. I was on furlough, so I certainly had the time.

One small problem. I couldn't find the computer folder containing the book and my research. Three months later, it turned up when archiving and reformatting a batch of old hard drives that I'd accumulated during my days of doing home computer support.

By then, Cris's book *Is that the Programme?* had just been published, to some critical acclaim among Palace fans. I read it in one sitting and thoroughly enjoyed it. Maybe I should take another look at what I had written fifteen years ago.

It was a complete dog's breakfast. I knew my decision to junk it had been the right one. Over the weekend, however, I came around to the idea of maybe starting again and completely rewriting the book. I got to work, with the sole focus of getting everything down, no stopping for edits or even grammar and spellchecking. That could all be done once there was a complete book.

2020 was one of those rare years where Palace's pre-season schedule had been arranged and announced well in advance. By the end of February the rumour mill was in full swing, at the away game against Brighton. There were many rumours afloat, related by many different sources, but all pointing to one destination, Australia. The club formally announced the tour early the following week.

Two games were scheduled in Queensland. The first, against Brisbane Roar in Townsville, in the northern part of the state and then a 'showpiece' (their words, not mine) game against West Ham at Brisbane Roar's stadium back in that city.

As excited as Sue and I were at the prospect of Palace's furthest-flung friendlies, it seemed just a tad ironic. We had only just returned from Australia after celebrating Sue's fiftieth birthday. The savings took another hammering as Eden Park Tours swung into action and flights were booked. Several familiar faces were up for this ground-breaking trip: Wags, Hoover, Tippo, Mr Cad, Dan and couple of new recruits: Dave Ashton a.k.a Camberley Dave and Tippo's pal, Ian.

No-one was prepared for the speed at which the COVID-19 virus changed the world. Less than a fortnight after booking, all football was suspended and we were in lockdown. The trip, though still almost four months away, seemed in serious doubt. It was no surprise when it was officially postponed in late-April. There were assurances that all parties would do their best to re-stage in 2021, but the virus had other ideas. They are still hopeful that it will take place in 2022. It took nearly six months to get our main flights refunded, although the money spent on Australian internal flights is still held in escrow.

When football finally returned in June, behind closed doors, I admit I had a tough time of it. An initial 2-0 win away at Bournemouth effectively cemented our position in the Premier League for another season. After that victory, the media pundits and some fans, were tentatively suggesting that Palace could have a run towards a European place. Manchester City had been banned from European Competition for falling foul of UEFA's Financial Regulations, although they were appealing this. It also seemed as though the FA Cup winners would probably come from the teams that would have already qualified for Europe.

Their argument ran that if Palace could continue their recent winning form, then they might have a shot at getting to eighth place. They had moved up to ninth and, with currently Man City out of the frame, were just four points off a Champions League spot, albeit with a poor goal difference compared to the teams above.

It seemed extremely unlikely to me that Europe was a realistic goal. Our run-in was particularly tough, with games against six sides currently above us out of the eight remaining. And so it proved. Palace went on a run of seven straight defeats, the awful sequence only slightly mitigated by a draw at home in the final game of the interrupted season.

In the final reckoning, Man City were successful in their appeal and Arsenal, who were outside the European League placings, won the FA Cup. Consequently, Palace would have needed to finish sixth to earn a place in a European competition. Effectively, that would have meant getting 18 points from the 24 available. That said, it would have been so typically Palace to have qualified for Europe when we weren't allowed to go.

I had watched every remaining game live, but simply couldn't get into it. This wasn't just down to our poor form, I just couldn't muster any enthusiasm or interest for Palace in this medium. I have limited experience of watching Palace live on television, as for most of my life I've usually been at the games. Up to that point, I had only ever watched a handful of live televised Palace games and I can't say I enjoyed many of those either. Meanwhile, I had started to rewrite this book and was getting far more stimulation from reliving these older games and journeys. I realised my love for the club was being kept alive by the past, not the present.

In mid-August, Palace announced that they were to face Danish side, Brøndby IF at home as our final pre-season friendly. The game would be behind closed doors, as everything else had been since early March. I was resigned to not going and, for reasons already outlined, had decided that I would rather go to watch a non-league game, than the stream of this match.

I did, however, put in a request to Terry Byfield – now Head of Production at the club – for a press pass for the game, citing research for this book as my reason. My press accreditations had long since lapsed, so it was an act of hope, rather than any expectation. However, on the eve of the game, I received an email confirming that I could come along, providing I complied with the club's COVID-19 policy and could meet the health conditions. I was beyond delighted, but the real bonus of being able to go was yet to reveal itself to me.

Matchday dawned and it felt strange going to a first team game at Selhurst when neither Sue, nor any of the friends who've filled these pages would be there. It was a truly odd sensation to walk up the traffic-free Holmesdale Road with so many conflicting emotions. Thus, I was pleased to see the familiar face of Carl Davies at the main gates. Carl was part of the matchday team at Selhurst maintaining the 'Behind Closed Doors' protocols. We took a few moments to reflect on the utterly bewildering events in the months since we had last seen each other at Brighton. After our catch-up his colleague, Alastair, walked me down to main reception.

"Are you a regular to Selhurst, then?" Alastair asked.

"Yes, man and boy…"

My next words died in my throat, as I came to an abrupt halt. A sudden realisation had hit home. Man and boy… today was exactly fifty years to the day from my first visit to Selhurst Park. I am not ashamed to admit I welled up.

"Are you alright, sir?" asked Alastair as I struggled to process this mental bombshell. I'm not sure he quite understood my explanation or the huge level of emotion it had provoked within me.

I was struggling to fathom why this major personal anniversary had not dawned on me before. I guess it was because the first Saturday in September is usually international weekend these days. I had not envisaged that a Palace game might be played on the actual date.

The shock may have raised my heart rate, but thankfully not my temperature as I passed the mandatory check at the door. Once signed in, it felt good to be a 'gentleman of the press' once again, albeit temporarily. I had always been proud to be asked to contribute. On the way up to the press box in the Main Stand, I walked up through the old Family Enclosure where pretty much my whole family had worked on a matchday back in the late eighties. Reaching the back of the stand, I passed where I worked for Pete King and James Coome in the Selhurst Six TV studio during the nineties.

I've seen my fair share of reserve and youth games from the Main Stand down the years, so the old place still looked much the same. I took my socially distanced seat in the press box, head still swirling with Selhurst memories and of those no longer with us: Dad, Ray and also Pete King, who had passed away in early summer. Terry was there and I thanked him profusely for the opportunity to see the game, explaining the greater personal significance this match had just taken on. The game had not exactly captured the imagination of the national press and there were very few places occupied, which had, no doubt, assisted my request for a pass.

With time to kill before kick-off, I did my homework on Brøndby. One of the most popular teams in Denmark, Drengene fra Vestegnen ('The boys from Vestegnen') had finished fourth in the Danish League in the previous season and just missed out on qualification for the Europa League. Their biggest and fiercest rivalry is with FC København, where Roy Hodgson once managed. If it had been a normally attended game, you would imagine that the away ultras may well have referenced that fact. And not with the kind of adulation that Roy had received on our last two pre-season tours.

The Danes started with the upper hand, with Palace countering on the break and having the best of the chances. As the game swayed in Palace's favour, Wilfried Zaha cut in from the left and drilled an unstoppable shot into the roof of the net. The second half was a litany of missed chances from Palace, some of which beggared belief. Brøndby survived three one-on-one's before somehow conjuring up an equaliser at the other end, totally against the run of play. Despite their dominance, Palace could not find a winner and the game ended 1-1.

As I packed away, I took a long, lingering look at the stadium. The previous March, in my rush to get down the pub and celebrate after a vital win against Watford, I'd had no real inclination that I wouldn't be back for six months. I needed a mental Polaroid this time. I had no clue when my next visit might be.

On the way home, it struck me that this book begins with a statement of my desire to see Palace compete in a 'proper' European Competition abroad. Now it ends in an era when I was delighted just to have got to see a Palace game live.

Mum and me on a CPFC Family Enclosure trip to Watford
- March 1989

While in the spirit of full disclosure, I must confess that last downbeat paragraph was where this book originally ended. I had written the final chapter out of order just after the Brøndby game. My intention was that the book would be finished soon afterwards, so this would not matter. As is often the way with the best-laid plans, things went astray.

In October, my beloved 94 year old Mum, who lived at home with us, fell ill and passed away a month later. In her final weeks, she needed almost constant care. To make matters worse all three of us came down with Covid, although Mum was asymptomatic; her issues were simply down to her advanced age. Thankfully, Sue and I both received a relatively mild viral load and were just about able to continue caring for Mum.

After she passed, my time was taken up making the necessary arrangements and sorting out her affairs, not helped by being back in a second lockdown. The book took a back seat and, if I'm being honest, I had no desire to write. It was not until the New Year that I felt ready to finish off the final chapters.

I did get to see another couple of games at Selhurst that season. In December 2020, the club was permitted to have 2,000 fans for the league match against Spurs and for our last home game against Arsenal, when 6,500 fans were allowed in. Palace finished in 14th and exited both cups at the first hurdle, thus did not qualify for a European Competition. A few days before the season ended Roy Hodgson confirmed that he would be leaving the club after the final game. And so a new chapter begins for Palace, although we did not ever come close to realising my dream under him, we have enjoyed a long period of Premier League stability under his guidance.

Even more so, watching Palace on television has simply become a duty; in part due to some ultra-cautious performances, but mainly simply the complete absence of any matchday atmosphere or experience. There has been the odd high spot: the victory away at Brighton, when Palace scored twice with their only two touches in the box, which still brings a huge smile to my face. Generally, however, it has become increasingly difficult to watch.

I am truly glad that I started to rewrite this book and have persevered until the end. The memories it has invoked and hearing the tales of friends have provided a large dose of the joy that Palace and football bring to my life. Ultimately, that is why I could not end the book on such a downbeat note.

I hope that you, too, have found some of that same enjoyment when reading the tales in this book. Maybe it has inspired you to follow Palace abroad in the future. Or perhaps to drastically increase your alcohol consumption.

So, here's to that next trip, whenever and wherever it may be.

Appendices

(Information as at 31st May 2021)

APPENDIX A : COMPLETE LIST OF FIRST TEAM MATCHES PLAYED AGAINST

DATE	OPPONENTS	VENUE	SCORE F-A	COUNTRY OF CLUB
16/05/1908	SK Slavia Praha	A	5-4	Bohemia
17/05/1908	SK Slavia Praha	A	4-1	Bohemia
20/05/1908	Smichov	A	7-1	Bohemia
21/05/1908	SK Slavia Praha	A	2-0	Bohemia
23/05/1908	Koniggratz	A	10-1	Bohemia
24/05/1908	Klando	A	6-1	Bohemia
08/05/1914	Copenhagen Select XI	A	1-2	Denmark
10/05/1914	Copenhagen Select XI	A	2-4	Denmark
15/05/1914	Örgryte IS	A	4-1	Sweden
17/05/1914	IFK Göteborg	A	3-1	Sweden
22/05/1914	Grenland Select XI	A	6-0	Norway
24/05/1914	Oslo/Kristiania Select XI	A	4-1	Norway
24/02/1937	Dutch National XI	A	2-2	The Netherlands
23/03/1938	Royal Netherlands Voetbalbond	A	2-3	The Netherlands
04/01/1939	Belgian National XI	A	4-5	Belgium
02/07/1947	Combined Services	N	2-2	Great Britian
05/07/1947	British Army	N	0-1	Great Britian
01/05/1948	Aberdeen	H	3-0	Scotland
16/05/1951	AS Nancy	H	1-2	France
12/05/1952	Dundee United	A	1-1	Scotland
13/05/1952	Inverness Select XI	A	1-3	Scotland
15/05/1952	Morayshire Select XI	A	4-1	Scotland
27/10/1953	Stade Français	H	4-2	France
23/02/1954	F.C. Vienna	H	4-3	Austria
16/03/1954	Queen of the South	H	2-2	Scotland
04/10/1954	Queen of the South	H	2-1	Scotland
13/10/1954	Clyde	H	1-1	Scotland
18/10/1954	Third Lanark	H	0-1	Scotland
26/10/1954	Wiener AC	H	2-2	Austria
01/11/1954	St. Mirren	H	0-1	Scotland

INTERNATIONAL OPPOSITION OR GAMES PLAYED OVERSEAS

COUNTRY OF VENUE	NOTES	CHAPTER
Bohemia		19
Bohemia		19
Bohemia		19
Bohemia		19
Bohemia		19
Bohemia		19
Denmark	at Parken Stadium, Copenhagen	19
Denmark	at Parken Stadium, Copenhagen	19
Sweden	at Walhalla Stadium, Gothenburg	19
Sweden	at Walhalla Stadium, Gothenburg	19
Norway	at Frogner Stadium, Oslo	19
Norway	at Frogner Stadium, Oslo	19
The Netherlands	at Sparta FC, Rotterdam	19
The Netherlands	at Sparta FC, Rotterdam	19
Belgium	at Union St. Gilliose, Brussels	19
West Germany	at Zoo Stadion, Wuppertal, West Germany	14
West Germany	in Bad Oeynhausen, West Germany	14
England		13
England	Festival of Britain exhibition match	26
Scotland		13
Scotland	in Inverness	13
Scotland	at Elgin City FC	13
England		26
England		22
England		13
England		13
England		13
England		13
England	Team name anglicised as 'WAS Vienna' in match programme	22
England		13

DATE	OPPONENTS	VENUE	SCORE F-A	COUNTRY OF CLUB
06/12/1954	Esbjerg fB	H	5-2	Denmark
04/04/1955	Hamilton Academicals	H	4-1	Scotland
08/04/1957	Clyde	H	3-4	Scotland
14/10/1959	Caribbean XI	H	11-1	Carribean
04/04/1961	Bangu	H	0-2	Brazil
31/01/1962	CHZJD Slovan Bratislava	H	3-2	Czechoslovakia
18/04/1962	Real Madrid	H	3-4	Spain
06/05/1962	Bermuda Football League	A	6-0	Bermuda
08/05/1962	Bermuda Football Combination	A	7-2	Bermuda
10/05/1962	Bermuda Football Association	A	11-2	Bermuda
13/05/1962	Toronto City	N	7-3	Canada
15/05/1962	West End Rovers	A	5-0	Bermuda
15/05/1964	Italia Montreal	A	1-0	Canada
17/05/1964	Hamilton Steelers	A	7-0	Canada
19/05/1964	Bermuda FA Representative XI	A	3-0	Bermuda
22/05/1964	Bermuda FA Representative XI	A	8-1	Bermuda
24/05/1964	Young Men's Social Club	A	6-1	Bermuda
27/05/1964	Bermuda FA Representative XI	A	4-0	Bermuda
30/03/1966	Alkmaar 54 (now AZ Alkmaar)	H	1-0	The Netherlands
17/05/1966	Aberdeen	H	1-0	Scotland
06/08/1966	VW DOS (now FC Utrecht)	A	1-0	The Netherlands
07/08/1966	Alkmaar 54 (now AZ Alkmaar)	A	2-0	The Netherlands
09/08/1966	SC Feijenoord (now Feyenoord)	A	1-3	The Netherlands
21/02/1967	CHZJD Slovan Bratislava	H	1-0	Czechoslovakia
05/04/1967	FC Metz	A	3-1	France
17/04/1967	Dundee United	H	1-1	Scotland
01/08/1967	MVV Maastricht	A	0-2	The Netherlands
03/08/1967	Go Ahead (now Go Ahead Eagles)	A	0-3	The Netherlands
06/08/1967	SC Feijenoord (now Feyenoord)	A	1-1	The Netherlands
02/05/1969	Morton (now Greenock Morton)	H	0-0	Scotland
14/05/1969	Benidorm	A	4-2	Spain

COUNTRY OF VENUE	NOTES	CHAPTER
England		27
England		13
England		13
England		19
England		21
England		19
England		11
Bermuda	at Somerset Park Cricket Field	16
Bermuda	at Devonshire Recreation Club	16
Bermuda	at National Sports Field	16
Bermuda	at National Sports Field	16
Bermuda	at Devonshire Recreation Club	16
Canada		16
Canada		16
Bermuda	at Devonshire Recreation Club	16
Bermuda	at Devonshire Recreation Club	16
Bermuda	at Devonshire Recreation Club	16
Bermuda	at Devonshire Recreation Club	16
England		12
England		13
The Netherlands		12
The Netherlands		12
The Netherlands		12
England		19
France		26
England		13
The Netherlands		12
The Netherlands		12
The Netherlands		12
England		13
Spain		11

DATE	OPPONENTS	VENUE	SCORE F-A	COUNTRY OF CLUB
21/05/1969	Aruella	A	3-2	Spain
22/05/1969	Hercules	A	0-0	Spain
30/07/1969	Asante Kotoko	H	3-1	Ghana
02/08/1969	Morton (now Greenock Morton)	H	1-1	Scotland
20/10/1969	Dallas Tornado	H	2-0	USA
07/05/1970	San Paulo	A	3-2	Spain
14/05/1970	Atletico Madrid XI	A	1-1	Spain
21/05/1970	Mahon	A	2-1	Spain
01/08/1970	St. Mirren	H	4-0	Scotland
05/08/1970	Paykaan	H	8-1	Iran
19/01/1971	Israel National XI	A	0-0	Israel
12/02/1971	PSV Eindhoven	H	2-4	The Netherlands
03/03/1971	ADO Den Haag	H	0-0	The Netherlands
08/03/1971	First Tower United	A	2-1	Jersey
13/05/1971	RFC Bruges (now Club Brugge)	H	1-3	Belgium
21/05/1971	Clyde	H	1-1	Scotland
26/05/1971	Cagliari	H	1-0	Italy
29/05/1971	Internazionale (Inter Milan)	H	1-1	Italy
01/06/1973	Cagliari	A	0-2	Italy
04/06/1973	Internazionale (Inter Milan)	A	2-1	Italy
28/07/1971	SC Feijenoord (now Feyenoord)	A	0-1	The Netherlands
01/08/1971	ADO Den Haag	A	0-0	The Netherlands
04/08/1971	PSV Eindhoven	A	3-2	The Netherlands
06/08/1971	Maccabi Netanya	H	4-1	Israel
26/02/1972	Partick Thistle	H	2-0	Scotland
29/07/1972	Dundee United	H	3-1	Scotland
30/07/1972	MVV Maastricht	A	0-1	The Netherlands
05/08/1972	Dundee	A	4-1	Scotland
13/09/1972	Heart of Midlothian	A	0-1	Scotland
26/09/1972	Heart of Midlothian	H	0-1	Scotland
24/10/1972	MVV Maastricht	H	2-1	The Netherlands

COUNTRY OF VENUE	NOTES	CHAPTER
Spain		11
Spain	in Alicante	11
England		21
England		13
England		16
Spain	Fishermans Cup	11
Spain		11
Spain	in Minorca	11
England		13
England		21
Israel		21
England		12
England		12
Jersey		12
England	John Sewell Testimonial	19
England		13
England	Anglo Italian Tournament Group 2	2
England	Anglo Italian Tournament Group 2	2
Italy	Anglo Italian Tournament Group 2	2
Italy	Anglo Italian Tournament Group 2	2
The Netherlands		12
The Netherlands		12
The Netherlands		12
England		21
England		13
England		13
The Netherlands		12
Scotland		13
Scotland	The Texaco International League Competition R1 L1	13
England	The Texaco International League Competition R1 L2	13
England		12

DATE	OPPONENTS	VENUE	SCORE F-A	COUNTRY OF CLUB
08/11/1972	Persepolis	A	5-1	Iran
14/11/1972	Leningrad Zenit (now Zenit St Petersburg)	H	1-1	Russia
09/01/1973	Aberdeen	A	0-2	Scotland
14/02/1973	Hellas Verona	H	4-1	Italy
21/03/1973	SSC Bari	A	1-0	Italy
04/04/1973	SS Lazio	H	3-1	Italy
02/05/1973	ACF Fiorentina	A	2-2	Italy
22/07/1973	IK Sirius	A	3-2	Sweden
25/07/1973	Sandvikens IF	A	1-1	Sweden
29/07/1973	Västerhaninge IF	N	3-0	Sweden
30/07/1973	Degerfors IF	A	1-0	Sweden
21/07/1974	Helsingborgs IF	A	1-1	Sweden
23/07/1974	IF Saab	A	2-1	Sweden
25/07/1974	IFK Norrköping	A	2-2	Sweden
24/07/1976	Alemannia Aachen	A	2-3	West Germany
28/07/1976	SC Heracles Almelo	A	2-0	The Netherlands
30/07/1976	Rijnsburgse Boys	A	6-0	The Netherlands
01/08/1976	WVV Wageningen	A	2-1	The Netherlands
18/07/1977	Jersey Under 23 XI	A	2-0	Jersey
21/07/1977	Jersey XI	A	9-3	Jersey
18/02/1978	Hibernian	H	0-1	Scotland
20/05/1978	Corfu Select XI	A	3-1	Greece
22/05/1978	Corfu Select XI	N	2-0	Greece
25/07/1978	Sandvikens IF	A	3-0	Sweden
27/07/1978	IK Brage	A	3-1	Sweden
31/07/1978	IF Brommapojkarna	A	4-0	Sweden
03/08/1978	IK Sirius	A	1-0	Sweden
22/05/1979	Memphis Rogues	A	3-1	USA
23/05/1979	Fort Lauderdale Strikers	A	2-0	USA
24/07/1979	Storms BK	A	1-0	Norway
26/07/1979	FK Ørn	A	1-1	Norway

COUNTRY OF VENUE	NOTES	CHAPTER
Iran		21
England		21
Scotland		13
England	Anglo Italian Tournament Group 1	2
Italy	Anglo Italian Tournament Group 1	2
England	Anglo Italian Tournament Group 1	2
Italy	Anglo Italian Tournament Group 1	2
Sweden	Juli-Cupen Group A	18
Sweden	Juli-Cupen Group A	18
Sweden	Juli-Cupen Final at Söderstadion, Johanneshov	18
Sweden		18
Sweden		18
Sweden		18
Sweden		18
West Germany		12
The Netherlands		12
The Netherlands		12
The Netherlands		12
Jersey		12
Jersey	at Springfield Stadium, St Helier	12
England		13
Greece		12
Greece	In Ingoumentisa (Greek mainland)	12
Sweden		18
Sweden		18
Sweden		18
Sweden		18
USA		16
USA		16
Norway		12
Norway		12

DATE	OPPONENTS	VENUE	SCORE F-A	COUNTRY OF CLUB
28/07/1979	FK Jerv	A	3-0	Norway
31/07/1979	FK Viking	A	1-0	Norway
02/08/1979	Lillestrøm SK	A	2-1	Norway
25/05/1980	Malaga	A	0-2	Spain
23/07/1980	Öviksallainsen	A	5-0	Sweden
25/07/1980	IKK Strömsund	A	3-0	Sweden
27/07/1980	Kramfors Alliansen	A	4-0	Sweden
30/07/1980	Edsbyns IF FF	A	8-0	Sweden
23/03/1981	Minnesota Kicks	H	1-1	USA
24/02/1982	IFK Göteborg	H	1-3	Sweden
30/07/1982	VfR Neumünster	A	4-3	Germany
31/07/1982	SV Lurup	A	1-3	Germany
01/08/1982	SV Börnsen	A	4-2	Germany
04/08/1983	US Gravelinoise (Gravelines)	A	5-1	France
06/08/1983	Calais Racing Union FC	N	2a0	France
09/08/1983	Japan National XI	H	1-2	Japan
20/08/1984	Hapoel Tel Aviv	H	3-0	Israel
03/02/1985	Qatar Under 21 XI	A	0-0	Qatar
26/07/1987	IFK Grängesberg	A	5-0	Sweden
28/07/1987	Smedjebackens FK	A	3-0	Sweden
29/07/1987	Frövi IK	A	8-0	Sweden
01/08/1987	Rossöns IF	A	6-1	Sweden
02/08/1987	Lycksele IF	A	8-0	Sweden
04/08/1987	Södertälje FK	A	1-0	Sweden
25/07/1988	FK Mjølner	A	1-3	Norway
27/07/1988	Kemin Pallaseura	A	5-1	Finland
28/07/1988	Hemmingsmarks IF	A	2-1	Sweden
30/07/1988	Gällivare SK	A	4-1	Sweden
02/08/1988	Luleå FF/IFK	A	4-0	Sweden
03/08/1988	Västerhaninge IF	A	9-0	Sweden
23/08/1988	'Tel Aviv'	H	1-0	Israel

COUNTRY OF VENUE	NOTES	CHAPTER
Norway		12
Norway		12
Norway		12
Spain		11
Sweden	At Skyttis, Örnsköldsvik	18
Sweden		18
Sweden		18
Sweden		18
England	(Lost on NASL shoot-out)	16
England		18
Germany	Oppostion uncertain (also listed as Combined Flensburg XI)	14
Germany		14
Germany		14
France		26
France	in Guînes Abandoned 88m - Crowd Trouble	26
England		21
England		21
Qatar		21
Sweden		18
Sweden		18
Sweden		18
Sweden		18
Sweden		18
Sweden		18
Norway		18
Finland		18
Sweden		18
Sweden		18
Sweden		18
Sweden		18
England	Behind closed doors - Opposition uncertain	21

DATE	OPPONENTS	VENUE	SCORE F-A	COUNTRY OF CLUB
23/07/1989	IF Norvalla	A	3-1	Sweden
25/07/1989	Billesholms GIF	A	7-2	Sweden
27/07/1989	Vederslöv/Dänningelanda IF	A	5-1	Sweden
29/07/1989	Virserums SGF	A	7-1	Sweden
31/07/1989	Skrea IF	A	7-1	Sweden
01/08/1989	Södra Vings IF	A	2-0	Sweden
30/08/1989	Derry City	A	4-2	N. Ireland
20/05/1990	Caribbean Select XI	A	2-2	Caribbean
23/05/1990	Trinidad & Tobago XI	A	0-4	Trinidad & Tobago
27/05/1990	Jamaican XI	A	2-0	Jamaica
30/05/1990	Cayman Islands XI	N	4-0	Cayman Islands
23/07/1990	Hamrånge GIF	A	6-0	Sweden
24/07/1990	Väsby IK FK	A	5-0	Sweden
26/07/1990	IF Sylvia	A	5-0	Sweden
28/07/1990	Hallsthammars SK	A	8-1	Sweden
30/07/1990	Nykvarns SK	A	6-0	Sweden
31/07/1990	Alnö IF	A	6-1	Sweden
20/08/1990	ACF Fiorentina	N	1-2	Italy
22/08/1990	UC Sampdoria	N	1-1	Italy
25/04/1991	Gibraltar FA XI	A	2-2	Gibraltar
22/07/1991	Smögens IF	A	8-1	Sweden
24/07/1991	Landskrona BoIS	A	3-1	Sweden
25/07/1991	Bankeryds SK	A	8-0	Sweden
27/07/1991	Mölnlycke IF	A	6-0	Sweden
29/07/1991	Sandefjord BK	A	1-1	Norway
30/07/1991	Fredrikstad FK	A	2-2	Norway
05/08/1991	AEK Athens	A	2-2	Greece
13/08/1991	Levski Sofia	N	3-1	Bulgaria
14/08/1991	Sporting Gijon	A	2-2	Spain
18/07/1992	Kaizer Chiefs	A	3-2	South Africa
19/07/1992	Orlando Pirates	N	1-2	South Africa

COUNTRY OF VENUE	NOTES	CHAPTER
Sweden		18
Sweden		18
Sweden		18
Sweden		18
Sweden		18
Sweden		18
N. Ireland		4
Trinidad & Tobago	In Port of Spain, Trinidad	16
Trinidad & Tobago	At Trinidad National Stadium	16
Jamaica		16
Cayman Islands		16
Sweden		18
Sweden		18
Sweden		18
Sweden		18
Sweden		18
Sweden		18
Italy	Cesar Pier Baretti Tournament at St Vincent	1
Italy	(won 5-4 on penalties) Cesar Pier Baretti Tournament at St Vincent	1
Gibraltar		3
Sweden		18
Sweden		18
Sweden		18
Sweden		18
Norway		18
Norway		18
Greece		3
Spain	(won 5-3 on penalties) Costa Verde Trophy at Sporting Gijon	3
Spain	Costa Verde Trophy	3
South Africa		4
South Africa	in Durban	4

DATE	OPPONENTS	VENUE	SCORE F-A	COUNTRY OF CLUB
26/07/1992	Horreds IF	A	1-0	Sweden
28/07/1992	Karlskrona AIF	A	1-0	Sweden
29/07/1992	Oskarshamns AIK	A	7-2	Sweden
30/07/1992	Bankeryds SK	A	11-2	Sweden
01/08/1992	Målilla GOIF	A	5-0	Sweden
20/07/1993	Ayamonte	N	4-0	Spain
23/07/1993	Louletano	A	0-0	Portugal
13/11/1993	Guernsey XI	A	8-0	Guernesy
26/01/1994	Derry City	A	2-1	N. Ireland
17/05/1994	Gibraltar Select XI	A	1-0	Gibraltar
19/05/1994	Marbella	A	0-2	Spain
21/05/1994	Malaga	A	1-0	Spain
25/07/1994	Local Portugese XI	A	3-1	Portugal
23/04/1995	Happy Valley	A	1-1	Hong Kong
12/07/1995	Muğlaspor	A	4-0	Turkey
14/07/1995	Altayspor	A	1-1	Turkey
26/07/1996	Årjängs IF	N	8-0	Sweden
27/07/1996	Førde IL	A	7-2	Norway
29/07/1996	Råde IL	A	2-0	Norway
30/07/1996	Skjetten SK	A	4-3	Norway
03/08/1996	Hallingdal FK	A	8-0	Norway
09/07/1997	JJK, Jyväkylän Jalkapalloklubi	A	4-0	Finland
11/07/1997	Kings SC	A	0-0	Finland
13/07/1997	AC Oulu	A	1-0	Finland
15/07/1997	Santa Claus	A	5-0	Finland
20/08/1997	China National XI	H	2-5	China
13/11/1997	IFK Göteborg	A	1-2	Sweden
19/07/1998	Samsunspor	H	0-2	Turkey
26/07/1998	Samsunspor	A	0-2	Turkey
06/07/1999	Beijing Guoan	A	2-1	China
10/07/1999	Shanghai 02	A	3-2	China

COUNTRY OF VENUE	NOTES	CHAPTER
Sweden		18
Sweden		18
Sweden		18
Sweden		18
Sweden		4
Portugal		4
Portugal		4
Guernsey		4
N. Ireland		4
Gibraltar		4
Spain		4
Spain		4
Portugal	Opposition uncertain	4
Hong Kong		4
Turkey		5
Turkey		5
Norway		5
Norway		5
Norway		5
Norway		5
Norway		5
Finland		5
Finland		5
Finland		5
Finland		5
England	Played at Mitcham Training Ground	8
Sweden		5
England	Intertoto Cup R3 1L	P,6
Turkey	Intertoto Cup R3 2L	P,6
China		7
China		7

DATE	OPPONENTS	VENUE	SCORE F-A	COUNTRY OF CLUB
13/07/1999	Yunnan Hongta	A	2-2	China
15/07/1999	Dalian WanDa	N	0-0	China
11/07/2000	Shan'xi GouLi	A	2-0	China
13/07/2000	China National XI	A	1-3	China
17/07/2000	Guangzhou Songri	N	2-1	China
23/03/2001	SC Bastia	A	3-4	France
11/07/2001	San Pedro	N	4-0	Spain
14/07/2001	Čakovec	N	2-0	Croatia
18/05/2002	Malmö IF	N	2-1	Sweden
21/05/2002	Real Betis Balompie	A	0-2	Spain
18/07/2003	Juventud de Torremolinos CF	A	3-0	Spain
30/07/2003	PSV Eindhoven	H	0-1	The Netherlands
06/09/2003	Brescia Calcio	H	3-4	Italy
13/07/2004	Crusaders	A	2-0	Northern Ireland
17/07/2004	Glentoran	A	5-0	Northern Ireland
28/07/2004	Sporting Clube de Portugal (Sporting Lisbon)	H	1-0	Portugal
07/08/2004	UC Sampdoria	H	0-1	Italy
20/07/2005	FK Teplice	N	1-2	Czech Republic
23/07/2005	Eintracht Frankfurt	N	1-1	Germany
27/07/2004	Internazionale (Inter Milan)	H	0-2	Italy
15/07/2006	Crystal Palace USA	A	3-1	USA
19/07/2006	L A Galaxy	N	1a1	USA
26/07/2006	Boavista	H	2-1	Portugal
24/07/2007	IFK Göteborg	N	2-1	Sweden
27/07/2007	IK Oddevold	A	4-1	Sweden
31/07/2007	RSC Anderlecht	H	1-1	Belgium
07/09/2007	Crystal Palace USA	H	1-0	USA
14/07/2009	Crystal Palace USA	N	5-2	USA
16/07/2009	Harrisburg City Islanders	N	3-1	USA
03/08/2013	Waterford United	A	4-0	Republic of Ireland
10/08/2013	SS Lazio	H	0-1	Italy

COUNTRY OF VENUE	NOTES	CHAPTER
China	(lost 8-7 on penalties)	7
China	(won 4-2 on penalties) in Da Qing	7
China	in Xi'an	8
China	in Xi'an	8
China	in NanChang	8
France		9
Spain	Marbella Cup	9
Spain	Marbella Cup	9
Spain	European Communities Trophy at Real Betis, Seville	10
Spain	European Communities Trophy	10
Spain		11
The Netherlands	Philips Cup	12
England		2
Northern Ireland		13
Northern Ireland		13
England		24
England	BT Cup	2
Germany	at ASV Miesbach, Germany	14
Germany	at FC Füssen, Germany	14
England	CPFC Centenary Challenge	2
USA	at US Naval Base, Annapolis, MD	15
USA	at Richmond Kickers FC, VA. Abandoned HT - electrical storm	15
England		15
Sweden	at Siljevi IP, Grebbestad	18
Sweden		18
England		18
England	Medd Cup	16
USA	Medd Cup in Waldorf, MD (on Baseball Field)	20
USA	in Lancaster, PA (on Baseball Field)	20
Republic of Ireland		21
England		2

DATE	OPPONENTS	VENUE	SCORE F-A	COUNTRY OF CLUB
10/09/2013	Oman National XI	H	2-0	Oman
16/07/2014	GAK Graz	A	13-1	Austria
23/07/2014	Columbus Crew	A	2-2	USA
25/07/2014	Philadephia Union	A	1-0	USA
28/07/2014	Richmond Kickers	A	3-0	USA
09/08/2014	FC Augsburg	A	0-0	Germany
26/05/2015	Dundee	H	4-3	Scotland
18/07/2015	1.FC Union Berlin	A	0-2	Germany
23/07/2015	SuperSport United	N	4-0	South Africa
26/07/2015	Sporting Clube de Portugal (Sporting Lisbon)	N	0-2	Portugal
13/07/2016	Philadephia Union	A	0-0	USA
16/07/2016	FC Cincinnati	A	2-0	USA
19/07/2016	Vancouver Whitecaps	A	2-2	Canada
06/08/2016	Valencia	H	3-1	Spain
19/07/2017	Liverpool	N	0-2	England
22/07/2017	West Bromwich Albion	N	2-0	England
29/07/2017	FC Metz	A	1-1	France
05/08/2017	FC Schalke 04	H	1-1	Germany
13/07/2018	Helsingør	A	2-2	Denmark
16/07/2018	BK Halmstads	A	6-1	Sweden
04/08/2018	Toulouse	H	4-1	France
09/07/2019	FC Luzern	N	1-1	Switzerland
13/07/2019	BSC Young Boys	N	0-2	Switzerland
03/08/2019	Hertha Berlin	H	0-4	Germany
05/09/2020	Brøndby IF	H	1-1	Denmark

COUNTRY OF VENUE	NOTES	CHAPTER
England		21
Austria		22
USA		23
USA		23
USA		23
Germany		23
England	Julian Speroni Testimonial	13
Germany		24
South Africa	Cape Town Cup at Cape Town Stadium	24
South Africa	Cape Town Cup at Cape Town Stadium	24
USA		25
USA		25
Canada		25
England		11
Hong Kong	Premier League Asia Trophy in Hong Kong	26
Hong Kong	Premier League Asia Trophy in Hong Kong	26
France		26
England		26
Denmark		26
Sweden		27
England		27
Switzerland	(won 6-5 on penalties) UhrenCup at FC Biel	27
Switzerland	UhrenCup at FC Bern	27
England		27
England	Behind closed doors	E

APPENDIX B : GEOGRAPHICAL ANALYSIS

i. By Club Nationality

NO. OF GAMES	CLUB NATIONALITY
55	Sweden
25	Scotland
20	The Netherlands
16	Spain
14	Italy, Norway, USA
9	Germany (including West Germany)
8	China, Bermuda, France
7	Czech Republic (including Bohemia)
5	Finland, Portugal, Denmark,
4	Canada, Channel Islands, Israel, Northern Ireland, Turkey
3	Austria, Belgium, Greece, South Africa
2	Caribbean, Gibraltar, Iran, Slovakia (formerly Czechslovakia), Switzerland
1	Brazil, Bulgaria, Cayman Islands, Croatia, Ghana, Hong Kong, Jamaica, Japan, Oman, Qatar, Republic of Ireland, Russia, Trinidad & Tobago

ii. By Country of Venue

NO. OF GAMES	COUNTRY OF VENUE
64	England (Home Games)
52	Sweden
16	Spain, The Netherlands
15	Norway
11	USA
10	Germany (incl. West Germany)
9	Bermuda
7	China
6	Czech Republic (including Bohemia), Italy, Scotland
5	Finland, France
4	Channel Islands, Northern Ireland, South Africa
3	Canada, Denmark, Greece, Hong Kong, Portugal, Turkey
2	Gibraltar, Switzerland, Trinidad & Tobago
1	Austria, Belgium, Cayman Islands, Iran, Israel, Jamaica, Qatar, Republic of Ireland

iii. By Extremes

Furthest North	FK Mjølner, Norway 1978
Furthest South	Cape Town Cup in Cape Town Stadium, South Africa, 2015
Furthest East	Dalian WanDa in Da Qing, China 1999
Furthest West	Vancouver Whitecaps, Canada, 2016
Highest Elevation	1897m: Yunnan Hongta, China, 1999
Lowest Elevation	0m: Den Haag, The Netherlands, 1971
Furthest away*	9567km: Cape Town Stadium, South Africa, 2015
Closest to home*	148km: Calais Racing Union FC in Guînes, 1983

* 'As the crow flies' from Selhurst Park

APPENDIX C : MOST PLAYED CLUBS

Overseas clubs which Crystal Palace have played more than twice (excluding Representative and Select XI's):

NO. OF GAMES	CLUB	NATIONALITY	RECORD
4	IFK Göteborg	Sweden	W2 D0 L2 F7 A7
3	PSV Eindhoven	The Netherlands	W1 D0 L2 F5 A7
3	SK Slavia Prague	Czech Republic	W3 D0 L0 F11 A5
3	Clyde	Scotland	W0 D2 L1 F5 A6
3	MVV Maastricht	The Netherlands	W1 D0 L2 F2 A4
3	Crystal Palace USA	USA	W3 D0 L0 F9 A3
3	SC Feijenoord (now Feyenoord)	The Netherlands	W0 D1 L2 F2 A5
3	Dundee United	Scotland	W1 D2 L0 F5 A3
3	Aberdeen	Scotland	W2 D0 L1 F4 A2
3	Internazionale (Inter Milan)	Italy	W1 D1 L1 F3 A3

APPENDIX D : CLUB RECORDS

Overall Record:

Total Games Played: 272*	Home: 64	Away: 182	Neutral: 26
*2 games abandoned	Won: 169	Draw: 49	Lost: 52
	Goals For: 744 (2.74 average per game)		
	Goals Against: 299 (1.10 avearge per game)		

Biggest Win & Most Goals Scored:

DATE	OPPONENTS	VENUE	SCORE F-A	COUNTRY OF VENUE
16/07/2014	GAK Graz	A	13-1	Austria

Biggest Defeats by Margin:

DATE	OPPONENTS	VENUE	SCORE F-A	COUNTRY OF VENUE
23/05/1990	Trinidad & Tobago XI	A	0-4	Trinidad & Tobago
03/08/2019	Hertha Berlin	H	0-4	England

Most Goals Conceded: Five

DATE	OPPONENTS	VENUE	SCORE F-A	COUNTRY OF VENUE
04/01/1939	Belgium National XI	A	4-5	Belgium
20/08/1997	China National XI	H	2-5	England

Games in which Palace scored ten or more goals:

DATE	OPPONENTS	VENUE	SCORE F-A	COUNTRY OF VENUE
23/05/1908	Koniggratz	A	10-1	Bohemia
14/10/1959	Caribbean XI	H	11-1	England
15/05/1962	West End Rovers	A	11-2	Bermuda
30/07/1992	Bankeryds SK	A	11-2	Sweden
16/07/2014	GAK Graz	A	13-1	Austria

APPENDIX E : DOMESTIC GAMES PLAYED IN INTERNATIONAL TOURNAMENTS

DATE	OPPONENTS	VENUE	SCORE F-A	COMPETITION
11/05/1973	Newcastle United	H	0-0	Anglo-Italian Tournament Semi-Final 1L
21/05/1973	Newcastle United	A	1-5	Anglo-Italian Tournament Semi-Final 2L
07/09/1993	Charlton Athletic	A	1-4	Anglo-Italian Cup Group Stage
14/09/1993	Millwall	H	3-0	Anglo-Italian Cup Group Stage

STOP PRESS

Quite literally, Stop the Press! On 15th June, just as I had been given final sign-off by Amazon to publish the book, Palace announced that they were now part of the Global Football Alliance. This association 'brings together clubs from six continents to share best practices, find synergies and reflect on the future of football.' I guess we will have to wait and find out what that really means.

The fifteen other GFA members are:

AS Saint Etienne, France

Associacao Chapeconese De Futebol, Brazil

Athletic Club Paradou, Algeria

AZ Alkmaar, Netherlands

Club Estudiantes De La Plaza, Argentina

Deportivo Independiente Medellin, Colombia

Deportivo Toluca FC, Mexico

FK Krasnodar, Russia

Kawaski Frontale, Japan

Melbourne Victory, Australia

New England Revolution, USA

Standard De Liege, Belgium

Villarreal, Spain

VFL Wolfsburg, Germany

Wadi Delga, Egypt

Is it wrong that my first thought about this announcement was 'Ooh, I hope this means we can get some friendlies/tournaments against our new partners?'

"All the world's a stage, and all the men and women merely players: they have their exits and their entrances; and one man in his time plays many parts..."
William Shakespeare

Principal Boys & Girls

Neil Witherow (Neil the Eagle)
Sue Witherow (The Missus)
Andy Carey (Hoover)
Andrew Wagon (Wags)
Neil Everitt (Mr Cad)
Dave Lewis (Safety)
Andy Gibson (Gibbo)
Tracy Peto
Pete Bonthrone
Darrell Bourne (Bourno)
Dave Hynes
Glenn Bastin (Colonel Britain)
Paul Withers (Baldy)
Robert Ellis (BVB Bob)
Dan Weir
Rick Ballantine
Andy Tipping (Tippo)
Mike & Mitch Copperwheat (Biggus Mickus)
Ian Chapman (Chocky)
Paul Field (Paf)
John O'Connor (Big Bad John)
Jane Vigus (SKATE)

And the 'Supporting Cast' of friends, family and those not already acknowledged that I have met along the way on these Palace journeys, both at home and abroad:

Peggy & Len Witherow, Ray Witherow, Christine Post, Dean Chandler, Donna Couch, Carly Hobdell, Hannah Witherow, Richard Post, Penny Nangle, Sheila & John Gibson, John & Mick Harrigan, Keeley, Jon & Daniel Bugg, Kate Thompson, Simon Higgins, Colin Moody, Collin Kenny, Kevin Ellis, Stuart Driver, Andy "Bungle" Brander, Graham & Ben Carter, Michelle Rodger, Pete King, James Coome, The Cooper & Megginson families from Oldham, Ken Warner, Johnny 'Bush' Wood, John Ellis, Tony Matthews, Jason Axell, Phil Huffer, John & Annette Pateman, Stuart Dunbar, Danny Whitmarsh, Laurie Dahl, John Scarlett, John Curran, The Orpington Pissheads: {Paul & John James; Kelvin Blackman; Claire Baker; Marcus Lawson, Malcolm Turner, Pete & Sarah Mahoney, the Young & Greenwood Brothers et al}, Robbie Tobin, Dave Stovell, Richard Moore, Nigel Campey, Shaun Ellis, Alan & Pete Jones, Nicki Carey, The Sniffer, Alan Smith, Spike Hill, Al & Trish Murray, Pete "the Pom" Lewis, Chris Plummer, Mick 'Thirsty' Hersey, Paul 'Moderate' Brown, Phil "Palace Fan in Alabama" Manning, Will "Winston the Dog" Block, Mark Evetts, Pete & Nick Redman, Richard Bamber, Sam Burch, Dave Campbell, Janet Kingdom, Nigel Moran, Inge Lauritzen, Andy "Essex" Curtis, Andy Wilson, Chris "Fred" Plaisted, Richie Davis, The Eagles Fitter Fans, Patrick & Christiane Rhefus, Rüdiger Schwarz, Sebastian Schalow, Simon "Wiz" Wisdom, Kev Mason, Grant Saunders, Georgina Halford-Aylard & family, Dave Hart, Dave Adamson, Andy "Puttsy" Puttock, Adrian "Agey Boy" McCulloch, Damo Farino, John Rolls, Mansur Enus, Terry Byfield, Grace Saunders, Ashley Royston & family, Chris Waters, Dave Ashton, Pete Carter, Mik Woolley.

Photography:

All pictures with associated credit have been kindly provided by Neil Everitt, Dan Weir, Gary Chapman, Dave London, Dom Fifield, Ian Weller, Dave Lewis and Derek Collison. The rest are from the personal collection of Neil & Sue Witherow.

Reference Material and Sources:

"Crystal Palace – The Complete Record" by Ian King

"We all Follow the Palace" by Eagle Eye Publications

"The Origins of Crystal Palace FC – Vol 2 & 4" by Steve Martyniuk

"Crystal Palace: 1905 to 1997" by the Reverend Nigel Sands

"Dark Days to Cup Finals" by Simon Higgins

The Anglo-Italian Inter-Leagues Competition 1971 & 1973 Souvenir Brochures

Crystal Palace Fanzines: Eagle Eye, Suffer Little Children, So Glad You're Mine, One More Point, Red & Blue Review

Crystal Palace Publications: Matchday Programmes, Official Newspapers, Club Handbooks and other periodicals

Internet Resoucres: www.cpfc.org – "The BBS", VAVEL.COM Crystal Palace content managed by Edmund Brack, CP-FRIS (Crystal Palace — Fast Results Information Service), Palace 'Til I Die (PTID) Facebook group, Wikipedia.

Magazines, Newspapers and radio stations: The Croydon Advertiser, South London Press, 90 Minutes, The Derry Journal, London Evening News & Star, Evening Standard, The London Paper, The Bermuda Recorder, The Voice, Daily Express, Daily Mirror, The Guardian, LBC, Talksport, Capital Gold, Drammens Tidende og Buskerud Blad, Svenska Dagbladet, Göteborgs-Posten, Provinciale Drentsche en Asser courant.

Facebook:

There is a Facebook group called Don't Mention The Spor where you can find more trip photos and memories from many of the people mentioned in the book. Please feel free to join and add any you may want to share.

About the Author:

Neil Witherow has been going to football matches for as long as he can remember and is usually at his local non-league club, Beckenham Town when Palace aren't playing. He is an avid collector of football jerseys from around the world, although he still can't seem to get his hands on a Beckenham Town shirt.

Away from the game, he divides his time between helping to run the family Mortgage Broking business and is an occasional band driver and roadie. He also enjoys running and writes the popular blog website: runspoonsrun.co.uk.

He relaxes by playing the ukulele, which apparently has the opposite effect on anyone within earshot.

Printed in Great Britain
by Amazon

63253226R00190